Reconsidering Confederation

Reconsidering Confederation

CANADA'S FOUNDING DEBATES
1864-1999

Edited by
DANIEL HEIDT

© 2018 Daniel Heidt

University of Calgary Press
2500 University Drive NW
Calgary, Alberta
Canada T2N 1N4
press.ucalgary.ca

This book is available as an ebook which is licensed under a Creative Commons license. The publisher should be contacted for any commercial use which falls outside the terms of that license.

LIBRARY AND ARCHIVES CANADA CATALOGUING IN PUBLICATION

Reconsidering confederation : Canada's founding debates, 1864-1999 / edited by Daniel Heidt.

Includes bibliographical references and index.
Issued in print and electronic formats.
ISBN 978-1-77385-015-3 (softcover).—ISBN 978-1-77385-016-0 (open access PDF).—ISBN 978-1-77385-017-7 (PDF).—ISBN 978-1-77385-018-4 (EPUB).—ISBN 978-1-77385-019-1 (Kindle)

1. Canada—History—Confederation, 1867. I. Heidt, Daniel (Daniel Henry), 1985-, editor

FC474.R37 2018   971.04'9   C2018-904065-3
                                         C2018-904066-1

The University of Calgary Press acknowledges the support of the Government of Alberta through the Alberta Media Fund for our publications. We acknowledge the financial support of the Government of Canada. We acknowledge the financial support of the Canada Council for the Arts for our publishing program.

This book has been published with the help of a grant from the Canadian Federation for the Humanities and Social Sciences, through the Awards to Scholarly Publications Program, using funds provided by the Social Sciences and Humanities Research Council of Canada.

This book has been published with the support of the Crabtree Foundation.

 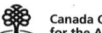 Canada Council   Conseil des Arts   CRABTREE FOUNDATION
                                        for the Arts   du Canada

Printed and bound in Canada by Marquis
♻ This book is printed on 57lb Enviro paper

Copyediting by Francine Michaud
Cover design, page design, and typesetting by Melina Cusano

Contents

Illustrations	*vii*
Acknowledgments	*ix*
1 | Introduction: Reconsidering Confederation Daniel Heidt	*1*
2 | Compact, Contract, Covenant: The Evolution of First Nations Treaty-Making J.R. Miller	*19*
3 | Ontario: The Centre of Confederation? Daniel Heidt	*53*
4 | Quebec and Confederation: Gains and Compromise Marcel Martel, Colin M. Coates, Martin Pâquet, and Maxime Gohier	*75*
5 | The Maritimes and the Debate Over Confederation Phillip Buckner	*101*
6 | Resisting Canada's Will: Manitoba's Entry into Confederation Robert Wardhaugh and Barry Ferguson	*145*
7 | "The interests of Confederation demanded it": British Columbia and Confederation Patricia E. Roy	*171*

8 | "It is better to have a half loaf than none at all": The Yukon and Confederation   193
P. Whitney Lackenbauer and Ken S. Coates

9 | Creating New Provinces: Saskatchewan and Alberta   213
Bill Waiser

10 | Newfoundland and Canada: Confederation and the Search for Stability   237
Raymond B. Blake

11 | "A More Accurate Face on Canada to the World": The Creation of Nunavut   263
P. Whitney Lackenbauer and André Légaré

Confederation Quotes: Sources and Further Reading   291

Contributors   297

Index   303

Illustrations

1.1	Canada, with its current provincial and territorial borders.	*14*
2.1	Historical Treaties of Canada. Developed from Canada, "Historical Treaties of Canada," *Indigenous and Northern Affairs Canada*, https://www.aadnc-aandc.gc.ca/DAM/DAM-INTER-HQ/STAGING/texte-text/htoc_1100100032308_eng.pdf.	*21*
3.1	British North America's settler political boundaries as they existed in 1867. Developed from Natural Resources Canada, "Map 1867," *Library and Archives Canada*, https://www.collectionscanada.gc.ca/confederation/023001-5005-e.html.	*55*
3.2	The Charlottetown delegates, 1 September 1864. photograph by George P. Roberts, LAC, C-000733.	*58*
6.1	The Red River settlement, 1870, showing the locations of the predominantly French and English parishes. Developed from: Gerhard J. Ens, *Homeland to Hinterland: The Changing Worlds of the Metis in the Nineteenth Century* (Toronto: University of Toronto Press, 1996), 11; Gerald Friesen, *The Canadian Prairies: A History* (Toronto: University of Toronto Press, 1987), 91; Norma Jean Hall, "The People," *The Provisional Government of Assiniboia*, https://hallnjean2.wordpress.com/resources/definition-provisional-government/the-people-electorate/; George Stanley, *The Birth of Western Canada: A History of The Riel Rebellions*, 2nd edition (Toronto: University of Toronto Press, 1961), 14.	*148*
6.2	Manitoba's expansion, 1870–1912. Reproduced with permission from John Welsted et al. "Manitoba: Geographical Identity of a Prairie Province," *The Geography of Manitoba: Its Land and Its People*, eds. John C. Everitt, Christoph Stadel and John E. Welsted (Winnipeg: University of Manitoba Press, 1996), 5.	*162*
7.1	The BC delegation of Dr. J.S. Helmcken, Dr. R.W.W. Carrall and J.W. Trutch departing for Ottawa to negotiate the terms of union with Canada. Image PDP00488 by Robert Banks, courtesy of the Royal BC Museum and Archives.	*183*

8.1	Yukon miners being chased from power by the Yukon Council and Ottawa "monsters." *Dawson Daily*, 19 May 1903.	198
9.1	The North-West demanding "justice" for the North-West. *The Grip*, November 1883.	224
9.2	The proposed province of "Buffalo." Reproduced with permission from Bill Waiser, *Saskatchewan: A New History* (Calgary: Fifth House, 2006).	228
9.3	Laurier as the proud father of two provincial "twins." *Montreal Daily Star*, 23 February 1905.	230
10.1	The Ottawa Delegation of the National Convention, 1947. Photographer: G. Hunter. LAC, MIKAN 3362966.	250
10.2	Anti-Confederate Campaign, 1948. Courtesy of the Rooms Provincial Archives Division, George Carter Collection, Box 5, MG910.	253
10.3	*The Confederate*, 31 May 1948, 3.	254
10.4	Rt. Hon. Louis St. Laurent speaking during the ceremony which admitted Newfoundland into Confederation. Ottawa, Ontario, 1 April 1949. LAC, MIKAN 3408569.	258
11.1	Canada at the beginning of the 20th century, before the federal government created Alberta as well as Saskatchewan, and extended the northern boundaries of Manitoba, Ontario, and Quebec. Developed from Natural Resources Canada, "Map 1898," *Library and Archives Canada*, https://www.collectionscanada.gc.ca/confederation/023001-5009-e.html.	265
11.2	Northern NDP MP Peter Ittinuar. NWT Archives/©GNWT. Department of Public Works and Services/G-1995-001: 0539.	274
11.3	Nunavut, as established in 1999. Reproduced from: "Nunavut with Names," *Natural Resources Canada*, http://ftp.geogratis.gc.ca/pub/nrcan_rncan/raster/atlas_6_ed/reference/bilingual/nunavut_names.pdf.	279
11.4	The Northwest Territories after the establishment of Nunavut in 1999. Reproduced from: "Northwest Territories with Names," http://ftp.geogratis.gc.ca/pub/nrcan_rncan/raster/atlas_6_ed/reference/bilingual/nwt_names.pdf.	283

Acknowledgments

This book's genesis can be traced to the origins of *The Confederation Debates*, which sought to familiarize Canadians with the debates that shaped their country's founding during the past one and a half centuries. The project digitized roughly nine thousand pages of text from local and federal legislatures debating the admission of each province or territory into Confederation, between 1865 and 1949, as well as the Numbered Treaties and records of their negotiation, and posted these records to our legacy website hosted by the University of Victoria (http://hcmc.uvic.ca/confederation/).

From the outset, contributors from across the country diligently worked to package portions of these records into educational mini-units, social media posts, and other deliverables, and the project's leadership recognized that the records would be much more meaningful if they were accompanied by primers concerning each province, territory, and Treaty area's entry into Confederation.

Towards this end, a group of Canada's leading historians congregated at St. Jerome's University in February 2017 to share and discuss papers detailing each province, territory, and Treaty areas' journeys into Confederation. Everyone was impressed by the collective strength of the research as well as the thoughtful analysis emphasizing a common (though diverse) pursuit of local autonomy, and the decision was quickly made to submit the papers for scholarly publication. The result is *Reconsidering Confederation*.

This book would not have been possible without the continuous support and guidance provided by Raymond B. Blake, Penny Bryden, Colin

M. Coates, P. Whitney Lackenbauer, and Marcel Martel. I am also deeply grateful to all of the chapter contributors for their carefully considered work and fast turnaround times. Support from the Crabtree Foundation, the Social Sciences and Humanities Research Council, St. Jerome's University, the University of Waterloo, and the Canada150@York fund helped to make this book a reality. Several research assistants, including Yuqian (Gloria) Fan, Sumedha Jain, and Phil Thompson also helped to prepare the manuscript for publication.

The book is also indebted to the University of British Columbia Press for granting us permission to reproduce J.R. Miller's chapter from *New Histories for Old: Changing Perspectives on Canada's Native Pasts*. The authors of this volume are also appreciative for the constructive feedback offered by the anonymous peer reviewers.

Introduction: Reconsidering Confederation

Daniel Heidt

> *July 1, 1867, was a beginning only, not an end. Nova Scotia had to be reconciled. Prince Edward Island and Newfoundland must be wooed, if there were to be unity in handling the fisheries. The Northwest had to be annexed if it were to be saved for Canada. Beyond the Rockies was British Columbia, which must be won to union to give Canada [an] outlet to the Pacific. These things, rather than the integration of the new governments, were still the main work of Confederation: union, to be union, had to include expansion.*[1]
>
> W.L. Morton, 1964

Anticipating Canada's centennial year, historian W.L. Morton wrote that the date of 1 July 1867 "was a beginning only, not an end." Canada, as we know it today, remained only a dream. On its first day, the new "dominion" was a fledgling amalgam of Nova Scotia, New Brunswick, Quebec, and Ontario constituting something more than a colony, but still less than an independent country. Even then, the move had been unpopular in the Atlantic colonies, and Nova Scotian voters would soon elect anti-Confederate MPs to all but one of their federal ridings. Prince Edward

Island and Newfoundland, meanwhile, had rejected the project, and the residents of Rupert's Land and British Columbia had yet to be consulted about membership. Canada's motto "*A Mari usque ad Mare*" (Latin for "from sea to sea"), instilling the image of a country spanning northern North America from the Atlantic to the Pacific, remained an unfulfilled aspiration. Confederation, to be successful, had to accommodate the interests and cultures of these diverse regions and Peoples.

The formation of a country, separate from the United States and bordering three oceans, ultimately required decades to achieve and over one hundred and thirty years to reach its current complement of three territories and ten provinces. While Canada grew to encompass much of its present-day geographical extent during the two decades after it was created, the political boundaries we recognize today were far from certain. Alberta, Saskatchewan, the Yukon, and Nunavut all took shape during the late nineteenth and early twentieth centuries—repeatedly and dramatically reshaping the Northwest Territories in the process. Voters in Newfoundland and Labrador remained wary of Confederation and the colony/dominion did not ultimately become a part of Canada until 1949. Treaty negotiations between the Crown and Indigenous Peoples also came in fits and starts, creating misunderstandings that still plague the country today. A twenty-first century understanding of Confederation must also include these foundational additions to the Canadian political framework.

Each proposed addition or change spawned debates in colonial, territorial, and federal legislatures as well as negotiations at meeting places on traditional territories. At these assemblies, leaders weighed the merits of deals that would bring their constituents into the Canadian fold. Their opinions, historian Peter B. Waite would later note when writing about the 1860s debates, "were held with stubbornness and expounded with conviction."[2] Very few of the participants, it is true, engaged in deep philosophical debates as American founders Thomas Jefferson and Alexander Hamilton did,[3] but, as Janet Ajzenstat and her co-editors point out in their collection of Canada's early debates, the so-called pragmatism of our country's founders has been misunderstood as a dearth of "strong commitment to political values" or a lack of "interest in political ideas."[4] Whether they convened during the 1860s or the late 1990s, these founding assemblies were opportunities to expand, reaffirm, or shift Canada's ideals and development. Participants from different parts of the country or cultural backgrounds repeatedly contested how Canada would navigate timeless concerns like local autonomy, minority rights, majority rule, nationalism, liberty, and equality. Their successes and failures at balancing these often-conflicting values created legacies that we live with today. During these discussions, the participants regularly recalled past precedents to justify their positions, creating a chain of interconnected dialogues that reveal the roots and evolution of Canadian attempts to balance inclusion and autonomy.

The Stakes

Political reputations were won and lost during these founding discussions and historians have expended considerable energy debating which politicians deserve the credit—or the blame—for Canada's past and present successes and failures. Sir John A. Macdonald, for example, has been portrayed as *The Man Who Made Us* (to borrow journalist Richard Gwyn's recent description) in dozens of biographies and books over the years.[5] Other authors emphasize the contributions of other political leaders who shaped Canada. The biographers of George Brown, George-Étienne Cartier, and Thomas D'Arcy McGee all point out the critical roles that these individuals played in convincing the Province of Canada and two initial Maritime provinces to join Confederation in 1867.[6] Books on Nova Scotia's Charles Tupper and Newfoundland's Joey Smallwood, make a similar case for the important contributions of these key founders.[7] In recent decades, Louis Riel's leadership of the opposition to the unilateral imposition of central Canadian designs on the Prairies has attracted nearly as much attention as Macdonald's attempts to create a country spanning the continent—and perhaps even more sympathy than Macdonald's expansionism.[8] In British Columbia, Amor de Cosmos' campaign to bring that colony into Confederation has also received some attention.[9] Those who opposed union, such as Albert Smith, William Annand, Antoine-Aimé Dorion, John Helmcken, and Kenneth Brown have not received as much attention despite their critical contributions to the debates and, consequently, the form of the subsequent union. "While the Antis lost the battle," historian Ged Martin notes, "they won at least some of the arguments" and their critiques of the Confederation deal often proved to be prophetic.[10]

John A. Macdonald
Attorney General West, Province of Canada, Ont. and Future PM

6 FEBRUARY 1865

CONFEDERATION QUOTE 1.1
Quotation from Province of Canada, Legislative Assembly, 6 February, 1865
Photograph from Library and Archives Canada, C-006513

" ... if we wish to be a great people ... commanding the respect of the world, able to hold our own against all opponents ... [with] one system of government, and...a commercial union ... obeying the same Sovereign ... and being, for the most part, of the same blood ... this can only be obtained by a union ... between the scattered and weak ... British North American Provinces. "

Kenneth McKenzie Brown
Member of Newfoundland National Convention

28 OCTOBER 1946

Confederation Quote 1.2
Quotation from Newfoundland National Convention, 28 October 1946
Photograph from *Who's Who in and from Newfoundland*, page 198.

> I am against confederation as I see it today. I came here with an open mind, with no preconceived ideas. I did not go to my district and preach confederation; I did not preach anything. Whatever government is best for the people, that is the government I would vote for and I will do it today regardless of resolutions brought in by Mr. Smallwood or by anyone else.

Interpreting Canada's Past

Over the past one hundred and fifty years, historians have described and analyzed how different parts of the country balanced their desires for autonomy against attempts to establish a national economy and common political values when assessing Canada's development. "The aim of Confederation was political—the creation of a great 'new nationality'," according to Donald Creighton. He saw it as the product of "a political agreement among several provinces" that would extend the economic reach of the "Empire of the St. Lawrence" across British North America.[11] While Creighton celebrated this expansionism, regional historians have questioned Central Canada's power and fairness. In 1986, David Bercuson aptly summarized the common contention among Prairie and Maritime historians that "the federal government has always been more representative of the desires and ambition of Central Canada than the Maritimes and the West together. Central Canada is where the votes are and where elections are won and lost; this was true at Confederation and it remains true today."[12] As a result of these power asymmetries, T.W. Acheson contends, the Maritimes were subsumed within "empire Canada."[13] W.L. Morton, writing during the 1940s, went even further by insisting that "Laurentian imperialism" marginalized the Prairies into a "colony of a colony" that suffered economic exploitation and Central Canadian political dominance.[14]

Centralist leaders perpetuated this sense of regional marginalization when they insisted on what Donald Creighton later described and defended as "Dominion paramountcy and national leadership."[15] Noting the bloody American Civil War over states' rights inspired by strong regional identities and disagreements, John A. Macdonald, Charles Tupper, and several other founders would have preferred the establishment of a single parliament (a unitary government, without provinces, resembling that of the United Kingdom) to govern all of the provinces and territories. Widespread desire within all of the colonies for some degree of local autonomy, however, made a legislative union impractical. Instead, they proposed a highly centralized federation with limited powers assigned to the provinces, which would remain subordinate to a federal government so that the latter could create a common sense of allegiance to the Crown while balancing each province or region's diverse expectations and interests.[16]

Many Canadians rejected this centralist vision. While the phrase "provincial compact" did not come into widespread use until 1869, several debaters described Confederation as an interprovincial "treaty" between 1865 and 1867. Pro-Confederation speakers emphasized the constitutional entrenchment of exclusive provincial jurisdictions when rebutting warnings by "antis" that union would infringe upon local autonomy. Each province, in this view, surrendered discrete jurisdictions—such as maintaining separate military forces—in return for the benefits of membership in a larger union. These benefits, they maintained, included each province's right to exclusive jurisdiction in other areas—such as private property—making these governments coordinate with, rather than subordinate to, the federal government. This concept of a provincial compact was also fundamental to the provincial rights movements of the nineteenth and early twentieth centuries, and it is also critical to understanding the subsequent and heated debates on education, Crown lands, and natural resource rights for Alberta and Saskatchewan during the late nineteenth and early twentieth centuries.[17]

Other visions of Confederation's purpose were more cultural. In the eyes of many French Canadians, Confederation entrenched Quebec as a safe-haven. During the late nineteenth and early twentieth century, Quebec's unique constitutional rights were sufficient to calm assimilationist concerns within the province. Events like Louis Riel's execution in 1885, however, contributed to "a new insistence in French-Canadian rhetoric on the need for the two races, English- and French-Canadian, to live together in peace and harmony, to share Canada between them on friendly and equitable terms."[18] This view of Canada as a bicultural compact of two "founding peoples" motivated French-Canadian leaders such as Henri Bourassa to advocate on behalf of French minorities across the country, and featured prominently in the lengthy parliamentary debates that led to the creation of the new provinces of Alberta and Saskatchewan in 1905. According to this vision, Canadians needed to preserve and cultivate bicultural identities or at least bilingualism to foster national unity.[19]

Indigenous Peoples are also contesting their place in Canada. "For over a century," the Truth and Reconciliation Commission recently observed, "the central goals of Canada's Aboriginal policy were to eliminate Aboriginal governments; ignore Aboriginal rights; terminate the Treaties;

and, through a process of assimilation, cause Aboriginal Peoples to cease to exist as distinct legal, social, cultural, religious, and racial entities in Canada."[20] Today, Canadians are increasingly sensitive to this longstanding mistreatment and to the need for reconciliation. It is now widely acknowledged that our country was founded by at least "three founding Peoples."[21] This volume embraces this important shift by recognizing that Indigenous Peoples were and continue to be "partners in Confederation" (as the Royal Commission on Aboriginal Peoples insisted)[22] and by affirming that their Treaties with the Crown remain a way to "harmonize" relations between Indigenous and non-Indigenous Peoples in Canada.[23] Despite the longstanding need for this sort of coming together, Indigenous legal scholar John Borrows observes that "many non-Indigenous leaders believe that treaties are about concluding old, unfinished business. They do not generally see treaties as creating structures for present and future Indigenous growth and interaction with the nation state."[24] The present anthology encourages Canadians to recognize the treaties as well as the oral agreements reached during the negotiations, as "foundational documents."[25] In so doing, it takes up the Truth and Reconciliation Commission's call to encourage Canadians to embrace the idea that, "by virtue of the historical and modern Treaties negotiated by our government, we are all Treaty people."[26]

Outline

J.R. Miller therefore begins this book's discussion of Confederation by outlining the precedents, practices, and agreements that inform Canada's Treaties with Indigenous Peoples. Indigenous-Crown agreements evolved over centuries into intricate relationships. The earliest agreements, Miller explains, were commercial compacts between European traders and Indigenous fur suppliers. As competition within the fur trade expanded and contestation of lands intensified, these compacts included written agreements promising peace and friendship. After the War of 1812, these treaties typically resembled contracts whereby the Crown acquired Indigenous Lands. Crown agents subsequently began viewing these treaties as "indentures"—or one-time deals. Despite these shifts, leaders from both sides attending negotiations and renewal meetings continued to follow Indigenous ceremonial practices. As the nineteenth century progressed, land-related treaties became the most frequent form of agreement which, by the 1870s, "took on the form of a covenant, a three-sided agreement to which the deity was a party" and which were "intended to be renewed annually, last forever, and be modified as circumstances required." While Miller cautions that all three forms of treaty-making are "authentic" within the right contexts, he points out that the present-day disconnect between Indigenous Peoples and the Crown owes to the fact that Indigenous Peoples continue to view their treaty relationship as a covenant, while the Crown has used its power to enforce a narrower interpretation of treaties as contracts with limited and unchanging obligations.

Subsequent chapters focus on the post-1865 era, reviewing each province, territory, or region's incorporation into Canada. Where and when applicable, they also integrate Indigenous-Crown Treaties into the discussion about Confederation. The next chapter of the book explains why Confederation was the most popular in Upper Canada. Future Ontarians, Daniel Heidt notes, did not yet think of themselves as "Canadians," and therefore assessed Confederation with a provincial consciousness that may seem foreign to present-day Ontarians. These assessments were informed by the colony's multi-decade pursuit of responsible government, representation by population, and the North-West. Confederation offered all of these rewards, making the deal almost irresistible. Only a few politicians opposed the 72 Resolutions, and their complaints about the potential financial burden of union for Ontario, doubts about national unity, and critiques of the government for refusing to allow the electorate to vote on union did not detract from the deal's overwhelming luster. But Confederation did not end in 1867 for Ontario. Expansion into the North-West required forging agreements with the Indigenous Peoples inhabiting present-day northern Ontario. During the late 1860s and early 1870s, these groups possessed considerable bargaining power and used this leverage to secure better terms than the Crown initially offered. This power eroded, however, by the turn of the century, and Crown officials frequently misled Cree and Ojibwa leaders who had little choice but to sign Treaty 9.

Marcel Martel, Colin M. Coates, Martin Pâquet, and Maxime Gohier then review the other side of the Province of Canada's story. Confederation, they contend, "happened because of Quebec, not in spite of it." When delegates gathered in Charlottetown in September 1864 and a month later in Quebec City, French-speaking representatives from the future province of Quebec were in a position of relative strength at the negotiating table despite being members of a linguistic and religious minority. During negotiations and debates, many French-Canadian representatives favoured federalism. They insisted on separation from Canada West and provincial control of political and social institutions that they judged instrumental to strengthening French-Canadian culture and identity. For their part, English-speaking representatives from Quebec obtained additional protections beyond those of language and education. While these cultural protections were rarely effective at protecting minorities residing in the rest of Canada, they protected French culture inside of Quebec.

The Atlantic region considered Confederation at the same time as the Province of Canada. In his sweeping chapter covering the reactions to Confederation in New Brunswick, Nova Scotia, and Prince Edward Island, Phillip Buckner highlights common fears including: lack of influence in a parliament dominated by Ontario and Quebec MPs, the possibility that the dominion would impose protectionist tariffs on the free-trading Atlantic colonies, and concerns that the new division of taxing powers would make it impossible for the provinces to fulfil their jurisdictional responsibilities. He reviews the unique combinations of arguments, outside developments, and political machinations that pro-Confederation leaders from each colony employed to sidestep or overcome these doubts.

With most of Atlantic Canada secured, Canada turned West to acquire the Hudson's Bay Company territories of Rupert's Land and the North-West as well as British Columbia. Barry Ferguson and Robert Wardhaugh explore Manitoba's entry into Confederation. The province's story, they point out, "is unique" because Manitoba "was the only province created against the designs of the Canadian government." In 1869, the Canadian government proposed the acquisition of the entire North-West Territories without consulting the region's inhabitants. Between September of 1869 and July of 1870, the Red River Settlement defended itself against Canada's acquisition first by denying Canada the right to administer the territory without legal agreement, and second by forming a Provisional Government that negotiated the terms for a new province. The Provisional Government's delegates thereafter forced a somewhat reluctant Canadian government to acknowledge their key demands, and the Manitoba Act of July 1870 recognized the institutions and ways of a French/English, Catholic/Protestant and Métis/Canadian province.

Recognition, however, came at the price of constitutional inferiority compared to the other provinces, a price that would later be extracted from Saskatchewan and Alberta. Recognition hastened treaty negotiations with First Nations on the Prairies between 1871 and 1877.

Next, Patricia E. Roy describes British Columbia's entry into Confederation. Canada's desire to extend its boundary to the Pacific Ocean as well as Britain's desire to rid itself of a colony with a contracting population, declining revenues, and mounting debts pushed the Pacific colony to consider three solutions to their problems: joining the United States, remaining a British colony, or becoming a Canadian province. The first was practical, but had limited support; the second appealed to the governor and his officials who controlled the Legislative Council; and the third was championed by two Canadian-born journalists, Amor de Cosmos and John Robson, who wanted responsible government. When the John A. Macdonald government completed arrangements to acquire Rupert's Land from the Hudson's Bay Company, it asked the British government to appoint a new governor of British Columbia and instruct him to encourage Confederation. This was done and the Legislative Council subsequently debated terms of union, sending three men to Ottawa to negotiate what they insisted must be "fair and equitable terms." Because Canada wanted British Columbia more than British Columbia wanted Canada, the new province secured virtually everything it wanted and British Columbia entered Confederation in 1871.

At the end of the nineteenth century, problems in administration of the North-West Territories led to the creation of the Yukon territory. The Yukon became a territory in 1898, in the midst of the Klondike Gold Rush, carved out from the North-West in a dispute between Regina and Ottawa over control of liquor revenues. The territory's constitutional evolution did not, therefore, follow Manitoba's example. By establishing the territory via an Order in Council, Sir Wilfrid Laurier's government avoided consulting local settlers and Indigenous Peoples. The Yukon was instead initially run by a council of government officials appointed in Ottawa. Although local protests resulted in the addition of elected council members and then the establishment of a wholly-elected Territorial Council in 1910, the subsequent collapse of the mining economy and the significant depopulation of the Yukon during the First World War led to the shrinking of both the elected Council and the territorial government. The battle for responsible government in the Yukon would not be won until 1979.

Determining governance of the Prairies also required decades, and Bill Waiser contends that the establishment of Alberta and Saskatchewan was not simply a story of achievement or celebration. It was a protracted and, at times, acrimonious experience. As Canada looked past Manitoba in anticipation of "settling" the Prairies, Indigenous leaders sought to preserve their People's cultures and places in the region via Treaties. The Crown, eager to avoid costly "Indian Wars," gradually obliged this desire by negotiating treaties when settlement reached new Indigenous communities. As this settler population grew during the succeeding decades, it also wanted to become part of Confederation. This new population complained about federal indifference and neglect, the glacial speed of constitutional evolution, and the limited or restricting terms of provincehood. While the North-West Legislature demanded full jurisdiction in all areas of provincial jurisdiction, Catholic-Protestant debates about education rights and the federal government's determination to control Crown lands and natural resources ultimately produced one of the longest and heated debates in Canadian parliamentary history, delaying the date for the entry of Saskatchewan and Alberta into Confederation, which had to be pushed back for two months, from 1 July to 1 September 1905.

A further forty years would pass before Canada's final province joined Confederation. Newfoundland had sent delegates to Quebec City in 1864 and the proponents of union promoted Confederation as a way to deal with Newfoundland's isolation, its rampant poverty, its reliance on the fishery, and as a way to spur economic diversification. The anti-Confederates, as Raymond B. Blake notes in his contribution to this volume, ultimately carried the day. Confederation arose periodically after 1869, but it was not until the late 1940s that voters reconsidered joining Canada. The proponents of union once again argued that Canada would provide economic and social security and rid Newfoundland of its long history of underdevelopment and poverty, while the opponents of union fought again to maintain independence. In 1949, Newfoundlanders opted by a slim margin for the security of union with Canada.

Confederation's most recent addition came with the creation of Nunavut in 1999. The establishment of Canada's newest territory, P. Whitney Lackenbauer and André Légaré note, required decades of negotiations and spawned from concurrent Indigenous demands for greater self-government. Between 1905 and the Second World War, the Canadian government showed little interest in the High Arctic. After the Second World War, however, the state extended its reach across the region in the name of strategic defence and economic development. Indigenous leaders soon organized, demanding greater self-government and a comprehensive land claims settlement. By reviewing the varied Indigenous proposals, government commissions, and negotiations, the authors explain how the creation of Nunavut laid the "foundation for new relationships" between the Crown, newcomers, and Inuit that provided the latter with "powerful mechanisms to control their future through a public territorial government."

Confederation's Common Pursuits

By concisely discussing the colonial, territorial, federal, and Indigenous aspirations, grievances, and jurisdictions for each province or region together, these chapters provide a primer for Canadians who want to better understand similarities and differences between provinces, regions, and Peoples. This book documents a common desire for autonomy and inclusion. At some point during each province's deliberations, debaters warned that other parts of the country would band together to force through policies that threatened their province's core interests. Nearly all groups, except for perhaps John A. Macdonald's followers, demanded guarantees for local autonomy within Confederation. Quebecers worried about protecting what would subsequently be called a "distinct society" and demanded measures that preserved their language, civil code, and culture. Atlantic Canadians desired federal support to preserve the continuation of local programs and, when federal offers were deemed insufficient, Newfoundland and Prince Edward Island rejected union. Prairie leaders sought provincial jurisdiction for Crown lands and natural resources. The territories pursued responsible and elected government for decades. Indigenous Peoples also tried to secure protections and safeguards from the Crown that would "assist them in making a transition from a declining hunting economy to one more compatible with the farming economy that was invading their territories."[27]

This push for autonomy, the failure of the Canadian government to honour its treaty commitments, and the degree of interprovincial and/or

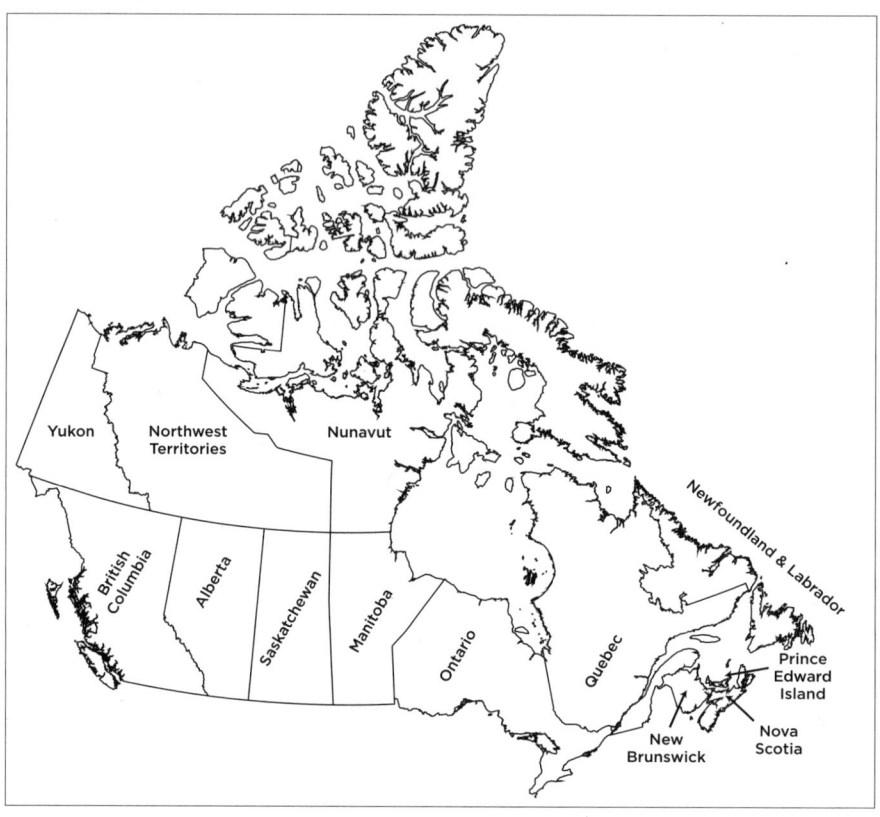

Fig 1.1 Canada, with its current provincial and territorial borders.

federal-provincial distrust that permeated the debates about each province's addition to Confederation are not causes for cynicism about Canada's future. The founders of most federations choose this structure of government because, as political scientist Ronald Watts notes, it "provide[s] a practical way of combining . . . unity and diversity."[28] Instead, Canadians should recognize the achievement of creating a country distinct from the United States, with a high (though unevenly distributed) standard of living that provides some degree of local autonomy. Balancing inclusion and autonomy while correcting past wrongs will continue to be challenging and, at times, divisive. By updating our understanding of Confederation to encompass a series of agreements between Indigenous Peoples, the Crown, as well as colonial, territorial, provincial, and federal authorities, this book seeks to inspire further discussions about Canada's founding and its future.

Further Reading

Ajzenstat, Janet, Paul Romney, Ian Gentles, and William D. Gairdner, eds. *Canada's Founding Debates.* Toronto: University of Toronto Press, 2003.

Friesen, Gerald. *The Canadian Prairies: A History.* Toronto: University of Toronto Press, 1987.

Heaman, Elsbeth A. *Tax, Order, and Good Government: A New Political History of Canada, 1867–1917.* Montreal: McGill-Queen's Press, 2017.

Krikorian, Jacqueline D., David R. Cameron, Marcel Martel, Andrew W. McDougall, and Robert C. Vipond, eds. *Roads to Confederation. The Making of Canada, 1867. Vols. 1 and 2.* Toronto: University of Toronto Press, 2017.

Moore, Christopher. *1867: How the Fathers Made a Deal.* Toronto: McClelland and Stewart, 1998.

Romney, Paul. *Getting It Wrong: How Canadians Forgot Their Past and Imperiled Confederation.* Toronto: University of Toronto Press, 1999.

Silver, A.I. *The French-Canadian Idea of Confederation, 1864–1900.* 2 ed. Toronto: University of Toronto Press, 1997.

Truth and Reconciliation Commission of Canada. *Honouring the Truth, Reconciling for the Future: Summary of the Final Report of the Truth and Reconciliation Commission of Canada.* Winnipeg: Truth and Reconciliation Commission of Canada, 2015.

Waite, P.B. *The Life and Times of Confederation,* 1864–1867, 3rd ed. Toronto: Robin Brass Studio, 2001.

NOTES

1. W.L. Morton, *The Critical Years: The Union of British North America, 1857–1873.* The Canadian Centenary Series (Toronto: McClelland & Stewart, 1964), 221–22.

2. Peter B. Waite, *The Life and Times of Confederation,* 1864–1867, 3rd ed. (Toronto: Robin Brass Studio, 2001), 1.

3. For examples of historians bemoaning the alleged pragmatism of Canada's founders, consult: Frank H. Underhill, *Image of Confederation* (Toronto: Canadian Broadcasting Corporation, 1964), 3; J.K. Johnson, "John A. Macdonald," in *The Pre-Confederation Premiers: Ontario Government Leaders, 1841–1867,* ed. J.M.S. Careless (Toronto: University of Toronto Press, 1980), 224; P.B. Waite, "The Political Ideas of John A. Macdonald," in *The Political Ideas of the Prime Ministers of Canada,* ed. Marcel Hamelin (Ottawa: University of Ottawa Press, 1969), 51–67.

4   Janet Ajzenstat, Paul Romney, Ian Gentles, and William D. Gairdner, *Canada's Founding Debates* (Toronto: University of Toronto Press, 2003), 1.

5   Some of the more popular studies of Macdonald's life and legacy include: Donald G. Creighton, *John A. Macdonald: The Young Politician* (Toronto: University of Toronto Press, 1952); Donald G. Creighton, *John A. Macdonald: The Old Chieftain* (Toronto: University of Toronto Press, 1955); Richard Gwyn, *John A.: The Man Who Made Us* (Toronto: Random House Canada, 2008); Richard Gwyn, *Nation Maker: Sir John A. Macdonald: His Life, Our Times, vol. 2, 1867–1891* (Toronto: Random House Canada, 2011); Patrice Dutil and Roger Hall, eds. *Macdonald at 200: New Reflections and Legacies* (Toronto: Dundurn, 2014).

6   J.M.S. Careless, *Brown of the Globe, vol. 2, Statesman of Confederation, 1860–1880* (Toronto: Macmillan Company, 1963); Alistair Sweeny, *George-Etienne Cartier: A Biography* (Toronto: McClelland and Stewart, 1976); David A. Wilson, *Thomas D'Arcy McGee: The Extreme Moderate, 1857–1868*, vol. 2 (Montreal: McGill-Queen's University Press, 2011).

7   Carl M. Wallace, "Sir Leonard Tilley: A Political Biography," PhD diss., University of Alberta, 1972; Joseph R. Smallwood, *I Chose Canada. The Memoirs of the Honourable Joseph R. "Joey" Smallwood* (Toronto: Macmillan of Canada, 1973).

8   A sampling of the vast research concerning Louis Riel includes: Hartwell Bowsfield, ed. *Louis Riel: Selected Readings* (Toronto: Copp Clark Pitman, 1988); Albert R. Braz, *The False Traitor: Louis Riel in Canadian Culture* (Toronto: University of Toronto Press, 2003); Thomas Flanagan, *Louis "David" Riel: Prophet of the New World* (Toronto: University of Toronto Press, 1996); Thomas Flanagan, *Riel and the Rebellion: 1885 Reconsidered* (Toronto: University of Toronto Press, 2000); Douglas Owram, "The Myth of Louis Riel," *Canadian Historical Review* 63, no. 3 (1982): 315–36; Jennifer Reid, *Louis Riel and the Creation of Modern Canada: Mythic Discourse and the Postcolonial State* (Albuquerque: University of New Mexico Press, 2008); George F.G. Stanley, *Louis Riel: Patriot or Rebel?* Historical Booklet no. 2 (Ottawa: Canadian Historical Association, 1974); Donald Swainson, "Rieliana and the Structure of Canadian History," *The Journal of Popular Culture* 14, no. 2 (1980): 286–97.

9   George Woodcock, *Amor de Cosmos: Journalist and Reformer* (Toronto: Oxford University Press, 1975); Gordon Hawkins, *The de Cosmos Enigma* (Vancouver: Ronsdale Press, 2015).

10 Ged Martin, "Painting the Other Picture: The Case Against Confederation," in *From Rebellion to Patriation: Canada and Britain in the Nineteenth and Twentieth Centuries*, ed. C.C. Eldridge (Cardiff: Canadian Studies in Wales Group, 1989), 67. The notable exception to this observation is Nova Scotia's Joseph Howe, who has been the subject of several biographies.

11 Donald Creighton, *Canada's First Century, 1867–1967* (Toronto: Macmillan of Canada, 1970), 11.

12 David Jay Bercuson, "Canada's Burden of Unity: An Introduction," in *Canada and the Burden of Unity*, ed. David Jay Bercuson (Toronto: Copp Clark Pitman, 1986), 3.

13 T. W. Acheson, "The Maritimes and 'Empire Canada'," in *Canada and the Burden of Unity*, ed. David Jay Bercuson (Toronto: Copp Clark Pitman, 1977), 87–114.

14 Morton's classic essay is reproduced in: W.L. Morton, "Clio in Canada: The Interpretation of Canadian History," in *Context of Canada's Past: Selected Essays of W.L. Morton*, ed. A.B. McKillop (Toronto: Macmillan of Canada, 1980), 109.

15 Creighton, *Canada's First Century*, 48.

16 For examples of centralist scholarship, consult: Creighton, *Canada's First Century*; Norman McLeod Rogers, "The Compact Theory of Confederation," in *Papers and Proceedings of the Annual Meeting of the Canadian Political Science Association* (1931), 205–30; W.L. Morton, "The Conservative Principle in Confederation," *Queen's Quarterly* 71 (1965): 528–46.

17 Ramsay Cook, *Provincial Autonomy, Minority Rights, and the Compact Theory, 1867–1921*, vol. 4 of Canada Royal Commission in Bilingual and Biculturalism (Ottawa: Information Canada, 1969), 9. See also: Paul Romney, *Getting It Wrong: How Canadians Forgot Their Past and Imperiled Confederation* (Toronto: University of Toronto Press, 1999).

18 Arthur I. Silver, *The French-Canadian Idea of Confederation, 1864–1900*, 2 ed. (Toronto: University of Toronto Press, 1997), 184.

19 For further studies concerning biculturalism, bilingualism, and separatism in Canada consult: Silver, *The French-Canadian Idea of Confederation*; Cook, *Provincial Autonomy, Minority Rights, and the Compact Theory*; A.D. Dunton and André Laurendeau, *Report of the Royal Commission on Bilingualism and Biculturalism*, Book 1: General Introduction (Ottawa: Queen's Printer, 1967); Ralph Heintzman, "The Spirit of Confederation: Professor Creighton, Biculturalism, and the Use of History," *Canadian Historical Review* 52, no. 3 (1971), 245–75; Matthew Hayday, *So They Want Us to Learn French: Promoting and Opposing Bilingualism in English-Speaking Canada* (Vancouver: University of British Columbia Press, 2015); Susan Mann, *The Dream of Nation. A Social and Intellectual History of Quebec* (Montreal: McGill-Queen's University Press, 2002).

20 Truth and Reconciliation Commission of Canada, *Honouring the Truth, Reconciling for the Future: Summary of the Final Report of the Truth and Reconciliation Commission of Canada* (Winnipeg: Truth and Reconciliation Commission of Canada, 2015), 1.

21 See for example: Citizenship and Immigration Canada, "Discover Canada: The Rights and Responsibilities of Citizenship," accessed 30 June 2017, http://www.cic.gc.ca/english/pdf/pub/discover.pdf.

22 Royal Commission on Aboriginal Peoples, "Partners in Confederation: Aboriginal Peoples, Self-Government, and the Constitution" (Ottawa: Canada Communication Group, 1993).

23 For discussion on "harmonizing" relations between Indigenous and non-Indigenous Peoples consult: John Borrows, *Freedom and Indigenous Constitutionalism* (Toronto: University of Toronto Press, 2016), 45.

24 Borrows, *Freedom and Indigenous*, 35.

25 J.R. Miller, *Compact, Contract, Covenant: Aboriginal Treaty-Making in Canada* (Toronto: University of Toronto Press, 2009), 300.

26 Truth and Reconciliation Commission of Canada, *Honouring the Truth, Reconciling for the Future*, 8.

27 J.R. Miller, *Shingwauk's Vision: A History of Native Residential Schools* (Toronto: University of Toronto Press, 1996), 98.

28 R.L. Watts, "Contemporary Views on Federalism," in *Evaluating Federal Systems*, ed. Bertus de Villiers (Boston: Juta & Co. 1994), 2.

2

Compact, Contract, Covenant: The Evolution of First Nations Treaty-Making†

J.R. MILLER

The history of treaty-making between First Nations and Europeans in Canada has had a lengthy history and many phases. The earliest agreements, usually informal and generally unrecorded in a lasting form that Europeans would recognize, were compacts governing commercial relations between European traders and indigenous suppliers of fur. Alongside these commercial pacts, treaties of peace and friendship emerged in the late seventeenth and eighteenth centuries as the dominant form of treaty-making in north-eastern North America. Like commercial agreements, these procedures for making and maintaining diplomatic and military associations largely followed Aboriginal practices. In the latter decades of the eighteenth century and throughout the first part of the nineteenth, land-related treaties emerged as the most frequent form of treaty-making between First Nations and Europeans in Canada. Very often these territorial agreements resembled, at least superficially, simple contracts for straightforward transactions. Perhaps because later record keeping has proven better and more enduring, it is clear that, in the latter part of the nineteenth century, land-related treaties shifted in character. From the 1870s onward, the agreements by which Europeans obtained access to First Nations territory took the form of a covenant, a three-sided agreement to which the deity was a party. Through the twentieth century, especially

19

in its latter decades, First Nations have insisted on the covenant nature of treaty-making as the norm, while for a long time the Government of Canada emphasized that land-related treaties were contractual in nature. In all the discussion, the original form of treaty as commercial compact tended to get lost. If, as the Supreme Court of Canada decreed in 1985, treaties between First Nations and the Crown were *sui generis*, unique, it might be because, historically, they had taken so many forms.

In sorting out the complex and shifting history of treaty-making in Canada, no scholar has been of greater assistance than Arthur J. Ray. As Ray has noted, First Nations' objectives in making treaty and the nature of treaties are important issues: "For Canada's First Nations it is a crucial question that has a bearing on the pursuit of treaty rights issues" that have become so important since the refashioning of the Constitution in 1982. With characteristic modesty, Ray has suggested that he contributed to the discussion about the nature of treaties by proposing an alternative to the interpretation "that the accords should be seen primarily as peace agreements through which Aboriginal nations agreed to share their lands with newcomers." His alternative interpretation stressed the economic aspects of treaty-making: "I closed *Indians in the Fur Trade* with the observation that the Aboriginal People of the prairie West sought to adapt through treaty negotiations to the radical economic developments that were taking place in western Canada in the late nineteenth century. In other words, I emphasized the economic dimension."[1]

In spite of Ray's modest statement, his contributions to scholarly understanding of First Nations treaties with Europeans throughout Canadian history extend far beyond his emphasizing the economic aspect of treaty-making. This is not to say that Ray's emphasis was not important and badly needed. Prior to his work, treaty-making had been but dimly understood in published scholarship. For a long time the prevailing view seemed to echo the federal government's position: treaties were simple contracts for land that in some cases—the Numbered Treaties, for example —were also distinguished by the inclusion of provident and far-sighted provisions to encourage agricultural development and schooling by a wise and benevolent government in Ottawa. While that perspective, celebrated most notably in George Stanley's 1936 *The Birth of Western Canada*,[2] was starting to be questioned in the late 1970s and early 1980s,[3] it had not been dislodged by the time Ray began to publish his work on First Nations in

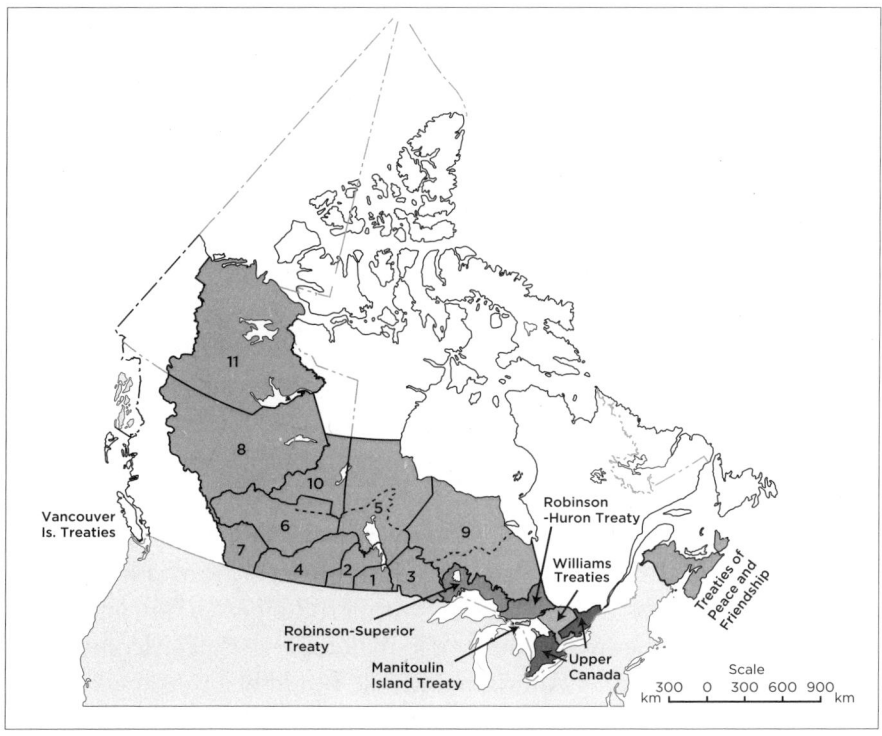

Fig 2.1 Historical Treaties of Canada. Developed from Canada, "Historical Treaties of Canada," *Indigenous and Northern Affairs Canada*, https://www.aadnc-aandc.gc.ca/DAM/DAM-INTER-HQ/STAGING/texte-text/htoc_1100100032308_eng.pdf.

the fur trade.

The second major contribution to treaty studies made by Arthur Ray's scholarship was its explanation of trade protocol and, later, how that protocol informed treaty talks in nineteenth-century Western Canada. More so than in *Indians in the Fur Trade*, in "*Give Us Good Measure*," his quantitative history written with Donald Freeman, Ray laid out the elaborate ceremonialism with which the trade was conducted, particularly at York Factory.[4] Quoting contemporary observer Andrew Graham, Ray and Freeman explained that, when a trading party got about three kilometres from a Hudson's Bay Company (HBC) post, they halted out of sight while their trading captains organized their approach. They "soon after appear in sight of the Fort, to the number of between ten and twenty in a line abreast of each other. If there is but one captain his station is in the centre, but if more they are in the wings also; and their canoes are distinguished from the rest by a small St. George or Union Jack, hoisted on a stick placed in the stern of the vessel."[5] When they got closer to the fort, a group of would-be traders would join other parties to form a flotilla of canoes. The approaching Natives saluted the post by firing "several fowling-pieces," while the HBC post master, having already given the order to hoist "the Great Flag" at the fort, returned the compliment with his twelve pounders. These opening salutations and honours were merely the prelude to more elaborate ceremonialism.

Once the Aboriginal traders had landed and the women had set up camp, the trading captains and their immediate subordinates engaged in a lengthy ceremony with HBC personnel. The man in charge of the post, on learning the leaders of the Natives had arrived, had his trader introduce them formally: "Chairs are placed in the room, and pipes with smoking materials produced on the table. The [Indian] captains place themselves on each side [of] the Governor, but not a word proceeds from either party, until everyone has recruited his spirits with a full pipe."[6] Then, and only then, the leaders of the two parties would make speeches of welcome. The spokesman for the visiting Aboriginal People would begin by explaining how many there were in the party, what had transpired with other traders who were not accompanying them this year, and general news since last the parties had met to trade. He likely would also make a call for fair and generous treatment in trade, and he would always ask how things had been with his English partners since they met last. For his part, the post factor would welcome them and assure them of his good will and generosity.

The factor would conclude his presentation by providing gifts to his Aboriginal trading partners. The presents usually consisted of clothing, food, smoking materials, and alcohol. The items of clothing were especially significant for the development of a treaty-making tradition in Canada:

> A coarse cloth coat, either red or blue, lined with baize with regimental cuffs and collar. The waistcoat and breeches are of baize; the suit ornamented with broad and narrow orris lace of different colours: a white or checked shirt; a pair of stockings tied below the knee with worsted garters; a pair of English shoes. The hat is laced and ornamented with feathers of different colours. A worsted sash tied round the crown, and

end hanging out on each side down to the shoulders. A silk handkerchief is tucked by the corner into the loops behind; with these decorations it is put on the captain's head and completes his dress. The lieutenant is also presented with an inferior suit.[7]

The factor would also present his gifts of food, tobacco, and liquor, and escort the Natives from the trading post to their encampment in a formal procession.[8] At the Aboriginal encampment, the other half of the reciprocal ceremonial welcome and exchange occurred. The factor and perhaps an officer or two would be invited into the carefully prepared lodge and seated in the place of honour. The Aboriginal trading captain would then make a speech and cause gifts to be distributed to his visitors.

After a period of a day or more during which the Natives indulged in liquor, songs, and dance in their encampment, both sides were prepared to move on to the main event: trading furs. However, before the truly commercial part of the visit got under way, more ceremony was required. The Natives came back to the trading post to smoke the calumet, or ceremonial pipe, with the Europeans and to complete trade preliminaries. An observer at York Factory reported:

> As the ceremony of smoking the calumet is necessary to establish confidence, it is conducted with the greatest solemnity, and every person belonging to that gang is admitted on the occasion. The Captain walks in with his calumet in his hand covered with a case, then comes the lieutenant and the wives of the captains with the present, and afterwards all the other men with the women and their little ones. The Governor is genteely dressed after the Indian fashion, and receives them with cordiality and good humour. The captain covers the table with a new beaver coat, and on it lays the calumet or pipe; he will also sometimes present the Governor with a clean beaver toggy or banian to keep him warm in the winter. The Puc'ca'tin'ash'a'win [gift of furs prepared in advance] is also presented. Then the Governor sits down in an arm-chair, the captain and the chief men on either hand on chairs; the others

sit round on the floor; the women and children are placed behind, and a profound silence ensues.[9]

The solemn smoking of the pipe then occurred, with the factor first lighting the pipe. The ceremonial smoking was followed by another exchange of speeches, quite lengthy this time, and the HBC man's distribution of food to the Natives.[10] On this occasion, the Aboriginal traders might also renew their calls for fair and generous treatment in trade with phrases such as "pity us" and "give us good measure," followed by an examination of the measures used in trading to satisfy themselves as to their "goodness." In some cases, as Arthur Ray pointed out more recently, the HBC representative would make gifts of medicines to those of his visitors who had responsibility for curing: "The captains and several others are doctors, and are taken singly with their wives into a room where they are given a red leather trunk with a few simple medicines such as the powders of sulphur, bark, liquorice, camphorated spirit, white ointment, and basilicon [ointment of 'sovereign' virtues], with a bit of diachylon plaster [an ointment made of vegetable juices]."[11]

As Ray and others have noted, the significance of these and other trade-related events that are known thanks to the richness of HBC records and researchers' efforts is great. In the ceremonies of welcome, speech making, gift-giving, and reassurance, the newcomers were adjusting to the Natives and their ways. These ceremonies and exchanges were part of Aboriginal protocol that governed interactions, including trade relations, between First Nations. In other words, the European newcomers had to accommodate Aboriginal values, observances, and practices in order to establish their sincerity and bona fides as trading partners. What was being created by these ceremonial observances was a commercial relationship that was enduring. They did not signal a one-time trade transaction. Further supporting this interpretation of HBC trade protocol was one further Aboriginal practice that Ray underlined. A First Nations trading captain who was content with how he and his party had been treated would leave his pipe at the post to be used the next year; if he was unhappy, he would take the pipe with him. The actions, respectively, signified maintaining or rupturing the commercial partnership.[12] The pipe was laden with symbolic significance. More generally, the entire protocol surrounding fur trade activity demonstrated European adjustment to Aboriginal ways.

Arthur Ray's scholarship on the fur trade also contributed one other important point relevant to the story of treaty-making: he outlined how HBC practice recognized First Nations occupancy and control of territory in Rupert's Land. Even though the Royal Charter of 1670, which authorized the "Gentlemen Adventurers" to monopolize trade in all the lands drained by Hudson Bay and James Bay, also purported to confer on the HBC freehold ownership of the lands, the company, in practice, behaved as though it had no foreordained territorial rights. Just as Cornelius Jaenen has explained that French claims and pretensions to ownership of Aboriginal lands in New France were a formality intended for European, rather than Aboriginal, ears,[13] so Ray demonstrated that the HBC recognized the necessity of securing First Nations permission to operate in their lands. The distinction is parallel to one of Walter Bagehot's insights about the British system of government. In *The English Constitution* (1867), Bagehot distinguished between two "two parts" of the Constitution: "First, those which excite and preserve the reverence of the population—the *dignified* parts, if I may so call them; and next, the *efficient* parts—those by which it, in fact, works and rules."[14] The same point was expressed, acidly as usual, by Goldwin Smith, who observed of the monarch and Governor General that: "Religious Canada prays each Sunday that they may govern well, on the understanding that heaven will never be so unconstitutional as to grant her prayer."[15] The distinction was between the formality of the strict letter of theory and the reality of practice on the ground.

Arthur Ray explained very clearly that this distinction applied to the HBC and the title to Rupert's Land that the company derived from its charter. He pointed out how, in 1680, the directors of the HBC instructed their representative in James Bay as follows:

> There is another thing, if it may be done, that wee judge would be much for the interest & safety of the Company. That is, In the several places *where you are or shall settle*, you contrive to make compact with the Captns, or chiefs of the respective Rivers & places whereby it might be understood by them that you had purchased both the lands & rivers of them, and that they had transferred the absolute propriety to you, *or at least the only freedome* of trade, And that you should cause them to do some act wch. By the Religion or Custome of their Country

should be thought most sacred & obliging to them for the confirmation of such Agreements...

As wee have above directed you to endeavour to make such Contracts with the Indians in all places where you settle as may in future times ascertain to us *all liberty of trade & commerce and a league of friendship & peaceable cohabitation*, So wee have caused Iron marks to be made of the figure of the Union Flagg wth. wch. wee would have you burn Tallys of wood wth. Such ceremony as they shall understand to be obligatory & sacred. The manner whereof wee must leave to your prudence as you shall find the mode & humours of the people you deal with, But when the Impression is made, you are to write upon the Tally the name of the Nation or person wth. Whom the Contract is made and the date thereof, and then deliver one part of the Stick to them, and reserve the other. This wee suppose may be sutable to the capacities of those barbarous people, and may much conduce to our quiet & commerce, and secure us from foreign or domestic pretenders.[16]

Ray's insight into the practical nature of HBC practice is the key element in demonstrating that the fur trade yielded the earliest form of First Nations treaties. Agreements of the sort that the directors instructed their man in James Bay to secure were, in effect, commercial compacts and, as such, a form of treaty. The record of the French fur trade of the seventeenth and eighteenth centuries also yields examples of Europeans entering into agreements with First Nations to further their exploration and fur commerce. The famous pact between Champlain and the Huron in the early years of the seventeenth century, whereby the French secured permission to operate in Huron country and the Huron received French help against their Iroquois enemies is only one of many.[17] The relationship between trade and peaceful relations was well expressed by an eighteenth-century Iroquois orator, who said "Trade and Peace we take to be one thing."[18] Ray and Freeman made the same point for the western trade: "Exchange between North American Indian groups was a political as well as an economic activity. Indians would not trade with groups with whom they were not formally at peace. Therefore, prior to the commencement of trade, ceremonies were held to conclude or renew alliances."[19] In Aboriginal society, trade relations were impossible outside a friendly relationship established and renewed according to First Nations protocols. There is even some evidence from the later period of ententes that were, in effect, fur trade compacts. According to Canon Edward Ahenakew, in the nineteenth century Chief Thunderchild noted that the HBC "gave one boat load of goods for the use of the Saskatchewan River" to Natives at Fort Carlton.[20] Hugh Dempsey documented the use of pre-trade ritual—including welcoming ceremonies, gift-giving, smoking of the pipe, and speeches—at Rocky Mountain House down to the 1850s.[21]

Arthur Ray further contributed to scholarly understanding of the treaty-making process by linking HBC practices to events of the latter part of the nineteenth century:

> The First Nations of western Canada forged their relations with Europeans in the crucible of the fur trade. Successful long-term commercial intercourse required the development of institutions and practices that accommodated the sharply different diplomatic, economic, political, and social traditions of the two parties. When First Nations treaty-making with Canada began in the nineteenth century, Aboriginal People carried over into negotiating practices and strategies many long-established fur trading customs that they incorporated into the treaties.[22]

Such practices as welcoming formalities, speeches, exchanges of gifts, smoking of the pipe, and assurances of good will figured as prominently in the making of the Numbered Treaties, for example, as they had in the earlier commercial exchange. Moreover, First Nations formed their opinions and expectations of nineteenth-century European or Euro-Canadian emissaries in accordance with earlier fur trade exchanges. Both because the agreements forged in the fur trade, especially the HBC trade, bore the characteristics of commercial compacts and because they bequeathed a tradition that manifested itself in the Numbered Treaties of the late nineteenth century and early twentieth century, these fur trade arrangements deserve to be recorded as the first phase of treaty-making in Canadian history.

Two other forms of treaty-making soon emerged. The first, which developed contemporaneously with the commercial relationships of New France, was the treaty of peace and friendship. Administrators, most notably the governor in New France, had constructed an elaborate system of alliances on the base of France's extensive fur trade networks during the seventeenth century. On occasion, in the case of the Huron Confederacy for example, the combined commercial-military alliance did not survive. With the Huron, repeated Iroquois attacks on Huronia, about which French forces were not able to do much, resulted in the dispersal of the Huron. In most other cases, however, the alliances that France forged with Nations such as the Montagnais, Algonkin, and a large variety of "western Indians" proved to be enduring and effective. As was the case with the HBC's commercial dealings with northern and western First Nations, the French style of treaty diplomacy featured essentially Aboriginal practices such as gift-giving, elaborate ritual, speeches, and ceremony. Onontio, as the governor of New France was known, was expected to strike an imposing figure and make both grand gestures and elaborate gifts to renew the alliances that were established. The giving of presents was especially important for both material and symbolic reasons. Presents sustained First Nations allies who might have been hard pressed by poor hunting or harrying attacks by their enemies. But, equally important, presents represented a renewal of alliance and another token of good will and intentions. In the diplomatic parlance of the seventeenth and eighteenth centuries, presents "dried the tears" of allies who had suffered losses, "opened the throats" of people so they could speak, and "opened the ears" of partners so that they would hear what was said. The speeches, gifts, and other rituals that were held regularly when French and forest diplomats[23] met were a mechanism for renewing the alliance.

The British south of the lower Great Lakes and St. Lawrence learned to practise diplomacy as the First Nations did as well. Indeed, from the Thirteen Colonies, and more particularly from New York, came one of the most remarkable artefacts of the era of treaties of peace and friendship: the Covenant Chain. In the late seventeenth century, England began to fashion an extended system of alliances with the Five Nations of the Iroquois. (Early in the eighteenth century, the Tuscarora would move north into Iroquoia, and the Iroquois Confederacy would become the League of the Six Nations.) In time, an extensive structure evolved that paralleled the French alliance with the western First Nations. By the late 1600s, the Covenant Chain linked the English, with greater or lesser effectiveness depending on the exigencies of the moment, to a vast range of First Nations. In this system, the governor of New York, known as Corlaer to the Natives, functioned as the counterpart of Onontio in New France. Indeed, Aboriginal diplomats frequently used "Onontio" or "Corlaer" as shorthand references for their links to the French or the English.[24]

Over time, the English developed methods of reaching arrangements with their First Nations allies that were very similar to those employed by the French. They, too, used elaborate ritual, speech making, gifts, and other ceremonies to maintain their links to their allies. Most remarkable, perhaps, was the way in which British diplomats learned and employed the elaborate rituals of the Iroquois, including the condoling and requickening ceremonies. When an Iroquois chief died, there were lengthy ceremonies to mourn his passing (the condoling ceremony) as well as rituals to recognize publicly the man who would succeed the deceased in office (the requickening ceremony). Another example of European adaptation to Aboriginal ways in the diplomatic field involves the use of wampum to record important actions. Wampum, belts made of shells or beads of different colours arranged in patterns, were for the First Nations of northeastern North America both a mnemonic, or memory-assisting, instrument and a way of recording events.

So, a First Nations diplomat—and in time European diplomats, too—would deliver a section of his speech and then lay a belt of wampum before the people to whom he was making his oral proposal. In an important conference diplomats might eventually present a dozen or more belts of wampum. Equally important was the use of wampum to record the results of conferences designed to secure peace or alliance. The principal terms of the deal would be commemorated graphically in a wampum belt. One of the most famous of these instruments was the *gus wenta*, or the two-row wampum, which the Five Nations of the Iroquois fashioned with the Dutch in the seventeenth century. The two-row wampum contained symbols that represented the two parties in separate water craft that travelled side by side. The meaning, Iroquois maintain even today, is that the two parties agreed to work together in partnership but to respect each other's difference and not to attempt to interfere with each other. Iroquois also insist that the British inherited the Dutch role after they took control of

New Netherlands in 1664.

These complex treaty-making systems came to a meeting of sorts in 1701. In that year, the French and a variety of First Nations, the Iroquois prominent among them, fashioned the Great Peace of Montreal, while the Iroquois also concluded a separate arrangement with the English at Albany. The motives of the various parties were complex but complementary.[25] The Iroquois, who were weakened by disease and population loss after some seven decades of off-again-on-again warfare with the French and their allies, wanted to relieve the pressure and replenish their ranks by an exchange of prisoners. The Five Nations were also anxious about the persistent worrying of their western flank by New France's Aboriginal allies. The French were similarly wearied by long periods of devastating guerilla warfare and sought peace for the respite and stability it would provide. The English hoped, by treaty-making, to maintain their ties with the Five Nations and spare themselves attacks by the Aboriginal allies of the French.

The complex treaty talks of 1700–1 revealed Native-newcomer treaty-making at a very sophisticated level. The Great Peace of Montreal, called "great" partly because over three dozen First Nations from a region stretching from the Maritimes to the edge of the Prairies signed it, established peace among the Iroquois, the French, and the allies of the French; promised a return of prisoners; and guaranteed the Iroquois the right to remain neutral in any hostilities between France and England. The last clause was enormously beneficial to both New France and the Five Nations, for both had been gravely weakened by the attrition of prolonged warfare.[26] If those terms understandably worried the English, who saw their Covenant Chain allies removed to a neutral category by the Peace of Montreal, further diplomatic action by the Iroquois in the same year attempted to reassure them. By a treaty often referred to as the Albany Deed, the Five Nations renewed their friendship with Corlaer and his people, while simultaneously purporting to convey hunting grounds north of the Great Lakes to English protection. While interpretations of the significance of this arrangement differ,[27] it clearly provided some reassurance to the English allies of the Iroquois, while simultaneously leaving untrammeled the Five Nations' right to stand neutral in a European imperial rivalry that seemed certain to play itself out in the interior of North America before very long. In any event, the Iroquois would choose their own course of action—neutrality or alliance with a European power—as their interests dictated whenever conflict broke out. That had always been the case with First Nations approaches to diplomacy and alliance in wartime; it would continue to be so during the war-torn eighteenth century in eastern North America.

Although the Great Peace of Montreal of 1701 and the Albany Deed were important instances of the genre of treaty-making known as the treaty of peace and friendship, they were by no means the only examples. European-First Nations diplomacy figured prominently in the succession of imperial clashes that culminated in the Seven Years' War (or the French and Indian War, as it is more commonly known in the United States) as well as the War of the American Revolution and, ultimately, the War of 1812. A particularly important and revealing theatre of the wars of imperial rivalry of the period to 1760 was the Atlantic. Acadia, the French colony in peninsular Nova Scotia, along with the St. Lawrence River Valley colony of Canada, constituted what the French called New France. If Canada stood for access to the fur trade and its attendant system of Indian alliances, Acadia represented the entrée to the Atlantic fishery and to strategically important sites. France would develop the latter in the early 1720s, after the 1713 Treaty of Utrecht forced it to concede "Acadia with its ancient limits" to Great Britain, by building the massive fortress of Louisbourg on Cape Breton. Acadia had one other strategic asset so far as the French were concerned: the Mi'kmaq.

The Mi'kmaq, an Algonkian people who dominated Nova Scotia, Prince Edward Island, and northern New Brunswick, were drawn to the French for both negative and positive reasons. As Cornelius Jaenen has well explained, the French presence in Acadia after 1604 did not threaten Mi'kmaq territorial interests because the settlers who would evolve into the Acadians settled in areas largely unused by the Mi'kmaq—farming land reclaimed from the waters by dyking and draining. To this compatibility of location and land usage was added the fact that French representatives from the earliest days of contact with the Mi'kmaq wove bonds of friendship and affinity between the two peoples. The most important of those links was religion: from the early conversion of Chief Membertou and his entire family in 1610, French Roman Catholic missionaries worked among the Mi'kmaq, ministering both to Acadians and Natives. Over time, the process of intermarriage and acculturation developed close ties between the two communities. This experience of the seventeenth century stood in dramatic contrast to events of the first half of the eighteenth. Following the Treaty of Utrecht, Britain moved to make good its claim to Nova Scotia, as it preferred to call what had been "Acadia" to the French, by settlement and military presence. Unfortunately for British-Mi'kmaq relations, the territorial compatibility that had figured so prominently in Acadian dealings with the Mi'kmaq did not exist in the portions of the colony where British and British-sponsored settlers chose to locate. Unlike the French, the British presence brought to the surface a strong territorial incompatibility between the Indigenous People and the new European power in the region.

Religion played an important role in the growing friction between the British and the Mi'kmaq. His Britannic Majesty, as head of a militantly Protestant country, took a dim view of Roman Catholicism in his new Atlantic colony and among an Aboriginal People who for so long had had close relations with His Most Catholic Majesty, the king of France. For their part, the Mi'kmaq had close ties to Roman Catholic missionaries from France and, according to at least one authority, even believed that they had entered into a concordat, a treaty-like agreement between the Vatican and their nation, as a result of the conversion of Membertou in 1610.[28] During the first half of the eighteenth century, and most especially after about 1720, the governor of New France regularly employed Catholic missionaries as emissaries in Acadia to influence the Mi'kmaq in ways that assisted French strategic designs of maintaining a presence in Nova Scotia. Such complications explain why the British had such difficulty making their hold on Nova Scotia good between the Treaty of Utrecht and the end of the Seven Years' War, as well as why British forces found it necessary to expel the Acadians in 1755. One measure of the greater difficulty the British had in the region compared to the French is that, over the century and a half that the French associated with the Mi'kmaq, France made precisely one formal treaty with the First Nation, whereas the British entered into no fewer than thirty-two treaties with them between 1720 and 1786.[29] The unusual treaty history of Canada's maritime region illustrates that treaty arrangements, which could be founded on factors such as trade and religion, took many forms and that a propensity to make treaty by itself did not guarantee stability in a country's treaty regime.

In contrast to the impermanence and ineffectiveness of its treaty system in eighteenth-century Nova Scotia, Britain's next foray in Native policy would have a profound and long-lasting impact. The Royal Proclamation of October 1763, which Britain issued to provide institutions of government and law for territories newly acquired in the Seven Years' War, contained extremely important provisions concerning First Nations lands. Although the Proclamation, which was a unilateral Crown document, is often described as the "Indians' Magna Carta" and is said to bestow many territorial blessings on First Nations, it was written as though the royal author assumed the territories all belonged to the Crown. When the Proclamation turned to the First Nations and their territorial rights, it described them as "the several Nations or Tribes of Indians with whom We are connected, and who live under our Protection," and said that they "should not be molested or disturbed in the Possession of such Parts of Our Dominions and Territories as, not having been ceded to or purchased by Us, are reserved to them, or any of them, as their Hunting Grounds." In other words, the Proclamation said that the Crown reserved from its dominions land for First Nation allies and associates as their grounds for hunting and maintaining themselves. Be that limited recognition as it may, it then went on to lay out a regime that was to govern those lands "reserved to them . . . as their Hunting Grounds." First, it forbade settlement in the interior beyond the height of land and regulated commercial penetration of the region by requiring traders to get licences from the governor before going beyond the mountains. The purpose of these clauses was to hold back and control non-Native entry into the interior so as to placate the First Nations and prevent clashes between them and intruding colonists intent on making Aboriginal "Hunting Grounds" into settlers' fields. The fact that Pontiac's War, a rising of interior First Nations against the newly victorious British, was raging when the Proclamation was issued underlined the need to control non-Native access to lands beyond the mountain ranges west of the Thirteen Colonies.

The Proclamation continued with important clauses concerning interior First Nations territories. It reserved "for the use of the said Indians, all the Land and Territories not included within the Limits of Our said Three new Governments, or within the Limits of the Territory granted to the Hudson's Bay Company," and the King did "hereby strictly forbid, on Pain of our Displeasure, all our loving Subjects from making any Purchases or Settlements whatever, or taking Possession of any of the Lands above reserved, without our especial leave and Licence for that Purpose first obtained." The objective of forbidding settlement or purchase of First Nations lands was to put an end to "great Frauds and Abuses [that] have been committed in purchasing Lands of the Indians, to the great Prejudice of our Interests, and to the great Dissatisfaction of the said Indians." Or, as American historian Francis Jennings was later to put it, the Proclamation aimed to put a stop to the "deed game," the dubious practice by which pioneers or land speculators—the distinction between the two categories was often a fine one in settler societies—obtained a transfer deed from a Native by fraud or employment of alcohol. When the colonists acted on the dubious deed, trouble ensued between the First Nations and incoming settlers.

The Proclamation's alternative to the "deed game" was a policy for acquiring First Nations land that would give the document its long-lasting influence:

> In order, therefore, to prevent such Irregularities for the future, and to the end that the Indians may be convinced of our Justice and determined Resolution to remove all reasonable Causes of Discontent, We do, with the Advice of our Privy Council strictly enjoin and require, that no private Person do presume to make any purchase from the said Indians of any Lands reserved to the said Indians, within those parts of our Colonies where We have thought proper to allow Settlement: but that, if at any Time any of the said Indians should be inclined to dispose of the said Lands, the same shall be Purchased only for Us, in our Name, at some public Meeting or Assembly of the said Indians, to be held for that Purpose by the Governor or Commander in Chief of our Colony respectively within which they shall lie.

Analogous rules were laid down for acquiring First Nations lands in colonies where there already was a colonial government. In other words, in both the lands beyond settlement that were reserved for First Nations and within settled colonies the Proclamation held that the only way Aboriginal lands could be obtained lawfully was by a representative of the Crown, not a private citizen or a company, and only through a public process that would help to avoid fraudulent dealings. As the Proclamation also said, these restrictions on acquiring lands were motivated in large part by Britain's desire that "the Indians may be convinced of our Justice and determined Resolution to remove all reasonable Causes of Discontent."

Although these terms of the Royal Proclamation of 1763 were important in their own right, they paled in significance with the implications and legacy of the document. For one thing, according to one Aboriginal law specialist, British officials in 1764 took actions that converted the Proclamation from a unilateral Crown document into a treaty. According to John Borrows, in 1764 William Johnson, Britain's superintendent of the northern First Nations, called together some two thousand First Nations representatives from districts stretching from Nova Scotia to the Mississippi, explained the contents of the Royal Proclamation, and procured their agreement to them.[30] The implication of the events, according to Borrows' interpretation, is that, through the Niagara conference of 1764, the Royal Proclamation became a treaty protected by Section 35 of Canada's 1982 Constitution Act. Although documentary sources such as the published Johnson Papers, *New York Colonial Documents*, and government-compiled collection of treaties do not explicitly support his argument, there is evidence that Johnson explained the Royal Proclamation's territorial guarantees to Iroquois groups early in 1764.[31] If he did this with relatively small groups of Iroquois in January 1764, it is reasonable to infer that he did the same thing with much larger numbers of First Nations at Niagara that summer. Borrows also points out that First Nations oral traditions and wampum do provide evidence for his view of the Proclamation.[32] If this interpretation is upheld, the Proclamation will itself be a key development in the Canadian treaty-making tradition.

Whether or not the courts treat it as a treaty, there is no doubt that, since the late eighteenth century, the Proclamation has profoundly influenced treaty-making. Although the requirements of the Proclamation were not followed scrupulously in every case, from 1764 until Confederation, treaties were made by the Crown with a variety of First Nations in central British North America to gain access to First Nations lands. For the first half century after 1763, the acquisitions were motivated by a desire to obtain lands on which to settle allies of the British and then immigrants to British territory. The former motive was exemplified by the acquisition of lands immediately north of Lake Erie and Lake Ontario for Mohawk allies defeated in the War of the American Revolution. The latter reason, the need to provide access to lands for immigrants, became especially compelling after the creation of Upper Canada as a separate political unit in 1791. In this first fifty years of Proclamation-style treaty-making, the documents that resulted provided for a straightforward transfer of territory in return for a one-time payment, often in goods. So, for example, Treaty No. 8 in 1797 provided access to 3,450 acres of land north and east of Burlington Bay. A group of Mississauga (Ojibwa) negotiated the pact with William Claus, superintendent of Indian Affairs "on behalf of the Crown," in return for "seventy-five pounds two shillings and sixpence Quebec Currency in value in goods estimated according to the Montreal price." A certificate attached to the government version of the treaty listed blankets, several types of cloth, butcher knives, and brass kettles to the specified value as having been conveyed to the First Nations signatories.[33]

The land-related treaties of this fifty-year period following the Royal Proclamation are the agreements that bear the closest resemblance to simple contracts in Canadian history. At least as explained in the government's version of them, they exchanged a specific tract of land, usually a relatively small piece, from the First Nation in return for a one-time payment. The treaties usually were negotiated, as the example (above) was, by an official who clearly represented the Crown. There were, however, exceptions. One was the so-called Selkirk Treaty of 1817, negotiated in the Red River area by a representative of Lord Selkirk, the landlord who had acquired a large tract of land from the HBC and established a struggling colony on it in the second decade of the nineteenth century. The origins of this agreement were anything but exemplary of Proclamation policy, which, in any event, was not intended to apply to Rupert's Land. The background of the Selkirk Treaty was a violent clash between mixed-ancestry[34] forces and colonists at Seven Oaks in 1816. Only then was Selkirk, who had acquired lands from the HBC in 1811 and started his colony in 1812, moved to have an arrangement with local Saulteaux (Western Ojibwa) negotiated. Also instructive was the fact that the Selkirk's text labelled the agreement "This Indenture," an indenture being a legal agreement or contract that bears a seal. The treaty or indenture conveyed 3.2 kilometres on either side of the Red and Assiniboine rivers to Selkirk on "the express condition that the said Earl, his heirs and successors, or their agents, shall annually pay to the Chiefs and warriors of the Chippewa or Saulteaux Nation, the present or quit rent consisting of one hundred pounds weight of good and merchantable tobacco."[35]

The Selkirk Treaty, whether or not it was part of a treaty-making tradition founded upon the Royal Proclamation of 1763, stands at a transitional point in the history of such agreements in Canada. Between 1763 and the War of 1812, the agreements that had been made covered small areas, provided for one-time compensation to the Aboriginal signatories, and resembled simple contracts. By means of such agreements, the Crown had dealt with First Nations territorial rights in a large portion of Upper Canada, now southern Ontario, in preparation for settlement by allies and immigrants. In retrospect, Selkirk was a harbinger of change that was on its way in British practice in Upper Canada. What the Selkirk Treaty unknowingly foreshadowed was a shift in the type of compensation provided by the Crown, a change that introduced an element to treaty-making that was both a novelty and a throwback. The change that was introduced by the British in 1818 was the use of annuities, annual payments to the First Nations in compensation for land rights obtained by treaty. From that time onward, the Crown used annuities mainly for reasons of economy. In another surge of treaty-making in preparation for immigration and settlement after the War of 1812, Britain moved to reduce its financial obligations by using annuities. The theory was that, once settlement commenced and colonists paid fees for the lands, income from this source would fund the annual payments to the First Nations. The annuity system would thereby reduce Britain's outlay.

However, annual payments to First Nations would be reminiscent of earlier transactions with allies, transactions that were still carried out down to 1858 in central British North America. Annuities resembled the annual presents that first the French and later the English had used to cement their alliances with First Nations. They "wiped the rust from the chain of friendship," "dried the tears" of bereaved partners, and "opened the ears and throats" for friendly dialogue. Moreover, to First Nations, the giving of presents, like the annual exchange of gifts at fur-trading posts, symbolized the renewal of a partnership, whether commercial or diplomatic and military. Introducing annuities into treaty-making linked land treaties in the nineteenth century to the commercial compacts and diplomacy of an earlier era. The action also complicated the view of Upper Canadian treaties as simple contracts and paved the way for a more complex form of treaty-making.

Before that complicated type of treaty emerged, however, the making of land treaties continued and evolved in Upper Canada. Between 1783 and the War of 1812, the Crown dealt with First Nations territorial rights in a band covering the "front" (river-front and lake-front). The depth back from the water that was embraced in these treaties was usually moderate, but in the regions at the east end of Lake Erie and along the river in the eastern part of the province the land treated for stretched noticeably further in-land.[36] These were the treaties in which the compensation for First Nations took the form of one-time payments. Between 1818 and the 1830s, the Crown dealt with a broader band of territory to the north in a series of treaties in which the compensation was annuities. For example, Upper Canadian Treaty No. 27 between the Crown and Mississauga dealt with a large tract in eastern Upper Canada that stretched to the Ottawa River, and it guaranteed the First Nation signatories "the yearly sum of six hundred and forty-two pounds ten shillings, Province Currency, in goods at the Montreal price to be well and truly paid yearly and every year by His Majesty, His Heirs and successors, to the said Mississaugua [sic] Nation inhabiting and claiming the said tract."[37] For the Upper Canadian treaties, a culmination occurred in 1850 with what are known as the Robinson Treaties.

The Robinson Huron and Robinson Superior treaties, named for the Great Lakes to which they were adjacent, advanced treaty-making in the pre-Confederation era. Geographically, they extended the Crown's claim to lands stretching well up into the Canadian Shield, where the attractions of mining had begun to draw non-Natives. They also advanced treaty-making practice by dealing with much larger tracts than had hitherto been the case in Upper Canada. The Robinson Treaties also broke new ground by specifying that provision of reserves was a Crown obligation flowing from the treaties. Prior to this time, reserves had existed as a result of missionary or Indian Department initiative, but they were not associated with treaties or Crown treaty obligations. From the time of Robinson onward, treaties and reserves normally went together. Finally, the Robinson Treaties reintroduced an element that had been present in some of the eighteenth-century Nova Scotia treaties: Crown recognition of the First Nations' continuing right to hunt and fish. As Commissioner Robinson explained to his superiors this concession was not altruistic: by acknowledging "the right of hunting and fishing over the ceded territory, they cannot say that the Government takes from their usual means of subsistence and therefore have no claims for support, which they no doubt would have preferred, had this not been done."[38] Commissioner Robinson gave the Ojibwa who signed the 1850 treaties the choice of a lump sum payment or a small upfront sum and annuities; they chose the latter. The Robinson Treaties combined elements that would form the template of later treaties in the West: they dealt with large territories, they established reserves for the First Nations, they included annuities, and they recognized a continuing Aboriginal right to hunt and fish.

By the time of Confederation, the Upper Canada treaty-making tradition had evolved into a sophisticated protocol that conformed in many respects to the requirements of the Royal Proclamation. That the Proclamation was not always followed was demonstrated in the background to both the Selkirk and Robinson treaties. In both instances, Native resistance had brought on overtures to make treaties. However, treaty-making in Upper Canada did involve the Crown and First Nations in public negotiations concerning territory. During the first fifty years after the Proclamation, the use of one-time payments had made the agreements resemble simple contracts for territory, although practice after the War of 1812 shifted to the use of annuities, which would prove to be the harbinger of a different style of treaty-making. Another exception to the general use of annual payments for compensation was to be found in colonial British Columbia. When Governor James Douglas responded in the 1850s to the pressure of encroaching settlement on Vancouver Island, he entered treaty talks with a variety of groups; this led, by 1854, to the conclusion of fourteen treaties for small parcels of land on the Island. In the talks, Douglas explained, he offered the First Nations leaders the choice of one-time compensation or annuities. The Natives chose a single payment upfront, making BC treaties unconventional in their compensation clauses as well as in the amount of territory they covered. Elsewhere in British North America, however, annuities were the norm, as were provision of reserves, large tracts, and guarantees of hunting and fishing.

The Numbered Treaties that were concluded in the West between 1871 and 1877 introduced a third category of treaty: the covenant. Of course, the official record, the government's version of the treaties that was published in 1880, continued to portray the agreements that covered the region from the Lake of the Woods to the foothills of the Rockies as simple contracts transferring territory from First Nations to the Crown. For example, Treaty No. 1, the Stone Fort Treaty in Manitoba, had the

"Chippewa and Swampy Cree Tribes of Indians . . . cede, release, surrender, and yield up to Her Majesty the Queen, and her successors for ever, all the lands included within the following limits, that is to say," in return for reserves, a signing payment, schools, and annuities of fifteen dollars paid in goods. Later, after the First Nations had successfully argued that there were other "outside promises" that did not turn up in the printed version of the treaty, Treaty No. 1 also increased annuities, made four rather than two headmen eligible for annual stipends, and provided livestock and equipment for the pursuit of agriculture.[39] The view of treaties between the Crown and First Nations as contracts for territory would prevail on the government side of transactions through the later negotiation of the northern Numbered Treaties between 1899 and 1921. The same interpretation informed the federal government's approach to dealing with claims arising from the treaties throughout the twentieth century.

Western First Nations in particular insisted upon a different view of the nature of their treaties. Rather than a contract involving two parties—Crown and First Nations—First Nations communities see the treaties as three-cornered agreements to which the deity is a party. A covenant is an agreement between humans, in which the deity participates and provides oversight. For Christians, for example, establishing a sacred relationship in marriage is generally described as a covenant because God is witness and participant in the solemn pact. In a similar fashion, First Nations argue that the western Numbered Treaties are covenants. One of the terms that Plains Cree use to describe treaties is *itîyimikosiwiyêcikêwina*, which means "arrangements ordained or inspired by our Father [Creator]."[40] Saskatchewan Saulteaux elder Danny Musqua told interviewers, "We made a covenant with Her Majesty's government, and a covenant is not just a relationship between people, it's a relationship between three parties, you [the Crown] and me [First Nations] and the Creator."[41] A contract between two or more parties is specific and relies on the precise letter of its terms; a covenant among two or more humans and the deity creates a special, solemn relationship in which the partnership is more important than its specific terms.

First Nations point to several forms of evidence to sustain their argument that the Numbered Treaties of the 1870s were covenants rather than contracts. In particular, with the exception of Treaty No. 4, the making of these seven treaties was preceded by observance of First Nations ceremonies and forms. (Apparently, First Nations negotiators at Fort Qu'Appelle in 1874 did not include Commissioner Alexander Morris in ceremonies—an omission on which Morris pointedly commented[42]—because they were angered by the transfer of Rupert's Land to Canada without their having been consulted or paid.) Morris described a typical instance of First Nations ceremonialism at Fort Carlton in August 1876:

> On my arrival, the Union Jack was hoisted, and the Indians at once began to assemble, beating drums, discharging fire-arms, singing and dancing. In about half an hour they were ready to advance and meet me. This they did in a semicircle, having men on horseback galloping in circles, shouting, singing and discharging fire-arms.
>
> They then performed the dance of the "pipe stem," the stem was elevated to the north, south, west and east, a ceremonial dance was then performed by the Chiefs and head men, the Indian men and women shouting the while.
>
> They then slowly advanced, the horsemen again preceding them on their approach to my tent. I advanced to meet them, accompanied by Messrs [W.J.] Christie and [James] McKay [fellow commissioners], when the pipe was presented to us and stroked by our hands.
>
> After the stroking had been completed, the Indians sat down in front of the council tent, satisfied that in accordance with their custom we had accepted the friendship of the Cree nation.[43]

The significance of the ceremonies was far greater than the commissioner apparently realized. While joining in friendship was certainly part of the ritual's meaning, there was far more to it than that. The use of the pipe invoked the Great Spirit as a participant at the talks that were to follow and bound everyone who smoked the pipe to tell only the truth. Moreover, any agreement produced by such solemn talks was sacred and could not be violated without grave ills befalling the violator. On the more positive side, according to two researchers who conducted many interviews in Saskatchewan, the ceremonies had an inclusive effect: "The treaties, through the spiritual ceremonies conducted during the negotiations, expanded the First Nations sovereign circle, bringing in and embracing the British Crown within their sovereign circle."[44] Inclusion in any sort of family relationship with Aboriginal Peoples was a potent development. The attribution or creation of kin relationships, as in the language used in the Covenant Chain of the seventeenth and eighteenth centuries, was a prelude to conducting business of any kind, commercial or diplomatic, in North American Aboriginal societies. By embracing the Queen's treaty commissioner through ceremonies, the western First Nations were establishing kinship with the Crown and, through the Crown, with the Queen's people. Little wonder that when Governor General Lord Lorne, the husband of a daughter of Queen Victoria, visited the Prairies in 1881, Kakishiway, a chief who had signed Treaty No. 4 in 1874, greeted him with, "I am glad to see you my Brother in Law" as both of them had a family relationship to the Queen.[45] The chief's link was through the treaties, while Lorne's was by marriage.

A second type of evidence supporting the interpretation of the western treaties as covenants came from the mouths and the actions of the Queen's treaty commissioners. First Nations would have been impressed by the presence and participation of Christian missionaries as interpreters or witnesses at the talks. There were Christian ministers or priests in attendance at the negotiation of treaties 4, 5, 6, and 7. Moreover, the treaty commissioner's insistence on suspending talks so that the Christians could observe the Sabbath properly testified to their adherence to spiritual practices and values.[46] The Queen's commissioners frequently involved the deity in their arguments, and for a variety of purposes. For example, at Treaty No. 4 talks, Commissioner Alexander Morris used a reference to the "Great Spirit" to counter Saulteaux arguments that the HBC had stolen their territory from them when it took the money Canada paid for the HBC lands: "Who made the earth, the grass, the stone, and the wood? The Great Spirit. He made them for all his children to use, and it is not stealing to use the gift of the Great Spirit."[47] At other times, the occasion of a reference to the deity was more positive. When summing up the Treaty No. 6 talks at Fort Carlton in 1876, Commissioner Morris noted: "What we have done has been done before the Great Spirit and in the face of the people."[48] At times, a treaty commissioner's language would have sounded as though the Queen's representative was explicitly accepting the First Nations understanding of treaty as covenant and kin relationship. For example, at Blackfoot Crossing in 1877, Commissioner David Laird said: "The Great Spirit has made all things—the sun, the moon, and the stars, the earth, the forests, and the swift running rivers. It is by the Great Spirit that the Queen rules over this great country and other great countries. The Great Spirit has made the white man and the red man brothers, and we should take each other by the hand. The Great Mother loves all her children, white man and red man alike; she wishes to them all good."[49] If western First Nations saw the Numbered Treaties as covenants involving the Great Spirit, the Crown, and themselves, and if they believed that the Queen's white-skinned children understood them the same way, it is hardly surprising.

For western First Nations leaders who invoked the Creator with their rituals, it would not have been difficult to conclude that the Queen's commissioners were acting in the same spirit. Their words and their actions both seemed to involve their god in the proceedings. In this way, treaty commissioners in the nineteenth-century West embraced the protocol that Aboriginal People had developed and that, earlier, the HBC had adopted. Other aspects of the customary rites were the Crown's provision of treaty uniforms ("suits of clothing") to chiefs and headmen, much as HBC post masters had issued clothing along with food to trading captains who brought furs to the HBC forts. All these practices illustrated the continuity of Aboriginal and HBC practices, a system of protocol that invoked and involved the deity through the ritual smoking of the pipe. Given this pattern of western treaty-making, it is not surprising that First Nations regard the agreements they made with the Queen's commissioners in the 1870s as covenants, establishing a sacred and permanent relationship between themselves and the Crown.

In the twentieth century, First Nations were to experience a great disillusionment with the way that the Queen's Canadian government interpreted and applied treaties. Indeed, the disappointment did not have to wait for the twentieth century. Once the treaties were concluded (by 1877) and the buffalo economy—the foundation of Plains culture and the source of Plains strength—collapsed (by 1879), Canada began to take a narrow, legalistic, and parsimonious approach to treaty-making and treaty implementation. As early as the 1880s, western First Nations leaders were complaining that the Crown's representatives had used "'sweet promises' . . . to get their country from them" and then ignored the Crown's obligations to them.⁵⁰ Another manifestation of the federal government's attitude was its refusal to act on petitions from a variety of First Nations in regions north of the seven Numbered Treaties to make treaties with them. Ottawa's attitude was that it was not interested in making further treaties, which would entail financial obligations to First Nations, unless and until the lands on which they resided became desirable in the eyes of non-Native economic interests that sought to develop them. Accordingly, numerous petitions for treaty were ignored, but when oil was discovered at Norman Wells in 1920, the wheels were set in motion to make Treaty No. 11, which covered the region in 1921.⁵¹ After the early 1920s, the federal government declined to make any further treaties. For the time being there were no southerners coveting the untreatied lands of the North and British Columbia, and, in any event, by 1920 Ottawa and its Department of Indian Affairs had entered a phase of pursuing coercive and controlling policies towards First Nations that would not lift until the middle of the century.

When treaty-making did resume, with the James Bay and Northern Quebec Agreement in 1975, it was only because better organized and highly assertive First Nations political organizations, specifically the James Bay Cree, went to court to secure a temporary injunction to halt the massive James Bay hydroelectric power development. That contretemps and the 1973 Supreme Court of Canada decision on Aboriginal title in *Calder*, the Nisga'a case, led the federal government to develop a comprehensive claims settlement process to deal with Aboriginal title claims in regions where there were no effective treaties. As the Indigenous and Northern Affairs Canada website once noted, the Comprehensive Claims Branch's purpose is "to negotiate modern treaties which will provide a clear, certain and long-lasting definition of rights to lands and resources for all Canadians."⁵² Comprehensive claims settlements were joined in the 1990s by individually negotiated agreements such as the Nunavut pact and the Nisga'a treaty to round out Canada's modern treaty-making processes. In the twenty-first century, Canada and First Nations must negotiate treaties concerning access to territory for Atlantic Canada, parts of northern Quebec, most of British Columbia, and portions of the Far North.

Through those times in the twentieth century when treaties were being made, and certainly since the resumption of treaty-making in the 1970s, the federal government's view of treaties as contracts whose contents are recorded in the government's version has been prominent. As

Cumming and Mickenberg pointed out in their 1970 *Native Rights in Canada*, the courts had often found that Aboriginal treaties were akin to contracts in law. As late as 1969, Pierre Trudeau, initially no friend of treaty or Aboriginal rights, in the aftermath of the uproar over his government's White Paper, said that while his government "won't recognize aboriginal rights[,] We will recognize treaty rights. We will recognize forms of contract which have been made with the Indian people by the Crown."[53] The implications of the government's attitude became clear in the 1980s in the context of comprehensive claim resolution discussions. As a review of the comprehensive claims process put it, "progress has, in the past, been blocked by the fundamental difference between the aims of each party. The federal government has sought to extinguish rights and to achieve a once-and-for-all settlement of historical claims. The Aboriginal Peoples, on the other hand, have sought to affirm their aboriginal rights and to guarantee their unique place in Canadian society for generations to come."[54] The federal position, which only slowly and grudgingly gave way by century's end to a policy that sought "certainty" rather than explicit extinguishment, was consistent with a view of treaties as contracts. The stand of the First Nations who opposed the extinguishment doctrine was the product of a view of treaty that emphasized treaties as the formalization of a relationship that was regularly renewed and might, if necessary, be modified in detail.

These twentieth-century differences in interpreting treaty are a reminder that, in the more than three hundred years that Europeans and Aboriginal Peoples have been making agreements in Canada, there have been several different views regarding what constitutes a treaty. In their earliest forms, which emerged in the commercial forum in which European fur trader and Aboriginal fur supplier met, treaties were commercial compacts. They arose from traders' common-sense recognition that, whatever rights royal charters or licences might purport to bestow on them, the practical thing to do was to secure permission from the occupants, on whom they relied heavily in any event, to establish themselves and carry on commerce. Making these commercial compacts drew the Europeans into the First Nations system of values and protocol as they learned to carry out the ceremonies of welcome, gift exchange, and pipe smoking that governed Aboriginal Peoples' relations with one another. Later, in the century after the Royal Proclamation of 1763 produced land-related treaties, the ensuing agreements often appeared to resemble contracts. At least according to the government versions of the ententes that have survived, a straightforward swap of land and title for compensation occurred. In the first half-century after 1763, the Crown's reliance on one-time payments strengthened that impression. By the time the Canadian state was established, this view of treaty as contract was firmly established in the minds of Canadian politicians.

As the Numbered Treaties of the West have shown, however, there was another, in many ways richer, view of treaty that vied with the contract interpretation for prominence. This was the conception of treaties that were ostensibly about access to territory as covenants. As treaty-related ceremonies suggest and oral history evidence confirms, western First Nations saw the agreements that they made between 1871 and 1877 as establishing relationships under the oversight of the Creator, relationships that were intended to be renewed annually, last forever, and be modified as circumstances required. As the number and power of First Nations declined and non-native Canada became correspondingly dominant, that interpretation of treaties was pushed back into the shadows. In an era when First Nations were viewed as "a vanishing race" that was "melting like snow before the sun," and when the government of Canada pursued aggressive policies to control and refashion them through the Indian Act and its attendant programs, an exclusive emphasis on treaties as contracts and an insistence that the government text was the valid version were championed by the government and usually acquiesced to by the courts.

As attitudes and power relationships between First Nations and non-Natives began to shift in the late years of the twentieth century, perceptions of treaty were modified, too. Thanks both to the revelations of oral history research and the efforts of a new generation of researchers, including in particular Arthur J. Ray, a more complex understanding of treaties as having taken a variety of forms has emerged. Compacts, contracts, and covenants have at different times and in different quarters been seen as the single authentic form of treaty. In British Columbia in the 1990s, when a stalled treaty-making process left uncertainty about ownership that deterred investment in resource industries, pragmatic resource-company executives and First Nations quietly negotiated local agreements to pave the way for investment and job creation on First Nations lands.[55] In a sense, the approach that fur traders had used in the earliest decades after contact to ensure peaceful and assured access to Aboriginal territory and resources emerged again in the Pacific province in the 1990s. Given such historical ironies, one looks forward eagerly to see what a postmodern age such as the twenty-first century holds for Canadians' understanding of treaties.

Further Reading

Blood Tribal Elders (with Walter Hildebrandt, Dorothy First Rider, and Sarah Carter). *The True Spirit and Original Intent of Treaty 7*. Montreal: McGill-Queen's University Press, 1996.

Friesen, Jean. "Magnificent Gifts: The Treaties of Canada with the Indians of the Northwest, 1869–76, *Transactions of the Royal Society of Canada*, Series 5, no. 1 (1986): 41–51.

Government of Canada. "Summaries of Pre-1975 Treaties." https://www.aadnc-aandc.gc.ca/eng/1370362690208/1370362747827.

Miller, J.R. *Compact, Contract, Covenant: Aboriginal Treaty-Making in Canada*, 4th ed. Toronto: University of Toronto Press, 2017.

Miller, J.R. *Skyscrapers Hide the Heavens: A History of Indian-White Relations in Canada*. Toronto: University of Toronto Press, 2000.

National Film Board. "Aboriginal Perspectives." http://www3.nfb.ca/enclasse/doclens/visau/index.php?language=english.

Treaty Elders of Saskatchewan. *Our Dream Is That Our Peoples Will One Day Be Clearly Recognized as Nations*. Edited by Harold Cardinal and Walter Hildebrandt. Calgary: University of Calgary Press, 2000.

NOTES

† Reproduced with slight revisions and with the publisher's permission from *New Histories for Old: Changing Perspectives on Canada's Native Pasts*, edited by Ted Binnema and Susan Neylan © University of British Columbia Press 2011. All rights reserved by the Publisher. The research on which this chapter is based was funded by a Standard Research Grant of the Social Sciences and Humanities Research Council of Canada. The chapter has also benefited from the research assistance of Rebecca Brain.

1 Arthur J. Ray, *Indians in the Fur Trade: Their Role as Trappers, Hunters, and Middlemen in the Lands Southwest of Hudson Bay, 1660–1870*, rev. ed. (Toronto: University of Toronto Press, 1998 [1974]), xxiv. The introduction to the revised edition provides valuable insights into Ray's intellectual development and his views on many topics of importance, including treaties, in Native-newcomer history.

2 G.F.G. Stanley, *The Birth of Western Canada: A History of the Riel Rebellions*, rev. ed. (Toronto: University of Toronto Press, 1961 [1936]).

3 John L. Taylor, "Canada's North-West Indian Policy in the 1870s: Traditional Premises and Necessary Innovations" (1978), and John L. Tobias, "Canada's Subjugation of the Plains Cree, 1879-1885" (1983), in *Sweet Promises: A Reader on Indian-White Relations in Canada*, ed. J.R. Miller, 212–40 (Toronto: University of Toronto Press, 1991).

4 Arthur J. Ray and Donald Freeman, *"Give Us Good Measure": An Economic Analysis of Relations between the Indians and the Hudson's Bay Company before 1763* (Toronto: University of Toronto Press, 1978), esp. 55–59.

5 A.J. Ray and D. Freeman, *"Give Us Good Measure,"* 55.

6 A.J. Ray and D. Freeman, *"Give Us Good Measure,"* 56.

7 A.J. Ray and D. Freeman, *"Give Us Good Measure."*

8 A.J. Ray and D. Freeman, *"Give Us Good Measure."*

9 A.J. Ray and D. Freeman, *"Give Us Good Measure,"* 57.

10 A.J. Ray and D. Freeman, *"Give Us Good Measure."*

11 A.J. Ray and D. Freeman, *"Give Us Good Measure,"* 59. See also Arthur J. Ray, Jim [J.R.] Miller, and Frank Tough, *Bounty and Benevolence: A History of Saskatchewan Treaties* (Montreal and Kingston: McGill-Queen's University Press, 2000), 8. Professor Ray drafted the chapter on Aboriginal-Hudson's Bay Company relations in *Bounty and Benevolence*.

12 "Each leader leaves his grand calumet at the Fort he trades at unless he is affronted, and not designed to return next summer, which is sometimes the case": Andrew Graham in Ray and Freeman, *"Give Us Good Measure,"* 70.

13 Cornelius J. Jaenen, "French Sovereignty and Native Nationhood during the French Regime," in Miller, *Sweet Promises*, 19–42.

14 Walter Bagehot, *The English Constitution*, with an introduction by R.H.S. Crossman (London: C.A. Watts, 1964 [1867]), 61.

15 Goldwin Smith, *Canada and the Canadian Question* (Toronto: Hunter, Rose, 1891), 147.

16 E.E. Rich and A.M. Johnson, eds., *Copy-book of Letters Outward &c: Begins 29th May, 1680, ends 5 July, 1687* (Toronto: Champlain Society for the Hudson's Bay Record Society, 1948), 4–13, emphasis added. For a second example, see *Copy-book*, 36.

17 On these early pacts and their relationship to the fur trade, see E.E. Rich, *The Fur Trade and the Northwest to 1857* (Toronto: McClelland and Stewart, 1967), 9–14.

18 Gilles Havard, *The Great Peace of Montreal of 1701: French-Native Diplomacy in the Seventeenth Century*, trans. Phyllis Aronoff and Howard Scott (Montreal and Kingston: McGill-Queen's University Press, 2001 [1992]), 16.

19 Ray and Freeman, "*Give Us Good Measure*," 22.

20 Edward Ahenakew, in *Voices of the Plains Cree*, ed. Ruth M. Buck (Toronto: McClelland and Stewart 1973), 72–73.

21 Hugh A. Dempsey, "Western Plains Trade Ceremonies," *Western Canadian Journal of Anthropology* 3, no. 1 (1972): 29–33, esp. 31–32.

22 Ray, Miller, and Tough, *Bounty and Benevolence*, 3. See also J.E. Foster, "Indian-White Relations in the Prairie West during the Fur Trade Period: A Compact?" in *The Spirit of the Alberta Indian Treaties*, ed. Richard Price (Edmonton: Pica Pica Press 1987 [1979]), 184. It should be noted that Foster's article refers to a general Aboriginal-European compact—similar to the compact between French Canada and English Canada that George Stanley champions in an article entitled "Act or Pact? Another Look at Confederation," Canadian Historical Association, *Report of the Annual Meeting 1956*, 1–25—rather than to commercial compacts in the fur trade.

23 "Forest diplomats" refers to Indigenous and non-Native representatives who engaged in talks in the northeast woodlands.

24 The literature on the English alliance system, including the Covenant Chain, is vast. The best approach is via the works of Francis Jennings: *The Invasion of America: Indians, Colonialism, and the Cant of Conquest* (Chapel Hill: University of North Carolina Press, 1975); *The Ambiguous Iroquois Empire: The Covenant Chain Confederation of Indian Tribes with the English Colonies from Its Beginnings to the Lancaster Treaty of 1741* (New York: W.W. Norton, 1984); and *Empire of Fortune: Crowns, Colonies and Tribes in the Seven Years War in America* (New York: W.W. Norton, 1988).

25 José Antonio Brandão, *"Your Fyre Shall Burn No More": Iroquois Policy toward New France and Its Native Allies to 1701* (Lincoln and London: University of Nebraska Press, 1997); J.A. Brandão and William A. Starna, "The Treaties of 1701: A Triumph of Iroquois Diplomacy," *Ethnohistory* 43, no. 2 (1996): 209–44; Havard, *Great Peace*.

26 A facsimile of the original 1701 treaty in French is found in Havard, *Great Peace*, 112–18 (an English translation is found in app. 3, 210-15, and a photograph of a wampum that some believe commemorates the 1701 Peace is found on page 129 [LAC reference number C-38948]).

27 Starna and Brandão regard it as part of a "triumph of Iroquois diplomacy" in 1701; Havard sees it as a French victory. The clash of interpretations derives, as is often the case, in large part from the different sources upon which the respective historians relied. Starna and Brandão used both British and French documents extensively, while Havard's account is based on a wider range of French sources than Starna and Brandão employed.

28 James Youngblood Sákéj Henderson, *The Mi'kmaw Concordat* (Halifax: Fernwood, 1997). Authorities on Rome's relations with Canada, including with First Nations in the early period, hold that whatever relations existed between the Mi'kmaq and the Roman Catholic clergy, the Vatican would not have considered their arrangement a "concordat." Rome had

no need of a concordat with the Mi'kmaq, and Rome in the early seventeenth century would not have considered the Mi'kmaq a society with a form of government with which it could have formal relations. Private correspondence with Luca Codignola, University of Genoa, 20 September 1999; and Roberto Perin, York University, 29 June 1999.

29 David L. Schmidt and B.A. Balcom, "The Règlement of 1739: A Note on Micmac Law and Literacy," *Acadiensis* 23, no. 1 (1993): 110.

30 John Borrows, "Wampum at Niagara: The Royal Proclamation, Canadian Legal History, and Self-Government," in *Aboriginal and Treaty Rights in Canada: Essays on Law, Equity, and Respect for Difference*, ed. Michael Asch (Vancouver: University of British Columbia Press, 1997), 155–72 and 256–67.

31 James Sullivan, ed., *The Papers of Sir William Johnson* (Albany: University of the State of New York Press 1921-65), 11:30–31, 34.

32 For a more equivocal portrait of wampum and the Niagara commitments, see Paul Williams, "The Chain" (LL.M. thesis, Osgoode Hall, York University, 1982), chap. 4, "The Ojibways, the Covenant Chain and the Treaty of Niagara of 1764," 72–94. I am indebted to Professor Brian Slattery of Osgoode Hall, who kindly made a copy of this chapter available to me.

33 Canada, *Indian Treaties and Surrenders*, vol. 1, *Treaties* 1–138 (Ottawa: Queen's Printer. 1891), 22–23.

34 "Mixed-ancestry" refers to all Métis individuals and communities in all regions of Canada.

35 Alexander Morris, *The Treaties of Canada with the Indians* (Saskatoon: Fifth House, 1991 [1880]), 299. The Selkirk Treaty is 299–300; the transfer of land from HBC to Selkirk is 300-01.

36 See Map 6.3 in Robert J. Surtees, "Land Cessions, 1763–1830," in *Aboriginal Ontario: Historical Perspectives on the First Nations*, eds. Edward S. Rogers and Donald B. Smith (Toronto: Dundurn, 1994), 103. Many of the later Upper Canadian treaties are depicted in Map 6.4, E. S. Rogers and D. B. Smith, eds., *Aboriginal Ontario*, 114.

37 Canada, *Indian Treaties and Surrenders*, vol. 1, 62-63.

38 Morris, *Treaties*, 19.

39 Morris, *Treaties*, 314–16. The inclusion of the "outside promises" is found on at 338–42. See also Ray, Miller, and Tough, *Bounty and Benevolence*, 81–85.

40 *Treaty Elders of Saskatchewan: Our Dream Is That Our Peoples Will One Day Be Clearly Recognized as Nations*, eds. Harold Cardinal and Walter Hildebrandt (Calgary: University of Calgary Press, 2000), 53.

41 *Treaty Elders of Saskatchewan: Our Dream Is That Our Peoples Will One Day Be Clearly Recognized as Nations*, 32.

42 Morris, *Treaties*, 97. Alexander Morris: "I held out my hand but you did not do as your nation [the Saulteaux] did at the [North West] Angle [last year]. When I arrived there the Chief and his men came and gave me the pipe of peace and paid me every honor."

43 Morris, *Treaties*, 182–83.

44 *Treaty Elders of Saskatchewan: Our Dream Is That Our Peoples Will One Day Be Clearly Recognized as Nations*, 41. For an elder's understanding of the binding nature of the pipe ceremony at Treaty No. 6 talks, *see The Counselling Speeches of Jim* Kâ-Nîpitêhtêw, ed. and

trans. Freda Aheanakew and H.C. Wolfart (Winnipeg: University of Manitoba Press 1998), 109–13.

45 Notes of Lord Lorne's meetings with chiefs, 1881, LAC, RG10, Records of the Department of Indian Affairs, vol. 3768, file 33,642.

46 For example, at Qu'Appelle in 1874. See Morris, *Treaties*, 86.

47 Morris, *Treaties*, 102,

48 Morris, *Treaties*, 221.

49 Morris, *Treaties*, 267.

50 J.A. Macrae to E. Dewdney, 25 August 1884, LAC, RG 10, vol. 3697, file 15,423.

51 For instances of government's rejecting First Nations requests for treaty, see the following: for Treaty No. 8, Ray, Miller, and Tough, *Bounty and Benevolence*, 148–55; and René Fumoleau, *As Long As This Land Shall Last: A History of Treaty 8 and Treaty 11, 1870-1939* (Toronto: McClelland and Stewart, 1975), 36–37. For Treaty No. 9, see John S. Long, *Treaty No. 9: The Indian Petitions, 1889–1927* (Cobalt, ON: Highway Book Shop, 1978), 2ff. For Treaty No. 10, see Ray, Miller, and Tough, *Bounty and Benevolence*, 170–73. And for Treaty No. 11, see Fumoleau, *As Long*, 134–49, 158, and 199–200.

52 Indian and Northern Affairs Canada, *Comprehensive Claims Branch*, accessed 16 February 2011, http://www.ainc-inac.gc.ca/ps/clm/ccb_e.html.

53 P.A. Cumming and N.H. Mickerberg, *Native Rights in Canada*, 2nd ed. (Toronto: Indian-Eskimo Association, 1972 [1970]), 56–57. The Trudeau quotation is from an 8 August 1969 speech delivered in Vancouver.

54 Murray Coolican, *Living Treaties*: Lasting Agreements: *Report of the Task Force to Review Comprehensive Claims Policy* (the Coolican Report) (Ottawa: Indian Affairs and Northern Development, 1985), 30.

55 I am indebted to my colleague Keith Carlson who drew this point to my attention.

3

Ontario: The Centre of Confederation?

Daniel Heidt

On 1 July 1867, celebrations of the new dominion of Canada broke out across Ontario. It was the only province to enjoy such widespread festivities. In Nova Scotia, by contrast, the *Morning Chronicle* mourned the event with the mock eulogy: "Died! Last night at 12 o'clock, the free and enlightened Province of Nova Scotia."[1] The widespread Ontarian celebrations stemmed, in part, from the belief that their wealthy and populous province would be at the centre of Canadian politics. In fact, this sort of influence became so commonplace that most of the province's inhabitants still do not readily identify as "Ontarians," preferring to instead think of themselves as "Canadians." Aside from this vague sense of centrality, however, many Ontarians disagreed about just how their province would benefit from the deal and there was also a smaller but nevertheless significant group who doubted the viability of the broader union. These varied and, at times, conflicting assessments of the proposed union arose from the way that the Province of Canada evolved out of the separate, yet connected colonies of Upper and Lower Canada. The ensuing debates in the colony's two legislatures reflected the largely French-English emphasis of that era's politics, ignoring additional ethnic and Indigenous voices. The Numbered Treaties that would subsequently govern Indigenous lands across much of Northern Ontario were not negotiated until the post-1867 era when the Dominion of Canada was well in place. The backgrounds to these events are critical to understanding how these key agreements came about. The discussions of the deals also reveal the strengths and weaknesses of the union—many of which persist today.

Background

Understanding Ontarian responses to Confederation requires knowing something about the colony's prolonged pursuits of autonomy and expansion. Upper Canada (present-day Ontario) was carved out of Quebec via the Constitutional Act of 1791 in response to complaints about the "rigorous Rules, Homages and Reservations, and Restrictions of the French laws and Customs."[2] The history of balking at the French-Catholic majority of the St. Lawrence region was a long one, and it was not surprising that this refrain would persist into the 1860s. The new colony of Upper Canada soon possessed an elected Assembly, but it lacked power because the British, guided by suspicions about the loyalty of Americans arriving from the independent states to the south, preferred to vest power with their appointed lieutenant-governors and councils.[3] Despite the colonial population proving its loyalty during the War of 1812 and by rejecting William Lyon Mackenzie's 1837 rebellion, the imperial government did not give Upper Canadian politicians the power to run their colony—responsible government. Instead, they united Upper and Lower Canada against the will of the majority of both populations. Each section received an equal number of seats in the new Legislative Assembly, and imperial authorities hoped that this unification would create an English-speaking majority that would encourage French-speaking colonists to assimilate.[4]

The new united Province of Canada eventually secured responsible government but not without incurring some maladjustments that arose from its unique features. The fact that half the colony was predominantly English and the other half predominantly French eventually created an expectation that the majority of politicians from both sections had to support measures effecting the entire colony. Such concurrence was rare and, thus, the achievement of responsible government wreaked havoc on political stability by the end of the 1850s. Divisions over land, language, religion, and defence ensured that governments did little or resigned on a regular basis. In this crippled state, the colony lacked the credibility to assume responsibility for additional territory. Over the preceding decades,

Fig 3.1 British North America's settler political boundaries as they existed in 1867. Developed from Natural Resources Canada, "Map 1867," *Library and Archives Canada*, https://www.collectionscanada.gc.ca/confederation/023001-5005-e.html.

Upper Canadian farmers had "settled" all available farmlands and a new generation of farmers looked to the North-West for additional lands. The Province of Canada's relative paralysis, however, made it a poor contender to assume responsibility for this territory from the Hudson's Bay Company.[5]

Nor was there much positive experience to glean from Upper Canadian relationships with Indigenous Peoples. After the Royal Proclamation of 1763 reserved the lands west of the Thirteen Colonies for Indigenous Peoples and gave the British Crown exclusive right to negotiate future land exchanges, the latter negotiated a series of Treaties with Indigenous groups in present-day Ontario to cement alliances, redistribute land, and maintain lasting relationships. These negotiations generally followed newcomer "settlement," and continued into 1850 with the Robinson-Huron and Robinson-Superior Treaties which "brought colonial treaty making to a new level: now land-related treaties dealt with large tracts, recognized continuing hunting and fishing rights, committed the Crown to annuities, and contained provision for reserves for the First Nations signatories."[6] Whereas the treaties established a way of securing peaceful co-existence, they did little to suggest a way forward in designing a new system of government for the Province of Canada.

Solutions had been floated regularly, and federalism was often among them. Embracing the "federal principle," as it was often called, by uniting some or all of British North American colonies and assigning divisive issues to provincial governments so that parliament could focus on areas of common interest, was a longstanding idea. Conservatives and Reformers both advocated the solution at different times, hoping to export Canadian manufactured goods to the Maritimes and the North-West.[7] In 1858, for example, the Macdonald-Cartier government kept itself alive by taking up Alexander Tilloch Galt's vague suggestion for a British North American (BNA) federation. At the Reform Convention of 1859, George Brown, the editor of the *Globe* and a leader of the Reformers, proposed a federal union with limited powers for the general government and local powers for two or more sections of the united province.

But other solutions initially seemed more attractive. One of the issues at the forefront of any discussion about a new form of governance was demographics. Although Canada West had been over-represented in the original division of seats in the united colony, the 1851 census revealed that mass immigration had reversed the situation. Demands in Upper Canada for representation by population (or "rep by pop") intensified as Canada West's population continued to grow at a far faster pace than that of Canada East's. Moreover, a variety of issues set the two sides of the united colony on a collision course that would result either in stalemated parliaments or endless government turnover. The Civil War to the south raised new and serious concerns about the plausibility and expense of defending against the North's immense standing army; and the commercial economy that had taken root in the western section of the colony increasingly required trading partners if growth was going to continue at the rate the inhabitants wanted. Over the next several years, the Brownites who had come to dominate the Reform side of the political spectrum frequently won a majority of the seats in the western part of Canada, but Brown's tendency to insult French-Catholic Lower Canadians put an end to any possibility of forming the sort of working coalition necessary to form a government.

The Conservatives had a great deal more experience with cooperation between the upper and lower sections of the colony. Robert Baldwin and Louis-Hippolyte La Fontaine had partnered during the 1840s to secure responsible government; John A. Macdonald and George-Étienne Cartier governed cooperatively during much of the late 1850s and early 1860s. By then, though, moderate Reformers and the *Rouges* (Liberals) formed their own alliances and Canada endured the rise and fall of three governments between 1862 and 1865. George Brown, an unlikely non-partisan, offered a solution to the impasse. He secured the establishment of a committee in the Legislative Assembly that studied constitutional reforms to resolve the deadlock, and he subsequently agreed to join and support the Great Coalition encompassing Upper Canadian Reformers and Conservatives as well as Lower Canadian *Bleus* (Quebec Conservatives).

This new alliance formed on the eve of a September 1864 conference in Charlottetown to discuss the possibility of uniting the Maritime provinces. After the conference agreed to hear the Canadian delegation, Macdonald and Cartier laid out the broad arguments in favour of a union of the British North American colonies—that through unity, concerns over defense and trade could be solved, while federalism would preserve each colony's autonomy in matters such as education where differences of opinion continued to complicate the Province of Canada's politics. Later, Alexander Galt offered an explanation of the financial settlement, noting that the general government would assume all debts and provide revenue to each of the provinces on the basis of their population. This was certainly an effort to sweeten the pot for the Maritimers, but it also created a new area of concern for Ontarians who were reluctant to assume their neighbours' debts. George Brown then summarized some of the constitutional issues.[8] Notably absent from these speeches—and the discussions that followed—was dialogue concerning the appointment of political offices, such as lieutenant-governors, and practices, like the federal disallowance of provincial legislation, which would both subsequently privilege federal

Fig 3.2 The Charlottetown delegates, 1 September 1864. photograph by George P. Roberts, LAC, C-000733. Front row from left to right: Alexander Tilloch Galt; Hector-Louis Langevin; John Hamilton Gray, N.B.; George-Étienne Cartier; John A. Macdonald; John Hamilton Gray, P.E.I.; Samuel Leonard Tilley; Adams George Archibald; Alexander Campbell; George Coles; George Brown; William H. Lee, Clerk Executive Council, Canada. Back row from left to right: Charles Drinkwater; Major Bernard; Sir Charles Tupper; Edward Barron Chandler; Edward Palmer; Robert Barry Dickey; Thomas D'Arcy McGee; William Alexander Henry; William Henry Steeves; John Mercer Johnson; Andrew Archibald Macdonald; William McDougall; William Henry Pope; Jonathan McCully.

over provincial power.

The meeting then adjourned, agreeing to resume discussions at Quebec City in October and it was here that all of the good intentions of the Charlottetown Conference were put to the test. The discussions followed the general agreements forged at the preceding conference, but many details still had to be worked out and the delegates "consistently underestimated how long [agreement] would take."[9] On some matters, though, agreement seemed fairly straightforward. For example, all agreed in Quebec, it seemed, that the new country could avoid the American error of vesting too much power in the states by providing for a strong central government, and only allowing "sectional prejudices and interests" to be "legislated by local legislatures."[10] After two weeks of sometimes lengthy discussions, the 72 Quebec Resolutions emerged, laying out the principles upon which Confederation would be based. Within another week, the 72 Resolutions were published in newspapers across British North America, and became the topic of debate in both public and private conversations.

Supporting Arguments

Once the delegates returned to their respective colonies, each legislature debated the merits of the deal. The vast majority of Upper Canadian politicians liked most of what they read. Unlike Lower Canada, whose representatives offered impressive speeches for and against union, Upper Canadian oratory and constitutional talent generally lay with the pro-Confederation camp.

"Rep by pop" was almost universally popular. Reformers and Conservatives alike rejoiced at the achievement of this long-sought goal.[11] In the new federal parliament, Ontarian representatives would constitute 45 percent of seats. If Ontario's population continued to grow, some speculated, the province could achieve an absolute majority of seats. Shrewd readers will recognize that such parliamentary majorities offered the possibility of Ontario dictating the federal government's policies against the collective wishes of the rest of Canada. While Upper Canadians hoped to achieve this sort of power,[12] they avoided expressing this aspiration during the debates to prevent Lower Canadians from fearing an Ontarian tyranny. Instead, advocates like George Brown echoed English Canada's long-held fears of French domination by describing "rep by pop" as a defensive measure that would allow Ontario MPs to unite and prevent Lower Canadians from "forcing through whatever we may deem unjust to us" in the House of Commons.[13] He also suggested that any Ontarian attempt to use its parliamentary preponderance of votes to overrule the objections of other provincial MPs would be countered in the Senate, where the rest of Canada held the majority of votes.

The opportunity to expand into the North-West was also extremely popular in Ontario. The establishment of the Dominion of Canada would

George Brown
President of the Executive Council, Grit Leader

8 FEBRUARY 1865

CONFEDERATION QUOTE 3.1
Quotation from Province of Canada, Legislative Assembly, 8 February, 1865. Photograph by William Ellisson, from Library and Archives Canada, C-008359

" We in Upper Canada have complained that though we paid into the public treasury more than three-fourths of the whole revenue, we had less control over [expenditures] than the people of Lower Canada. Well, sir, the scheme in your hand remedies that . . . we are to have seventeen additional members in the house that holds the purse. "

create a country with sufficient resources to convert the region into a new economic hinterland. Rural Upper Canadians looked forward to their sons and daughters "settling" what George Brown called the "vast Indian Territories" as an agricultural frontier, while urbanites anticipated that the region would offer new demand for Central Canadian manufacturers. This territorial growth, many Upper Canadians also assumed, would be critical to establishing a vast country capable of maintaining British rule across the continent and checking American expansionism.

In addition to "rep by pop" and expansionism, Confederation supporters in Ontario also embraced the "federal principle" as a practical way of hiving off divisive issues from national politics. Comparing the speeches of different speakers, however, will leave some readers wondering whether they were talking about the same constitution. In some cases, the differing messages were the result of confusion. To that date, only Switzerland and the United States had created modern federal governments, and many Ontarians struggled to grasp the complexity of the still novel system. In addition, the continuation of the long and bloody American Civil War into 1865 led many British North Americans to question the advisability of institutionalizing strong regional identities by creating provincial governments. John A. Macdonald, for example, blamed the Civil War on excessive states' rights and localism, preferring a legislative union similar to that governing England and Scotland because he and his Ontario followers believed that it was more likely to win the loyalty and respect of all citizens by subverting regional disagreements. A legislative union was, however, inconceivable for a British North American union since Lower Canada and the Atlantic colonies would never resign control of key local concerns such as education and legal codes to a national parliament that could be dominated by Ontario votes. Macdonald and his Ontario followers, therefore, accepted provincial jurisdictions while insisting that they be kept to a minimum. These centralizers also noted that the 72 Resolutions empowered the federal government to disallow (think veto) provincial legislation. In addition, the federal government retained "residual" powers—or the jurisdiction to pass legislation concerning "all matters of a general character, not specially and exclusively reserved for the Local Governments and Legislatures."[14] The federal parliament, they concluded, would be supreme in all important jurisdictions and would have the power to assume responsibility for new national concerns that would arise in future decades (like air travel). Provincial governments would, by comparison, be "subordinate" to their federal counterpart.[15]

Upper Canadian Reformers rejected this interpretation. Like many leaders from the Atlantic colonies, these future Ontarians feared the establishment of a federal government that could interfere with local concerns. While few favoured the extreme states' rights demanded by the American Confederacy, Brown and other local rights advocates had ensured that the 72 Resolutions incorporated a series of local jurisdictions including direct taxation (e.g., property tax), education, local works, and municipal institutions. The same terms of union also, somewhat confusingly, promised each province jurisdiction over "all matters of a private or local nature, not assigned to the General Parliament." As Paul Romney suggests, Upper Canadian Reformers expected these articles to collectively ensure that "Ontario's local affairs would be a matter for Ontarians alone."[16]

The political union of British North America, Confederation advocates insisted, would also bolster the defence of each colony. This argument typically amounted to "united we stand, divided we fall." Britain, all hoped, would still help to defend the fledging dominion; but by uniting, the new country could aggregate its forces and deploy them where necessary via an Intercolonial railway that would soon be constructed. The Confederation would, in short, cause the colonies to become "a great nationality, commanding the respect of the world,"[17] and deter American manifest destiny.

Opposing Arguments

Not all Upper Canadian politicians voted in favour of the 72 Resolutions. Opposition to the terms of union was not strong or unified in Upper Canada, but the critiques often centred distinct assessments of Upper Canadian interests. Most critics favoured union in principle, but were unimpressed by the Quebec Resolutions. The Great Coalition's insistence that the Province of Canada debate the terms of union as a "treaty" that could not be amended, however, deterred all but the most ardent critics from matching their complaints with negative votes.[18] The Upper Canadian opponents, therefore, must be understood as a disparate lot who recognized several shortcomings of the deal, but were ultimately unable to do more than delay its affirmation.

Because their colony imported the most goods and paid the most taxes, Upper Canadians such as Matthew Crooks Cameron (the Conservative representative for North Ontario in the Assembly and future leader of the province's Conservatives) complained that Ontarians would ultimately pay a disproportionate share of the dominion's future costs, and therefore objected to the increased expenses envisioned in the terms of union. The new dominion government would, for example, assume all of the member colonies' debts and pay a subsidy to each province (somewhat like equalization payments today). Establishing a House of Commons, a Senate and separate provincial legislatures, also seemed redundant as well as expensive to many who preferred the current system.[19]

The cost argument extended to other subjects as well. Perhaps the most consistently unpopular article of the terms of union was the promise to construct an Intercolonial railway. Until the 1870s, no rail link connected the Province of Canada to the Atlantic colonies, and trade was limited to what could be shipped via the St. Lawrence during the spring, summer, and fall months. Negotiations to construct a railway linking these regions had gone on for years, but repeated disagreement about how much of the cost each colony would bear consistently spoiled agreement. At the most recent negotiations in 1862, the government of John Sandfield Macdonald and Louis-Victor Sicotte agreed that the Province of Canada would pay 5/12 of the railway's construction cost, but then abruptly pulled out.[20] This linkage, viewed as a nation-building necessity by pro-Confederation politicians across the country, and an especially important incentive for Nova Scotia and New Brunswick, was generally unpopular in Upper Canada because, as David Reesor of Kings complained, the Province of Canada's taxpayers would shoulder "twice as great an expenditure as was formerly contemplated."[21] Knowledge of the great political contest in New Brunswick concerning the future railway's route, in addition to the Grand Trunk Railway's recent financial struggles, also led these critics to worry that the construction guarantee was tantamount to writing a blank cheque.[22]

Critics also worried that the construction of the railway, and the union scheme more generally, was a poor defensive measure. Railways located so close to the American border were vulnerable to attack, and would require significant defensive forces—if the line could be defended at all. The idea that British North America could be better defended by establishing a single border stretching from the North-West to Nova Scotia also seemed doubtful. "This union," John Sanborn mocked,

> was to strengthen us so marvellously that we would be able to intimidate all the rest of the world, and guarantee us a lasting peace with all mankind. It might increase facilities for communication, but could not increase our real strength. How the people of New Brunswick could be expected to come up to Canada to defend us, and leave their own frontier unprotected, he could not comprehend.[23]

John Macdonald (the Reform MLA for West Toronto, not the future Prime Minister) similarly doubted that "we in Upper and Lower Canada, with a population less than that of the city of London, will be called upon to defend such a frontier—a territory, we are told, as great as the continent of Europe?"[24] Local defences, it seemed, needed to be constructed regardless of each colony's political status and the proposed union, therefore, would be an ineffective deterrent or even entangling.

Other objections to the Quebec Resolutions were more philosophical. There was, for example, considerable doubt about the "federal principle." The union of Upper and Lower Canada had brought immense discord. How would bringing Atlantic Canada into the mix while giving each province autonomy improve the situation?[25] In a private letter to Macdonald, Matthew Cameron complained that "the scheme itself based on the federal principle does not inspire me with a feeling of confidence that it will succeed in making us live more in harmony . . . or work with an eye solely to the common good."[26] He elaborated on this fear during his parliamentary critique of the Quebec Resolutions. Cameron advocated a legislative union because "if we are to be united, it ought to be in fact as well as in name; that we ought to be one people, and not separated from each other by sections."[27] Conscious of how the Southern desire for local autonomy sparked the American Civil war, Cameron concluded that if Canadians joined the British North American union proposed in the Quebec Resolutions, they "would be sowing the seeds of discord and strife, which would destroy our union."[28] Suggestions by Thomas D'Arcy McGee and other advocates that the union would create a "new nationality" were frequently disparaged.

The colonies jealously guarded their local laws, the Quebec Resolutions protected local autonomy, and many doubted that a federal system could promote unity by preserving difference.

A few Ontario politicians even doubted their province's potential influence within Confederation. Cameron, for example, hypothesized that "sixty-five members from Lower Canada and forty-seven from the Lower Provinces, whose interests are identical, will be united against us."[29] Reform Legislative Council member John Simpson similarly warned that, even with the seventeen additional MPs that representation by population would give Ontario, "Upper Canada would still be in a large minority of the whole" and vulnerable to the spending whims of the rest of the country's federal representatives.[30]

The decision to fill the Legislative Council (aka Senate) with lifetime appointees, rather than elected officials, also received considerable criticism. After 1856, the Province of Canada opened several of its Council seats to elections.[31] Many Ontarians therefore objected to this move, suggesting that this would make the federal Senate unaccountable to voters and a tool of partisan patronage. As Ged Martin notes, critics interpreted the decision to appoint the first senators from existing councillors as "a transparent bribe to curb the upper houses in discharging the very task of disinterested second thoughts for which they were supposed to exist."[32]

Finally, most anti-Confederates objected to the lack of public consent for the deal. The Great Coalition formed in 1864 without a general election, and one would not be called until 1867. While the Province of Canada's voter franchise was still based on wealth and gender, and some critics undoubtedly used the lack of public pronouncement on the union plan as an excuse for delay, many critics disliked implementing radical constitutional change without securing the approval of this limited franchise. John Sandfield Macdonald, who would become Ontario's first premier, even cast the electoral defeat of New Brunswick Premier Samuel Leonard Tilley during the summer of 1865 as an example for those who pushed forward with Confederation against public opinion, but his argument had little effect.[33]

Matthew Crooks Cameron
Member of the Legislative Assembly, Province of Canada, Ont.

24 FEBRUARY 1865

CONFEDERATION QUOTE 3.2

Quotation from Province of Canada, Legislative Assembly, 24 February 1865
Photograph by Notman & Fraser, from Library and Archives Canada, PA-028639

"I regard the scheme itself as having been got up hastily, for it bears upon its face the evidence of haste and of compromise. Indeed, it is a complete piece of patchwork, and as we are all aware, it is a piece of patchwork in which we are not to be at liberty to change the patches in any respect so as to make it look better to the eye or more enduring to those who will have to wear it."

Afterwards

Ultimately, both of the province's legislatures approved the Quebec Resolutions. In the Assembly, majorities from Upper and Lower Canada approved the deal, though *Rouge* opposition ensured that the Lower Canadian majority was slim. The lack of a clear alternative plan, disunity, and a vote that required a clear yes or no stand made it impossible for Upper Canadians opposing the Quebec Resolutions to mount an effective opposition to the relatively popular push for union.

Readers should recognize that pro- and anti-Confederation advocates offered thoughtful assessments of the terms of union. Over the next one hundred and fifty years, for example, major nation-building projects like the Intercolonial railway were critical to establishing interprovincial trade. Yet Ontario, traditionally a "have" province, provided funds that brought national programs to other provinces. Similarly, a legislative union was not politically feasible in Canada, and our federal structure has provided considerable flexibility for varied ways of being Canadian. Yet these same divisions have, at times, been rallying points for those who wanted to leave the country in provinces like Quebec and Nova Scotia. Such observations do not disparage subsequent events or imply single causes; instead they recognize that both sides of the debates made legitimate observations.[34]

But Ontario's founding debates did not end in 1865. In 1869, the federal government secured the North-West from the Hudson's Bay Company, and the Red River Métis' subsequent reaction to the federal government's failure to recognize their presence illustrated the danger of ignoring the authority of Indigenous inhabitants. This realization, in addition to the imperative of constructing a transcontinental railway, avoiding further expensive conflicts, and the knowledge that Indigenous Peoples all along the suggested routes expected to negotiate prior to the arrival of "settlers," led the Crown to take up past precedents of the previous decade and negotiate a series of Numbered Treaties that would eventually stretch from Ontario to the Yukon.[35] These were, as historian J.R. Miller explains elsewhere in this volume, not just written treaties, but *covenants* which involved the deity that bound all parties to lasting commitments and relationships.[36] Although Ontario's borders did not reach their present state until 1912, a portion of Treaty No. 3 falls within these modern boundaries. Negotiations began in 1870 and continued each year, and Indigenous leaders held out each time for more generous terms. The breakthrough did not come until 1873 when Governor Alexander Morris met with the Saulteaux, Lac Seul, and English River First Nations leaders at the North-West Angle (where the borders of Manitoba, Ontario, and Minnesota meet today) with terms that aligned more closely with Indigenous expectations. After difficult negotiations, Chief Kakatcheway agreed to sign the treaty and Morris threatened to negotiate with each band individually if they did not follow suit. After further negotiations, the Crown agreed to increase the one-time cash payment from ten to twelve dollars, provide tools, farming implements, supplies, cattle, and certain clothing. It also accepted continued Indigenous hunting and fishing on Crown lands, and promised to allow Indigenous relatives from the United States to join the Treaty if they arrived within two years. Several of these commitments were verbal, rather than written, and were subsequently contested but, at the time, both sides agreed to the terms and Treaty No. 3 was signed on 3 October 1873.[37]

Newcomer settlement, however, continued to expand, and by the turn of the century, extended further into northern Ontario. The negotiations for Treaty No. 9 from 1905 to 1906 were a very different experience. Unlike Alexander Morris, Treaty No. 9's Commissioners did not deviate from the provisions already drafted in Ottawa. Instead, they worked to explain and convince Cree and Ojibwa leaders to sign the treaty. Unfortunately, the commissioners' explanations frequently oversimplified or even "flatly contradict[ed] the written provisions."[38] At Mishkeegogamang (previously Osnaburgh), for example, the commissioners emphasized obedience of Crown laws. Reassurances that bands could continue hunting and farming on all "surrendered" lands, on the other hand, were given without adequately explaining that these activities would be "subject to such regulations" made by the government and that this pledge also excepted "such tracts as may be required or taken up from time to time for settlement, mining, lumbering, trading or other purposes."[39] At Eabametoong (formerly Fort Hope), one of the Commissioners even suggested that the bands were only surrendering title to their "unused lands."[40] With these inaccurate reassurances and comparatively little bargaining power, the bands signed the Treaty.

While the meaning of the Indigenous and parliamentary records will continue to be discussed for decades to come, it is important that

Mawedopenais
Fort Francis First Nations Chief

2 OCTOBER 1873

CONFEDERATION QUOTE 3.3
Quotation from Alexander Morris, *The Treaties of Canada with the Indians of Manitoba and the North-West Territories Including the Negotiations on Which They Are Based, and Other Information Relating Thereto.* Toronto: Willing & Williamson, 1880, page 59
Photograph from Library and Archives Canada, Acc. No. 1986-79-1638

> This is what we think, that the Great Spirit has planted us on this ground where we are, as you were where you came from. We think that where we are is our property. I will tell you what he said to us when he planted us here; the rules that we should follow—us Indians— He has given us rules that we should follow to govern us rightly.

Ontarians, and Canadians have the opportunity to access and assess these discussions. The Province of Canada's debates, the Numbered Treaty texts, and accounts of the negotiations of those Treaties are all critical founding records. The Canadian state did not ultimately honour the terms of the Numbered Treaties and reconciliation remains an ongoing process that can only be aided by awareness of past agreements and wrongs. While the parliamentary debates on Confederation have a different flavour and purpose, they provide useful insights into the strengths and weaknesses of Canada's political structure and Ontario's past and present role within Confederation. With these insights, we can consider Canada's past, correct mistakes, and build on existing achievements.

Further Reading

Ajzenstat, Janet, Paul Romney, Ian Gentles, and William D. Gairdner, eds. *Canada's Founding Debates*. Toronto: University of Toronto Press, 2003.

Baskerville, Peter A. *Sites of Power: A Concise History of Ontario*. Don Mills: Oxford University Press, 2005.

Careless, J.M.S. *Brown of the Globe. Vol. 2, Statesman of Confederation, 1860–1880*. Toronto: Macmillan Company, 1963.

Gwyn, Richard. *John A.: The Man Who Made Us. Vol. 1, 1815–1867*. Toronto: Random House Canada, 2008.

Heaman, Elsbeth A. *Tax, Order, and Good Government: A New Political History of Canada, 1867–1917*. Montreal: McGill-Queen's Press, 2017.

Long, John S. "How the Commissioners Explained Treaty Number Nine to the Ojibway and Cree in 1905." *Ontario History* XCVIII, no. 1 (Spring 2006): 1–29.

Romney, Paul. *Getting It Wrong: How Canadians Forgot Their Past and Imperiled Confederation*. Toronto: University of Toronto Press, 1999.

Waite, P.B. *The Life and Times of Confederation, 1864–1867*, 3rd ed. Toronto: Robin Brass Studio, 2001.

NOTES

The author wishes to express his gratitude to Penny Bryden for her extensive suggestions for this chapter.

1. *Halifax Morning Chronicle*, 1 July 1867.
2. Quoted in Gerald M. Craig, *Upper Canada: The Formative Years, 1784–1841* (Toronto: McClelland and Stewart, 1963), 9.
3. For a discussion of the recent literature on loyalty, revolution, and the long nineteenth century, see Jeffrey McNairn, "As the Tsunami of Histories of Atlantic and Liberal Revolutions Wash up in Upper Canada: Worries from a Colonial Shore—Part One," *History Compass* vol. 14, no. 9 (2016): 407–17.
4. See Alan Taylor, *The Civil War of 1812: American Citizens, British Subjects, Irish Rebels and Indian Allies* (Toronto: Random House, 2010).
5. Douglas Owram, *Promise of Eden: The Canadian Expansionist Movement and the Idea of the West, 1856–1900* (Toronto: University of Toronto Press, 1992).
6. J.R. Miller, "Compact, Contract, Covenant: Canada's Treaty-Making Tradition," Keenan Lecture, 2003.
7. For a detailed discussion of pre-1864 federal proposals in Upper Canada, consult Daniel Heidt, "'First Among Equals': The Development of Preponderant Federalisms in Upper Canada and Ontario to 1896," PhD diss., Western University, 2014, ch. 1 and 2.
8. P. B. Waite, *The Life and Times of Confederation, 1864–1867: Politics, Newspapers, and the Union of British North America* (Toronto: University of Toronto Press, 1962), 76–85.
9. Waite, *The Life and Times of Confederation, 1864–1867*, 89.
10. John T. Saywell, *The Lawmakers: Judicial Power and the Shaping of Canadian Federalism* (Toronto: University of Toronto Press for the Osgoode Society for Canadian Legal History, 2002), 6–7; see also G. P. Browne, *Documents on the Confederation of British North America* (Toronto: McClelland and Stewart, 1969), 94–95.
11. While George Brown pioneered the "rep by pop" movement, many Upper Canadian Conservatives joined the chorus. John Hillyard Cameron, for example, broke with Macdonald in 1861, and brought a growing number of Conservatives with him, forcing Macdonald to eventually make "rep by pop" an open question among his followers.
12. Daniel Heidt, "'First Among Equals'," ch. 2.
13. Province of Canada, Legislative Assembly, 8 February 1865, 88, reproduced by *The Confederation Debates*, http://hcmc.uvic.ca/confederation/en/lgPCLA_1865-02-08.html.
14. For classic texts on the centralist interpretation of Canada's constitution, consult: Donald Creighton, *John A. Macdonald: The Young Politician* (Toronto: University of Toronto Press, 1952); Norman McLeod Rogers, "The Compact Theory of Confederation," in *Papers and Proceedings of the Annual Meeting of the Canadian Political Science Association* (1931), 205–30; Richard Gwyn, *Nation Maker: Sir John A. Macdonald: His Life, Our Times, Vol. 2, 1867–1891* (Toronto: Random House Canada, 2011); W.L. Morton, *The Kingdom of Canada: A General History From Earliest Times* (Toronto: McClelland and Stewart Limited, 1963).
15. Province of Canada, Legislative Assembly, 6 February 1865, 42, reproduced by *The Confederation Debates*, http://hcmc.uvic.ca/confederation/en/lgPCLA_1865-02-06.html.

16 Paul Romney, *Getting It Wrong: How Canadians Forgot Their Past and Imperiled Confederation* (Toronto: University of Toronto Press, 1999), 103. See also J.M.S. Careless, *Brown of the Globe. Vol. 2: Statesman of Confederation, 1860–1880* (Toronto: Macmillan Company, 1963).

17 Province of Canada, Legislative Assembly, 6 February 1865, 27, reproduced by *The Confederation Debates*, http://hcmc.uvic.ca/confederation/en/lgPCLA_1865-02-06.html.

18 Unlike the debates in Atlantic Canada where Confederation proponents often advocated further negotiations that would amend the Quebec Resolutions, the Great Coalition, warry of further delays or disagreement, limited voting to accepting or rejecting the deal. This tactic did not deter critics from proposing amendments but none were successful. The London Conference delegates, ironically, subsequently deviated from the Quebec Resolutions on several occasions.

19 Province of Canada, Legislative Assembly, 24 February 1865, 453-63; 6 March 1865, 681; and 7 March 1865, 756, reproduced by *The Confederation Debates*, http://hcmc.uvic.ca/confederation/en/lgPCLA_1865-02-24.html, http://hcmc.uvic.ca/confederation/en/lgPCLA_1865-03-06.html and http://hcmc.uvic.ca/confederation/en/lgPCLA_1865-03-07.html.

20 Gene Lawrence Allen. "The origins of the Intercolonial Railway, 1835–1869," PhD diss., University of Toronto, 1991.

21 Province of Canada, Legislative Council, 13 February 1865, 164, reproduced by *The Confederation Debates*, http://hcmc.uvic.ca/confederation/en/lgPCLC_1865-02-13.html.

22 For detailed histories of the Intercolonial Railway, consult: Andy Albert den Otter. *The Philosophy of Railways: The Transcontinental Railway Idea in British North America* (Toronto: University of Toronto Press, 1997); Allen, "The Origins of the Intercolonial Railway."

23 Province of Canada, Legislative Council, 9 February 1865, 123, reproduced by *The Confederation Debates*, http://hcmc.uvic.ca/confederation/en/lgPCLC_1865-02-09.html.

24 Ged Martin, "Painting the Other Picture: The Case Against Canadian Confederation," in *From Rebellion to Patriation: Canada and Britain in the Nineteenth and Twentieth Centuries*, ed. C.C. Eldridge (Whales Canadian Studies in Wales Group, 1989), 56–57.

25 For more on this perspective, consult Martin, "Painting the Other Picture," 49.

26 M.C. Cameron to JAM, 3 December 1864, LAC, MG26-A, Vol. 338, Pt 2.

27 Province of Canada, Legislative Assembly, 24 February 1865, 455, reproduced by *The Confederation Debates*, http://hcmc.uvic.ca/confederation/en/lgPCLA_1865-02-24.html.

28 Province of Canada, Legislative Assembly, 24 February 1865, 463, reproduced by *The Confederation Debates*, http://hcmc.uvic.ca/confederation/en/lgPCLA_1865-02-24.html.

29 Quoted in Martin, "Painting the Other Picture," 60.

30 Province of Canada, Legislative Council, 16 February 1865, 232, reproduced by *The Confederation Debates*, http://hcmc.uvic.ca/confederation/en/lgPCLC_1865-02-16.html.

31 Janet Ajzenstat, "Bicameralism and Canada's Founders: The Origins of the Canadian Senate," in *Protecting Canadian Democracy: The Senate You Never Knew*, ed. Serge Joyal (Montreal: McGill-Queen's University Press, 2003), 12.

32 Martin, "Painting the Other Picture," 65.

33 Bruce W. Hodgins, *John Sandfield Macdonald, 1812–1872* (Toronto: University of Toronto Press, 1971), 78–79.

34 Readers will also appreciate a brief note on topics that these debates do not include. Separate schools for Catholic and Franco Ontarians, as well as English and Protestant Lower Canadians, was a key concern during the 1860s, and the 72 Resolutions preserved the rights of both groups as they existed "at the time when the Union goes into operation." Yet education was rarely discussed during the legislatures' Confederation debates. This is because Alexander Galt promised to propose legislation improving separate school rights in both sections of the colony after the Legislative Assembly voted on the Confederation deal, effectively separating the two subjects for a few key months.

35 Miller, "Compact, Contract, Covenant: Canada's Treaty-Making Tradition," 20–21.

36 Miller, "Compact, Contract, Covenant: Canada's Treaty-Making Tradition," 32.

37 Wayne E. Daugherty, "Treaty Research Report: Treaty Three, 1873" (Treaties and Historical Research Centre Self-Government, Indian and Northern Affairs Canada 1986). Bands that were not present at the negotiations signed adhesion agreements during the succeeding two years. It should be noted that Treaty No. 3 is the only Numbered Treaty to allow Métis to sign adhesion agreements.

38 John S. Long, "How the Commissioners Explained Treaty Number Nine to the Ojibway and Cree in 1905," *Ontario History* XCVIII, no. 1 (Spring 2006): 13.

39 Treaty No. 9: Long, "How the Commissioners Explained Treaty Number Nine to the Ojibway and Cree in 1905," 14–19.

40 Long, "How the Commissioners Explained Treaty Number Nine to the Ojibway and Cree in 1905," 19. See also: John S. Long, *Treaty No. 9: Making the Agreement to Share the Land in Far Northern Ontario in 1905* (Montreal: McGill-Queen's University Press, 2010).

4

Quebec and Confederation: Gains and Compromise

MARCEL MARTEL, COLIN M. COATES,
MARTIN PÂQUET, AND MAXIME GOHIER

Confederation happened because of Quebec, not in spite of it. When delegates gathered in Charlottetown in September 1864 and a month later in Quebec City, French-speaking representatives from the future province of Quebec occupied a position of some strength at the negotiating table despite being members of a linguistic and religious minority. Their concerns had to be addressed in order to proceed with the reorganization of the colonial order in North America. Without significant support from French-Canadian politicians, a new constitutional arrangement was unlikely to succeed. For their part, English-speakers, who constituted a minority in the future province of Quebec, counted on their representatives to protect their interests.

Reconciling the rights and concerns of French- and English-speaking colonists had been a major political and constitutional issue in British North America since the Treaty of Paris in 1763, which ceded New France to the British. For over a century, British authorities had imposed constitutional reorganizations on their Empire in North America without substantial input from colonists. A series of constitutional changes attempted to wrestle with the issue of integrating a large Catholic and French-speaking population into a colonial political structure administered from London. In 1774, Britain enlarged the boundaries of the province of Quebec, recognized French civil law, and permitted Catholics to take oaths that allowed them to occupy state offices. Only seventeen years later, British authorities again modified constitutional arrangements: they divided the province of Quebec into two distinct territories, Lower Canada and Upper Canada, and gave both colonies representative parliamentary institutions.

Following the 1837–38 rebellions, Britain attempted to assimilate French Canada by decreeing the union of Lower Canada and Upper Canada. Despite being less populous, Canada West (the former Upper Canada) received the same number of representatives as Canada East (Lower Canada) in the new legislature that would govern both sections of the colony. The use of French in the colonial parliament was also initially disallowed, though it was subsequently restored in 1848. This attempt to assimilate French-Canadian society into a broader British North American polity was also unsuccessful. French-Canadian politicians had to address complaints from reform politicians in Upper Canada. Anxious to flex their increasing demographic muscle, Protestant political leaders wished to enhance their autonomy from the large number of Catholic voters. However, French-Canadian politicians like Louis-Hippolyte La Fontaine brilliantly used ideological differences among their English-speaking counterparts to develop workable coalitions that relied on substantial support from Francophone legislators to maintain power. For example, after the 1851 census had proved that Upper Canada had become more populated than Lower Canada, Protestants demanded "representation by population" hoping that it would guarantee their section greater autonomy from Catholic political influence. But French-Canadian allegiances with moderate Upper Canadian politicians allowed them to stonewall all attempts to implement this policy throughout the 1850s and early 1860s. This recognition among French-Canadian leaders that the French- and British-Canadian duality could be harnessed to serve their interests shaped their political thought and strategy throughout the next fifteen years.

The "Quebec" Delegation in Action

By the time colonial politicians met to discuss the idea of a broader union of British North American colonies in the 1860s, French Canadians occupied important positions at the negotiating table. Without the involvement of these key political figures from Canada East, the project could not have moved forward. The union of the British North American colonies became a possibility when George-Étienne Cartier, leader of the *Bleus* (Conservatives) in Canada East (the future province of Quebec), joined John A. Macdonald and George Brown from Canada West to form a coalition to end political deadlock in the colony of the Province of Canada. For some of the political leaders in that colony, one way of dealing with the ongoing disputes was to include the other British colonies in a larger federation.

Taking advantage of a meeting to discuss the union of the three Maritime colonies (Nova Scotia, New Brunswick, and Prince Edward Island) scheduled for September 1864 in Charlottetown, Canadian political leaders presented the broader project of uniting all the colonies into a new polity. The French-Canadian delegates were George-Étienne Cartier and Hector-Louis Langevin, alongside Irish-Catholic Montrealer Thomas D'Arcy McGee and Scottish-Protestant Alexander Galt from the Eastern Townships.

After working out broad strokes of a deal for British North American union, thirty-three colonial leaders reconvened at Quebec City to refine the terms of union. The compromises that they worked out became the 72 Resolutions—also known as the "Quebec Scheme"—and it was this agreement that eventually became the basis for the final negotiations in London, England and the eventual British North America Act.

The "Quebec" delegation included four French Canadians, Cartier, Langevin, Jean-Charles Chapais, and Étienne-Paschal Taché, along with two Anglophones: Galt and D'Arcy McGee. No members of the opposition *Rouge* party (Liberals) attended the Quebec talks and their absence meant that one of their key tenets—the separation of Church and state—was not reflected in the new agreement. If Quebec gained a significant, though not absolute, degree of autonomy with the Confederation deal, so did the French-language Catholic Church, albeit within the boundaries of the province.

At the negotiating table, the French-Canadian representatives made specific demands. It is important to situate their positions within the context of the limited state activities of the nineteenth century. Governments throughout the Western world played fairly minor economic and social roles at the time compared to the latter half of the twentieth century. During Canada's early years, for example, federal employees only numbered in the hundreds and federal revenues amounted to only fourteen million

George-Étienne Cartier
Attorney General East, Province of Canada, Que.

7 FEBRUARY 1865

CONFEDERATION QUOTE 4.1
Quotation from Province of Canada, Legislative Assembly, 7 February 1865
Photograph from Library and Archives Canada, MIKAN 2242461

> Some parties . . . pretended that it was impossible to carry out Federation, on account of the differences of races and religions. . . . It was just the reverse. It was precisely on account of the variety of races, local interests, &c., that the Federation system ought to be resorted to, and would be found to work well.

Thomas D'Arcy McGee
Liberal-Conservative Member of the Legislative Assembly, Province of Canada, Que.

9 FEBRUARY 1865

CONFEDERATION QUOTE 4.2

Quotation from Province of Canada, Legislative Assembly, 9 February 1865
Photograph by William Notman, from Library and Archives Canada, C-016749

" ... with a good deal of moderation and a proper degree of firmness, all that the Protestant minority in Lower Canada can require, by way of security to their educational system, will be cheerfully granted to them by this House ... if there are to be any special guarantees or grants extended to the Protestant minority of Lower Canada, I think the Catholic minority in Upper Canada ought to be placed in precisely the same position— neither better nor worse. "

dollars, almost all of which came from excises and duties. Confederation did not, in other words, lead immediately to a vast expansion in the scope of government. When negotiating Confederation at Quebec City, French-Canadian politicians expected to gain provincial control of political and social institutions that they judged instrumental to the strengthening of French-Canadian culture and identity. The Maritime delegates also generally shared the French-Canadian distrust of the centralizing tendencies. Federalism, with the provincial autonomy and diversity it offered, was therefore a political necessity. A legislative union with a strong central government, which Macdonald personally preferred, was therefore out of the question. While discussing the powers to be allocated to the federal government and the provinces, French-Canadian representatives insisted that education be controlled by the future provincial governments because denominational divides across the country ran deep, and local circumstances required accommodation. French-Canadian leaders, furthermore, expected some assurances regarding the use of the French language in federal institutions and in the future province of Quebec.

D'Arcy McGee and Galt were instrumental in protecting the rights of the English-speaking population of Quebec, and Cartier and Langevin agreed with their position. The issues of bilingualism and schooling were crucial. In fact, Quebec became the only bilingual province where French and English both became official languages in the legislature and courts. For education, denominational Protestant and Catholic schools (not language-based) were guaranteed. Anglophones, both Protestant and Catholic, as well as Catholic Francophones, thereby secured essential protections for many of the institutions they considered key to their cultural survival.

Indigenous Rights

This interest in minority rights did not extend to Indigenous Peoples. French-Canadian and English-speaking representatives from the future province of Quebec did not discuss Indigenous People's rights at all, even though some constitutional provisions would have major impacts on them. The Province of Canada had adopted a number of laws impacting Indigenous Peoples since 1851, but it was only in 1860 that it officially received from London the responsibility over "the Management of the Indian Lands and Property."[1] In fact, Indigenous Affairs was the final power London devolved to the colony before Confederation. Thus, when discussions began over a possible legislative or federal union of the Canadas in the late 1850s, Indigenous peoples and their rights were still officially a prerogative of the Crown.[2] At Charlottetown, no one broached the subject and, at Quebec, it was only on October 25—after two days of deliberations on the respective powers of the federal and local governments—that Oliver Mowat proposed that the "General Legislature" have jurisdiction over "Indians."[3] The delegates do not appear to have even discussed the proposal[4] and no objections were raised when "Indians and Lands reserved for the Indians" was finally added as one of the 37 "powers" of the "General Government."[5] The subject of Indigenous Peoples was also absent from the subsequent debates on the 72 Resolutions that took place in the Canadian Assembly and Legislative Council in 1865.

The fact that Indigenous People were not at the negotiating table (either physically or symbolically) does not mean they were not a concern for leaders in British North America, although it is hard to grasp the thoughts of the Fathers of Confederation on the subject. Many of the framers of the 72 Resolutions had been involved in Indian Affairs over the previous decade. In his position as Attorney General of Canada East, George-Étienne Cartier had often worked on issues relating to Indigenous rights, as did John A. Macdonald in his capacity as Attorney General for Canada West. Both had been responsible for introducing bills relative to Indigenous People to the Assembly, including the *Gradual Civilization Act* of 1857 and the bill securing the devolution of responsibility over Indian Affairs to the United Canadas in 1860. As Commissioner of Crown Lands, Alexander Campbell was the acting head of the Indian Department from March 1864 up to Confederation, a position previously occupied by William McDougall (1862–64), also present at the Quebec Conference.[6] For his part, Hector-Louis Langevin would become the first Superintendent General of Indian Affairs after Confederation, while Macdonald would serve more time in this position than anyone else in Canadian history (1878–87). During his time as Superintendent, Macdonald was also one of the main promoters of the federal system of residential schools.[7]

Indigenous Affairs thus mattered to Canada's founders, although these men obviously considered it self-evident that its supervision and management be vested in the "national" government. A newly obtained jurisdiction—one the Maritime colonies also exercised, though unofficially—it was still perceived as a symbol of Crown sovereignty and a legitimate imperial power over local legislatures, a political model Conservatives such as Macdonald wished to perpetuate.[8] For the Fathers, management of Indigenous Affairs was an important part of their nation-building project, being one of the main symbolic links that would unite the new "Federal Union" with "the Crown of Great Britain," ensuring the "perpetuation of [the] connection with the Mother Country" they sought to preserve.[9]

As a result of this omission, the same issues that had characterized relations between Indigenous Peoples living in Canada East and their non-Indigenous neighbours would extend into the future. Unlike the policy initiated in Canada West that was to be followed in the Plains and the North-West, no formal treaties with Indigenous nations governed land use. The Confederation agreement of the 1860s did not, consequently, resolve any outstanding issues between non-Indigenous Quebecers and the Mohawk, Wendat, Anishinaabeg, Abenaki, Atikamekw, Wolastoqiyik (Maleseet), Mi'kmaq, and Innu. With the expansion of Quebec's borders to the north in 1898 and 1912, the territory of other Indigenous nations, including the Cree, the Naskapis, and Inuit, would also be integrated into the province without any treaty being negotiated for the acquisition of their lands.

Debating the Merits of Confederation

Once approved by all delegates attending the October conference, the Confederation pact triggered important debates in the various colonial legislatures. In the Province of Canada's rotating capital at Quebec City, the Legislative Council (the upper body of the assembly, which since 1856 had included some elected members) held debates between 3 and 20 February 1865, and the entirely elected Legislative Assembly between 3 February and 13 March 1865.

Many French-Canadian politicians considered the Quebec Resolutions to be an improvement on the previous constitutional arrangement. Cartier and his *Bleu* allies in the Legislative Assembly agreed to support a coalition government until the political and institutional reorganization of British North America was a *fait accompli*. Since the Cartier-Macdonald-Brown coalition formed a majority, the passage of the deal was fairly certain. However, no one took the results for granted, and French-Canadian society was divided—like other British North American colonies—on the strengths and weaknesses of the new constitutional deal. In addition to convincing the colony's political representatives to vote for the Quebec Resolutions, supporters also had to reassure the broader population through the press that the creation of the new federation was the best available course of action. This imperative for wider public support, along with the historical gravity of the occasion, prompted the legislatures to commission the publication of a record of their debates soon thereafter for public consumption.[10]

During the debates in the legislature, proponents focused on the difficult challenges involved in creating a federation as well as the various economic and political benefits that the new union supposedly offered to all the colonies. For many supporters, Confederation was a visionary project. The integration of the Maritimes offered the promise of broader markets for agricultural and manufactured goods. A railway linking Canada West and East with the Maritimes was a key feature of the vision of future prosperity. According to advocates, this railway was indispensable to creating a larger consolidated market of four million consumers. Confederation, they contended, would thereby encourage French-Canadian political and business elites to take part in the creation of a continental nation. The new country would, furthermore, soon acquire the North-West Territories—then under the nominal control of the Hudson's Bay Company and occupied largely by Indigenous Peoples—and this vast territory would be thrown open to immigrants and native-born settlers alike.

Some doubters worried that the 72 Resolutions would erase local distinctiveness. So Cartier reassured his listeners that different religious and ethnic traditions would survive in the new country and proclaimed that Canada would constitute a new "political nationality with which neither the national origin, nor the religion of any individual, would interfere."[11] The protection of French Canadians' rights under the new constitutional arrangement would, according to Cartier and his supporters, depend on the shape of the new political institutions, the freedom to exercise their religion, limited language guarantees, and the preservation of their system of civil law. The presence of two national communities, they recognized, created tensions that had complicated colonial governance in the United Canadas, rendering the formation of stable governments which enjoyed the confidence of the House almost impossible, particularly in the 1860s.

Étienne-Paschal Taché
Premier, Province of Canada, Que.

3 FEBRUARY 1865

CONFEDERATION QUOTE 4.3
Quotation from Province of Canada, Legislative Council, 3 February 1865
Photograph from Library and Archives Canada, PA-074100

" If a Federal Union were obtained it would be tantamount to a separation of the provinces, and Lower Canada would thereby preserve its autonomy together with all the institutions it held so dear, and over which they could exercise the watchfulness and surveillance necessary to preserve them unimpaired. "

The time had come, they contended, to divide the United Canadas into two. This would allow voters in the future province of Quebec to regain the political institutions that they used to control until the dissolution of the Legislative Assembly in 1838. This notion of "separation from" was central for proponents of Confederation in both Canada East and Canada West. Taché, who attended the Quebec Conference, stated that Confederation was "tantamount to a separation of the provinces, and Lower Canada would thereby preserve its autonomy together with all the institutions it held so dear, and over which they could exercise the watchfulness and surveillance necessary to preserve them unimpaired." The individual who transcribed Taché's remarks added that these words were repeated in French, "for the express purpose of conveying his meaning in the clearest and most forcible manner to his fellow-members for Lower Canada, who might not have apprehended so well the English."[12] The new federal government would have limited control over issues at the heart of French-Canadian concerns. Langevin explained that at the level of the federal government, "there will be no questions of race, nationality, religion or locality, as this Legislature will only be charged with the settlement of the great general questions which will interest alike the whole Confederacy and not one locality only."[13]

Proponents of the Quebec Scheme also insisted that not one single drop of blood was shed in its accomplishment. British North Americans did not need to wage war to achieve political unity. George-Étienne Cartier reminded his counterparts that colonists were able to double the size of their population without strife, in distinct contrast to bellicose France. Although Napoleon III, argued Cartier, had become a major player on the European scene, he did it "after great expenditure of blood and treasure," which led to the incorporation of Savoy and Nice and "an addition of nearly one million inhabitants to France."[14]

Opponents of the Quebec Scheme dismissed the congratulatory rhetoric of those who favoured Confederation, and criticized many of their claims. Christopher Dunkin, the MLA for Brome in Quebec's Eastern Townships, was one of the few Conservatives to oppose the Quebec resolutions. In a very long speech that required two days to present, he raised a series of concerns about the Confederation deal. He was not convinced, for example, that a new nationality would emerge from the union. The British North American colonies, he contended, were divided by religion,

Christopher Dunkin
Member of the Legislative Assembly, Province of Canada, Que.

27 FEBRUARY 1865

CONFEDERATION QUOTE 4.4

Quotation from Province of Canada, Legislative Assembly, 27 February 1865. Photograph by Topley Studio, from Library and Archives Canada, PA-026325

> Talk . . . of . . . "a new nationality"—of your creating such a thing—of your whole people here rallying round its new Government at Ottawa. Mr. SPEAKER, is such a thing possible? We have a large class whose national feelings turn towards London . . . Paris . . . the Emerald Isle . . . and . . . Washington; but have we any class of people who are attached . . . to the city of Ottawa, the centre of the new nationality that is to be created?

Antoine-Aimé Dorion
Rouge Leader, Member of the Legislative Assembly, Province of Canada, Que.

16 FEBRUARY 1865

CONFEDERATION QUOTE 4.5
Quotation from Province of Canada, Legislative Assembly, 16 February 1865
Photograph by Topley Studio, from Library and Archives Canada, PA-025755

> I thank God, sir, I never insulted Upper Canada, like some of those who reviled me. I never compared the people of Upper Canada to so many codfish. I showed on the contrary that I was always willing to meet the just claims of Upper Canada.

ethnicity, and language. He also denied that united British North American military forces would be able to repel an American invasion. Given the size of the Northern US Army then engaged in the Civil War, the limited joint forces available to British North America, whether united under a single banner, or united in common defence, could do little to stop an attack.[15]

Among the strongest opponents were the *Rouges*, who were considered radical liberals because of their views on the separation between church and state. Their leader, Antoine-Aimé Dorion, led the *Rouge* charge against the new constitutional package. Noting that the majority of elected officials in the Assembly did not understand French, he delivered his criticisms in English. Dorion questioned whether Confederation would actually establish a federal union. No, he argued, the federal power to disallow provincial legislation would allow the former to overrule "laws passed by the local legislatures and demanded by a majority of the people of that locality."[16] He reminded his audiences that he was a longstanding advocate of a true Confederation and "to leave to a general government questions of trade, currency, banking, public works of a general character, &c., and to commit to the decision of local legislatures all matters of a local bearing."[17] The Quebec Scheme, he warned, would pave the way to a legislative union that would be detrimental to French Canadians. Dorion also denounced the anti-democratic nature of the proposed appointed Senate.[18] Like other opponents in New Brunswick and Nova Scotia, he challenged the government to let the electorate decide the fate of the 72 Resolutions.

Some of Dorion's concerns were well founded. It may have been difficult to foresee in 1867, but the federal government sometimes used its disallowance powers in the way that Dorion warned about (although such actions have not occurred since 1943). Nonetheless, the potential threat to minority rights that the greater constitutional authority of the federal government poses remains a key argument in favour of Quebec acquiring greater autonomy within, perhaps even separation from, the Canadian union.[19]

The largest group of opponents to the terms of union were the *Violets* (Purples) or moderate liberals. One representative of this group was Henri-Gustave Joly de Lotbinière, who spoke for an entire day on February 20 against the Confederation deal.[20] His speech was "distinctive," according to his biographer J.I. Little, because of his "erudition with

Henri-Gustave Joly de Lotbinière
Member of the Legislative Assembly, Province of Canada, Que.

20 FEBRUARY 1865

CONFEDERATION QUOTE 4.6

Quotation from Province of Canada, Legislative Assembly, 20 February 1865
Photograph by Topley Studio, from Library and Archives Canada, PA-025470

" Let us begin with Lower Canada; its population is composed of about three-fourths French-Canadians, and of one-fourth English-Canadians. It is impossible, even for the blindest admirers of the scheme of Confederation, to shut out from their view this great difference of nationality, which is certainly fated to play an important part in the destinies of the future Confederation. "

copious references to political philosophy and history."[21] Joly de Lotbinière found nothing reassuring in the proposed constitutional deal. It would weaken relations between British North America and the Imperial government. The "so-called" economic advantages offered by the constitutional package could have been achieved without amalgamating all the British North American colonies, de Lotbinière contended. He also offered harsh criticisms for those who celebrated the merits of the proposal. Federal models of governance had failed in various part of the world, the United States being a case in point since a civil war had torn the country apart, but de Lotbinière reviewed the political evolution of countries in Europe and Latin America as well. Like Dunkin, de Lotbinière tried to undermine Cartier's vision of a new Canadian nationality. The colonists who were about to be united under a similar political structure lacked commonalities. As one of the few French-speaking Protestants in public life in Canada, he reminded elected officials that there was no common language, nor common religion between English and French-speaking people. Disagreeing with his French-Canadian colleagues who had taken part in the negotiations over the constitutional package, he rejected their self-congratulatory statements on the supposed political gains they had made. Far from securing institutions to protect French language and culture, for Joly de Lotbinière the constitutional framework did not safeguard the distinctiveness of French Canada. On the contrary, it threatened the survival of French Canadians. "Let us not give to the world," he exhorted, "the sad spectacle of a people voluntarily resigning its nationality."[22]

The Results of the Votes

The Legislative Council voted first on the terms of union on 20 February 1865, passing the motion to adopt the terms of union forty-five to fifteen. On March 10, at 4:30 a.m., members of the Legislative Assembly cast their votes. This latter vote took place in a tense atmosphere, since it occurred after Samuel Leonard Tilley's pro-Confederation government lost the election in New Brunswick a few days earlier. This popular rejection was a major setback for the proponents of Confederation in the Province of Canada. Nonetheless, Macdonald, Brown, and Cartier won the vote with ninety-one members voting for and thirty-three against. In Canada East, thirty-seven members, including six *Violets*, voted in favour of the Quebec

Scheme, and twenty-five rejected it. Among the opponents in Canada East, all *Rouge* MPs voted against it, along with eleven *Violets* and four *Bleus*. The opponents represented Montreal Island ridings and those near the American borders since they believed in North-South trade with the United States rather than what they called the "illusionary" East-West trade that was part of the federation proposal.[23]

In the end, most opponents of the Confederation deal chose to pursue their careers within the new political framework. For instance, de Lotbinière voted against the constitutional package, but he accepted the result. After Confederation, he was elected to both the House of Commons in Ottawa and the Quebec Legislative Assembly (it was possible to hold seats in both legislatures during the years immediately after 1867).[24] Leader of the provincial Liberal Party from 1869 to 1882, he briefly served as Quebec premier from 1878 to 1879. From 1900 to 1906, he became the lieutenant-governor of British Columbia. Likewise, Antoine-Aimé Dorion was elected a Liberal member of parliament in 1867, and was appointed minister of justice when Alexander Mackenzie became the first Liberal prime minister in 1873, but he retired from active political life a year later. For his part, Christopher Dunkin pursued his career in provincial politics by becoming the first minister of finance. In 1869, he agreed to join the federal government led by John A. Macdonald, but then left the position when he received a judicial appointment in 1871. In short, opposition to the Confederation proposals in 1865 did not indicate an unwillingness to accept the legitimacy of the new polity.

Debating Confederation Outside of Parliament

While elected and appointed politicians examined the terms of the Confederation deal in the legislature, debate raged in public as well. Following the Quebec conference, newspapers in the British colonies published favourable or critical assessments of the 72 Resolutions, reflecting their political affiliations. *Rouge* newspapers such as *Le Journal de Saint-Hyacinthe*, *Le Défricheur*, *L'Ordre*, *Le Canadien*, *La Tribune*, and *Le Pays* were highly critical. They depicted the deal as a threat to French-Canadian culture and language, and questioned the degree of autonomy that French Canadians would enjoy through the creation of the new provincial political institutions. In 7 June 1865, *L'Ordre*, for example, contended that joining the United States would better protect French Canada because, within the United States, Quebec "would be a sovereign state."[25] In Canada, by contrast, Quebec might become a mere municipality. The newspaper *Le Pays* warned of dire repercussions: "the French language drowned, religion persecuted, nationality submerged, the French-Canadian race violated and mistreated, its rights ravished, its liberties trampled."[26] Between the Quebec conference and the debate in the Canadian parliament in 1865, public meetings, many of them organized by the *Rouges*, denounced the deal.[27]

On the other hand, newspapers that supported Cartier and his political group defended the Confederation deal. *La Minerve*, for example, insisted on the gains that Quebec and in particular French Canadians had achieved with the constitutional provisions. Writing at the time of the Charlottetown Conference, *La Minerve* set out its position: "if the plan seems to us to safeguard Lower Canada's special interests, its religion and its nationality, we'll give it our support; if not, we'll fight it with all our strength."[28] *La Minerve* and other newspapers concluded that Quebec would benefit from the proposed union. For Joseph-Édouard Cauchon, who founded the *Journal de Québec*, Confederation would protect the French language, Catholicism, and French-Canadian culture. American annexation—the only logical alternative—would lead to linguistic and cultural assimilation.[29] In an 1865 pamphlet considering the Quebec Resolutions, Cauchon adopted a fairly similar stance. For him, the re-establishment of a local and autonomous legislature was key, whether it took place within a new federation with Canada West or with all the British North American provinces. "[A] local government," he argued, "... would certainly offer a measure of protection to us, as Catholics and Frenchmen. ... [A]s a religious minority, we would become, and always remain, a national and religious majority."[30] In his analysis of newspaper coverage of the Confederation debates in the public domain, historian Arthur Silver observed that "*separation*" from Canada West and "*independence* (of Quebec within its jurisdictions) were the main themes of *Bleu* propaganda."[31]

In the battle for public opinion, proponents of Confederation could count on a powerful ally: the Roman Catholic Church, a religious institution with tremendous political influence. Ecclesiastical officials continued to exert influence over the chief French-Canadian proponents of Confederation, Cartier and Hector-Louis Langevin, during the negotiations in 1864 and 1866. Langevin, for instance, corresponded regularly with his brother Edmond—who was the secretary and confidential adviser to the Archbishop of Quebec City—while in London overseeing the passage of the terms of union through Britain's parliament. Hector-Louis assured his brother that he would prevent British politicians from removing education from the list of powers given to provinces.

During the debates in the Legislative Assembly, opponents to Confederation discussed the role of the Catholic Church. If the higher clergy supported Confederation, this was not necessarily the case among the lower clergy who were more closely connected to their parishioners. The *Rouge* member for Verchères, Félix Geoffrion, challenged the claim that the Catholic Church in Quebec unanimously supported Confederation.[32] He asserted that numerous priests opposed the deal, which led Joseph-Édouard Cauchon to accuse Geoffrion of dragging the Church into the debate. In his sharp reply, Geoffrion noted that George-Étienne Cartier was the first to invoke the Church during his speech on 7 February 1865.[33] Without identifying the individual, Geoffrion referred to a news article published in *Le Canadien* where a priest denounced the federal government's jurisdiction over marriage, because it would allow it to interfere with Quebec civil law. In his attempt to undermine the credibility of this religious opponent, Édouard Rémillard—who was a *Rouge* but supported Confederation[34]—wondered if the views of two or three priests were sufficient to support the claim that the clergy was divided. After all, these two or three priests had contributed to the newspaper as citizens rather than as members of the Catholic Church.[35] Opponents to Confederation would not let Rémillard have the last word. Maurice Laframboise, for example, read a letter to the Legislative Assembly written by a priest and published in *Le Canadien* on 6 March 1865. The priest had opposed Confederation because he believed that French Canadians would lose their "liberty of action" in the new political structure. French Canadians, the priest had also contended, would have exercised almost no influence in federal institutions.[36]

References to the views of some clergy members did not change the outcome of the debates in the Legislative Assembly, but the Catholic Church hierarchy mobilized the clergy in 1867. Several Quebec bishops, including Jean Langevin of Rimouski, Edmond's and Hector-Louis' eldest brother, praised Confederation. For Bishop Langevin, "the new constitution ... is given ... as the expression of the supreme will of the legislator of the legitimate Authority, and thus of God himself." For him, Catholicism and French-Canadian culture and language would be preserved, and therefore he asked his flock to support Confederation.[37] Bishop Ignace Bourget of Montreal sent a letter on 25 July 1867 requesting the clergy pronounce favourably on Confederation. For his part, Bishop Louis-François Laflèche of Trois-Rivières included a strong warning: anyone opposing Confederation would be committing a sin. Priests in his diocese were expected to read his letter during Sunday mass.[38]

The British parliament passed the British North America Act, and it took effect on 1 July 1867. Elections took place in the fall of 1867. Quebec voters overwhelmingly elected Cartier and his Conservative team, controlling forty-seven seats to the opposition Liberals' seventeen.

Minority Rights: An Example for the World?[39]

During the 1864 negotiations, French- and English-Canadians from the future province of Quebec addressed concerns about rights for minorities. The Canadian parliamentary debates of 1865 covered the same ground. At a distance of over one hundred and fifty years, a close reading of these 1865 debates reveals that the participants had a limited conception of minority rights. Can we blame them? After all, most of these politicians participated in a legal culture based on the supremacy of Parliament that afforded the courts little scope for reviewing governmental action. It was also the age of empire building and the assertion of nationalism, with the emergence of new countries such as Germany and Italy. Despite such developments, on a day-to-day basis in most countries, governments played a fairly small role in citizens' lives in any case. Indeed, with some of the key political divides in countries like Canada being focused on religious denominations, antipathies between Protestants and Catholics also made it difficult to address some topics openly. In these circumstances, the precept that minority rights should enjoy strong constitutional and judicial recognition and protection was much weaker than it is today.

And yet, despite their backgrounds and biases, the legislators did address the issue of minority rights to some extent. Power relations between the main linguistic and religious groups in the colonies often shaped their discussions. French Canadians and Catholics, who formed minority communities in every colony except Canada East, were often the focus of these discussions. The vast majority of French-Canadians—more than 85 percent—lived in Canada East; about ninety thousand Acadians lived in New Brunswick, Nova Scotia, and Prince Edward Island. There were about forty thousand French Canadians living in Canada West (the future province of Ontario), and fifteen thousand French-speaking Métis on the Prairies. Catholics, in fact, constituted about 18 percent in Canada West, 20 percent in New Brunswick, and 25 percent in Nova Scotia. In Prince Edward Island, Catholics comprised about half of the population.[40] The rights of a second linguistic group also preoccupied the Fathers of Confederation: English speakers in Canada East. While Anglophones formed a majority outside of Canada East, their minority status within that province led their representatives to seek a measure of protection in the new constitutional order. (It is worth keeping in mind that around the time of Confederation, the percentage of Anglophones—and in particular Protestants in Canada East—was at its historic peak, about one-quarter of the total population. They therefore constituted an electoral force in Canada East that would only decline in subsequent decades, though the colony's political leaders did not anticipate this demographic shift at the time.) Other minority groups, such as Jews and non-French or English ethnic groups were almost entirely ignored during the debates.

The compromises forged between 1864 and 1867 were ultimately inadequate to protect most Catholic and French minorities outside of Quebec. Historian Arthur Silver has argued that the rights of French Canadians were not expected to extend beyond the boundaries of the future province of Quebec[41] and, indeed, the rights of French-speaking people, except those who lived in the future province of Ontario, rarely came up for discussion during the 1864 to 1867 negotiations and debates. French-Canadian politicians were ultimately unwilling to sacrifice the autonomy and control that the future province of Quebec would have over its "local affairs" in exchange for stronger constitutional guarantees for minority groups residing in other parts of the country. Education constituted one of the clearest battlegrounds, and Hector-Louis Langevin came under some pressure to adopt a different approach. Before leaving for London in 1866, Langevin met with Catholic bishops from the Maritimes, including Archbishop of Halifax Thomas Louis Connolly. In Nova Scotia, Catholics constituted a quarter of the population, and Connolly asserted their interests. Fearing that a non-confessional provincial school system would endanger the faith of Catholics, Connolly asked for the constitutional recognition of separate schools. However, the premier of Nova Scotia opposed the idea, and Connolly lobbied British politicians in London, suggesting that the federal government should take constitutional responsibility for education.[42] Hector-Louis Langevin, like many of his Canada-East peers, rejected the proposal because he feared that it would jeopardize French Canadians' rights in the future province of Quebec.

When considering language and education, Confederation proponents—and especially the French-speaking members of the parliament—understood what the new constitutional package meant, despite its limited focus on minority rights. Constitutional guarantees applied specifically to language and religion. In the British North America Act, section 133 recognized French and English as official languages, but only in Quebec and federal institutions. Concerning education, section 93 protected public and separate schools. It gave Catholic and Protestant minorities the right to appeal to the Governor General in Council (i.e., the federal cabinet) if a provincial legislature restricted access to schools or separate schools to less than what was offered at the time of union. Anglophones in Quebec received additional protections beyond language and education. Quebec's provincial parliament initially included both an elected Legislative Assembly and an appointed Legislative Council (which was only abolished in 1968). Moreover, in twelve provincial ridings largely comprising Anglophone populations at the time of Confederation, the "boundaries could not be changed without the additional approval of a majority of their own MPPs."[43] These, too, had a long life, and the twelve "protected" ridings retained their constitutional protection until 1970. It is unlikely that such provisions fulfilled their promise of a meaningful defence of Anglophone rights, but they were significant parts of the compromises of the 1860s. In any case, the rights of Quebec's minority Anglophones to control their own schooling system never faced the same challenges that Francophone minorities experienced outside the province.

After 1867, it did not take long for Canadian Catholics, and especially French-speaking Canadians, to discover that the delicate balance of power and influence enshrined in the constitution did not favour those living outside of Quebec. In 1871, the province of New Brunswick decided to fund only non-denominational schools. Ignoring protests by Acadians and other Catholics, the federal government chose not to intervene.

Equally dramatically, and despite the clear protections contained in the Manitoba Act of 1870, that province's government made English its only official language and abolished funding for denominational schools within two decades of its founding. Subsequent court decisions favoured Catholic and French rights, but the provincial government ignored them while the federal government, led by Wilfrid Laurier, compromised on the issue of separate schools by allowing the Manitoba government to provide religious instruction for an hour a day. Finally, in 1912, the government of Ontario limited the use of French as a language of instruction in schools. Although French-Canadians in Ontario contended that section 93 protected French as a language of instruction, the courts decided otherwise. These school crises demonstrated the limitations of constitutional guarantees for minority groups and greatly influenced discussions, starting in the 1960s, that led to the patriation of the Constitution in 1982. In 1864, Canada West leader and staunch Protestant George Brown had tried to reassure delegates that such delicate issues had been resolved. He suggested that the constitutional package should be understood as inspirational. However, when put to the test, the guarantees to minority groups outside Quebec failed miserably.

Nonetheless, the substantial powers over key sectors such as education, health, and welfare served to solidify the power and autonomy of the largest number of French Canadians within Canada: Quebecers. The Confederation agreement therefore largely fulfilled Cartier's dream of protecting French-Canadian culture and society in his home province. To the extent that Quebec provided a jurisdictional framework for the survival and promotion of French-Canadian and Catholic society, Cartier's image of a bicultural Canada ultimately prevailed over the unitary model that Macdonald had favoured.

Further Reading

Bellavance, Marcel. *Le Québec et la Confédération: un choix libre? Le clergé et la constitution de 1867*. Québec: Septentrion, 1992.

Bonenfant, Jean-Charles. *The French Canadians and the Birth of Confederation*. Canadian Historical Association, Booklet 21. Hull: Leclerc, 1966.

Brouillet, Eugénie. *La négation de la nation. L'identité culturelle québécoise et le fédéralisme canadien*. Québec: Septentrion, 2005.

Brouillet, Eugénie, Alain-G. Gagnon, and Guy Laforest, eds. *La conférence de Québec de 1864: 150 ans plus tard*. Québec: Les Presses de l'Université Laval, 2016.

Kelly, Stéphane. *Les fins du Canada: selon Macdonald, Laurier, Mackenzie King et Trudeau*. Montréal: Boréal, 2001.

Moore, Christopher. *Three Weeks in Quebec City: The Meeting that Made Canada*. Toronto: Allen Lane, 2015.

Paquin, Stéphane. *L'invention d'un mythe. Le pacte entre deux peuples fondateurs*. Montréal: VLB, 1999.

Silver, A.I. *The French Canadian Idea of Confederation, 1864–1900*. Toronto: University of Toronto Press, 1997.

NOTES

1 *An Act Respecting the Management of Indians Lands and Property* (23 Victoria, ch. 151). This law was adopted on 19 May 1860, and sanctioned by the Crown on 30 June 1860.

2 See, for instance, Joseph-Charles Taché, *Des provinces de l'Amérique du Nord et d'une Union fédérale* (Québec: Des presses à vapeur de J. T. Brousseau, 1858); Joseph Cauchon, *Étude sur l'union projetée des provinces britanniques de l'Amérique du Nord* (Québec: Augustin Côté et Cie, 1858). The only real discussion of Indigenous Peoples during the 1858 discussions was by Cartier, Ross, and Galt who proposed assigning the federal government jurisdiction over "unincorporated and Indian territories." G. E. Cartier, J. J. Ross, and M. East [A. T. Galt] to Sir Edward Bulwer Lytton, 25 October 1858, in *Documents on the Confederation of British North America*, ed. G. P. Browne (Toronto: McClelland and Stewart, 1969), 18.

3 Hewitt Bernard's Minutes of the Quebec Conference, 10–29 October 1864, in Browne, *Documents on the Confederation*, 85.

4 Christopher Moore, *Three Weeks in Quebec City: The Meeting That Made Canada* (Toronto: Allen Lane, 2015), 179.

5 The Quebec Resolutions, October 1864, in Browne, *Documents on the Confederation*, 159.

6 Brian Gettler, "Indigenous Policy and Silence at Confederation", *Earlycanadianhistory.ca*, https://earlycanadianhistory.ca/2017/06/26/indigenous-policy-and-silence-at-confederation/.

7 Donald B. Smith, "Macdonald's Relationship with Aboriginal People," in *Macdonald at 200: New Reflections and Legacies*, eds. Patrice Dutil and Roger Hall (Toronto: Dundurn Press, 2014), 58–93; J.R. Miller, "Macdonald as Minister of Indian Affairs: the Shaping of Canadian Indian Policy," in Dutil and Hall, *Macdonald at* 200, 311–40.

8 Robert C. Vipond, "1787 and 1867: The Federal Principle and Canadian Confederation Reconsidered," *Canadian Journal of Political Science / Revue canadienne de science politique* 22, no. 1 (1989): 3–25.

9 The Quebec Resolutions, October 1864, in Browne, *Documents on the Confederation*, 154; see Phillip Buckner, "L'élaboration de la constitution canadienne au sein du monde britannique," in *La Conférence de Québec de 1864: 150 ans plus tard. Comprendre l'émergence*

de la fédération canadienne, eds. Eugénie Brouillet, Alain-G. Gagnon and Guy Laforest (Québec: Presses de l'Université Laval, 2016), 84–85 and David E. Smith, *Federalism and the Constitution of Canada* (Toronto: University of Toronto Press, 2010), 48–49.

10 *Parliamentary Debates on the Subject of the Confederation of the British North American Provinces, 3rd Session, 8th Provincial Parliament of Canada* (Quebec: Hunter, Rose & Co Parliamentary Printers, 1865), reproduced by *The Confederation Debates*, http://hcmc.uvic.ca/confederation/en/lgPCLAssem.html and http://hcmc.uvic.ca/confederation/en/lgPCLCoun.html.

11 Province of Canada, Legislative Assembly, 7 February 1865, 60, reproduced by *The Confederation Debates*, http://hcmc.uvic.ca/confederation/en/lgPCLA_1865-02-07.html.

12 Province of Canada, Legislative Council, 3 February 1865, 9, reproduced by *The Confederation Debates*, http://hcmc.uvic.ca/confederation/en/lgPCLC_1865-02-03.html.

13 Province of Canada, Legislative Assembly, 21 February 1865, 368, reproduced by *The Confederation Debates*, http://hcmc.uvic.ca/confederation/en/lgPCLA_1865-02-21.html.

14 Province of Canada, Legislative Assembly, 7 February 1865, 60, reproduced by *The Confederation Debates*, http://hcmc.uvic.ca/confederation/en/lgPCLA_1865-02-07.html.

15 François Rocher, "Sur les opposants au projet de Confédération de 1864: critiques sur la finalité du régime," in Brouillet, Gagnon and Laforest, *La conférence de Québec de 1864*, 221–24; Stéphane Kelly, "L'argumentaire économique des opposants québécois," in Brouillet, Gagnon, and Laforest, *La conférence de Québec de 1864*, 255.

16 Province of Canada, Legislative Assembly, 16 February 1865, 258, reproduced by *The Confederation Debates*, http://hcmc.uvic.ca/confederation/en/lgPCLA_1865-02-16.html.

17 Province of Canada, Legislative Assembly, 16 February 1865, 246, reproduced by *The Confederation Debates*, http://hcmc.uvic.ca/confederation/en/lgPCLA_1865-02-16.html.

18 Province of Canada, Legislative Assembly, 16 February 1865, 255, reproduced by *The Confederation Debates*, http://hcmc.uvic.ca/confederation/en/lgPCLA_1865-02-16.html.

19 Michel Seymour, "Le Canada reconnaît-il l'existence des droits collectifs linguistiques du peuple québécois?" in *Légiférer en matière linguistique*, eds. Marcel Martel and Martin Pâquet (Québec: Les Presses de l'Université Laval, 2008), 426–28; Marcel Martel, "Ils n'étaient pas à la table de négociations: les francophones en milieu minoritaire et leur expérience concernant le pacte confédératif," in *Le Canada français et la Confédération: Fondements critiques*, eds. Jean-François Caron and Marcel Martel (Québec: Les Presses de l'Université Laval, 2016), 71–79.

20 His remarks in the Legislative Assembly were reprinted in a pamphlet.

21 J. I. Little, *Patrician Liberal. The Public and Private Life of Sir Henri-Gustave Joly de Lotbinière, 1829–1908* (Toronto: University of Toronto Press, 2013), 103.

22 Province of Canada, Legislative Assembly, 20 February 1865, 362, reproduced by *The Confederation Debates*, http://hcmc.uvic.ca/confederation/en/lgPCLA_1865-02-20.html.

23 P. B. Waite, *The Life and Times of Confederation, 1864–1867: Politics, Newspapers, and the Union of British North America* (Toronto: University of Toronto Press, 1962), 154–56; Kelly, "L'argumentaire économique des opposants québécois," 247–48.

24 The double mandate was abolished in 1874.

25 Waite, *The Life and Times of Confederation*, 147.

26 Waite, *The Life and Times of Confederation*, 148 (quotation).

27 Rocher, "Sur les opposants au projet de Confédération de 1864," 221–24.

28 *La Minerve*, 9 September 1864, quoted in Arthur I. Silver, *The French-Canadian Idea of Confederation, 1864–1900* (Toronto: University of Toronto Press, 1982), 33.

29 Eric Bédard, "Éviter ce 'gouffre d'inique liberté': Le fédéralisme centralisateur de Joseph-Édouard Cauchon," in Brouillet, Gagnon, and Laforest, *La conférence de Québec de 1864*, 109–22.

30 Joseph Cauchon, *The Union of the Provinces of British North America*, trans. George Henry Macaulay (Québec, Hunter, Rose & Co., 1865), 42–43.

31 Silver, *The French-Canadian Idea of Confederation*, 41.

32 Province of Canada, Legislative Assembly, 8 March 1865, 778, reproduced by *The Confederation Debates*, http://hcmc.uvic.ca/confederation/en/lgPCLA_1865-03-08.html.

33 Province of Canada, Legislative Assembly, 8 March 1865, 778, reproduced by *The Confederation Debates*, http://hcmc.uvic.ca/confederation/en/lgPCLA_1865-03-08.html.

34 Biography of Edouard Rémillard, Assemblée nationale du Québec, http://www.assnat.qc.ca/fr/deputes/remillard-edouard-5055/biographie.html.

35 Province of Canada, Legislative Assembly, 8 March 1865, 786, reproduced by *The Confederation Debates*, http://hcmc.uvic.ca/confederation/en/lgPCLA_1865-03-08.html.

36 Province of Canada, Legislative Assembly, 9 March 1865, 842–43, reproduced by *The Confederation Debates*, http://hcmc.uvic.ca/confederation/en/lgPCLA_1865-03-09.html.

37 Yvan Lamonde, *The Social History of Ideas in Quebec, 1760–1896*, trans. Phyllis Aronoff and Howard Scott (Montreal: McGill-Queen's University Press, 2013), 303.

38 Marcel Bellavance, *Le Québec et la Confédération: un choix libre ? Le clergé et la constitution de 1867* (Québec: Septentrion, 1992), 82–92, 122–24.

39 Some paragraphs of this sub-section were published by Marcel Martel, "An Example for the World? Confederation and French Canadians," in "Debating the Confederation Debates of 1865," eds. Colin M. Coates and Philip Girard, *Canada Watch* (Spring 2016): 7–8.

40 Waite, *The Life and Times of Confederation*, 117, 179, 195, 229.

41 Silver, *The French-Canadian Idea of Confederation*.

42 David B. Flemming, "Thomas Louis Connolly," in *Dictionary of Canadian Biography*, vol. 10 University of Toronto/Université Laval, 2003, accessed 10 March 2017, http://www.biographi.ca/fr/bio/connolly_thomas_louis_10E.html; Marcel Martel and Martin Pâquet, *Speaking Up: A History of Language and Politics in Canada and Quebec* (Toronto: Between the Lines, 2012), 52.

43 Silver, *The French-Canadian Idea of Confederation*, 56.

5

The Maritimes and the Debate Over Confederation

PHILLIP BUCKNER

On 1 September 1864 fifteen delegates from Nova Scotia, New Brunswick, and Prince Edward Island met in Charlottetown, ostensibly for the purpose of discussing a proposal for Maritime Union. In reality, the delegates were aware that their chances of working out a scheme of Maritime Union acceptable to the three Maritime legislatures were negligible. Quite probably they would not have met at all, if a delegation from the Province of Canada had not asked to attend the meeting in order to present a proposal for a larger union of British North America. Within just over a week the delegates at Charlottetown agreed to the general outline for the creation of a continental union that would ultimately stretch from the Atlantic to the Pacific. In October nineteen delegates from the Maritimes met in Quebec City with delegates from the Province of Canada and Newfoundland and hammered out seventy-two resolutions designed to provide a framework for the constitution of the union. The Maritime delegates then returned to their respective provinces to attempt to get legislative approval for the Quebec Resolutions (or the Quebec Scheme, as it was called by its opponents).

The Negotiations

In recent historiography it has become an article of faith that the Maritimes were persuaded to enter a union that they neither needed nor wanted, a union that was essentially designed to favour the interests of the Province of Canada. It is certainly true that the levels of trade between the Maritimes and Canada in the early 1860s were low. It is also true that many Maritimers could see few benefits from increased economic activity between two regions that had very similar economies, based primarily upon agriculture and the extraction of raw materials for export markets in Britain and the United States. Moreover, during the early 1860s the Maritimes were experiencing comparatively rapid economic growth, generated by the Reciprocity Treaty of 1854 with the United States and the increased demand for raw materials created by the American Civil War. There were, however, fears that the end of the War would also mean an end to the prosperity of the region, especially if the United States abrogated the Reciprocity Treaty.

There were other signs of a bumpy economic future. The population of the Maritimes continued to grow during the 1860s, reaching a total of 768,000 in 1871. But this growth disguised an important underlying reality that some Maritimers recognized. Population growth in the 1860s was generated largely by natural increase as the number of immigrants to the region began to decline and a growing number of the native-born emigrated, mainly to the United States. This was a sign that the limits for the expansion in the Maritimes of a traditional economy based upon the production of raw materials and the wooden ships built and operated by local merchants would soon be reached. Some members of the economic and political elites (and there was considerable overlap between the two) had already begun to see the economic future of the region in terms of the development of railways to the south to Maine and to the west to Canada. These railway links, the railway enthusiasts hoped, would increase the potential for trade and lead to the development of secondary manufacturing industry. Yet the building of long-distance railways involved more capital investment than any of the Maritime colonies could raise on their own. The attempt to build a railroad (usually described as the Western Extension) linking Saint John, the largest city in the Maritimes, with Bangor, Maine, floundered because of the failure of New Brunswick to find a partner in Maine willing to undertake any construction. The construction of an intercolonial railway linking the Maritimes with Canada also floundered because of the failure to reach an agreement with the Canadian and British governments over how the railway should be financed. Increasingly, it seemed obvious that the Intercolonial would never be built unless the British North American colonies united and made a firm commitment to the project.

The enthusiasm for railways was not universal. It was strongest in the larger urban centres that were likely to be on the route of the Intercolonial or could easily be connected by feeder lines, and in the areas that had substantial coal reserves and deposits of iron and therefore the greatest industrial potential. There was much less enthusiasm for vastly expanded expenditures on railways in communities that relied on agriculture, the fisheries, and the traditional seaborne trades and that preferred to keep taxes and tariffs as low as possible, and it was in these areas where Confederation had the least appeal. Without doubt for the Maritimes the decision to join what was designed to become a continental union involved a far greater risk than it did for the Canadas. The Maritime delegates at Quebec hoped that the economic advantages of the central provinces could be partly offset by the building at federal expense of the Intercolonial railway, but many Maritime merchants and bankers feared that the railway would lead to increased Canadian domination of their regional economy and many farmers, fishers, and shipowners feared that it would lead to increased taxation.

Confederation was, however, about a great deal more than trade. The English-speaking population in both the Maritimes and the Province of Canada may have been separated (as the opponents of Confederation pointed out) by a vast expanse of wilderness, but they still had a great deal in common. They had a sense of a shared ancestry and a deep commitment to the British Empire, to the British monarchy, to the British constitution, and to British liberal values. It was this shared cultural identity that enabled the delegates from Canada and the Maritimes at the Charlottetown Conference to accept the need for a confederation of the British North American Colonies and to agree at Quebec City upon a detailed plan of union. The timing of the conferences was critical. In 1862 the removal of two Confederate envoys to London from a British ship, the *Trent*, by the American navy, had brought America and Britain perilously close to war and aroused fears across all of British North America. As the American Civil War gradually drew to a close and the victory of the North became inevitable, it was increasingly clear that the balance of power on the North American continent had permanently shifted and that the political and economic viability of the British colonies on the northern half of the North American continent was threatened. The belief that British Americans had to choose between continued membership of the British Empire or gradual absorption into an expanding American Empire was the strongest force driving the movement for Confederation.[1] Initially the anti-Confederates played down these fears, insisting that the end of the war would mean an end to tensions along the American-Canadian border. But the decision of the American government in 1865 to abrogate the Reciprocity Treaty, a decision made on political, not on economic, grounds, seemed a clear sign of American hostility to the long-term survival of British North America. These fears were intensified by the raids on British North American soil from across the American border by the Fenians, an Irish nationalist movement with substantial support among Irish Americans and even some, very limited support, among Irish Canadians. The Fenian Raids have traditionally been viewed as something of a joke rather than a serious threat, a threat the pro-Confederates exaggerated in order to arouse anti-American and anti-Catholic sentiment and gain support for Confederation. There is some truth in this argument, but it greatly underestimates how seriously the Fenian threat was viewed throughout British North America and how worried British Americans were that the raids might provoke an incident that could lead to another Anglo-American War.

Recent scholarship on Anglo-American relations emphasizes that the aftermath of the American Civil War would lead to a growing rapprochement between the United States and Great Britain, culminating in the Treaty of Washington in 1871. But this is an interpretation based largely upon hindsight, for contemporaries both in Britain and British North America took the threat of American expansionism seriously. Even the Treaty of Washington did not bring an end to tensions in the Anglo-American relationship. It is also a myth that the Imperial Government was looking for a way to abandon its commitment to defend its North American colonies. If a war should take place (and the Imperial Government certainly hoped it could be avoided through diplomacy), the British were confident that they could rely on the Royal Navy to win it. But the Imperial Government was seeking to devolve more of the expense of defending its North American colonies on the British Americans themselves. The belief that the British North American colonies would be better able to protect their borders and survive American continental dominance if they were united was the primary reason why the Imperial Government strongly supported Confederation. Without Imperial support Confederation could not have taken place in the 1860s, but the extent of Imperial influence should not be exaggerated (as it has been in much of the recent literature).[2] British Americans could not have been coerced into Confederation. If a majority, or in the case of Nova Scotia at least a majority in the existing Assembly, had not been convinced that it was in the long-term interests of the British North American colonies to unite against the American threat in order to preserve their connection with the British Empire, Confederation could never have taken place. If anything showed that clearly, it was Prince Edward Island's refusal to join Confederation until it was ready to do so on its own terms, despite the Imperial Government bringing to bear all the pressure it could.

Some anti-Confederates in the Maritimes argued that the colonists would be better off if they abandoned the imperial tie and were annexed to the United States rather than to Canada. But this was the view of a small minority. Some anti-Confederates actually argued the opposite case, that the danger in the creation of a new national state was that it would weaken the loyalty of the colonists to the Empire and lead to independence (which it would eventually, but not in the lifetime of anyone living in 1864). But the majority, even of the anti-Confederates, in the Maritimes accepted that British American union was both necessary and desirable in the long run to preserve the imperial tie. Some of them objected to the timing of Confederation, arguing that union was premature and should not take place until the Intercolonial was built and closer links were forged between Canada and the Maritimes. But the primary objection of many, if not most, Maritimers (certainly of the Maritime political elites) was to the terms upon which union was to take place. Their objection was not to a union, but a union on the basis of the Quebec Resolutions.

With the hindsight of 150 years, it is easy to accept the argument made by the anti-Confederates that the Maritime delegates to the Quebec Conference had made a bad deal which led to the Maritimes entering an unequal union in which the interests of the region were inadequately protected. Again, there is an element of truth in this argument. Clearly the much larger colony of Canada was bound to have a disproportionate influence in the negotiations leading to union and in the politics of the nation that was being created—a nation that symbolically would be called Canada. Yet, as the leading pro-Confederates from the region recognized, the Maritimes were negotiating from a position of increasing weakness. The Imperial Government clearly intended to devolve more of the responsibility for defending and for governing its North American territories on the colonists. Without a union this would mean placing effective control in the hands of the largest and most powerful colony, the Province of Canada. In negotiations over the renewal of reciprocity with the United States, the regulation of the fisheries, the settlement of Western Canada, and many other important issues with serious consequences for the Maritimes, the Imperial Government was almost certain to follow Canadian advice and pay limited attention to the concerns of the Maritimes. The pro-Confederate leadership also believed that unless the Intercolonial was built and the Maritimes were able to become a part of a rapidly expanding Canadian economy, the region would fall behind and languish. If Canada survived and if it did gain control over the vast imperial territories in the West (and it was in the long-term interests of the Maritimes that both of these things should happen), the Maritimes might be at an even greater disadvantage if it sought to enter Confederation at a later date. The Maritime delegates at Quebec were also aware of the fragility of the Canadian coalition and that there were limits to the compromises the Canadians could accept over the terms of union.

Nonetheless, the delegates from the Maritimes at Quebec did seek to ensure that the interests of the region would be protected as best they could within the new federal structures. The measure that was hardest for the anti-Confederates to accept was the decision to establish representation by population as the basis of representation in the proposed House of Commons, thus ensuring that the Canadians would inevitably form a substantial majority in the new House of Commons, a majority likely to grow even larger over time. But it was clear from the beginning that no other system would be acceptable to the Upper Canadians and the anti-Confederates failed to come up with an alternative that was not patently self-serving and unrealistic. In any event the belief of the anti-Confederates that the Canadians would form a united bloc in the new House of Commons was rather ridiculous in light of the political history of the United Province of Canada and the obvious divisions between the English-speaking majority and the French-speaking minority. Indeed, George Brown, the political leader of the majority party in Canada West, tried to persuade the Maritime Liberals to support Confederation in order to create a majority in the Canadian House of Commons which would put an end to French-Canadian domination of the united Province. That alliance did not take place, but astute Maritime politicians like Samuel Leonard Tilley and Charles Tupper were right in the assumption that the Maritime contingent to Ottawa would have the ability to play a major role in federal politics, at least during their lifetimes (and Tupper did not die until 1915 at the age of 94).

To offset the principle of representation by population in the House of Commons, the Maritime delegates at the Quebec Conference had insisted on the creation of an appointed second chamber or Senate based upon the principle of regional representation. Unlike the American Senate, however, the Canadian Senate was to be a body appointed for life and appointed by the new federal government, not the provincial governments. Much of the week-long debate over the structure of the Senate at the Quebec Conference focused not on the method of appointment, but on the issue of how many senators would be given to the region.[3] In the end it was agreed that New Brunswick and Nova Scotia would have ten senators each, Prince Edward Island and Newfoundland four each. This meant that the Atlantic Provinces collectively would have twenty-eight senators, four more than the twenty-four each given to Ontario and Quebec. For the Maritime anti-Confederates this did not seem a sufficient number to prevent the senators from the Maritimes being overwhelmed by those from Ontario and Quebec. Ironically, in the long run the Senate would prove ineffective at protecting Maritime regional interests, not because there were too few senators from the region, but primarily because an appointed house had no credibility in an increasingly democratic society. With hindsight perhaps this should have been obvious to the Maritime delegates at Quebec. But they were used to functioning in political systems that were at best quasi-democratic, where the appointed legislative councils still played an active part in politics. Moreover, regardless of how senators were appointed, the centralization of power in the hands of the party controlling the

House of Commons was virtually inevitable under the system of responsible government, a system preferred by both the pro-Confederates and the anti-Confederates to the American republican system of government.

Most of the anti-Confederates were also critical of the highly centralized federal system that was to be created by the Quebec Resolutions. The intention to transfer the major powers of the colonial assemblies to Ottawa was made clear not only by the division of powers and the decision to give the residual authority to the new federal government (a decision later overturned by the Judicial Committee of the Privy Council), but also by the financial arrangements agreed upon at Quebec. The provinces would be left with responsibility for education, for property and civil rights, and for the building of local public works, but with very limited financial resources since control over the most important source of public revenue, import tariffs, was to be surrendered to the federal government. In return for this surrender the provinces were to receive a rather meagre annual subsidy, which, except in the case of the province of Ontario, was, as the anti-Confederates predicted, unlikely to meet provincial needs and in time would force the smaller provinces to impose an income tax to fill the gap between their income and expenditures.

For some anti-Confederates even this constitution was not highly centralized enough and they advocated a legislative union. But this was undoubtedly a minority view. During the nineteenth century all three Maritime provinces had evolved distinct corporate identities. A strong sense of local patriotism—a commitment to their "country"—was not incompatible with other loyalties, certainly not with a commitment to membership in the British Empire, a commitment shared by the vast majority of Maritimers. But some of the anti-Confederates argued that their provincial identity was incompatible with loyalty to the new nation that was being created by Confederation. This was undoubtedly a minority view among the anti-Confederates. The majority of the anti-Confederates objected not to the union, but to the fact that power was being centralized in a far-away government that would be dominated by the Canadians. They also worried that their provincial assemblies would be denuded of any real power and that their provincial identities would gradually erode. It was this fear—a fear of the political as well as the economic domination of Canada—that the Maritime delegates at Quebec had to confront when they returned home to their legislatures, for the Imperial Government had made clear that only with the consent of the colonial legislatures could Confederation take place.

Debating Confederation in New Brunswick

The delegates from New Brunswick at the Quebec Conference had returned relatively confident that the majority of New Brunswickers would support the Quebec Resolutions. New Brunswick, after all, had a long border with the United States, a deeply-rooted suspicion of the American government, and a strong commitment to membership in the British Empire. Indeed, its provincial identity was constructed around its Loyalist heritage and rooted in historical memories of the War of 1812 and the so-called Aroostook War over the boundary with Maine in the 1830s. The Reciprocity Treaty of 1854 had greatly benefitted the province and temporarily weakened anti-Americanism, but fears of American aggression were easily aroused during the American Civil War, particularly since many New Brunswickers harboured pro-southern sympathies. One of the New Brunswick delegates to the Quebec Conference, John Hamilton Gray (not to be confused with the Prince Edward Island delegate with the same name), had lost a brother who had died fighting for the Confederacy.[4] New Brunswick was also bound to benefit from the building of the Intercolonial railway, though which communities would benefit depended on whether the railway took the southern route through the most heavily populated parts of the province, or the northern route which would be more defensible in case of another Anglo-American war. Neither New Brunswick's timber trade nor its flourishing shipbuilding industry were likely to be harmed by union with Canada and its largest city, Saint John, had already begun to industrialize, helped by a tariff on imports that was nearly as high as the Canadian tariff.

The New Brunswick pro-Confederates were led by Samuel Leonard Tilley, a druggist with extensive property holdings in Saint John. Since 1857 Tilley had been provincial secretary and, since March 1861, the head of the provincial government. Tilley was responsible for a controversial programme of building railways at state expense and for a provincial tariff that included a degree of incidental protection to encourage industrial development in the province, particularly in his hometown of Saint John. He was deeply convinced of the economic importance of the Intercolonial and

Samuel Leonard Tilley
Premier, Reform Leader, NB

28 JUNE 1866

> Those who have been engaged in negotiating for the extension of the trade of British North America, know that peculiar difficulties exist when negotiating out of Union, compared with the facilities which would exist in negotiating when united.

CONFEDERATION QUOTE 5.1
Quotation from New Brunswick, Legislative Assembly, 28 June 1866
Photograph by Topley Studio, from Library and Archives Canada, PA-026347

of the need for Confederation to preserve the imperial connection. Unlike the majority of the leading pro-Confederates in the Maritimes, Tilley was nominally a Liberal and he had expressed some reservations about the highly centralized constitution created at the Quebec Conference, but in the end he was content with some slight modifications in the division of powers in favour of the provinces.[5]

Party loyalties had always been fluid in New Brunswick and the delegation Tilley selected to go to Quebec, although theoretically bipartisan, was composed mainly of men who had supported his government and who were united in their support for Confederation. The only New Brunswick delegate to express any serious concerns about the Quebec Resolutions was Edward Barron Chandler, a lawyer of Loyalist descent and a former premier of the province, who felt that the proposed constitution would be too highly centralized. Chandler, however, was strongly in favour of Confederation, even on the basis of the Quebec Resolutions, and he led the fight for union in the New Brunswick Legislative Council, alongside two other delegates to the Quebec Conference, William Henry Steeves, a lumber merchant from Saint John, and Peter Mitchell, another lumber merchant (and lawyer and shipbuilder) from Newcastle, who was a strong proponent of the Intercolonial railway. Throughout the battle ahead, the Legislative Council never deviated in its support for Confederation. In the Assembly Tilley's Liberal government was effectively transformed into a unionist coalition with the delegates from the Quebec Conference at its centre. Those delegates included Liberals like Charles Fisher, a Fredericton lawyer and former head of the government whom Tilley had forced from office in 1861, and the English-born John Mercer Johnson, a lawyer from Chatham. But it also included Conservatives like John Hamilton Gray, a Saint John lawyer and former leader of the Conservative party (who had supported Tilley since 1861). So strong was Tilley's hold over his government that only one member resigned, George Luther Hatheway, a merchant and lumberman in Fredericton, the provincial capital whose status would be much diminished by Confederation. Hatheway was so appalled by the terms of union agreed at Quebec that he became one of the leaders of the anti-Confederate movement.[6]

Tilley accepted that the issue of Confederation should be put to the people in an election, but he wished to delay it until the pro-Confederates had the time to sell the deal that had been agreed upon at Quebec. He was, however, pushed by an overconfident Lieutenant-Governor Arthur Hamilton Gordon into calling an election on 30 January 1865.[7] The result of the election in March 1865 was a disaster for the Tilley Government. All four of the delegates to Quebec in the Assembly, Tilley, Gray, Johnson, and Fisher, were defeated and so were all but six of Tilley's supporters. This left a dearth of leadership for the pro-Confederate cause in the Assembly, which was now composed of about twenty-six anti-Confederates, four independents, and perhaps eleven unionists. The victory of the anti-Confederates was so widespread that it cannot be explained in terms of any single factor. Tilley's railway and taxation policies were already unpopular in parts of the province and he procrastinated over the route of the Intercolonial, thus alienating both those who supported the northern route and those who supported the southern, and raising suspicions that the Intercolonial might never be built at all. Indeed, one of Tilley's most outspoken critics was another of his former Liberal allies, John W. Cudlip, a Saint John businessman who had split with Tilley over the building of the Intercolonial and become a committed supporter of the Western Extension. Cudlip won more votes in Saint John in the 1865 election than were won by any other candidate in the province, although Tilley himself was defeated by only 113 votes.[8] The anti-Confederates did particularly well in Saint John and in the counties along the American border, arguing that the province should concentrate on building the Western Extension to Maine and maintaining close economic links with the United States rather than take the risk of Canadian domination of the New Brunswick economy. The only region of the province where the pro-Confederates won a majority was in the north shore counties, which had fewer economic links with the United States, which relied on mining and the timber trade, and which were more easily persuaded of the advantages offered by the Intercolonial railway. In Restigouche County John McMillan, one of the most important timber merchants in the region and the former surveyor-general, was the only member of Tilley's administration to be re-elected. Restigouche County returned another merchant, Abner Reid McClelan, who had supported Tilley's Liberal Government, as did Carleton County where the timber merchant Charles Connell won by acclamation. McMillan, McClelan, and Connell became by default leaders of the pro-Confederate movement in the Assembly, a task for which none of them was particularly well suited.[9]

In the election the pro-Confederates did particularly badly in areas

Albert J. Smith
Anti-Confederate Leader, NB

1 JUNE 1865

CONFEDERATION QUOTE 5.2
Quotation from New Brunswick, Legislative Assembly, 1 June 1865
Photograph by Topley Studio, from Library and Archives Canada, PA-025258

> How could Mr. Tilley, or any other man, say what this Confederation would do? After it was once organized they could not control it. How then could they say how much per head our taxes were to be under Confederation? These delegates might be there, and they might not. Men die and pass away, but the Constitution would live after them, and Mr. Tilley or anybody else could not say what they would do, and what they would not do, after the Constitution was once adopted.

with substantial Catholic minorities. Many Irish Catholics were not enthusiastic about entering a union which might be dominated by the large Protestant majority in Ontario led by George Brown, while the Acadians, who formed just over 10 percent of the population and who had only the weakest of ties with their French-Canadian neighbours, feared that their interests would be sidelined in a federal parliament in which they would at best have one representative. Bishop John Sweeny of Saint John supported the anti-Confederates, as did the two leading Irish Catholic politicians in the province, the conservative John Costigan from Victoria County and the more radical Timothy Warren Anglin from Saint John.[10] Editor of the *Saint John Weekly Freeman*, the most influential Catholic newspaper in the province, Anglin was a controversial figure. He was accused by his opponents of being motivated by his hatred of Britain. In fact, although Anglin never accepted the British domination of Ireland, he had no desire to see British North America incorporated into the United States. He believed that a political union of the British North American colonies was probably desirable at some point in the future, but that it was premature and would bring few immediate military or economic advantages in 1864. He was also extremely critical of the centralist implications of the Quebec Resolutions.

These were also the views of Albert J. Smith, a lawyer from Westmorland County, a county with a substantial Acadian minority. Smith was another Liberal who had once been one of Tilley's colleagues, but he had resigned from the cabinet in 1862 because he was opposed to public financial support for railways. Smith saw Confederation as a scheme dreamed up by the Canadians to solve their internal problems. He was convinced that New Brunswick would be wiser to continue reciprocity with the United States than to enter into an unequal union with Canada, and he was a strong supporter of the Western Extension.[11] The anti-Confederates had no clear leader and no party structure, but Smith agreed to form a coalition government with a Conservative anti-Confederate, Robert Duncan Wilmot, a wealthy Saint John merchant, shipbuilder, and railway promoter.[12] It was an unequal partnership and Smith quickly became the dominant figure in the anti-Confederate government. From the outset it was clear that the anti-Confederates in the Assembly differed greatly over the policies that the Smith-Wilmot Government should pursue. On the critical question of railways some anti-Confederates wished the Government to focus on building the Western Extension, some still hoped for the building of the Intercolonial, some wanted both railways, and some were opposed to any further public expenditure on railways. In fact, although work was begun on the Western Extension, little progress was made because of the failure to raise sufficient capital. On other issues, like the regulations governing the militia and the amount to be spent on colonial defence, there was also little agreement among those elected as anti-Confederates, though the government was able to push through a bill substantially increasing the budget for provincial defence. Even on the issue of Confederation the anti-Confederates were not united. Some—including Anglin, Hatheway, and Arthur Hill Gillmor,[13] a prominent lumber merchant and farmer from Charlotte County—were opposed to the whole idea of union, at least for the moment, if not for all time. Others were prepared to consider a revised scheme for Confederation but disagreed over the nature of that scheme. Some—like Wilmot—favoured a legislative union; others—like Smith—wanted increased status for the provinces. The anti-Confederate government's majority in the 1865 session of the Assembly fluctuated widely, but it did carry by twenty-seven to ten a resolution to send a delegation to London to make clear that New Brunswick was opposed to Confederation for the foreseeable future.

Smith went to London to meet the Colonial Secretary but came back aware that the Imperial Government was committed to Confederation on the basis of the Quebec Resolutions and that the battle for Confederation was not over. Smith also found that the tide of public opinion was changing. Little progress had been made on the Western Extension and in the spring of 1865 the American Government announced its decision to abrogate the Reciprocity Treaty. Smith's cabinet was torn apart by dissension. In September Wilmot met with delegates from the Province of Canada in Quebec City to discuss how to respond to the abrogation of the Reciprocity Treaty. He returned convinced that legislative union was impracticable given the hostility of the French Canadians and convinced that Confederation was now necessary. In November Anglin resigned because the contract for the Western Extension was awarded to a private company. That same month Charles Fisher won a by-election in York County by a substantial majority and became the leader of the pro-Confederates in the Assembly.

In February 1866 Smith went to Washington to try to renegotiate reciprocity, but he returned empty-handed and began to hint that he had never been opposed to the concept of British North American Union, only to the greatly reduced status of the provinces under the Quebec Scheme and above all, to the principle of representation by population. His seeming conversion to some form of Confederation further alienated Anglin and antagonized committed anti-Confederates like Hatheway and Cudlip. The die-hard anti-Confederates in the Assembly continued (reluctantly in some cases) to support the government after the Assembly reconvened in March 1866, but a number of independents and even a few of those clearly elected to oppose Confederation withdrew their support. During the winter of 1865–66 New Brunswick also became increasingly concerned by the activities of the Fenians, particularly when a small force briefly camped out on Indian Island until driven off by the New Brunswick militia and a handful of British regulars. The committed anti-Confederates had always claimed that there was no real threat from the United States, but this argument seemed increasingly hollow as the Fenian threat continued along the Upper Canadian frontier.

On April 7 the Legislative Council, which was dominated by pro-Confederates, moved a resolution in favour of Confederation. When Lieutenant-Governor Gordon approved the resolution, against the advice of his ministers, the anti-Confederate government resigned as a body and Gordon asked Peter Mitchell, leader of the pro-Confederates in the Legislative Council, to form a government. Wilmot defected to the new government and Tilley became the attorney general, although he could not take his true place as the head of the government until re-elected to the Assembly. Gordon had in effect dismissed his ministry. The constitutionality of that act was dubious at best. Indeed, the twenty-two members of the Assembly who still supported Smith petitioned the Imperial Government for Gordon's recall. Gordon responded by dissolving the Assembly and calling an election.

Gordon's conduct became a source of controversy during the election, but it seems unlikely that it had much influence on its outcome. Neither, for that matter, did the sums of money given by the Canadians to support Tilley's campaign. The reality was that the pro-American and isolationist policies that had been at the centre of the anti-Confederation campaign in the previous election lay in shatters. The strong support given to Confederation by the Imperial Government undoubtedly played a part in undermining the support for the anti-Confederates, partly by allowing the pro-Confederates to call into question the loyalty of their opponents. Some anti-Confederates did not forgive the Imperial Government's intervention. But if anyone was responsible for the collapse of the anti-Confederation movement, it was the Government of the United States. Its refusal to renegotiate the reciprocity treaty undermined the viability of the Western Extension and an economic future for New Brunswick outside Confederation. The Fenian raid into New Brunswick, although easily put down, and the slowness with which the American Government moved against the Fenians reinforced fears of American hostility and the need for collective action on the part of British Americans to maintain the imperial connection.

Undoubtedly the Fenian raid was used as an excuse for an attack on the loyalty of the Irish Catholic minority in New Brunswick, particularly by the Protestant religious press. But it is easy to place too much stress on the importance of religious bigotry in the campaign.[14] Anti-Catholic sentiment had been a staple of politics in New Brunswick for decades. Perhaps more important for the pro-Confederates was the desire of many Irish Catholics to distance themselves from the Fenians, who had little support in New Brunswick's Irish communities. Bishop John Sweeny of Saint John, although still privately opposed to Confederation, stayed quiet during the election of 1866, while Bishop James Rogers of Chatham abandoned his previous neutrality and openly defended Confederation.[15] The Irish Catholic vote had never been monolithic and it now swung decisively into the Confederation camp, unseating both Anglin and Costigan. Only the Acadian vote held steady, enabling six anti-Confederates to be elected in Westmorland, Kent, and Gloucester Counties, including Smith and Amand Landry, the spokesperson for the Acadians in the Assembly.[16] Elsewhere the result was largely a disaster for the anti-Confederates, with the pro-Confederates carrying thirty-three of the forty-one seats, mainly with very high majorities. During a short legislative session in June and July 1866 Smith brought forward a series of motions, calling for a public referendum on Confederation and equal provincial representation in the Senate, but they were easily defeated by the Tilley Government, which pushed through the necessary resolutions to send a delegation to London to negotiate the final terms of union. In the election of 1866 Tilley had hinted that there might be some changes in the Quebec Resolutions, but he did not seek any substantial changes at the London Conference in December 1866 where the 72 Resolutions were transformed into the British North America Act, which was hurriedly passed through the British Parliament. Most of the leading anti-Confederates had always claimed that they were not against British North America union in principle and they abandoned their opposition to Confederation once it was enacted by imperial legislation. Smith, Anglin, and Costigan were all elected to the Canadian House of Commons in 1867. Smith eventually became the minister of marine and fisheries and Costigan the minister of inland revenue, while Anglin ended his political career as speaker of the House of Commons. Only John Cudlip remained defiant to the end. Although defeated in the 1866 election, he was re-elected to the New Brunswick legislature in 1868 where he put forward a motion for annexation to the United States, an act which effectively ended his political career. New Brunswick would join the provincial rights movement of the 1880s, but it had long since effectively been integrated into Confederation.

Avoiding Opposition in Nova Scotia

In Nova Scotia the delegates to the Quebec Conference also faced substantial and growing opposition to the Quebec Resolutions when they returned home. The same five delegates had attended both the Charlottetown and Quebec Conferences and, although the delegation was bipartisan, it was hardly representative of the whole of Nova Scotia. Three of the five were from Cumberland County; four of the five were lawyers and the fifth a doctor. The doctor was Charles Tupper from Amherst who had effectively been the head of the government since the Conservatives had won a sweeping victory in 1863 (although he did not actually become premier until May 1864). Tupper was a proponent of modernization, strongly supporting the building of railways and a more effective education system, and since 1860 he had enthusiastically endorsed the idea of British North American union. He played a key role at both the Charlottetown and Quebec Conferences. Although he would have preferred a legislative union of the colonies, he was a political realist and so was prepared to settle for the highly centralized federal union he helped to craft at Quebec.[17] The other four Nova Scotia delegates made only a minimal contribution at the Quebec Conference. The two Liberals, Adams George Archibald, a

Adams George Archibald
Liberal Leader, NS

12 APRIL 1865

CONFEDERATION QUOTE 5.3
Quotation from Nova Scotia,
Legislative Assembly, 12 April 1865
Photograph from Library and Archives
Canada, MIKAN 3214517

> Whether united with Canada by Confederation or not, we are bound together by a common fate and a common interest, and we must stand or fall together.

William Annand
Anti-Confederate Leader, NS

12 APRIL 1865

> Only those who are to be elevated from this country to Ottawa can be satisfied with a state of things so disastrous to the Province of Nova Scotia.

CONFEDERATION QUOTE 5.4
Quotation from Nova Scotia,
Legislative Assembly, 12 April 1865
Photograph from Nova Scotia Legislature,
Province House Collection

wealthy lawyer and landowner from Colchester County and a former premier, and Jonathan McCully, a lawyer and journalist from Cumberland County, were staunch pro-Confederates.[18] McCully was a legislative councilor and he effectively led the pro-Confederates in the Council. Archibald strongly defended the Quebec Scheme in his speeches in the Assembly but, although he remained leader of the Liberal party, only one other Liberal in the Assembly supported Confederation in the 1865 legislative session. The two Conservatives who had gone to Quebec were divided. William Alexander Henry, a Conservative from Antigonish, supported the Quebec Resolutions,[19] but Robert Barry Dickey had refused to accept the final terms of union agreed upon at Quebec, particularly the financial terms, which he felt were unfair to Nova Scotia.

With most Liberals opposed to the Quebec Resolutions and his own party divided, Tupper quickly realized that he would have great difficulty persuading the Nova Scotia legislature to accept the Quebec Resolutions. Tupper did have the support of the leaders of the Liberal opposition, Archibald in the elected Assembly and McCully in the appointed Council. He also had the support of those who feared the potential threat to British America from an increasingly hostile United States, including Archbishop Thomas Connolly, the spiritual leader of the large Irish Catholic community in Halifax and an outspoken opponent of American republican influences in the province.[20] Tupper could also count on the support of those who believed that Confederation would bring economic development and progress, an argument that had considerable support in Halifax, in communities like Amherst (Tupper's hometown) and Truro which would be along the line of the Intercolonial railway, and in the coal mining areas of Cape Breton and Pictou in eastern Nova Scotia. But more than two hundred petitions against Confederation flooded into the Assembly during the 1865 legislative session, showing that there was little enthusiasm for a union with Canada on the basis of the Quebec Resolutions.

In the winter of 1864–65 many Nova Scotians continued to believe that American threats, particularly the threat to cancel the Reciprocity Treaty, were simply wartime rhetoric and that the end of the Civil War would bring a return to business as usual. In any event the potential of clashes along the border with the United States did not arouse the same fears in a province that had no border with the United States as they did in its continental neighbours. As the anti-Confederates argued, the defence of Nova Scotia would inevitably depend not on local militias but on the Royal Navy. Some anti-Confederates even suggested that the creation of a British North American union would lead to separation from the Empire and end Britain's commitment to defend its North American colonies. The economic arguments of the pro-Confederates also seemed unconvincing to many coastal communities, particularly in the western half of the province, which were dependent on agriculture, shipbuilding, and the shipping industry. Their priority was to ensure that the reciprocity treaty remained in force. They saw few benefits from an Intercolonial railway and they feared that a union with Canada would cripple the Nova Scotian economy by leading to higher tariffs and increased taxation. This was the view of Thomas Killam, a major shipowner in Yarmouth, who quickly emerged in the Assembly as the leader of those who opposed Confederation on any terms.[21] Even in Halifax Tupper faced considerable opposition from mercantile and banking interests who did not share his enthusiasm for creating a continental nation.

Indeed, Tupper's most outspoken opponent in the Assembly was William Annand, a prominent Halifax businessman and Liberal who owned one of the most influential papers in Halifax, the *Morning Chronicle*. Annand was, however, open to the charge of inconsistency since he fluctuated between opposing Confederation on any terms and arguing that a new conference should be held to amend the Quebec Scheme.[22] A far more effective opponent of Confederation was Joseph Howe. Howe was the former head of the Liberal party and a Nova Scotia legend, but he was now serving as the Imperial Fisheries Commissioner in Washington and he was not a member of the Assembly. He too was open to the charge of inconsistency since he had previously promoted the idea of Confederation. In early 1865 Howe published twelve articles against Confederation known as the "botheration letters," arguing that Nova Scotia would be a subordinate unit within the proposed union.[23] Indeed, all the anti-Confederates agreed that under the Quebec Scheme Nova Scotia would effectively be annexed by Canada and that it would have little influence in a House of Commons with 194 members of which only nineteen would come from Nova Scotia, or in an appointed Senate also dominated by the Canadians. They also agreed that the surrender of all tariff revenues to the federal government would leave the government of Nova Scotia with inadequate resources to promote provincial development. Agreement on these issues allowed for the creation of an anti-Confederate coalition that included both those who rejected Confederation in principle upon any terms, and those who simply felt British North American union was either premature or who rejected not the idea of union but the Quebec Scheme.

Tupper was lucky. With the election of an anti-Confederate government in New Brunswick, there was no immediate necessity to hold a vote on the Quebec Resolutions and on 22 March 1865 he temporized by introducing a motion to renew the negotiations over Maritime Union. This led to an indirect debate over whether Maritime Union should be seen as simply a step toward the larger union, but the debate ended without any real resolution when the legislature was prorogued in April 1865. By the time that the Nova Scotia legislature met in 1866, much had changed. The American Civil War had ended and the American Government had made clear its intention to cancel the Reciprocity Treaty, raising fears about the economic future of a Nova Scotia cut off from American markets and particular fears about the future of the fisheries if American fishermen had access to the inshore waters of the province. It had also become clear that the Imperial Government was going to give Canada a leading role in any negotiations with the United States and that the interests of the Maritimes would take second place, thus strengthening Tupper's argument that there was no logical alternative to union if the Maritimes wanted to influence Canada's decisions. Tupper was also able to get a promise from the Canadians that a guarantee for the building of the Intercolonial railway would be included in the Act of Union. The Fenian threat and American talk of annexing Canada had greatly strengthened the argument for building the Intercolonial as quickly as possible and of the need for a unified British North American response to American aggression. The Imperial Government had also thrown its full weight behind a union based upon the Quebec Scheme, thus weakening the argument that British North American union would lead to the collapse of the imperial connection.

Gradually in the winter of 1865-66 the anti-Confederate coalition began to disintegrate. William Miller, from Richmond County, one of the original opponents of Confederation, admitted that he had come to believe that union was inevitable and, on 3 April 1866, he proposed a conference be held in London to discuss the terms of union. A number of the opponents of union now switched sides and on 10 April 1866, Tupper moved a motion declaring that it was desirable that a Confederation of the British North American Provinces should take place and authorizing the appointment of delegates to arrange the terms of union with the other colonies at a conference in London. Opposition to Confederation now appeared futile and the remaining anti-Confederates in the Assembly focused on demanding that the terms of union should be submitted to the people for their approval. An amendment to Tupper's resolution to this effect was rejected by a vote of thirty-one to eighteen and the original resolution accepted by thirty-one to nineteen. There was a clear regional pattern in the vote. Of the nineteen who opposed Tupper's motion, sixteen represented the western counties, a region with close ties to the United States and relatively little involvement in the fisheries. The pro-Confederates, on the other hand, came mainly from the central and eastern counties and included four Liberals and five Conservatives who had previously opposed union.

Tupper's motion had not included any mention of the Quebec Resolutions, but the opposition argued that there would be few changes made at the London Conference which was held in December 1866 and they were correct. The Canadian delegates would not have agreed to any substantial changes in the Quebec Resolutions, even if Tupper had demanded them, which he did not. A clause was inserted into the British North America Act guaranteeing the construction of the Intercolonial railway, and the twenty-four Maritime seats in the Senate were divided between New Brunswick and Nova Scotia, even though four of them had been intended for Prince Edward Island. Some minor changes were made to the subsidies to be given to the provincial governments. The regulation of the fisheries now became a federal rather than a shared federal-provincial responsibility and, at Tupper's request, the provinces lost the authority to levy an export duty on coal on the grounds that such levies would deter capital investment in Nova Scotia. At least one Nova Scotian delegate remained dissatisfied with the final agreement. William Alexander Henry, who had expressed similar concerns at the Quebec Conference, remained convinced that the Maritimes should have greater weight in the Senate and that more power should be given to the provinces to offset Canadian dominance in the new House of Commons, but in the end he abandoned his opposition and supported Confederation.

The opponents of Confederation in the Nova Scotia Assembly, led by Annand and Killam, were furious with the content of the British North

America Act. The result was a particularly bitter legislative session in 1867, as both sides traded insults and called into the question the loyalty of their opponents. The anti-Confederates denied that any real improvements had been made in the Quebec Scheme and demanded that the people of Nova Scotia be consulted in a general election before the British North America Act, which had already been passed by the Imperial Parliament, came into effect. In the end the anti-Confederates were defeated by a vote of thirty-two to sixteen. This was a larger margin than in the previous session, reflecting in part the belief that further opposition would be pointless. On the actual day of Confederation, 1 July 1867, flags of mourning joined banners of celebration in Nova Scotia's urban centres. Annand and Howe had travelled to London to try to persuade the British Parliament not to pass the British North America Act and now they organized a movement to repeal the Act. Although the anti-Confederates carried an overwhelming majority of both the federal and the provincial seats in Nova Scotia in the elections of 1867, there was never any real chance that the Imperial Government would agree to let Nova Scotia secede from the Dominion of Canada. In the end Howe broke with the repeal movement, negotiated a deal with Ottawa that included an increase in the federal subsidy to the province of Nova Scotia, and entered the federal cabinet in January 1869 as president of the Council. In a few parts of the province, anger against the way that union had been achieved in Nova Scotia led to a movement advocating annexation to the United States, but outside of Yarmouth where the movement was led by Killam, there was little enthusiasm for joining the United States. Annand, after becoming premier of Nova Scotia in 1867, continued to protest against Confederation until the Liberals came to power in Ottawa in 1873. The sense of grievance in Nova Scotia would persist in the province's political culture, surfacing again during another (rather weaker) secession movement in 1886, but in reality most Nova Scotians wanted better terms within Confederation rather than independence.

Holding Out for More: Prince Edward Island

From the outset it was clear that Confederation was going to be an even harder sell in Prince Edward Island than in the mainland provinces. Because it was an Island and had no border with the United States, many

Islanders could comfort themselves with the assumption that they could remain aloof from developments taking place on the continent because they could rely on the Royal Navy to protect them. One of the key arguments of the anti-Confederates on the Island was that there was no reason why they should pay taxes to defend Canada and the vast territories it hoped to acquire in the West. In the short run this argument was undoubtedly true, but in the long run the commitment of the Imperial Government to protect Prince Edward Island was bound to be determined by what happened on the mainland. In that sense, whether they liked it or not, their fate was, as the pro-Confederates argued, bound up with the fate of Canada. Moreover, there were short term costs in isolationism. Prince Edward had some serious checks on its autonomy before 1873. After the collapse of the Reciprocity Treaty the Island could not negotiate a free trade agreement on its own with the Americans without Imperial consent (which it was never going to get) and it had almost no control over one of its most important resources, the fisheries. In these and many other important areas Britain would inevitably seek advice from the Canadian government, but would pay little attention to the needs of Prince Edward Island. Even on purely internal matters Prince Edward Island was so insignificant in British eyes that it had less influence over Colonial Office decisions than lobbies representing interest groups based in Britain, as had repeatedly been shown in the successful efforts of the absentee landlords in Britain to block attempts on the Island at land reform.

One of the most persuasive arguments of the anti-Confederates was that the Island would have little influence in a Parliament at Ottawa where they would have only a handful of members. But what would become gradually clear after 1867 to a growing number of the Island political elite was that little influence was better than none. The alternative, of course, was for the Island to reject the limitations on its autonomy and declare its independence from Britain. But while Islanders might refer to Prince Edward Island as their "country" (a term also used in New Brunswick and Nova Scotia), the vast majority of Islanders never thought of Prince Edward Island as potentially a separate nation. They wished to remain part of the Empire. In this sense they were no different than the majority of the English-speaking British Americans on the mainland.

There is an unfortunate tradition in both Island and Canadian historiography of treating Prince Edward Island as a fundamentally different place from the mainland British North American colonies. Of course, the Island had some distinctive features. It was a small Island with a very large proportion of arable land. But, as in the other British North American colonies, most of the non-Francophone migration to the Island had come from the British Isles. In one sense it was the most British of all the Maritime colonies since it had received hardly any migrants from other places in Europe, had only small numbers of Francophones, Blacks, and Indigenous People, and contained perhaps the smallest proportion of Irish Catholics in the region (though it did have a large number of Scottish Catholics). Moreover, the roots of its British population did not go back many generations, since the vast majority of its immigrants had arrived after 1815, which is why so many members of its political elite were first or second generation immigrants from Britain, as compared with New Brunswick and Nova Scotia which had received far larger numbers of immigrants from both America and Britain prior to 1812.

The Island was different from the mainland Maritime colonies in one other important respect: in the 1760s the Island had been divided into a series of lots distributed by ballot to absentee landlords in Britain. The tenant system explains why migration to the Island came overwhelmingly from the British Isles. It also explains why the Island did not attract many middle class immigrants with the capital to purchase freehold estates. While there was a growing number of wealthy merchants and landlords on the Island and there was certainly inequality among the tenant farmers who formed the majority of the population, inequality was less pronounced than in the other British North American colonies. Given this social reality and the mobilization of the population in various campaigns to sweep away the landlord system, it is hardly surprising that the Island had the most democratic political system in British North America. In 1865 it was the only colony to have both an elected upper chamber and an Assembly elected upon the basis of nearly universal male suffrage. Many Islanders therefore did not like the decisions made at Quebec to have an appointed Senate (especially one appointed by Ottawa) and a House of Commons in which the members would be elected in all the other provinces under much more restrictive franchises.

In late 1864 Islanders had good reason for believing that there was no pressing need to join an economic union with the rest of Canada. In the previous decade the population of the Island had increased by no less than 29 percent to a population of 80,857 and even in the 1860s it would increase by 16.3 percent. This growth reflected the strength of Prince Edward Island's traditional economy based upon exporting agricultural products and fish as well as its thriving shipbuilding industry. Most of the ships built on the Island were destined for sale in Britain, but many were also owned by Island merchants and used to carry Prince Edward Island products to markets in New England and the other Maritime colonies. The Island had not started building railways and Islanders could not see how the building of an Intercolonial railway would bring any benefits to them, particularly since they would be taxed to pay for it. The end of the American Civil War in 1865 and the collapse of the Reciprocity Treaty would dramatically curtail the Island's trade with the United States, but it did not dent the rather optimistic assumption that the golden days of the previous decade would return.

Even at Quebec Conference it was apparent that the Island delegation was less than happy with the Quebec Resolutions. On a number of issues the Islanders found themselves isolated. They thought that the Senate should be based on the principle of provincial rather than regional equality and were dissatisfied that only four senators would be given to Prince Edward Island. They were also not happy with the undemocratic nature of the Senate, even when the property qualification for senators was slightly reduced at their (and Newfoundland's) request. The Prince Edward Island delegation was also the most disturbed that the House of Commons would be elected on the basis of representation by population, particularly when the compromise of allowing them one extra member, so that they would have six rather than five members, was rejected. Finally, they did not like the centralized nature of the new constitution and they believed that Prince Edward Island, with its small debt, was not going to receive adequate compensation for the transfer of its customs revenues to Ottawa. They had come to the Conference anticipating that they would be given a grant to enable the Prince Edward Island Government to purchase the remaining proprietorial estates, but this proposal was rejected by the other delegations.

Unlike the other delegations, the Island delegation had disagreed with each other on a number of issues. Partly this was a reflection of personal animosities. The two men most critical of the proceedings at Quebec were Edward Palmer and George Coles. Coles was a prominent Charlottetown merchant who wished to put an end to the proprietorial system. Although an Anglican, he was the leader of the Liberal party which relied heavily upon Roman Catholic support.[24] Palmer was both a lawyer and a large landholder who defended proprietorial rights and opposed many of the reforms introduced by the Liberals, including universal male suffrage. He had led the Conservatives to power in 1859 and again in January 1863 by arousing anti-Catholic sentiment among the Island's Protestants and forming an all Protestant government.[25] So deep was the antagonism between the two men that they had once fought a duel (a bloodless one). Palmer was a mercurial figure and there was also little love lost between him and Colonel John Hamilton Gray. Gray had served in the British Army for over twenty years before returning to the Island. In March 1863 he had replaced Palmer as leader of the Conservative party and prime minister. Gray and his fellow Conservative, William Pope, a lawyer and editor of the most important Conservative newspaper on Prince Island, were enthusiastic supporters of Confederation. They were prepared to defend—even if reluctantly—the Quebec Resolutions. They were supported by another Conservative delegate at Quebec, Thomas Heath Haviland, a major landowner, another spokesman for proprietorial rights, and an even more enthusiastic supporter of Confederation. Haviland believed that unless British Americans united to create a nation stretching from the Atlantic to the Pacific, they would in time be annexed to the United States. Throughout the late 1860s and the early 1870s he consistently attacked the insularity of the anti-Confederates as misguided.[26]

It is possible that under different circumstances the Conservative pro-Confederates might also have been assisted by Coles, the leader of the Liberal party, who was not against Confederation in theory, but who was completely antagonized by the decision not to give the Island the funds with which to liquidate leasehold tenure. That decision would cost the pro-Confederates on the Island dearly for there were a substantial number of tenant farmers and their advocates who might have been willing to support Confederation if it resolved the land issue. Coles, however, led the Liberal party into opposition to Confederation, with the support of another of the Liberal delegates at Quebec, Andrew Archibald Macdonald, a member of one of the wealthiest shipbuilding families and part of the Catholic aristocracy on the Island.[27] Macdonald was the opposition leader in the Legislative Council, where he and Palmer would conduct a relentless campaign against the Quebec Scheme.

The seventh of the Island's delegates to Quebec, Edward Whelan, was almost the only Liberal to support Confederation. Whelan had been born in Ireland and had trained as a journalist in the office of Joseph Howe before moving to Charlottetown and establishing the Island's most important Reform newspaper. In the 1850s he became a member of the Liberal government, strongly supporting the attempts of Coles to end the proprietorial system and speaking out on behalf of Catholics. Prior to the Charlottetown conference he had been skeptical of the proposed union, but like Coles he had come to believe that only Confederation could put an end to Colonial Office meddling and give the Island the resources to finally resolve the land question. Although he was unhappy with the Quebec Resolutions and the unwillingness of the Conference to provide the necessary funds to buy out the proprietors, he continued to advocate union, but his influence in the Liberal party, even over Irish Catholic Liberals, was in decline. Like many moderate Liberals, he did not approve of the tactics of the Tenant League in the 1860s—an organization which encouraged the Island's tenants to ignore the law and refuse to pay the rents they owed— and he supported the Island government's decision to request British troops to put an end to the agitation. Although he had always supported the independence of Ireland, he strongly disapproved of the Fenians, believing—like D'Arcy McGee in Canada and Timothy Warren Anglin in New Brunswick (though the first approved and the second disapproved of Confederation)—that Irish Catholics were better off living in British North America under the British constitution than in the United States.[28] These policies, as well as his support for Confederation, weakened his hold over his Irish Catholic constituents, who were increasingly influenced by the younger and Island-born journalist, Edward Reilly. In 1862 Reilly founded the *Vindicator*, a newspaper which vigorously supported the Catholic Church, did not condemn the Tenant League, was non-committal about the Fenian Raids, and vehemently attacked the Quebec Resolutions. In a by-election in 1867 Reilly defeated Whelan, thus removing from the Assembly the most articulate, in fact almost the only Liberal defender of Confederation, and permanently, as it turned out, since Whelan died a few months later.[29]

The Conservative pro-Confederates did not fare much better. Gray was forced out of office in January 1865 and replaced as premier by James Colledge Pope, the younger brother of William Pope. The younger Pope

William Henry Pope
Colonial Secretary, PEI

24 MARCH 1865

CONFEDERATION QUOTE 5.5
Quotation from Prince Edward Island, House of Assembly, 24 March 1865
Photograph by Topley Studio, from Library and Archives Canada, PA-027027

> Why shall we not unite our resources, and enter upon the career of prosperity which is clearly open to us? What Confederation did for the older Colonies, it would do for us. We have Railways and Steamboats, and machinery which they had not. We have a country in many respects equal to theirs. Are we prepared to admit that our people are inferior to the old Colonists, or to the Americans of the present day?

James Colledge Pope
Conservative Leader, Premier, PEI

7 MAY 1866

Confederation Quote 5.6
Quotation from Prince Edward Island, Legislative Assembly, 7 May 1866. Photograph by Topley Studio, from Library and Archives Canada, PA-027027

" [Moved:] Even if a Union of the Continental Provinces . . . should have the effect of strengthening and binding more closely together those Provinces . . . this House cannot admit that a Federal Union . . . could ever prove . . . advantageous to the interests and well-being of the people of this Island, cut off . . . by an immovable barrier of ice for many months in the year. "

had become one of the largest shipping contractors on the Island and the owner of some very large estates. He entered politics later than his brother but became part of the Conservative Government elected in 1859.[30] William was enthusiastic about Confederation but James was not. James did not disagree with the abstract principle of union but he did not think that the Quebec Resolutions offered fair terms to the Island and, although William remained a member of the new Government that James formed, it was decidedly an anti-Confederate government. How anti-Confederate would become clear in the debates in the 1865 session of the legislature, when William Pope, supported by Haviland, moved eight Resolutions in favour of Confederation. Gray, Haviland, and William Pope passionately defended the need for Confederation on the grounds that the choice was between union and annexation to the United States. The anti-Confederates denied that the Island was faced with such a stark choice and attacked the Quebec Resolutions, particularly the decision to give the Island only five members in the proposed House of Commons, a number which the anti-Confederates predicted would shrink to none as the population of Canada continued to increase through immigration. Speaker after speaker predicted that Confederation would destroy not only the Island's autonomy but its economy. These speakers included not just prominent Conservatives like James Pope and Frederick Brecken, but almost all of the leading Liberals, including George Howlan, another Irish Catholic and a major shipowner, who was emerging as the leader of the Catholic Liberals.[31] Whelan was the only important Liberal to defend Confederation. The end result was never in doubt and James Pope's amendment to his brother's resolutions, substituting five resolutions which attacked the idea of union, was carried by a vote of twenty-three to five. The Pope Government then prepared an address to the Queen indicating its determination to stay out of Confederation, an address carried by twenty-three to four in the Assembly and unanimously in the Upper House.

When Charles Tupper, the prime minister of Nova Scotia, tried to persuade Prince Edward Island to renew discussion of Maritime Union in 1865, the Government of Prince Edward Island declined to participate. Nor did the Pope Government pay any heed to British Imperial pressure. In 1865 the Imperial Government informed Prince Edward Island that without union the Island would have to pay the salary of the lieutenant-governor and it also tried—unsuccessfully—to make the Island pay for the British troops sent to the Island from Halifax to control the Tenant League. In response to this pressure, when the Assembly met in 1866, James Pope angrily presented his famous "no terms resolution," one of three resolutions declaring that Prince Edward Island would never agree to Confederation. Some of the members of the Assembly, such as Francis Kelly, another Irish immigrant who had become a land surveyor and farmer and who was elected as a running mate of the Liberal leader George Coles in Queen's County, declared that he wished the resolution could be made even stronger.[32] During the debate Cornelius Howatt, a tenant farmer from Prince County,[33] made the comment that the issue for Prince Edward Island was "a question of 'self or no self'" (a comment resurrected in the 1970s by a group of Prince Edward Island academics who were critical of what had happened to Prince Edward Island under Confederation and who described themselves as the "Brothers and Sisters of Cornelius Howatt").[34] A handful of pro-Confederates, including Whelan, Colonel Gray, and Haviland objected to the finality of the resolution and the insult it offered to the Imperial Government, and William Pope resigned from his brother's government in protest at the resolutions. The anti-Confederates were confident that there was no reason to fear the Imperial Government's reaction since the Assembly was fully within its constitutional rights to pass the resolutions. And pass them it did by a vote of twenty-one to seven.

The resolutions and the address to the Queen based on them certainly indicate that a large majority in the Assembly were opposed to Confederation, but one should be careful of taking the resolutions at face value. Even James Pope, who moved the resolutions, indicated in private that his personal opinion was less dogmatic than the resolutions he sponsored and that there might come a time when more advantageous terms might be offered to the Island and it might have to reconsider its position. He also rejected Edward Palmer's suggestion that the Island send a delegate to London to support Howe in lobbying against Confederation.

James Pope was in London on private business in late 1866 at the same time as the delegates from New Brunswick and Nova Scotia, who were there to participate in the London Conference. Pope talked with them about the possibility of an $800,000 grant from Canada to enable the Island to purchase the remaining proprietary estates, but the Canadian delegates indicated that no decision could be made without the prior consent of the new Canadian Parliament, in effect vetoing the proposal. When news of the offer leaked to the public on the Island, the anti-Confederate press condemned the grant as a bribe from Canada that the Island should reject on principle. Several anti-Confederates felt so strongly a sense of betrayal that they resigned from Pope's cabinet, thus weakening the Conservatives as they prepared for the election of February 1867, in which they were soundly defeated by the Liberals. Anti-Confederation sentiment certainly played a part in the Liberal victory. Edward Palmer bragged to Joseph Howe that the number of pro-Confederates in the Assembly had been reduced from eight to five, while the number of anti-Confederates had been increased to twenty-five and that even the five pro-Confederates had been forced to pledge not to attempt to revive the issue of joining Confederation until after another election. With Coles, a dedicated anti-Confederate in control, the Liberal Government did not include a single supporter of Confederation. But the refusal of the Imperial Government to provide the Island with a guarantee for a loan to purchase the remaining proprietorial estates meant that the issue of union was not dead. Moreover, the Island was beginning to feel the impact of the closing of the American market. In 1868 it entered into some rather pointless informal negotiations with General Benjamin F. Butler, a congressional representative from Massachusetts, about Prince Edward Island negotiating a separate free trade and fisheries agreement with the United States. It is unlikely that the American government took the discussions seriously since it was quite clear that Prince Edward Island did not have the authority to negotiate a separate treaty with the United States, a fact it was forced publicly to acknowledge.

In August 1869 the Governor General of Canada, Sir James Young, and three members of the Canadian cabinet came to Charlottetown to see if they could negotiate Prince Edward Island's entry into Canada. By this time the English-born Robert Poore Haythorne, a wealthy land proprietor, had replaced Coles, who had been forced to retire because of ill health, as head of the Liberal government.[35] The Canadians did offer "better terms," including an increase in the annual subsidy and efficient steam communication between the mainland and the Island. But the negotiations broke down early in 1870 over the settlement of the land question since Haythorne insisted that the Canadian government should persuade the British Government, which had created the problem, to give the Island the $800,000 it needed to buy the remaining estates, something that was never likely to happen. The Island also indicated that any offer of better terms should include a grant for the construction of a railway on Prince Edward Island, a proposal the Canadian Government was not prepared to accept.

In the Assembly in 1870 the anti-Confederates rejoiced over the failure of the negotiations but there was a difference in their tone. It was still triumphalist. But while the anti-Confederates congratulated themselves on their success in rejecting the Canadian offer, they also seemed to accept that even "better terms" might be on offer in the future, which implied a growing recognition that time was not on their side. And it wasn't. Increasingly the Island found its autonomy constrained. The Island government had no alternative but to accept Canadian regulation of its fisheries and the more direct subordination of the Island's lieutenant-governor to the governor general in Ottawa. In 1871 it agreed to adopt the Canadian decimal system of coinage. The final and decisive factor that would bring Prince Edward Island into Confederation was the decision to build a railway across the Island. This was a controversial decision, since it would lead to a huge and ultimately unsustainable increase in the provincial debt. This was a risk that the other Maritime colonies had accepted two decades earlier, and the reasons why the Island entered the railway age were much the same. Island entrepreneurs and politicians were not carried away with enthusiasm for a technology they did not need, but were motivated by a growing recognition that the limits for the expansion of the traditional economy had been reached, if not exceeded. In the 1870s the wooden shipbuilding industry was beginning a slow but steady decline and, with it, would come the decline of the shipping industry. As it became apparent that the Americans were never going to renew reciprocity, the Island had to find ways to lower transportation costs so that it could compete more effectively in Canadian markets. Moreover, many Island farmers located some distance from the capital wanted greater access to the market in Charlottetown.

Even Haythorne, who headed the anti-Confederate Liberal government, reluctantly accepted the need for a railway and it is conceivable that he might have embarked on building one, despite the reservations of some of his most outspoken anti-Confederate supporters, such as David Laird, the editor of the most influential Protestant newspaper on the Island.[36] But although the Haythorne Government was re-elected in July 1870, it only had a small majority in the Assembly and the defection of a block of Catholic Liberals into the Conservative party brought James Pope back into power. The new government included William Pope and a number of

Conservatives suspected (probably with good reason) of being sympathetic to Confederation, but the Catholic Liberals who had defected, led by the anti-Confederate George Howlan, insisted that no change should be made in the Island's constitutional status without consulting the people in an election. Howlan had previously been unsympathetic to the building of a railway, but he had come to the conclusion that the Island had no choice given the changing economic conditions. And so the construction of the railway began in 1871. Like all railways built in this period the project was accompanied by accusations of corruption, mismanagement, and over-expenditures, some of them fair and some of them not.

Partly because of these charges, the Conservatives were defeated in 1872 by the Liberals. In opposition the Liberals had claimed that they would bring the costs of the railroad under control but they were unable to resist the political pressure for further expansion. In November 1872, with the Island facing imminent financial collapse, the Haythorne Government approached the Canadian Government about joining Confederation. Some of the anti-Confederates had opposed building the railway because they saw it as leading inevitably to Confederation and they claimed that this was the main reason why the government had embarked upon the project. Indeed, it has become an unchallenged assumption in Canadian historiography that the Island was "railroaded" into Confederation. Yet there is no evidence that there was a conspiracy to force the Island into Confederation against its will through bankruptcy. It is true that a growing number of the Island's politicians were beginning to accept that Confederation was probably inevitable and that it would be in the Island's interest to build the railway before Confederation took place, since it would then become a debt that the Dominion Government would have to accept. But it was not only the railway debt that convinced many anti-Confederates that Confederation was increasingly desirable. For some, it was the knowledge that the Island was never likely to have the resources to buy out the remaining proprietors; for others, a desire to put an end to the 15 percent duty that the Island had placed on imports from Canada, by far the Island's major trading partner. By 1873 it also seemed clear that the Dominion was here to stay and that far from weakening the tie with Britain, Confederation had led to an even stronger bond with the United Kingdom.

In February 1873, Haythorne and Laird, previously a vehement anti-Confederate, travelled to Ottawa to discuss terms and found the

Canadian Government (influenced by Maritime Conservatives like Tilley) relatively generous in its proposals. But Haythorne had always promised that any deal would be put to the voters and an election was held in March 1873. The Conservatives under Pope won the election by campaigning that they would be able to negotiate even better terms with their fellow Conservatives in Ottawa. After the election Pope, Howlan, and Haviland, one of the few politicians who had continuously supported Confederation, returned to Ottawa, where they did gain slightly better terms. These terms included much of what the Island had sought at Quebec in 1864 and even a bit more. Canada agreed to assume the Island's railway debt and to give the Island $800,000 to purchase the estates of the remaining landlords. Its annual grant from Ottawa was raised to fifty dollars a head, a larger grant than was given to the other provinces, which was justified on the basis that Prince Edward Island had no Crown Lands which it could sell to raise revenue. The Canadian Government guaranteed (a promise it would later have difficulty in fulfilling) continuous steam communication with the mainland. The Island also received the six members in Parliament its delegates had asked for at Quebec (though it was probably entitled to that number because of its population growth over the previous decade).

In the Assembly only two members voted against the deal, one of them Cornelius Howatt who kept his anti-Confederate faith to the end. The other was a fellow farmer from Bedeque, Augustus Edward Crevier Holland. The other twenty-four members supported the agreement, some of them (like James Pope) declaring that they had been convinced of the need for Confederation for some time, others declaring that they had become pro-Confederates not out of choice but out of necessity. Certainly everyone—even Howatt—accepted that further resistance was futile. Some, like the only remaining delegate to the Quebec Conference still sitting in the Assembly, Thomas Heath Haviland, welcomed the Island's decision, declaring that Islanders would now become part of a nation extending "from the blue waters of the Atlantic, to the shores of the bright and sparkling Pacific Ocean," and that they should be "proud to form part of a Dominion that has a form of government so superior to that of the United States."[37] On 1 July 1873 Prince Edward Island entered Confederation. There were no protests against the union, certainly not in Charlottetown where many Islanders joined in celebrations and buildings were decorated with the Canadian flag. Even among most of those who had previously resisted

Confederation, there was little animosity since Prince Edward Island had entered Confederation on something close to its own terms. Ironically the Maritime province which had protested the most against Confederation entered it in the end with the least resentment.

Further Reading

Bolger, Francis W. P. *Prince Edward Island and Confederation, 1863–1873.* Charlottetown: St. Dunstan's University Press, 1964.

Buckner, Phillip. "Beware the Canadian Wolf: The Maritimes and Confederation." *Acadiensis*, XLVI (2017): 177–95.

Buckner, Phillip. "British North America and a Continent in Dissolution: The American Civil War and the Making of Canadian Confederation." *The Journal of the American Civil War Era* 7 (2017): 512–40.

Buckner, Phillip. "The Maritimes and Confederation: A Reassessment." *Canadian Historical Review*, 71 (1990): 1–35.

Buckner, Phillip and John G. Reid, eds., *The Atlantic Region to Confederation: A History.* Toronto: University of Toronto Press, 1994.

Conrad, Margaret. "'A Cacophony of Drumbeats': The Maritime Provinces in Confederation, 1867–2017." http://www.margaretconrad.ca.

Creighton, Donald G. *The Road to Confederation: The Emergence of Canada, 1863–1867.* Reprinted. Toronto: Oxford University Press, 2012.

MacNutt, W. S. *New Brunswick: A History, 1784–1867.* Toronto: University of Toronto Press, 1963.

Moore, Christopher. *1867: How the Fathers Made a Deal.* Toronto: McClelland and Stewart, 1998.

Pryke, Kenneth G. *Nova Scotia and Confederation 1864–1874.* Toronto: University of Toronto Press, 1979.

Waite, Peter B. *The Life and Times of Confederation, 1864–1867.* Toronto: University of Toronto Press, 1962.

NOTES

1   See Phillip Buckner, "'British North America and a Continent in Dissolution': The Role of the American Civil War in the Making of Canadian Confederation," *The Journal of the Civil War Era* 7, no. 4 (December 2017): 512–40.

2   For example, see Ged Martin, *Britain and the Origins of Canadian Confederation, 1837–1867* (London: Macmillan Press, 1995) and Andrew Smith, *British Businessmen and Canadian Confederation: Constitution-Making in an Era of Anglo-Globalization* (Montreal and Kingston: McGill Queen's University Press, 2008). The reasons for my disagreement with their approach can be found in Phillip Buckner, "L'élaboration de la constitution canadienne au sein du monde britannique," in *La Conférence de Québec de 1864: 150 Ans plus tard*, eds. Eugénie Brouillet, Alain-G. Gagnon, and Guy Laforest (Québec: Les Presses de l'Université Laval, 2016), 71-108.

3   The discussions at the Charlottetown and Quebec Conferences can be found in G. P. Browne, ed., *Documents on the Confederation of British North America* (Toronto: McClelland and Stewart, 1969).

4   C. M. Wallace, "Gray, John Hamilton (1814-89)," in *Dictionary of Canadian Biography*, vol. 11, University of Toronto/Université Laval, 2003–, accessed April 4, 2018, http://www.biographi.ca/en/bio/gray_john_hamilton_1814_89_11E.html.

5   C. M. Wallace, "Tilley, Sir Samuel Leonard," in *Dictionary of Canadian Biography*, vol. 12, University of Toronto/Université Laval, 2003–, accessed April 4, 2018, http://www.biographi.ca/en/bio/tilley_samuel_leonard_12E.html.

6   On these individuals, see: Michael Swift, "Chandler, Edward Barron," in *Dictionary of Canadian Biography*, vol. 10, University of Toronto/Université Laval, 2003–, accessed April 4, 2018, http://www.biographi.ca/en/bio/chandler_edward_barron_10E.html; W. A. Spray, "Steeves, William Henry," in *Dictionary of Canadian Biography*, vol. 10, University of Toronto/Université Laval, 2003–, accessed April 4, 2018, http://www.biographi.ca/en/bio/steeves_william_henry_10E.html; W. A. Spray, "Mitchell, Peter," in *Dictionary of Canadian Biography*, vol. 12, University of Toronto/Université Laval, 2003–, accessed April 4, 2018, http://www.biographi.ca/en/bio/mitchell_peter_12E.html; C. M. Wallace, "Fisher, Charles," in *Dictionary of Canadian Biography*, vol. 10, University of Toronto/Université Laval, 2003–, accessed April 4, 2018, http://www.biographi.ca/en/bio/fisher_charles_10E.html; W. A. Spray, "Hatheway, George Luther," in *Dictionary of Canadian Biography*, vol. 10, University of Toronto/Université Laval, 2003–, accessed April 4, 2018, http://www.biographi.ca/en/bio/hatheway_george_luther_10E.html. On John Hamilton Gray, see note 4 above.

7   J. K. Chapman, "Gordon, Arthur Hamilton, 1st Baron Stanmore," in *Dictionary of Canadian Biography*, vol. 14, University of Toronto/Université Laval, 2003–, accessed April 4, 2018, http://www.biographi.ca/en/bio/gordon_arthur_hamilton_14E.html.

8   C. M. Wallace, "Cudlip, John Waterbury," in *Dictionary of Canadian Biography*, vol. 11, University of Toronto/Université Laval, 2003–, accessed April 4, 2018, http://www.biographi.ca/en/bio/cudlip_john_waterbury_11E.html.

9   On McMillan and Connell, see: William Arthur Spray, "McMillan, John (1816-86)," in *Dictionary of Canadian Biography*, vol. 11, University of Toronto/Université Laval, 2003–, accessed April 4, 2018, http://www.biographi.ca/en/bio/mcmillan_john_1816_86_11E.html; Charles F. MacKinnon, "Connell, Charles," in *Dictionary of Canadian Biography*, vol. 10, University of Toronto/Université Laval, 2003–, accessed April 4, 2018, http://www.biographi.ca/en/bio/connell_charles_10E.html.

10 Terrence Murphy, "Sweeny, John," in *Dictionary of Canadian Biography*, vol. 13, University of Toronto/Université Laval, 2003–, accessed April 4, 2018, http://www.biographi.ca/en/bio/sweeny_john_13E.html; David Shanahan, "Costigan, John," in *Dictionary of Canadian Biography*, vol. 14, University of Toronto/Université Laval, 2003–, accessed April 4, 2018, http://www.biographi.ca/en/bio/costigan_john_14E.html; William M. Baker, "Anglin, Timothy Warren," in *Dictionary of Canadian Biography*, vol. 12, University of Toronto/Université Laval, 2003–, accessed April 4, 2018, http://www.biographi.ca/en/bio/anglin_timothy_warren_12E.html.

11 C. M. Wallace, "Smith, Sir Albert James," in *Dictionary of Canadian Biography*, vol. 11, University of Toronto/Université Laval, 2003–, accessed April 4, 2018, http://www.biographi.ca/en/bio/smith_albert_james_11E.html.

12 W. A. Spray, "Wilmot, Robert Duncan," in *Dictionary of Canadian Biography*, vol. 12, University of Toronto/Université Laval, 2003–, accessed April 4, 2018, http://www.biographi.ca/en/bio/wilmot_robert_duncan_12E.html.

13 Kathryn Wilson, "Gillmor, Arthur Hill," in *Dictionary of Canadian Biography*, vol. 13, University of Toronto/Université Laval, 2003–, accessed April 4, 2018, http://www.biographi.ca/en/bio/gillmor_arthur_hill_13E.html.

14 For a different view, see William M. Baker, *Timothy Warren Anglin, 1822–96: Irish Catholic Canadian* (Toronto: University of Toronto Press, 1977), ch. 7.

15 Laurie C. C. Stanley, "Rogers, James," in *Dictionary of Canadian Biography*, vol. 13, University of Toronto/Université Laval, 2003–, accessed April 4, 2018, http://www.biographi.ca/en/bio/rogers_james_13E.html.

16 W. A. Spray, "Landry, Amand," in *Dictionary of Canadian Biography*, vol. 10, University of Toronto/Université Laval, 2003–, accessed April 4, 2018, http://www.biographi.ca/en/bio/landry_amand_10E.html.

17 Phillip Buckner, "Tupper, Sir Charles," in *Dictionary of Canadian Biography*, vol. 14, University of Toronto/Université Laval, 2003–, accessed April 4, 2018, http://www.biographi.ca/en/bio/tupper_charles_14E.html.

18 K. G. Pryke, "Archibald, Sir Adams George," in *Dictionary of Canadian Biography*, vol. 12, University of Toronto/Université Laval, 2003–, accessed April 4, 2018, http://www.biographi.ca/en/bio/archibald_adams_george_12E.html; P. B. Waite, "McCully, Jonathan," in *Dictionary of Canadian Biography*, vol. 10, University of Toronto/Université Laval, 2003–, accessed April 4, 2018, http://www.biographi.ca/en/bio/mccully_jonathan_10E.html.

19 Phyllis R. Blakeley, "Henry, William Alexander," in *Dictionary of Canadian Biography*, vol. 11, University of Toronto/Université Laval, 2003–, accessed April 4, 2018, http://www.biographi.ca/en/bio/henry_william_alexander_11E.html.

20 David B. Flemming, "Connolly, Thomas Louis," in *Dictionary of Canadian Biography*, vol. 10, University of Toronto/Université Laval, 2003–, accessed April 4, 2018, http://www.biographi.ca/en/bio/connolly_thomas_louis_10E.html.

21 K. G. Pryke, "Killam, Thomas," in *Dictionary of Canadian Biography*, vol. 9, University of Toronto/Université Laval, 2003–, accessed April 4, 2018, http://www.biographi.ca/en/bio/killam_thomas_9E.html.

22   David A. Sutherland, "Annand, William," in *Dictionary of Canadian Biography*, vol. 11, University of Toronto/Université Laval, 2003–, accessed April 4, 2018, http://www.biographi.ca/en/bio/annand_william_11E.html.

23   J. Murray Beck, "Howe, Joseph," in *Dictionary of Canadian Biography*, vol. 10, University of Toronto/Université Laval, 2003–, accessed April 4, 2018, http://www.biographi.ca/en/bio/howe_joseph_10E.html.

24   Ian Ross Robertson, "Coles, George," in *Dictionary of Canadian Biography*, vol. 10, University of Toronto/Université Laval, 2003–, accessed April 4, 2018, http://www.biographi.ca/en/bio/coles_george_10E.html.

25   Ian Ross Robertson, "Palmer, Edward," in *Dictionary of Canadian Biography*, vol. 11, University of Toronto/Université Laval, 2003–, accessed April 4, 2018, http://www.biographi.ca/en/bio/palmer_edward_11E.html.

26   David E. Weale, "Gray, John Hamilton, (1811-1887)," in *Dictionary of Canadian Biography*, vol. 11, University of Toronto/Université Laval, 2003–, accessed April 4, 2018, http://www.biographi.ca/en/bio/gray_john_hamilton_1811_87_11E.html; Ian Ross Robertson, "Pope, William Henry," in *Dictionary of Canadian Biography*, vol. 10, University of Toronto/Université Laval, 2003–, accessed April 4, 2018, http://www.biographi.ca/en/bio/pope_william_henry_10E.html; Andrew Robb, "Haviland, Thomas Heath (1822-95)," in *Dictionary of Canadian Biography*, vol. 12, University of Toronto/Université Laval, 2003–, accessed April 4, 2018, http://www.biographi.ca/en/bio/haviland_thomas_heath_1822_95_12E.html.

27   G. Edward MacDonald, "MacDonald, Andrew Archibald," in *Dictionary of Canadian Biography*, vol. 14, University of Toronto/Université Laval, 2003–, accessed April 4, 2018, http://www.biographi.ca/en/bio/macdonald_andrew_archibald_14E.html.

28   Ian Ross Robertson, "Whelan, Edward," in *Dictionary of Canadian Biography*, vol. 9, University of Toronto/Université Laval, 2003–, accessed April 4, 2018, http://www.biographi.ca/en/bio/whelan_edward_9E.html.

29   Ian Ross Robertson, "Reilly, Edward," in *Dictionary of Canadian Biography*, vol. 10, University of Toronto/Université Laval, 2003–, accessed April 4, 2018, http://www.biographi.ca/en/bio/reilly_edward_10E.html.

30   Ian Ross Robertson, "Pope, James Colledge," in *Dictionary of Canadian Biography*, vol. 11, University of Toronto/Université Laval, 2003–, accessed April 4, 2018, http://www.biographi.ca/en/bio/pope_james_colledge_11E.html.

31   H. T. Holman, "Brecken, Frederick De St Croix," in *Dictionary of Canadian Biography*, vol. 13, University of Toronto/Université Laval, 2003–, accessed April 4, 2018, http://www.biographi.ca/en/bio/brecken_frederick_de_st_croix_13E.html; Boyde Beck, "Howlan, George William," in *Dictionary of Canadian Biography*, vol. 13, University of Toronto/Université Laval, 2003–, accessed April 4, 2018, http://www.biographi.ca/en/bio/howlan_george_william_13E.html.

32   D. B. Boylan, "Kelly, Francis," in *Dictionary of Canadian Biography*, vol. 10, University of Toronto/Université Laval, 2003–, accessed April 4, 2018, http://www.biographi.ca/en/bio/kelly_francis_10E.html.

33   David Weale, "Howatt, Cornelius," in *Dictionary of Canadian Biography*, vol. 12, University of Toronto/Université Laval, 2003–, accessed April 4, 2018, http://www.biographi.ca/en/bio/howatt_cornelius_12E.html.

34 See Harry Baglole and David Weale, *Cornelius Howatt: Superstar!* (Summerside, P.E.I.: William & Crue, 1974) and *The Island and Confederation: The End of an Era* (Charlottetown: Williams & Crue, 1973).

35 Andrew Robb, "Haythorne, Robert Poore," in *Dictionary of Canadian Biography*, vol. 12, University of Toronto/Université Laval, 2003–, accessed April 4, 2018, http://www.biographi.ca/en/bio/haythorne_robert_poore_12E.html.

36 Andrew Robb, "Laird, David," in *Dictionary of Canadian Biography*, vol. 14, University of Toronto/Université Laval, 2003–, accessed April 4, 2018, http://www.biographi.ca/en/bio/laird_david_14E.html.

37 T. H. Haviland in Prince Edward Island *Parliamentary Reporter* for 1873, 226–27. Reproduced by *The Confederation Debates,* https://hcmc.uvic.ca/confederation/en/lgPEILA_1873-05-26.html.

6

Resisting Canada's Will: Manitoba's Entry into Confederation

ROBERT WARDHAUGH AND BARRY FERGUSON

The story of Manitoba and Confederation is unique in that it was the only province created against the designs of the Canadian government. Manitoba emerged from the Red River Resistance of 1869–70. Canada was unprepared for the acquisition of Rupert's Land from the Hudson's Bay Company (HBC) and the country blundered its way into the vast territory of the North-West. The Red River Settlement of twelve thousand people—a diverse community the majority of whom were Métis—stood up to Canada's haphazard approach, opposed its peremptory occupation, reconstituted local power with a provisional government, and demanded a British form of representative government through negotiation. Manitoba was the only province where a portion of its Indigenous population was involved in its creation. The Manitoba Act of 1870 guaranteed a land grant for the Métis "to extinguish Indian title." But while the Red River Resistance that resulted in the creation of Canada's fifth province provided a temporary victory for the Métis, it laid the foundation for a full-blown Rebellion fifteen years later, as well as serious provincial and regional grievances. Manitoba entered Confederation in 1870 on an unequal basis with the other provinces. Saskatchewan and Alberta in 1905 would experience the same inequality, thereby establishing a powerful sense of western alienation.

Canada's Claim to the North-West

Canada's acquisition of "Rupert's Land and the North-Western Territory" was conducted under the "power to admit" provision in Article 146 of the Constitution Act of 1867.[1] As a project of settler colonialism, Canadian politicians were certain that the vast territories were theirs for the taking.[2] What Canada and Britain did not comprehend was that the area had its own economic and social structures and, in the case of the Old Settlement (as it was called) of Red River, a political system that could resist the plans and terms imposed from outside. When the Canadian and British governments negotiated the terms of the dominion's expansion, they neglected to consider the region, the people, and the institutions they were so confident of acquiring.

A significant amount of historical work has been done on the Red River Resistance and Manitoba's entry into Confederation. Recent work, however, has shed the nation-building perspective that permeated older studies, offering a chance for a refreshed understanding of the political issues that shaped the course of events in 1869–70.

Red River under the Hudson's Bay Company

The Old Settlement of Red River was not new to political, economic, and cultural conflict at the time Canada federated in 1867.[3] After the HBC's authority over the region was reconfirmed in 1835, Red River acquired its own political order in the form of the non-elected Council of Assiniboia and a legal system, the General Quarterly Court of Assiniboia. The Council and Court emerged gradually from HBC control.[4] Red River asserted political and economic rights in the form of self-regulation; it developed a capitalist market economy and an agricultural colony apart from HBC sway. The Settlement, however, was not an autonomous self-governing colony by the 1860s, and it suffered from all the ambiguities of Company authority and British Imperial scrutiny.[5]

The rule of the Hudson's Bay Company over Rupert's Land was controversial for decades prior to the transfer. In 1857, its tenure was reviewed by a Select Committee of the United Kingdom Parliament. The review was thorough and the Company was critically interrogated for its commercial practices, its failure to sponsor settlement, and its inability to assist in acquiring educational, religious, or social services.⁶ The Select Committee reviewed a petition signed by 575 "inhabitants and natives of the Settlement situated on the Red River." The petition claimed that, contrary to contractual relations with the HBC, the rights of settlers were crimped, including land tenure, crop sales, and trading rights. The petition also asserted that legal authority over the North-West lay not with the HBC but with the Crown under the Proclamation of 1763.⁷

The 1857 Committee Report recommended a limited renewal of the HBC "license" to trade in the North-Western Territories. The Company was ordered to vacate Vancouver Island for failing to promote settlement and to cede the Red River and North Saskatchewan River districts to the Province of Canada.⁸ Desultory negotiations to acquire the North-West commenced but little headway was made.⁹

Negotiations to Acquire the North-West

After 1867, Great Britain informed Canada that urgent action was needed.[10] The new dominion passed a series of resolutions on the matter, including authorizing the Imperial government to negotiate with the HBC. The minister of Public Works, William McDougall, proclaimed that Canada must acquire the entire North-West and indeed all the lands to the Pacific coast. "If we did not expand," he warned, "we must contract." Through expansion, Canada would realize its destiny as a "new nationality."[11] The British government forced the pace by passing the Rupert's Land Act in July of 1868 which stated that the Company would surrender its "Lands, Rights, Privileges, Liberties, Franchises, Powers, and Authorities" upon transfer to the new dominion.[12] In March 1869, the British government imposed the terms of a settlement.[13] In return for control of Rupert's Land, Canada would pay the HBC £300,000 and 1/20th of all arable lands. Nothing specific was stipulated about the rights to land ownership or political representation for the residents of Red River.[14]

In May of 1869, the Canadian government introduced legislation to take over the North-West. Already on the defensive for sending out preliminary exploratory/survey crews, cabinet minister George-Étienne Cartier extolled the move as a project that would accomplish in a few years what the United States had taken half a century to achieve. Cartier boasted that the acquisition cost was modest: the purchase price was in the form of a

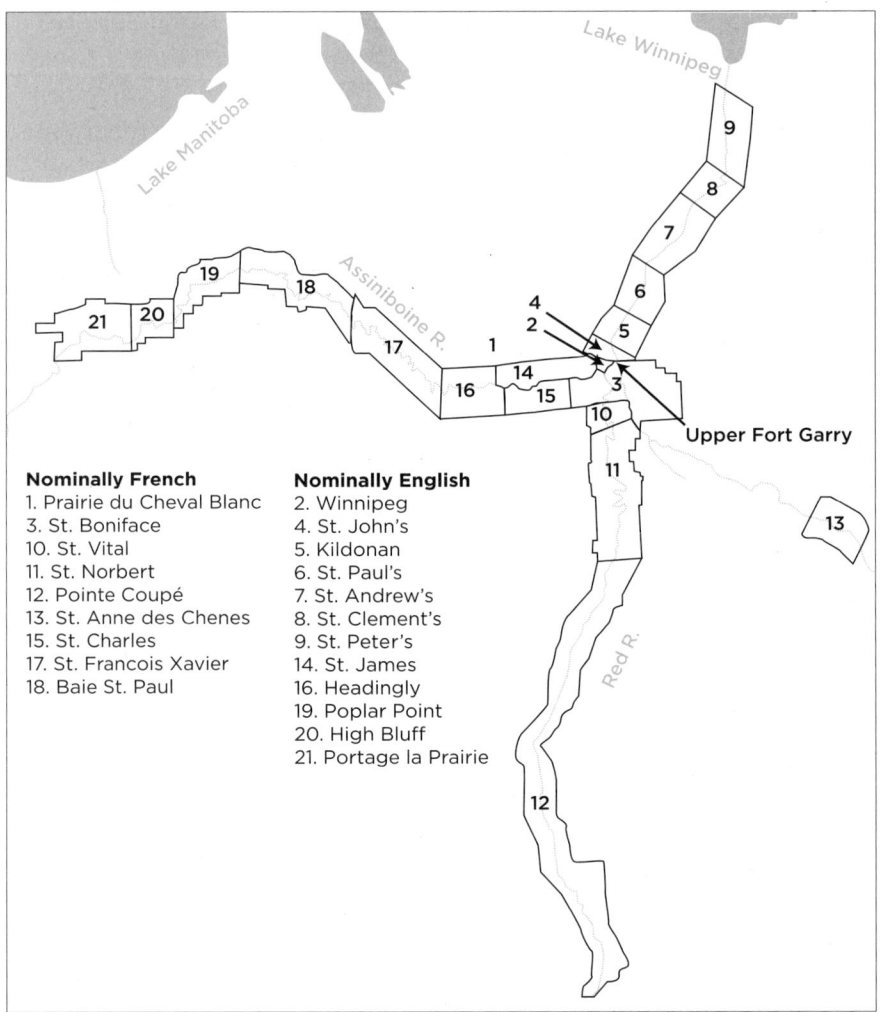

Fig 6.1 The Red River settlement, 1870, showing the locations of the predominantly French and English parishes. Developed from: Gerhard J. Ens, *Homeland to Hinterland: The Changing Worlds of the Metis in the Nineteenth Century* (Toronto: University of Toronto Press, 1996), 11; Gerald Friesen, *The Canadian Prairies: A History* (Toronto: University of Toronto Press, 1987), 91; Norma Jean Hall, "The People," *The Provisional Government of Assiniboia*, https://hallnjean2.wordpress.com/resources/definition-provisional-government/the-people-electorate/; George Stanley, *The Birth of Western Canada: A History of The Riel Rebellions*, 2nd edition (Toronto: University of Toronto Press, 1961), 14.

loan from the British to the Canadian government, payable over forty-five years. Prime Minister John A. Macdonald introduced an "Act for the temporary Government of Rupert's Land and the North-Western Territory when united with Canada." The legislation gave the lieutenant-governor complete authority to make arrangements as he saw fit for governing Red River and the North-West. The only concession to the residents of Red River was a clause stating that existing laws and current officials would continue at the pleasure of Canada (although Ottawa had no records of them). The legislation was approved with government assurances that the formal take-over would occur sometime later in the year.[15] Canada and Great Britain then dithered over the final terms.

The Failed Canadian Take-Over

In the summer of 1869 Canadian survey crews moved into the Red River area. Local concern turned into anger by late August when surveyors, acting on instructions from William McDougall, began staking out 800-acre farm plots over existing occupied lands. A month later, William MacTavish, president of the Council of Assiniboia and HBC Governor of Rupert's Land since 1858, informed the Catholic Bishop of St. Boniface, Alexandre-Antonin Taché, that the locals (particularly the Métis) were disturbed by these violations and were threatening "trouble."[16]

Prior to the official transfer, on 28 September 1869 Canada named McDougall as lieutenant-governor of Rupert's Land. He was ordered to proceed "with all convenient speed to Fort Garry" and make "preliminary arrangements for the organization" of territorial government by liaising with existing officials of the Council and the HBC. He was also ordered to review conditions among the Indigenous Peoples as well as the role of the HBC. In particular, McDougall was instructed to conduct an inventory of existing laws and ordinances, taxes and licenses and, finally, land holding. His instructions demonstrated that the Canadian take-over was conducted with almost no idea about the existing administration.[17]

McDougall slowly made his way to Red River via the United States. Meanwhile, Joseph Howe, now minister responsible for the provinces, also traveled to the Settlement on an informal, hurried visit. His meetings with representative groups led him to a very sympathetic understanding of why Red River was agitated over the activities of the Canadians at Red River and the prospects of Canadian administration. Howe carried back a copy of the records and legislation of the Council of Assiniboia. During his return trip, he met McDougall in Minnesota. They spoke for a brief time due to inclement weather. Howe cautioned McDougall and later wrote a strong letter warning him to avoid aligning himself with the "Canadians" or otherwise provoking the sensitivities of a divided Settlement.[18]

The moribund Council of Assiniboia, headed by a seriously-ailing William MacTavish, reconvened on October 16 and addressed a statement to McDougall. It welcomed the new lieutenant-governor but apprised him of the "mixed feelings" in the Settlement about the transfer and the "misgivings" over the future. The Council was concerned that "all just rights of the old settlers will be respected [and] that the transition will be made as easy for them as possible."[19] Simultaneously, a group of Métis had put together a *Comité National des Métis de la Rivière Rouge*.[20] On October 21 the *Comité National* sent a notice forbidding McDougall from setting foot in the North-West without its permission.[21]

A few days later, the Council of Assiniboia again met. It expressed "reprobation of the outrageous" act of the group that had threatened to bar McDougall. The heads of the *Comité National*, Louis Riel and John Bruce, were called to explain their actions. Riel claimed that the Métis Committee objected to Canada's imposition of authority without consultations and demanded that the whole Settlement—and not only the *Comité National*—send "delegates" to negotiate Canada's entry. The Council tried but failed to convince Riel of the "erroneous nature" of his arguments and warned him about the "highly criminal character" of Métis actions.[22]

Governor MacTavish also wrote McDougall about the serious "discontent" among the Métis in the Settlement, arguing that it was impossible to divert the Métis from their course of action. He recommended that McDougall remain at Pembina, North Dakota until "conciliatory negotiations" occurred.[23] McDougall also received information from others, including the head of the Canadian survey party, Colonel J.S. Dennis, about increasing hostility to Canada and tensions within the Settlement. McDougall concluded that he should press on to Red River. He started out but was barred at the Pembina border by an armed Métis force. A perplexed McDougall urged MacTavish to establish authority for him.[24]

After the confrontation, public life in Red River grew tumultuous. On November 2, the *Comité National* seized the HBC's Upper Fort Garry headquarters (present-day central Winnipeg), the symbolic centre of commercial and political authority. The Métis called for the creation of a council of equal representation from each of the French and English communities including the leader of the nearby Saulteaux, Henry Prince. This "Council of Twenty-Four" met between November 9 and December 1. Its deliberations were marked by debate as to whether the Council should remain an advisory body or declare itself a provisional government.[25]

In late November, the Canadian government postponed final agreement with the HBC and Britain. It cited growing evidence of unsettled conditions in the North-West and Canada's inability to effectively control the area. The British government was not pleased at being left in charge of an area it could not immediately control. The Colonial Secretary, the Earl of Granville, tried to insist on the take-over and stated that Canadian actions had led to the unsettled conditions.[26]

McDougall, meanwhile, was cautioned not to act hastily. Howe again warned him that "as matters stand you can assert or claim no authority" until informed by the Canadian government that it had "annexed" the territory. Prime Minister Macdonald was more blunt. The situation had become "grave" and McDougall was ordered to avoid any precipitous action, including public statements. If civil strife broke out at Red River, the prime minister warned, Britain and Canada would be unable to maintain public order, which would show that there was "no legal government" in the Settlement and that the residents would be entitled "by the law of nations" to form their own administration "for the protection of life and property." Hasty action could legitimize a provisional government under customary law. The United States, moreover, might well use such events as a pretext for intervention.[27]

McDougall did not receive either of these letters from Howe and Macdonald before undertaking a second and final attempt to impose his authority over Red River. On December 1, he ordered the posting of a Proclamation at Fort Garry in the name of the Crown claiming he was now the lieutenant-governor of the North West Territories. It was a disastrous claim made worse by further pronouncements. McDougall appointed Colonel Dennis as "Conservator of the Peace" against unspecified "bodies of armed men" and commanded him to create a force authorized "to attack, arrest, disarm or disperse the said armed men so unlawfully assembled and disturbing the peace." Bellicose words led to a second

Proclamation apprising the public of the new authority. But McDougall remained in Dakota, with almost no public sympathy, support, or recognition. For his part, Dennis struggled to contain the incitements to confrontation and balked at the order to take up arms.[28] McDougall had evoked the authority of the Crown without authorization, moved in defiance of the Canadian government's authority, and threatened the use of a force he did not possess.

Red River's Initiative: Political Convention & Provisional Government

Canadian and British officials recognized the situation they had created. The Governor General, Sir John Young, was well aware that British military forces could not be deployed to Red River due to the lack of efficient transportation links. Young issued a proclamation offering amnesty to all those "misguided persons" who had violently blocked "ingress" to the area as long as they abandoned their course of resistance. The proclamation presumed that the agitators were acting in good faith, were loyal to the Crown, and had acted solely in order to express legitimate concerns over the preservation of their civil, religious, and property rights, all of which would be guaranteed.[29]

Howe informed McDougall of the Governor General's proclamation and ordered him to withdraw his previous expressions of authority. On Christmas Eve 1869, Howe wrote to rebuke McDougall for his "entirely illegal actions," including invoking the Queen's authority without permission. While McDougall continued to issue reports and to defend his actions, he retreated to Minnesota and then back to Canada.[30] The Canadian government tried to regain the initiative by appointing two commissions. One was a duo of French Canadians, Fr. J-B. Thibault and Colonel Charles de Salaberry, both former residents of Red River who were sent to assess and calm the populace. The other was a single commissioner, Donald A. Smith, a senior HBC official resident in Montreal, who was instructed to conduct an inquiry and report on the means to resolve the situation by ensuring negotiations between Red River and Canada.[31] These appointments began the process of negotiation that should have occurred six months earlier.[32]

Meanwhile, on December 2, the Council of Twenty-Four had issued a "List of Rights," enumerating fifteen tenets as the basis for Red River's entry into Confederation as a territory of Canada. It demanded political representation in local and national legislatures, the creation of administrative and legal institutions, equal standing of the French and English languages, recognition of existing "customs, privileges and usages," and the negotiation of "Treaties" with the "several tribes of Indians" in the Territory. It would be the first of four such Lists devised by the Settlement's political representatives.[33] The Council then proclaimed itself a provisional government and issued its own "Proclamation" on December 8. As a result of the abortive sale by the HBC and the efforts of Canada to "subjugate" the residents of Red River, the Proclamation invoked the fundamental principle that a people who had no government was free to give or refuse allegiance to authorities by its own choosing.

Red River now possessed an effective government. Regardless of whether it was supported by the majority of its inhabitants or recognized by Canada, it plausibly claimed to be in charge.[34] The new regime raised a flag consisting of the fleur-de-lis and shamrock, although it also raised the Union Jack.[35]

The Provisional Government in Operation

The next four months proved to be a time of trouble, marked by civil unrest, violent incidents, and mass arrests undertaken by the Provisional Government. It was also a time of political deliberations that resulted in a programme for negotiations with the Government of Canada. The *Comité National*, meanwhile, organized a paramilitary force that could muster two hundred to three hundred men. It was used to patrol the perimeters of the Settlement and ensure the occupation of Upper Fort Garry. A serious confrontation occurred over the December proclamation of the Provisional Government. Members of the Canadian Party—a combination of long-disgruntled residents of Portage la Prairie and Canadians at Fort Garry—organized a force of armed men to overthrow the new government. The Métis responded by promptly arresting forty-five men, including their ringleader, Canadian adventurer Dr. John Christian Schultz, and jailing them in Fort Garry. The provisional government and *Comité National*, led by Louis Riel, had become the *de facto* law and order in Red River.[36]

Political deliberations continued in this tense atmosphere. Local Convention meetings and provisional government deliberations worked out terms and procedures to resolve the impasse. In late January, a new popular Convention was called comprising of twenty delegates each from the English-Protestant and French-Catholic parishes. This "Convention of Forty" promoted by leaders in each community and by the Canadian commissioner, Donald Smith, deliberated on negotiations with Canada. The new organization, starting with a subcommittee including James Ross, John Black, Louis Riel, and Louis Schmidt, drew up a new list of rights that was more extensive and specific than the previous version. There was heated debate in the Convention over the question of seeking territorial or provincial status (the latter would have meant more local expenses but also promised local control of public lands). Riel favoured provincial status but he could not carry the Convention. The "Second List of Rights" was subsequently revised on two occasions, but it was this second list that constituted the core of Red River's goals. They included local and national political representation, an elected legislature within three years, adequate local government revenues, and provision by Canada of communication and transportation links and local public works such as public buildings and funds for schools, roads, and bridges. The List demanded recognition of property and other rights, including the use of French and English in the legislature and courts, and recognition and acquisition of citizenship rights for the residents of the new territory.[37]

February saw a renewal of conflict. Riel's frustration at the defeat of provincial status led to further incarcerations, including the mortally-ill William MacTavish and several of Riel's rivals amongst the Métis. The "Canadian Party" again organized themselves to overthrow the provisional government. The Métis force moved in and captured a group of about fifty members of the Canadian Party. Several prisoners were threatened with execution, including the leader, former militia Major Charles Boulton. Feverish negotiations ensued and most prisoners were released, but Riel and his closest associates decided to make an example of one prisoner and force Canada to "respect" the new government. Thomas Scott, a member of the Canadian Party, was executed by military court martial on March 4 for threatening the life of Riel, President of the provisional government.[38] Scott's death became a grave symbol to Protestant Ontario

Louis Riel
Convention of 40 Representative and Métis Leader

27 JANUARY 1870

CONFEDERATION QUOTE 6.1

Quotation from Convention of Forty, Second Provisional Government of Manitoba, 27 January 1870
Photograph by Duffin and Co., from Library and Archives Canada, C-052177

"Of course I am a British subject; but I am not a Canadian subject yet: and for that reason the Governor-General of Canada has no business with me yet, and I have no business with him—only with his Commissioner. If he has a proclamation, let him proclaim."

in later months and years. It weakened the legitimacy of the Red River government and marred Riel's standing for the rest of his days.

The Convention of Forty was shocked by the turn of events. It turned immediately to revise the terms for negotiation with Canada. Five days after Scott's execution, the influential Bishop Taché returned to Red River from an epochal Ecumenical Council in Rome, called back at the request of the Canadian government. Taché met with George-Étienne Cartier and John A. Macdonald in Ottawa on his return journey, and he brought with him assurances on behalf of the Canadian government to do justice to the demands of the people of Red River. The Council spent mid-March honing the List of Rights. This "Third List" now included Riel's demand for provincial status. The Council commissioned three delegates to depart immediately for Ottawa to negotiate terms. The first was John Black, formerly Recorder and vice-president of the Council of Assiniboia, an active representative in the provisional government, and a leader of the "English" community. The second delegate was Rev. Noël-J. Ritchot, a parish priest at La Salle since 1862 and close advisor to the Métis throughout the fall of 1869 and winter of 1870. The third representative was Alfred H. Scott, identified as a young "American" merchant and member of the provisional government. By March 24, the three delegates had left for Ottawa. Ritchot possessed a revised copy of the List of Rights—a "Fourth List"—that was reworked by the provisional government executive to strengthen demands for "denominational schools."[39]

Negotiating the Manitoba Act

The arrival of the Red River delegation in Ottawa in mid-April caused a major uproar in Ontario where Thomas Scott's execution had spawned widespread indignation. The Canadian Party in Red River was supported and represented in Ontario by a group of ardent nationalists, the Canada First Movement. The province's press also played up the "murder" of a loyal Anglo-Ontarian by the French-Catholic "half-breeds," and French-English and Catholic-Protestant antagonism reached a fevered pitch. Mass demonstrations were held in Toronto on April 7 and the Canada First movement subsequently secured a warrant for the delegation's arrest. Upon their arrival in Ottawa on April 11, and after an initial meeting with cabinet ministers George-Étienne Cartier and Joseph Howe, Noël-J.

Ritchot and Alfred Scott were held by Ottawa police for a week, swept up by the campaign to punish those responsible for the death of Thomas Scott. The warrants were eventually declared beyond the authority of Ontario and the two delegates freed. Meanwhile, Black resided unmolested in the Russell Hotel in a room adjacent to Commissioner Donald A. Smith.[40]

The Canadian government was wary of recognizing the delegates in any official capacity but Cartier and Macdonald met with them. Negotiations continued at Cartier's private residence between April 22 and May 2. The List of Rights formed the basis for the goals advanced by Black and Ritchot. Scott was not an active participant. It was pitted against a draft document less generous to the Manitobans advanced by Cartier and Macdonald who were guided by Smith's unsympathetic Report on the grievances of Red River.[41]

The most contentious issues under discussion were provincial status and public lands. Macdonald and Cartier conceded provincial status but not local control of natural resources, including public lands. Instead, they insisted that lands and natural resources must be vested in the dominion government so it could foster homestead and railway policies. Ritchot was alarmed because control of public lands was a tenet of the List of Rights and was the crux of the demand for provincial status. Existing land tenure would be threatened and the means for future settlement and public revenues would be lost. Realizing that he did not have the support of John Black and was likely to lose on the issue, Ritchot sought an alternative: "We could not give up control of the lands," he wrote in his journal, "unless we had compensation or conditions that, for the people there now, would be the equivalent to control of the lands of their province."[42] Ritchot then brought up a proposal that, although not part of the delegates' official instructions, had been discussed in Red River. As descendants of the Indigenous Peoples, the Métis believed they had inherited some form of share in the Aboriginal title to the lands. While it was not necessary to sign treaties with the Métis because they were not and did not think of themselves as "Indians," an argument could be made that they were deserving of special recognition. Ritchot viewed a grant of large blocs of land for the Métis as an acceptable form of compensation for loss of provincial control. The land grant or reserve would ensure continued Métis and French-Canadian farm populations and security of tenure. Macdonald and Cartier accepted the compromise, but they offered only a grant of one

Donald Alexander Smith (1st Baron Strathcona)
Canadian Special Commissioner
27 JANUARY 1870

CONFEDERATION QUOTE 6.2
Quotation from Convention of Forty, Second Provisional Government of Manitoba, 27 January 1870
Photograph from Library and Archives Canada, C-5489

" I need hardly say now, that Canada is not only disposed to respect the people of this country, but is most desirous of according to them every privilege enjoyed by any Province of the Dominion— all the rights of British subjects, in fact, which are enjoyed in any portion of the Dominion. "

hundred thousand acres for the descendants of the Métis.

On April 28, after three days of negotiations, Macdonald and Cartier presented the delegates with another draft of the bill. But when discussion recommenced, Macdonald suddenly left the table. As it turned out, the prime minister was withering under personal problems and anxieties. He lapsed into a drinking bout that lasted several days.[43] The prime minister's absence meant that Cartier had to orchestrate the remaining negotiations. Between Ritchot's insistence and Cartier's sympathetic outlook, the two sides agreed upon the grant of a very large bloc of 1.4 million acres or one-sixth of the land area of the new province for current and future Métis people. Other matters, including fiscal arrangements, economic links, as well as legal, linguistic, and educational rights on the basis of dualism between French and English, and Catholics and Protestants, were negotiated amicably. It was in Macdonald's absence, however, that the final terms were struck.[44]

On May 2, John A. Macdonald returned to present a surprisingly cogent summary of the newly agreed-upon Manitoba bill, which was still being printed. The prime minister reviewed the legislation deftly enough, explaining that a province would be created since a "territory" was apparently unknown in the British colonial system. "Manitoba" would replace "Assiniboia" as a more euphonious, poignant aboriginal name ("the meeting of spirits," he claimed). His account was thorough, although he relied upon Cartier's clarification of such points as the guarantee of legal occupation of land by existing populations, and a peculiar comparison of the Métis land grant to that provided the United Empire Loyalists. The new legislation would "be satisfactory to the people of all classes and races of that country." Macdonald ended by announcing the subsidiary legislation that would support a small military "expedition" of British regulars and Canadian militia to alleviate the fears of the local population about Indian hostility and foreign threats to peace.[45]

Macdonald's announcement drew the first of many critical Opposition responses to what Liberal leader Alexander Mackenzie described as the "reprehensible" payment to the HBC for a territory that Canada had by right and "ludicrous" legislation making a province out of two or three "counties." William McDougall, now back on the Liberal side of the House, offered the first of several speeches that criticized the proposal and defended his own previous actions, a tactic that drew sharp comments from cabinet ministers such as Sir Francis Hincks and a strong rebuke from Joseph Howe.[46]

The day the Manitoba Act was to be debated, Macdonald fell seriously ill with gallstones, and would remain out of the fray for months. On May 7, Alexander Mackenzie argued that the Manitoba Act was a question of "vast political importance to the future of the country" and in effect agreed to quick passage.[47] During the debates, members questioned but did not strongly oppose provisions for denominational schools and they did not challenge recognition of French and English as languages of government and law. Many, however, spoke against the reservation of 1.4 million acres for the Métis population. Many MPs criticized the generous fiscal terms and both Conservatives and Liberals revealed their confusion over whether the Métis land was an aboriginal settlement or a grant of land in recognition of the resident population. On May 12 the bill was given final assent.[48] When the provisional government of Assiniboia was informed and apprised of the Act, it too gave formal approval.[49]

The new province created by the Manitoba Act was proclaimed on 15 July 1870, the same day the sale of Rupert's Land was completed. In December the election of the first provincial legislature occurred. The Manitoba Act departed radically in some respects from the British North America Act that had created Confederation in 1867. The provisions for the province to receive four members of parliament and two senators, as well as provision for federal control of Crown lands contravened sections on the Senate, House representation, and most importantly provincial powers under the Constitution Act. Not surprisingly, the acquisition of Manitoba was later placed upon the footing of a separate Imperial Statute, the British North America Act of 1871.[50]

The Canadian take-over of Red River was irregular from start to finish. Parliament's last move in the process caused further unease and trouble. It authorized a military Expedition—sought by the Macdonald government for some time—of 400 British regulars and 800 Ontario and Quebec militiamen, infantry, and artillery. The Red River Expedition set off in the summer of 1870 with the avowed purpose of protecting the Settlement. Led by British Army Col. Garnet Wolseley, it was touted as a presence to buttress the transfer. As the Expedition neared Red River in late August of 1870, in advance of the new civilian lieutenant-governor, Adams Archibald, Wolseley wrote the locals that the "mission is one of peace" whose purpose was to "secure Her Majesty's sovereign authority." He also promised the "strictest order and discipline" amongst the troops. Wolseley led the British battalion in advance of the Canadian militia and it marched into Red River on August 24 in military formation "prepared for a fight." The Settlement was in effect turned into an armed camp. Large numbers of Métis men had departed for the buffalo hunt. Riel consequently lacked military or civilian support, and Manitoba's "Father of Confederation" was forced into hiding. On September 2, Adams Archibald arrived as did the Canadian militia battalions. Wolseley's forces left a week later. Tension and sporadic conflict ensued, including several Métis deaths, notably Riel's associate Elzéar Goulet who was run into the Red River and drowned.[51]

The Canadian official now in charge, Adams Archibald, was a moderate Nova Scotian and an ally of Joseph Howe, who had some sympathies for the stated positions of the Manitobans. Archibald undertook the laborious process of negotiating the structures of government and politics. He spent two arduous years implementing the formation of a provincial legislature (divided equally between French and English parish-based constituencies) and the formation of courts and administrative agencies of government. During his time in office, he was effectively the head of a colonial and not a "responsible" form of government. The formation of a responsible government under a premier did not emerge until the mid-1870s.[52]

Manitobans gained the core of what they had sought in 1870: representative government, federal representation, institutions based on local society, a fiscal base, assurances about communication links, and a land reserve for the resident population. Offsetting these gains, however, were three factors. The first was the issue of the amnesty for the actions of the Provisional Government. Amnesty was repeatedly sought during and after 1870, but neither Canada nor Britain accepted responsibility. The former absolved itself of anything but sympathy, and the latter claimed that certain criminal actions remained open to prosecution, so the amnesty issue became a perpetual cloud over Louis Riel and a blight on politics. The second issue was the entrenchment of dominion control over natural resources and public lands. The administration of the promised Métis lands was vested in Ottawa. The fairness of the administration of Métis lands became a matter of dispute during the 1870s, when substantial numbers of the locals dispersed to the west, and has remained so since. This form of jurisdiction subordination led to a third point: the guarantees of

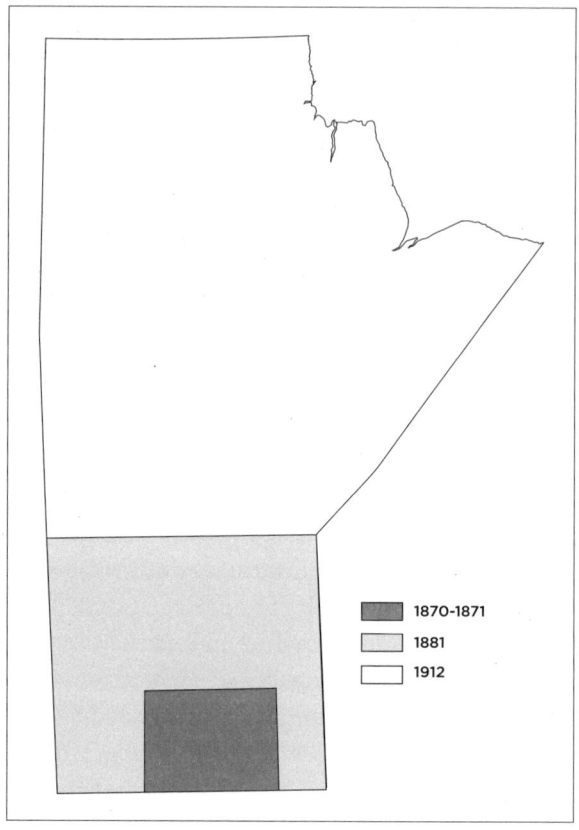

Fig 6.2 Manitoba's expansion, 1870–1912. Reproduced with permission from John Welsted et al. "Manitoba: Geographical Identity of a Prairie Province," *The Geography of Manitoba: Its Land and Its People*, eds. John C. Everitt, Christoph Stadel, and John E. Welsted (Winnipeg: University of Manitoba Press, 1996), 5.

religious and linguistic rights for Roman Catholics and French-language Manitobans were dependent upon the goodwill and intent of subsequent governments of Canada and Manitoba. As later events would prove, the guarantee of denominational and language rights and the fair administration of provisions enshrined in the Manitoba Act were not fully entrenched. Manitoba was not a province like the others and would not be so for sixty years. Its subordination was a constitutional watershed, as historian Chester Martin argued a century ago and was echoed by almost every historian since. The Act was a "second Confederation" establishing a model for subordinate provinces that created problems for decades. As Martin put it, the Manitoba Act as validated by the British Parliament in 1871, meant that "Canada was transformed from a federation of equals into an Empire."[53]

Treaty-Making, 1871–76

Canada's acquisition of Manitoba and the North-West was not completed by the take-over of 1870. As the Provisional Government's List of Rights had stipulated, "treaties" with the "Indian tribes" of the region still needed to be negotiated, and both the First Nations of the entire North-West and the Government of Canada were motivated to proceed. The First Nations were well aware of Canada's grandiose plans for their homelands. They had already experienced Canada's bumptious and insensitive approach to Indigenous Peoples as well as the increasingly serious concerns about outbreaks of disease and declining food sources.[54] They were aware of the experience of the Red River Métis with the Canadians. For its part, Canada had already shown its determination to absorb the North-West into its expansion strategy, while realizing it lacked the capacity to enforce its schemes in the way the United States was doing through a policy of warfare and mass settlement.[55]

The First Nations had a history of mutual accommodation during the HBC era and they were prepared to pursue the same approach with the Canadians. Accordingly, Indigenous Peoples in the areas in and around the new province sought treaty negotiations almost as soon as Adams Archibald arrived in Manitoba. They were stalled by the habitual disorganization of the Canadian government and by the lieutenant-governor's focus on creating a political and administrative structure for the new province.

By mid-1871, Archibald and a newly-appointed Indian commissioner, Wemyss Simpson (former HBC trader and Conservative MP), engaged in treaty talks. The first agreement, Treaty No. 1 or the "Stone Fort Treaty," was signed at Lower Fort Garry, downriver from Winnipeg, on 3 August 1871 with the "Chippewa and Swampy Cree Tribes of Indians" of Manitoba. This was an area of 43,250 square kilometres encompassing, but spilling over from the new province to east and west. The ceremonial aspects of the signing reflected the momentousness of the agreement and the negotiations were intense at times. About one thousand Anishinaabeg people gathered while their leaders concluded talks with the Canadians.[56] Treaty No. 2 was signed on August 21 at the "Manitoba Post" on Lake Manitoba. It was for an area of 92,000 square kilometres in an arc north and west of Treaty 1.

The terms of the Treaties No. 1 and No. 2 reflected the seriousness of the situation. Like all later treaties, they were reciprocal agreements—not with Canada—but between Her Majesty the Queen and peoples of the region. In return for a general acceptance of opening the specified lands for "settlement and immigration" and an agreement to observe the treaty and maintain the peace, First Nations were guaranteed grants of lands—160 acres [64.75 ha.] per family of five, an annual payment of fifteen dollars per family, a ban on the sale of "intoxicating liquor," and the provision of a school "on each reserve" at the desire of the inhabitants.[57]

Archibald introduced the signings for each treaty by emphasizing the Crown's commitment to "justice to all" and the dominion's promise of seeking the "good of all races." He stated that the Queen "though she may think it good for you to adopt civilized habits, has no idea of compelling you to do so. This she leaves to your choice, and you need not live like the white man." To underline this point, he stated that the reserves provided an abundance of land for their perpetual use either "by tilling" or by "the chase."[58] Commissioner Simpson stated in his speech to First Nations and in his report to the minister that it had also taken some convincing to disabuse band leaders of what he claimed were excessive demands for land grants, such as a demand by the Chiefs in the Treaty 1 area for a reserve of two-thirds of the province. He also noted that Métis in the areas along the Assiniboine who were eligible for land grants under the Manitoba Act had tried to gain reserve lands, though they were stymied.[59]

While Archibald and Simpson expressed fine sentiments on behalf of Queen Victoria, the government they represented promptly neglected its Treaty obligations, which led to agitations among the signatory First Nations during the next four years. This agitation led to a revision of the treaties by 1875. As Archibald's and Simpson's successor in negotiations, Alexander Morris admitted: "Certain verbal promises . . . were not included in the written text of the treaties, nor recognized or referred to, when these Treaties were ratified by the Privy Council." A memorandum was subsequently signed that raised the annuity to five dollars per capita and stipulated special gratuities to Chiefs and Headmen.[60]

Two other treaties were signed with First Nations in areas that became part of Manitoba by the 1880s. Alexander Morris became lieutenant-governor of Manitoba and the North-West Territories from 1873 to 1876 and J.A.N. Provencher became Indian commissioner. Treaty No. 3, the "North-West Angle" agreement, was signed in 1873 principally with bands of Saulteaux from north-western Ontario. These negotiations, for an area of 124,450 square kilometres, were characterized by more pointed demands from the Chiefs based on their understanding that the lands they possessed contained valuable timber and minerals, and that the signatories to Treaties No. 1 and No. 2 already were dissatisfied. They negotiated better terms, including a larger annuity of five dollars per person, a family land grant of 640 acres (259 hectares), the supply of equipment and stock for farming, and equipment for fishing as well as the promise that they had the right to "pursue their avocations of hunting and fishing throughout the tracts surrendered."[61] This promise of access for hunting and fishing rights, not uncommon in previous treaties throughout British North America, was entrenched in each subsequent treaty.

The final agreement pertaining to Manitoba was Treaty No. 5, the "Winnipeg Treaty" of 1875–76 (Treaty No. 4 impinged on the western edge of the province). It encompassed Indigenous Nations of the northern ends of Lakes Winnipegosis and Manitoba over a region of 259,000 square kilometres, an area specifically including waterways as well as lands. It was even more precise than previous treaties in accounting for entitlements to land, annuities, schooling, prohibition, and equipment and stock for farming. The Treaty was later extended in 1908 via further adhesions which added the rest of northern Manitoba, an area of some 345,500 square kilometres.[62]

The four treaties negotiated between 1871 and 1876 were based on the recognition of the autonomy and significance of the Indigenous Peoples that no amount of subsequent administrative sloth or perfidy could deny. The texts alone, apart from the rich context of prior agreements and the recorded discussions that framed the negotiations, reveal the complexities of the treaties. They were agreements between the Crown (not merely the Government of Canada) and the Indigenous Peoples. Canada was obliged to recognize perpetual obligations through annual ceremonies and commemorations, the payment of the annuities, a commitment to recognize Indigenous rights of possession and use of lands and waterways for their material well-being, and purported respect for both existing and new ways of life. First Nations were obliged to maintain treaties by keeping the peace and cooperating with settlement and development. All of the treaties were made possible by the willingness of Indigenous Peoples and the Crown's representatives to negotiate, and by the essential work of credible

Métis interpreters like James McKay, Charles Nolin, and others from Red River, and by the involvement of Catholic and Protestant clergy who had the trust of many Indigenous leaders.[63] These agreements ensured that the framework for Canadian control of the North-West and Manitoba did not collapse, although it nearly fell apart during the Rebellion of 1885.

NOTES

1. British North America Act 1867.

2. See Doug Owram, *The Promise of Eden* (Toronto: University of Toronto Press, 1980), and W.L. Morton, *The Critical Years: The Union of British North America 1857–1873* (Toronto: McClelland & Stewart, 1963).

3. See E.E. Rich, *The Fur Trade and the Northwest to 1857* (Toronto: McClelland & Stewart, 1967), W.L. Morton, *Manitoba: A History*, revised edition (Toronto: University of Toronto Press, 1966), and, for a more recent account, J.M. Bumsted, *Fur Trade Wars: The Founding of Western Canada* (Winnipeg: Great Plains, 2003).

4. E.H. Oliver, *The Canadian-North-West*, I (Publications of the Canadian Archives, no. 9, Ottawa, Government Printing Bureau, 1915), 35ff., "minutes", 266–618.

5. Besides Morton's *Manitoba* and D. and L. Gibson's *Substantial Justice: Law and Lawyers in Manitoba* (Winnipeg: Peguis Press, 1972), the more thorough analyses are: G.A. Friesen, *The Canadian Prairies: A History* (Toronto: University of Toronto Press, 1985) and Gerhard Ens, *Homeland to Hinterland: the Changing Worlds of the Red River Metis in the Nineteenth Century* (Toronto: University of Toronto Press, 1996). Dale Gibson has recently compiled a massive history of court records with a lengthy introduction that is in part a political history: *Law, Life and Government at Red River, Vol. I, 1812–1872* (Montreal: McGill-Queen's University Press, 2015).

6. See United Kingdom Parliament, "Select Committee . . . under the Administration of the Hudson's Bay Company," *Report*, London, 1857, passim. Witnesses included churchmen from Red River (Rev. David Anderson, Rev. G.O. Corbett), former residents (Alexander Isbister and Dr. John Rae), Canadian officials (Alfred Roche and W.H. Draper), and British officials.

7. *Report*, London, 1857, Appendix 15.

8. *Report*, London, 1857, Recommendations 7, 10, 12, 3.

9. John S. Galbraith, *The Hudson's Bay Company as an Imperial Factor 1821–1869* (Los Angeles: University of California Press, 1959), 341–54, W.L. Morton, *The Critical Years*, 30–40.

10. Galbraith, *The Hudson's Bay Company*, 355ff. and 413ff. and Morton, *The Critical Years*, 60–3, 69–70.

11. McDougall in Canada, *House of Commons Debates*, 6 December 1867.

12. United Kingdom Parliament, "Rupert's Land Act," 31–32 Victoria, c. 105, 1868, see article 3.

13. Galbraith, *The Hudson's Bay Company*, 413–24, Morton, *The Critical Years*, 223–25, 233ff.

14 The specific agreements are printed as "Memorandum of Agreement" 22 March 1869, and "Memorandum" of the Speakers of the House and Senate and the "Deed of Surrender" 29 and 31 May 1869, in Oliver, *The Canadian North-West*, II, 949ff. and 945ff.

15 Canada, *House of Commons Debates*, 1869: Cartier, 28 May 1869, McDougall, 28 May 1869, Galt, 28 May 1869. John A. Macdonald, 4 June 1869, John Rose, 9 June 1869, A. Mackenzie and L.H. Holton, 18 June 1869.

16 Morton, *Manitoba*, 118–20; William McDougall to J.S. Dennis, 10 July 1869 and Dennis to McDougall, 21 August 18769, in Canada, Sessional Paper #12, 1870; MacTavish to Bp. Taché, 4 September 1869, in Canada, "Committee . . . " 1874). Communication between Red River and Ottawa was awkward. Ordinary mail could take weeks, while telegraphy through the United States was broken by a three-day trek into Assiniboia: see D.N. Sprague, *Canada and the Metis* (Waterloo: Wilfrid Laurier University Press, 1988), 44.

17 Joseph Howe Secretary of State, to William McDougall, Lt.-Gov., 29 September 1869, "Papers Relating to Canada 1867–1874," *Irish University Press Series of British Parliamentary Papers* (Shannon: Irish University Press, 1968), vol. 27 and Oliver, *The Canadian North-West*, II, 878–80.

18 Murray Beck, *Joseph Howe, Vol. II: The Briton Becomes Canadian* (Montreal: McGill-Queen's University Press, 1983), 255–63; Howe in *House of Commons*, 21 February 1870 reproduced by *The Confederation Debates,* https://hcmc.uvic.ca/confederation/en/lgHC_MB_1870-02-21.html; Howe to McDougall, 19 October 1869, tabled in *House of Commons Debates* 1870, 1473.

19 Council of Assiniboia, Minutes, 19 October 1869, "Address to Governor McDougall," in Oliver, *The Canadian North-West* I, 610–13, 613–14.

20 The triumph of this particular group out of a complicated Métis politics was analyzed by Gerhard Ens, "Prologue to the Red River Resistance: Pre-liminal Politics and the Triumph of Riel," *Journal of the Canadian Historical Association* 5, no. 1 (1994), 111–23.

21 John Bruce and Louis Riel to Wm. McDougall, 21 October 1869, in Oliver, *The Canadian North-West*, II, 880.

22 Council of Assiniboia, Minutes, 25 October, in Oliver, *The Canadian North-West*, I, 616–18.

23 MacTavish to McDougall, 30 October 1869, in Oliver, *The Canadian North-West*, II, 884–87.

24 Morton, *Manitoba*, 121–23; J.S. Dennis to McDougall, 27 October 1869, in Oliver, *The Canadian North-West*, II, 881–83, McDougall to Howe, 4 November 1869, British Parliamentary Papers, 27, Canada 1867–74, McDougall to MacTavish, 2 November 1869, in Oliver, *The Canadian North-West*, II, 887–89.

25 The sequence of events may be pieced together from W.L. Morton, editor, *Alexander Begg's Red River Journal* (Toronto: Champlain Society, 1956), 163ff. and Alexander Begg's own book, *The Creation of Manitoba*, (Toronto: 1871), ch. 1–3.

26 See Galbraith, *The Hudson's Bay Company*, 426–27; British Parliamentary Papers, 27, Canada 1867–74, Granville to Young, 25 November and 30 November 1869.

27 Howe to McDougall, 19 November 1869 in British Parliamentary Papers, 27, Canada 1867–74; Macdonald to McDougall, 27 November 1869, Howe to McDougall, 29 November 1869, William McDougall Papers, LAC.

28 The text is found in many places: see Oliver, *The Canadian North-West* II, 893–95, and subsequent Orders to Col. J.S. Dennis and a second "Proclamation" announcing the

authority of Dennis: "Commission Appointing Col. Dennis" 1 December 1869, Proclamation, 2 December 1869, Oliver, *The Canadian North-West* II, 896–98 and 898–99.

29   Proclamation, 6 December 1869, Oliver, *The Canadian North-West*, II, 899–900.

30   Joseph Howe to William McDougall, 7, 11 December, and 24 December 1869; McDougall to Howe, 16 December 1869, 1 January 1870, 20 January 1870, Canada, *House of Commons Sessional Papers* #12, 1870.

31   Howe to McDougall, 7 December 1869, Canada, *House of Commons Sessional Papers* #12, 1870; Howe to Fr. Thibault, 4 and 6 December 1869, Canada 1874, 190.

32   Joseph Howe to Fr. Thibault, 4 December 1869, in *House of Commons Sessional Papers*, 1874, Howe to Smith, 10 December 1869; LAC William McDougall Papers, Commission issued to Donald A. Smith, 17 December 1869, Oliver, *The Canadian North-West*, II, 906–07.

33   See "List of Rights," December 1869, published in many places, Morton ed. *Alexander Begg's Red River Journal* (Toronto: Champlain Society, vol. 34, 1955), 193ff., Begg's own 1871 book *Creation of Manitoba*, 110ff. J.M. Bumsted rightly points out that this List, usually described as the 1st List, was actually the second version of a shorter List drafted in November by the Council of Twenty-Four: J.M. Bumsted, *Red River Rebellion* (Winnipeg: Great Plains, 1996), 93–95.

34   "Declaration of the People of Rupert's Land and the North-West," signed John Bruce, Pres., and Louis Riel, Sec., 8 December 1869, in Oliver, *The Canadian North-West*, II, 905–06. The Catholic conservatism of the document is explained by Thomas Flanagan, "Political Theory of the Red River Resistance: The Declaration of December 8, 1869," *Canadian Journal of Political Science* 11, no. 1 (March 1978), 153–64; legal historian Dale Gibson argues in favour of its legality: the Provisional Government met the three main tests of a legitimate provisional government: *Law, Life and Government at Red River, vol. I, 1812–1872*, 243–44.

35   The battle of the pennants is recounted in Morton, ed. *Alexander Begg's Red River Journal*, for March of 1870: 361–62 and 372–74.

36   There is no convenient single source, but see Alexander Begg's 1871: *The Creation of Manitoba*, passim, and D.N. Sprague, *Canada and the Metis*, 33–52.

37   Begg transcribed the 2nd List in W.L. Morton, editor, *Alexander Begg's Red River Journal* (Toronto: Champlain Society, vol. 34, 1955), 291–95, reprinted as "Second List of Rights" in *Manitoba: Birth of a Province*, ed. W.L. Morton (Altona: Manitoba Record Society, 1965), Appendix I, pp. 242–44.

38   First-hand accounts are D.A. Smith's melodramatic "Report . . . ," *House of Commons Sessional Papers*, #12, 1870, in Morton, *Manitoba: Birth of a Province*, 38–42 and the more neutral report of Alexander Begg in Morton, *Alexander Begg's Red River Journal*, 3–9 March 1870, 327–32. J.M. Bumsted has investigated the matter in *Thomas Scott's Body* (Winnipeg: University of Manitoba Press, 2000), 3–10 and 197–209.

39   Thomas Bunn, Secretary of Provisional Government, to Fr. N. Ritchot, 22 March 1870, in Canada, Select Committee . . . 1874, 71.

40   The episode may be followed at first hand in Fr. Ritchot's *Journal* for April 1870, in Morton, *Manitoba: Birth of a Province*, 133–6 and Philippe Mailhot's invaluable "Ritchot's Resistance: Abbé Noel Joseph Ritchot and the Creation and Transformation of Manitoba," PhD diss., University of Manitoba, 1986.

41 D.A. Smith, *House of Commons Sessional Papers,* #12, 1870 and Smith to Howe, 12 April 1870.

42 Ritchot's *Journal,* 27 April 1870, both in Morton, *Manitoba: Birth of a Province,* 140; see also Thomas Flanagan, *Métis Lands in Manitoba* (Calgary: University of Calgary Press, 1991), 33–34.

43 Stafford Northcote, "Diary," 29 April 1870, in Morton, *Manitoba: Birth of a Province,* 91 and Patricia Phenix, *Private Demons: The Tragic Personal Life of John A. Macdonald* (Toronto: McClelland & Stewart, 2006), 204–05.

44 See the journal entries of Northcote and Ritchot for late April and early May of 1870 in Morton, *Manitoba: Birth of a Province,* 90–101 and 139–43.

45 John A. Macdonald, *House of Commons,* afternoon session, 2 May 1870. Reproduced by *The Confederation Debates,* https://hcmc.uvic.ca/confederation/en/lgHC_MB_1870-05-02.html.

46 Alexander Mackenzie, William McDougall, Francis Hincks, Joseph Howe, Louis-R. Masson, Canada, *House of Commons,* 2 May 1870. Reproduced by *The Confederation Debates,* http://hcmc.uvic.ca/confederation/en/lgHC_MB_1870-05-02.html.

47 Canada, *House of Commons Debates,* 21 February 1870 and 9 May 1870, reproduced by *The Confederation Debates,* http://hcmc.uvic.ca/confederation/en/lgHC_MB_1870-02-21.html and http://hcmc.uvic.ca/confederation/en/lgHC_MB_1870-05-09.html.

48 Canada, *House of Commons Debates,* 7 May 1870, reproduced by *The Confederation Debates,* http://hcmc.uvic.ca/confederation/en/lgHC_MB_1870-05-07.html. Canada, *House of Commons Debates,* 9 May 1870, reproduced by *The Confederation Debates,* http://hcmc.uvic.ca/confederation/en/lgHC_MB_1870-05-09.html.

49 Morton, *Manitoba: A History,* 142. See Oliver, *The Canadian North-West, II.*

50 United Kingdom, Parliament, British North America Act c. 28, 1871.

51 G.F.G. Stanley, *Toil and Trouble: Military Expeditions to Red River* (Toronto: Dundurn, 1989), 160–70; David W. Grebstad, "Rowboat Diplomacy: The Dominion of Canada's Whole of Government Approach to the Red River Rebellion," *Canadian Military Journal* 13, no. 3 (2013): 57–66, argues that the Expedition was an early version of state occupation.

52 See letter of appointment: E.A. Meredith, under-secretary of state, to A.G. Archibald, 4 August 1870, Oliver, *The Canadian North-West,* II, 974.

53 Chester Martin, "The First 'New Province' of the Dominion," *Canadian Historical Review* I, no. 4 (1920): 377; Martin's more extensive argument is found in *The Natural Resources Question* (Winnipeg: King's Printer, 1920).

54 J.R. Miller, *Compact, Contract, Covenant: Aboriginal Treaty-Making in Canada* (Toronto: University of Toronto Press, 2009), 155; on Indigenous conditions, see James Daschuk, *Clearing the Plains: Disease, Politics of Starvation, and the Loss of Aboriginal Life* (Regina: University of Regina Press, 2013).

55 Miller, *Compact, Contract, Covenant,* ch. 6, Friesen, *The Canadian Prairies,* ch. 5, and Aimee Craft, *Breathing Life into the Stone Fort Treaty: An Anishinabe Understanding of Treaty One* (Saskatoon: Purich, 2013).

56 In addition to summaries in Miller and Friesen, see Alexander Morris, *The Treaties of Canada with the Indians of Manitoba and the North-West Territories* (Toronto: Belford, Clarke & Co. 1880), 15ff. reproduced by *The Confederation Debates,* http://hcmc.uvic.ca/confederation/en/lgTreatyNeg.html, and a government of Canada website, Canada, Aboriginal

Affairs and Northern Development Canada (AANDC), "Treaties in Manitoba," 2015: https://www.aadnc-aandc.gc.ca/eng/1100100020406/1100100020407; the first boundaries of Manitoba covered but 33,000 square km., expanded to 189,000 square km. in 1881.

57 Specific details are found in the Treaty documents: Canada, Aboriginal Affairs and Northern Development Canada, "Treaty Texts: Treaties No. 1 and No. 2", 2013: https://www.aadnc-aandc.gc.ca/eng/1370373165583/1370373202340 and AANDC, "Treaties in Manitoba."

58 Specific details in AANDC, "Treaty Texts, Treaties No. 1 and 2," and "Treaties in Manitoba." Comments on the negotiations are in Morris, *The Treaties of Canada*, 28–29.

59 Morris, *The Treaties of Canada*, citing Archibald to Howe, 20 July 1871, 33–35, and 3 November 1871, 37–43, reproduced by *The Confederation Debates*, http://hcmc.uvic.ca/confederation/en/Morris_Chapter_04.html.

60 Morris, *The Treaties of Canada*, 126–27, reproduced by *The Confederation Debates*, http://hcmc.uvic.ca/confederation/en/Morris_Chapter_07.html.

61 AANDC, "Treaty Texts, Treaty No. 3," and AANDC, "Treaties in Manitoba."

62 AANDC, "Treaty Texts, Treaty No. 5," and AANDC, "Treaties in Manitoba."

63 Miller, *Compact, Contract and Covenant*, 184–86.

7

"The interests of Confederation demanded it": British Columbia and Confederation

PATRICIA E. ROY

> [Canada] promised what she did to British Columbia less because British Columbia demanded it than because the interests of Confederation demanded it.
>
> Colonist, 20 July 1871

On 14 May 1870 in Victoria, three men—J.W. Trutch, Dr. R.W.W. Carrall, and Dr. J.S. Helmcken—specially selected by Governor Anthony Musgrave—himself nominated by John A. Macdonald—boarded the *Active* for the five-day journey to San Francisco. From there, the recently completed Union Pacific Railroad took them to Chicago and a transfer to the Grand Trunk Railway of Canada. In Ottawa, they expected to meet Prime Minister Macdonald and the federal cabinet to discuss the "fair and equitable" terms by which British Columbia might enter Confederation. Accompanying them was Henry Seelye, the correspondent of the *Victoria British Colonist*. On the instructions of John Robson, his editor, he was to use his influence with the Canadian government, particularly fellow New Brunswicker S.L. Tilley, to ensure that the terms of union included responsible government. Macdonald was critically ill,[1] so the acting prime minister, George-Étienne Cartier greeted the British Columbians. Macdonald, however, had laid the groundwork for a Canadian nation "From Sea unto Sea."

Talk of a continent-wide British North America was not new, but for British Columbia the story begins at the Quebec Conference of 1864, when George Brown proposed that the 72 Resolutions provide "for the admission into the Union on equitable terms of the North West Territory, British Columbia and Vancouver." Adopted unanimously,[2] the motion became Section 146 of the British North America Act of 1867. Section 146 did not refer to Vancouver Island. A year earlier, the British government had forced it into an unhappy union with the mainland colony of British Columbia in the hope of saving on administrative costs since revenues and population were falling and debt, rising.[3] In 1867 the united colony, with a non-Indigenous population generously estimated at fifteen thousand and steadily declining, had a debt of $1,300,000 incurred mostly by road building on the Mainland.[4] The Mainland was jealous of Victoria being the commercial centre; the Island was affronted by losing its name, Victoria's status as a free port, and a Legislative Assembly that provided a form of representative, but not responsible, government. Instead, it got a variation on the Mainland constitution, a Legislative Council in which the governor chose fourteen of twenty-three members. Nevertheless, some wanted to maintain the status quo. Others wanted change, either annexation to the United States or joining Canada.

The idea of annexation was not far-fetched given that most communication with the outside world was via San Francisco, and the American purchase of Alaska in 1867 had sandwiched the colony between two American territories. At least two petitions for annexation circulated in Victoria, but not on the Mainland, and secured signatures mainly of Americans and Europeans. They attracted little attention in Washington, D.C.,[5] but may have encouraged the Colonial Office to promote Confederation more vigorously and strengthened the Canadian argument for admitting British Columbia to Confederation.

Supporters of the status quo had more influence than their numbers warranted because, led by Governor Frederick Seymour, they dominated the government. Engineering the union of the colonies had taxed his health; he seemed unwilling to face the problems of creating another union.⁶ He did not oppose Confederation, but these reservations may explain his reluctance to act. The civil servants who formed the majority of the Legislative Council also favoured the status quo. They included Trutch, an English-born engineer, surveyor and Chief Commissioner of Lands and Works; Royal Naval officers; and former Hudson's Bay Company employees, such as Dr. Helmcken who came to Victoria in 1850 as the HBC surgeon. Helmcken thought Confederation "another leap in the dark" given the distance from Canada and its high tariffs.⁷ Officials such as Judge Matthew Baillie Begbie feared for their jobs and worried about their pensions. Being generally better educated and from higher social classes, the British officials considered themselves superior to the Canadians whom they regarded as "a poor mean slow people" or "North American Chinamen" because of their thriftiness.⁸

Pushing for Confederation

Canadians were likely in a numerical minority, but included two major newspaper editors: Amor de Cosmos and John Robson. De Cosmos, whose hero was Joseph Howe for championing British liberalism, was born William Smith in Windsor, Nova Scotia. He came to Victoria in 1858, having already changed his name a few years before, and founded the *Colonist*.⁹ His early editorials called for responsible government and a federation of the British North American colonies. In 1863, when an elected member of the Island's legislative assembly, he sold the *Colonist* and for a time concentrated on political activities. In June 1867 at the Reform Convention in Toronto, he issued a well-received call for British Columbia's entry into Confederation.¹⁰ The other key editor was John Robson. As early as 1862, in the New Westminster *British Columbian*, Robson, a native of Perth, Upper Canada, declared that the British American provinces must be linked "into one United Federation which shall extend from ocean to ocean."¹¹ He too wanted responsible government.

On 18 March 1867, British Columbia's Legislative Council unanimously passed de Cosmos' motion that given events in British North America and the views of British Columbians, Seymour should take immediate steps to insure British Columbia's admission into the Confederation "on fair and equitable terms."¹² According to Dr. Helmcken, they expected Canada to cover British Columbia's expenses, including debts, and "give

Amor de Cosmos
Member of the Legislative Council, BC

10 MARCH 1870

Confederation Quote 7.1
Quotation from British Columbia, Legislative Council, 10 March 1870
Photograph courtesy of the Royal BC Museum and Archives, Image A-01224

> " I am in favour of Confederation, provided the financial terms are right in amount, and if the other terms will contribute to the advancement and protection of our industry. If we cannot get favourable terms, which I believe we can, it will then be for the people of this country to say whether we shall remain in isolation or seek some other more favourable union. "

her a bonus into the bargain."[13] Seymour did not send the resolution to Canada. Belatedly sending it to London, he called it "the expression of a despondent community looking for a change." He ambiguously suggested that both he and the colonists wanted "a fusion or an intimate connection with the Eastern Confederation," but building a road through "rugged" mountains would be difficult.[14] The Colonial Office replied that union must wait until Canada acquired Rupert's Land.[15]

On 22 January 1868, S.L. Tilley, Canada's Minister of Customs, telegraphed H.E. Seelye, of the *Colonist's* staff, to inform him that Canada had had no communications from British Columbia.[16] A week later the telegram was read at a public meeting in Victoria which requested that Canada ask the Imperial government to instruct Seymour to inaugurate negotiations with Canada.[17] Suggested terms included: Canada accepting responsibility for an estimated debt of $1,500,000, providing fixed and per capita subsidies, responsible government, and, the "essential condition," the construction of a wagon road from the head of navigation on the Fraser River to Lake Superior within two years of admission.[18] On 7 March 1868, the Canadian cabinet asked the Colonial Secretary to instruct Seymour "to take such steps as may be deemed proper" to let the Legislative Council act towards Confederation.[19]

Two weeks later Seymour told the Council that he supported Confederation which might lead to overland communication with Canada, but union must wait until Rupert's Land was part of Canada.[20] The next day, Tilley wired that Canada had initiated discussions with the Imperial government on British Columbia joining Confederation and that the Council should pass an address to Her Majesty favouring union.[21] Public meetings in New Westminster and Yale asked Seymour to present a message to the Council calling for immediate union on "fair and equitable terms."[22]

When Seymour did not respond, de Cosmos introduced a resolution calling for the admission of British Columbia to Confederation "without delay" and listing terms including financial arrangements, the construction of "a good Overland Wagon Road" from Lake Superior to the head of navigation on the Fraser River, representation in parliament, and the transfer of colonial civil servants to the federal service if their duties fell within its responsibilities. The appointed members of Council passed an amendment that they lacked sufficient information about "the practical working of Confederation" to define advantageous terms. Only de Cosmos, Robson, and two other elected members opposed the amendment.[23] Seymour interpreted this as reason to postpone discussions about Confederation.[24]

Beyond the Council chambers, in September 1868, twenty-six individuals from most British Columbia communities convened for three days at Yale, the head of navigation on the Fraser River. Joshua Thompson of Barkerville claimed an "almost unanimous feeling throughout the colony in favour of Confederation." Complaining that the governor and his councillors were "generally antagonistic to the well-being of the colony," the delegates demanded that Seymour work for the admission of British Columbia to Confederation on favourable terms or publicly explain why this was not possible.[25]

In Victoria, the resolutions of the Yale Convention attracted ridicule because "a coloured man," an American, was a delegate.[26] That man was Mifflin Wistar Gibbs who had served on Victoria's City Council. Seymour sent the Yale resolutions to London. He included advertisements from the *Colonist* saying that the resolutions did not represent the views of all Victorians and added that he saw no way of introducing responsible government.[27] Nevertheless, recognizing the support for Confederation, in the equivalent of the Throne Speech on 17 December 1868, Seymour asserted that every Englishman would "rejoice to see a vast State, still under his own flag, extending from the Atlantic to the Pacific," but there were "extremely formidable" obstacles.[28] The reply to the Speech noted satisfaction with the Confederation discussions.[29]

Elections in the fall of 1868 changed the situation on the Council slightly. Island voters rejected supporters of Confederation, including de Cosmos. Seymour, who had rigged the results by enfranchising aliens and non-property owners, said support for Confederation was not universal. He did not report that Confederation supporters swept the election on the Mainland and that the press uniformly favoured Confederation. Among the Mainland members elected was John Robson. Another was Dr. Robert William Weir Carrall, a native of Woodstock, Upper Canada, who practised medicine in Barkerville, who had said: "We will span the continent with a cordon of thinking that a railroad will follow." In Cariboo, Confederation was the main election issue.[30] Seymour's appointees, however, still dominated the Legislative Council. On 17 February

Robert William Weir Carrall
Member of the Legislative Council, BC

11 MARCH 1870

" Who, I ask, are Confederates? The people most unquestionably; and could we, the people of this Colony, ever have made Confederation a successful issue unless it had been taken up by Government? "

CONFEDERATION QUOTE 7.2
Quotation from British Columbia, Legislative Council, 11 March 1870
Photograph by Topley Studio, from Library and Archives Canada, PA-026366

1869, the Council resolved, eleven to five, that Confederation was not desirable, "even if practicable," and urged Britain not to take any decisive steps towards union.[31]

According to Donald Creighton, British Columbia was "a mere speck on... [Macdonald's] mental horizon" until he concluded the agreement to purchase Rupert's Land from the Hudson's Bay Company in April 1869.[32] Carrall and others, including Seelye, kept Macdonald aware of pro-Confederation sentiment in British Columbia. In May 1869, Macdonald asked the Colonial Office to recall Seymour because "a good man" was "needed at the helm" in British Columbia. Such a man was Anthony Musgrave who worked hard, albeit unsuccessfully, for Confederation in Newfoundland.[33] The recall was unnecessary; Seymour had already requested a medical leave. While touring the coast, he died at Bella Coola on 10 June 1869.[34] News of his death reached Victoria on June 14 and was immediately cabled to London. The next day, the Colonial Office informed British Columbians that Musgrave was their new governor.

Musgrave arrived in August with instructions that the Colonial Office understood that the "prevailing opinion" in British Columbia favoured Confederation and, when appropriate, he should inform the people that Her Majesty's Government favoured it.[35] Musgrave found support for Confederation on "fair and equitable terms." The New Westminster City Council, for example, formally welcomed him as "a warm supporter of the great scheme of Confederation."[36] Musgrave published his instructions in the *Government Gazette* on 20 October 1869. Some legislative councillors resented their publication before presentation to the Council and were offended by an unnamed Canadian cabinet minister, likely Tilley, who wrote to a British Columbian, likely Seelye, that "Canada expects to lose money for some years by the admission of British Columbia, and is prepared to deal most liberally with her."[37]

The main opponents of Confederation were colonial officials who feared losing their jobs and farmers who worried that the Canadian tariff would not protect them from American imports. Most British immigrants, Musgrave observed, were indifferent, and only non-British subjects preferred Annexation. Musgrave won the Council over to Confederation by assuring officials of positions in the Canadian or provincial government and about pensions. He also appointed two elected members of the Legislative Council, Drs. Carrall and Helmcken, to his Executive Council.

Musgrave privately told Helmcken that Her Majesty's government favoured Confederation, but desired it to "be brought about by the desire of B. Columbians . . . that no force shall be exercised in the Council or the Legislature. . . . The Canadian Government wants B.C. to join—these [Her Majesty's government and Canada] are afraid that B.C. may, if left alone, choose to join the U.S. and the annexation cry makes them anxious."[38]

Musgrave and his executive then drafted the terms of union. They had little to guide them, apart from the terms granted to other provinces.[39] Because Musgrave had broken his leg, Philip Hankin, the Colonial Secretary, read the speech opening the Legislative Council session on 15 February 1870. It advised that "careful consideration" of union with Canada could no "longer be deferred with courtesy to Her Majesty's Government, or advantage to the Colony . . . on certain terms, which . . . would not be difficult to arrange, this Colony may derive substantial benefit from such an Union." Musgrave proposed to add more elected members to the Council, but did not think what is "commonly called 'Responsible Government'" suited a "community so young."[40]

Before the debate began, Musgrave informed the Governor General of Canada that the terms would be passed "as it will be pressed as a measure of the Government" because of "much divided" opinion among the elected members of the Council. He warned that "no important modification would obtain acquiescence" and that the Canadians must be "prepared to be liberal if they desire Union."[41]

Debating Terms of Union

On 9 March 1870, the debate on the draft terms or what Attorney-General Henry Crease described as "Confederation or no Confederation" began. No one seriously questioned the idea of Confederation, but the Council debated the details for eleven days.[42] Based on time spent, responsible government was the most contentious issue. Few opposed the principle; the question was timing. Should it be a *sine qua non* of union or should it be deferred until the population was larger and British Columbia was more ready for it? Robson claimed that if responsible government were not granted, British Columbia might see an uprising as had recently occurred at Red River. More representative was Carrall who called responsible government "the wisest and best form of government, but it is too cumbrous

John Sebastian Helmcken
Member of the Legislative Council, BC

9 MARCH 1870

Confederation Quote 7.3
Quotation from British Columbia, Legislative Council, 9 March 1870
Photograph courtesy of the Royal BC Museum and Archives, Image A-01351

> Confederation would make the Dominion territorially greater, but would, in case of war, be a source of weakness. It is people, not territory, that makes a country strong and powerful. To be strong, the union must be of people, and in my opinion that condition is wanting.

for this colony,"[43] with its small and scattered population. The Council agreed that the constitution of British Columbia's Legislature should remain until changed under the authority of the BNA Act. This meant, as Helmcken and others observed, "the people can have responsible government when they want it."[44]

The tariff was controversial. Helmcken warned the Canadian tariff would ruin farmers and "deprive the Government of the power of regulating and encouraging those interests" upon which the colony's prosperity depended."[45] Truich replied that Confederation would benefit Canada only if it was advantageous to British Columbia and British Columbia could have a special tariff.[46] That won over the Council.[47]

Financial terms were important. The draft terms proposed that Canada should assume the debts and liabilities of British Columbia of slightly over a million dollars; provide the debt allowance to provinces whose per capita debt was less than average; make an annual grant of $35,000, and give a subsidy of eighty cents per person based on a population of one hundred and twenty thousand. No one knew the size of the population. Many speakers speculated that the number was closer to forty thousand. Helmcken took credit for the idea of calculating the financial terms on the basis of a fictional number of people by a complicated formula based on the customs revenue.[48] Truich, who helped to draft the terms, explained that the cost of living in British Columbia was higher than in Canada and inflating the population would account for "undeveloped resources." (Robson noted that a population of one hundred and twenty thousand would mean more representation in Parliament.)[49] Henry Holbrook, of New Westminster, a magistrate and official member, rightly observed there was "no objection to getting all the money we can from Canada."[50]

That one day Canada would link British Columbia's seaboard with the rest of the country by rail was understood. The terms, however, simply asked Canada to "use all means" in its power to complete a railway "at the earliest possible date." Surveys should begin immediately and, beginning three years after Union Canada should spend at least a million dollars a year on building the line from the seaboard towards the railway system of Canada.[51] Foretelling later debates was a discussion of routes and a terminus, and doubts of Canada's ability and willingness to build the railway. The term was adopted after a relatively short debate. In the meantime, the terms only called for a subsidized passenger and mail steamship service to

Puget Sound and San Francisco and, within three years, the completion of a coach road from the main trunk road of British Columbia to Fort Garry. Terms such as urging Great Britain for a loan to help pay for a graving dock and the continued maintenance of the Esquimalt naval base, making a geological survey, and encouraging the development of a volunteer force passed with little or no debate.

The draft terms made no provision for Indigenous Peoples. Their numbers had declined sharply after approximately a third of them died of smallpox in 1862.[52] Given that the total population was estimated at forty thousand (including the Chinese), the estimated thirty thousand "Indians" were the majority.[53] No one considered them part of the body politic and no one consulted them. In the printed debates, the two motions relating to Indigenous Peoples occupy just over one of 131 pages. Holbrook asked that the terms specify the ability of Indigenous Peoples to occupy the land and enjoy equal protection of the law. Robson agreed that they should be properly cared for. Asserting that Canada's Indigenous policy was considered good, but "our own policy is not worthy of the name," he proposed extending Canadian policy to British Columbia and having it establish the "necessary agencies" for the "efficient administration of Indian affairs." "We should," he declared, "let the Indian mind at rest and let them feel that Confederation will be a greater boon to them than to the white population." Robson withdrew his amendment, but despite Helmcken's warning that "if the Indians are to be stuck in reservations, there will be a disturbance," the Council defeated Holbrook's motion twenty to one.[54] No clause relating to Indigenous Peoples went to Ottawa.

Finally, the Council agreed to pay for a delegation, to be chosen by Musgrave, to negotiate Union in Ottawa. Trutch, its unofficial leader, represented the "officials" who had opposed Confederation but who had been converted to the cause. His personal interests straddled Island and Mainland. Carrall represented the Mainland and had always favoured Confederation. Helmcken, who represented the Island, had consistently opposed Confederation.[55] The rail journey through mountains from San Francisco convinced him that Confederation was practical.[56]

At a dinner in Ottawa, the Governor General told the British Columbians: "They want you and British Columbia in very badly." The delegates found that the cabinet "knew as much of the subject as we did." Together they went through the terms, explaining reasons and answering

Fig 7.1 Using the symbolism of trains, the artist Robert J. Banks imagined British Columbia delegates Dr. J.S. Helmcken, Dr. R.W.W. Carrall, and J.W. Trutch arriving in Ottawa. Image PDP00488 by Robert Banks, courtesy of the Royal BC Museum and Archives.

questions. Cabinet ministers warned they could only offer what Parliament would accept. Cabinet members and prominent people in Montreal, however, told the delegates that a railway was needed to keep the country together. The railway to British Columbia would be an extension of the railway to Fort Garry; the difficult journey of Col. Wolseley and his men had proven its need. Canada's concern was how to pay for it. When Tilley asked, Helmcken replied: "Make everybody smoke a couple of cigars a day and take a glass or two of whisky, the duties on those will pay the interest on the outlay!" Helmcken did not know that Tilley strongly opposed liquor and tobacco.[57]

During a meeting with the cabinet, Trutch, who had surveyed much of the interior, explained how the railway could be built through the mountains and along the Fraser River; Carrall spoke of the interior, and, with Helmcken, sketched how the railway might come to Vancouver Island. The Canadians sensibly would not specify a route or terminus until the surveys were done. They would not guarantee to spend at least a million dollars a year on construction since they planned to have a private contractor build it. It is not clear if Cartier,[58] Trutch, or someone else suggested beginning construction within two years and completing it within ten. The British Columbians agreed to rely on Canada's honour "to fulfill the treaty" and dropped the demand for a wagon road.[59]

Devising financial terms took time. No one believed that British Columbia had a population of one hundred and twenty thousand. The cabinet generously conceded there might be sixty thousand residents, but Francis Hincks, the Minister of Finance, knew that British Columbia needed an annual subsidy of $150,000 to balance its books. Cartier then had the "brilliant idea" that British Columbia surrender land to subsidize the railway in return for annual compensation.[60]

Probably at Trutch's suggestion,[61] Ottawa inserted Article Thirteen concerning Indigenous Peoples. Members of Parliament did not question it.[62] Reminiscent of Robson's idea, it provided that Canada have charge of Indigenous Peoples, manage lands reserved for them, and continue "a policy as liberal as that hitherto pursued by the British Columbia Government." The clause did not benefit Indigenous Peoples. British Columbia's "Indian policy" was mainly creating reserves. The Chief Commissioner of Lands and Works, J.W. Trutch, who was in charge from 1864 to 1871, believing that Indigenous Peoples had no right to the lands they claimed, kept the reserves small.[63]

Several issues were contentious. Canada was unwilling to set a precedent of a province having its own tariff. The solution was a compromise. British Columbia could retain its own tariff until the railway was built. Similarly, Canada would not assist with the dry dock lest other provinces want one. Another compromise was that for ten years, Canada would guarantee the interest on a loan to build it. Canada said a lunatic asylum was a local responsibility and sailors could be cared for in ordinary hospitals so a marine hospital was unnecessary, but it was obliged to build a penitentiary. As for responsible government, British Columbia could adopt it at any time after Confederation.[64] Helmcken recalled, "The Council yielded nearly everything asked for—indeed we told them we had come to get the terms proposed or nothing. Everyone was courteous and always open in private to learn or discuss."[65]

With the terms agreed upon, the British Columbians went their separate ways. Only Helmcken returned immediately to Victoria. He was cautioned to say nothing about the terms beyond, "everything asked for has been granted" before delivering them to Musgrave. Musgrave, who learned of the terms by telegram, advised the Colonial Office that if Canada promised a railway, "scarcely any other question" would be as difficult, but without "the certainty of overland communication through British territory" in a reasonable time, he was not confident that "the community will decide upon Union."[66]

When the terms were made public at the end of August, Helmcken was disappointed by the response that the terms "were too good to be true," and the lack of enthusiasm in Victoria except in the press. In November over five hundred Victoria residents signed a petition asking that the terms state that the transcontinental railway terminate at Victoria or Esquimalt. At New Westminster, a public meeting deprecated this action as "hurtful to the cause of Confederation" and expressed perfect satisfaction with the terms, "feeling sure" that the Fraser Valley "presents such natural advantages for the route of the Transcontinental Railway as will not be overlooked."[67]

As promised, Musgrave reconstituted the Executive Council so members elected in November 1870 were the majority. Confederation was the main issue. All of the elected members, who included de Cosmos and Robson, favoured Confederation, as did some defeated candidates.[68] When the Council met in January 1871, Trutch explained the financial terms and the railway; Helmcken seconded the motion. It had been determined that the terms were a Treaty and so must be accepted as a package.[69] No one else spoke; the motion for Confederation passed unanimously.

Such unanimity was not present in the Canadian parliament. The Throne Speech on 15 February 1871 reported that British Columbia had sought admission to the union. Members would be asked to provide funds for exploring and surveying a route for "an Interoceanic Railway" and would be shown "all the papers" to justify extending Canada's boundaries "from the shores of the *Atlantic Ocean* in the one side, to the shores of the *Pacific* on the other."[70] Macdonald expected a hard fight in Parliament on the grounds that the terms were a burden on the Dominion, but he was in Washington negotiating on the fisheries.[71]

In introducing the bill to admit British Columbia, Cartier quoted Lord Lytton, who when creating the colony of British Columbia in 1858, hoped that British North America might "be ultimately peopled in an unbroken chain from the Atlantic to the Pacific." Cartier said that the arrangement was like a treaty and, having been approved by British Columbia's Legislature, could not be amended. Anticipating controversy about the railway, he advised that a private company, financed mainly by land grants, would build it so there would be little charge on the exchequer. He explained how the size of British Columbia's population was determined and urged haste since growth would increase the amount of the per capita subsidy.[72]

The debate was bitter. Many amendments were proposed and defeated. Alexander Morris, the Minister of Inland Revenue, called it the government's "worst fight" since Confederation.[73] Alexander Mackenzie, the opposition leader, moved that while the House would consider reasonable terms, the terms were "so unreasonable and so unjust to Canada," they should not be approved. Mackenzie's motion was defeated sixty-eight to eighty-six.[74] Opposition members complained of the unknown cost of the railway (Timothy Anglin quoted the *Colonist* as saying the proposed route was through a "sea of mountains"[75]); the ten-year time limit on its completion;[76] and the burden on Canadian finances.[77] No one, however, objected to British Columbia becoming a Canadian province. On 1 April 1871, the bill passed.[78] The Senate considered similar issues and approved it four days later.

In British Columbia, the government proclaimed 20 July 1871 a public holiday. It provided no funds for celebrations so the festivities relied on volunteer organizers. In Barkerville, where Canadian sentiment was strong, residents had celebrated on July 1 with decorated buildings, a royal salute at noon, and an afternoon concert.[79] In New Westminster, "flags of every shape and nationality floated from every possible pole" as families enjoyed sunshine and a programme of sports. An evening ball rounded out the day.[80] Without financial aid, the committee planning a celebration in Victoria disbanded. Nevertheless, at midnight on July 19 the fire department rang its alarm bells, scaring people who rushed downtown where they saw an impromptu display of fireworks. According to the *Colonist*, at midnight "there were manifestations of great rejoicing in the city. Bells were rung, guns fired, blue lights and Roman candles burned and crackers snapped ... Everybody seemed happy and jolly and the manifestations were kept up long." Reflecting the interest of John Robson in responsible government, it observed, "[t]hey were celebrating the birth of Liberty." During the day, others raised flags of several countries, including

Canada, the H.M.S. *Zealous* fired a salute, and the Mechanics Institute sponsored a picnic with foot races, dancing, refreshment, and an "address on Confederation" by Amor de Cosmos.[81]

Save for a passing comment in the *Cariboo Sentinel*, published in Barkerville by Robert Holloway who had come overland in 1862 from Canada West, that "a new nation has been born," editorial comment in the province's four newspapers emphasized the practical advantages of Confederation, not sentimental attachments to Canada. Both the *Victoria Daily Standard*, of which Amor de Cosmos was a proprietor, and the *Colonist*, whose new editor was John Robson, cited the presence of surveyors from the Geological Survey of Canada and the railway as manifestations of Canada's bona fides in fulfilling the terms of Confederation. The *Standard* neatly summarized the main advantages: "The new constitution grants to the people self-government; so with the management of our own affairs in our own hands, and a surplus revenue of $200,000, with a railway and steamship lines, we are indeed glad to welcome Confederation and cheerfully become Canadians."[82] Yet, the *Mainland Guardian* after admonishing Canadians that "young" British Columbia required "nourishment to develop our infant limbs," advised that they had "added the brightest jewel to their crown."[83] British Columbians were a proud people who, though manoeuvred into Confederation by the British and Canadian governments, had entered largely on their own "fair and equitable" terms.

Further Reading

Still the best overview of British Columbia's entry into Confederation is in chapters 8 and 9 of Margaret A. Ormsby, *British Columbia: A History* (Toronto: Macmillan, 1958, rev. ed. 1971). The only book specifically on the subject is W. George Shelton, ed. *British Columbia & Confederation* (Victoria: University of Victoria, 1967), a collection of essays written mainly by former students of the University of Victoria. The British Columbia debates on the terms of Union have been reprinted in James E. Hendrickson, ed. *Journals of the Legislative Council of British Columbia, 1866–1871* (Victoria: Provincial Archives of British Columbia, 1980). The memoirs of one of the key participants, Dr. John Helmcken, including his diary of the Confederation negotiations, have been published as *The*

Reminiscences of Doctor John Sebastian Helmcken, edited by Dorothy Blakey Smith (Vancouver: University of British Columbia Press, 1975). Although First Nations formed the majority of British Columbia's population during the 1860s and 1870s, they were not consulted about Confederation. In addition to providing a few suggestive comments on Confederation and the First Peoples of British Columbia, Cole Harris in *Making Native Space* (Vancouver: University of British Columbia Press, 2002), provides an excellent overview of the land question with two chapters devoted to the period around that time. The views of Joseph Trutch, one of the delegates to Ottawa and the man largely responsible for Indian land policy before and after Confederation, are explained in Robin Fisher, "Joseph Trutch and Indian Land Policy," *BC Studies* 12 (Winter 1971–72): 3–33.

NOTES

1. Donald Creighton, *John A. Macdonald: The Old Chieftain* (Toronto: Macmillan, 1955), 70–71.
2. Quoted in J.M.S. Careless, *Brown of the Globe: The Statesman of Confederation, 1860–1880* (Toronto: Macmillan, 1963), 164.
3. F.W. Howay, "The Attitude of Governor Seymour Towards Confederation," *Transactions of the Royal Society of Canada RSC Trans. 3rd ser., XIV* (1920): 33.
4. Cited in Margaret A. Ormsby, "Frederick Seymour: the Forgotten Governor," *BC Studies* 22 (Summer 1974): 13.
5. Willard E. Ireland, "The Annexation Petition of 1869," *British Columbia Historical Quarterly* (hereafter BCHQ) IV (October 1940), 269.
6. Susan Dickinson Scott, "The Attitude of the Colonial Governors and Officials Towards Confederation," in *British Columbia & Confederation*, ed. W. George Shelton (Victoria: University of Victoria, 1967), 147.
7. *The Reminiscences of Doctor John Sebastian Helmcken,* ed. Dorothy Blakey Smith (Vancouver: University of British Columbia Press, 1975), 242, 253.
8. Helmcken, *Reminiscences*, 247. See also: *Victoria Daily Standard,* 17 July 1871. The latter comment was a serious insult. There was considerable antipathy to the Chinese in colonial British Columbia largely because of a belief that as sojourners who sent most of their earnings to China, they did not contribute to the colony's development. For details, see Patricia E. Roy, *A White Man's Province: British Columbia Politicians and Chinese and Japanese Immigrants* (Vancouver: University of British Columbia Press, 1989), ch. 1.
9. H. Robert Kendrick, "Amor De Cosmos and Confederation," in Shelton, *British Columbia and Confederation*, 68; Robert A. J. McDonald and H. Keith Ralston, "Amor De Cosmos," *Dictionary of Canadian Biography* (hereafter *DCB*), vol. 12 (Toronto: University of Toronto

Press, 1990), 239–30, also available online at: http://www.biographi.ca/en/bio/de_cosmos_amor_12E.html.

10 McDonald and Ralston, "Amor De Cosmos," 240; Kendrick, "Amor De Cosmos," 80.

11 *British Columbian*, 15 October 1862.

12 Legislative Council, *Journals*, 18 March 1867 reprinted in James E. Hendrickson, *Journals of the Legislative Council of British Columbia, 1866–1871* (Victoria: Provincial Archives of British Columbia, 1980), 73.

13 Helmcken, *Reminiscences*, 239–40.

14 Seymour to the Duke of Buckingham and Chandos, 24 September 1867 in Great Britain, Parliament, House of Commons, *Papers on the Union of British Columbia with the Dominion of Canada*, 1869), 390.

15 Quoted in Howay, "The Attitude of Governor Seymour," 36.

16 *Colonist*, 31 January 1868.

17 This draws on Howay, "The Attitude of Governor Seymour," 37.

18 James Trimble et al. to the Governor General and Privy Council, Memorial of 29 January 1868 attached to Privy Council Report, 6 March 1868. Printed in *Papers on the Union of British Columbia with the Dominion of Canada* (London: House of Commons, 1869), 6-7.

19 Report of a Committee of the Privy Council, approved by the Governor-General, 6 March 1868, enclosure with Monck to Duke of Buckingham and Chandos, 7 March 1868. Printed in *Papers on the Union of British Columbia with the Dominion of Canada*, 5.

20 Legislative Council, 21 March 1868, in Hendrickson, *Journals*, 110.

21 Margaret A. Ormsby, "Frederick Seymour: The Forgotten Governor," *BC Studies* 22 (Summer 1974): 17; Howay, "The Attitude of Governor Seymour," 38.

22 Howay, "The Attitude of Governor Seymour," 39.

23 Legislative Council, *Journals*, 24 April 1868, in Hendrickson, *Journals*, 143–45.

24 Legislative Council, *Journals*, 1 May 1868, in Hendrickson, *Journals*, 164.

25 Quoted in Howay, "The Attitude of Governor Seymour," 44–45.

26 Helmcken, *Reminiscences*, 246.

27 Howay, "The Attitude of Governor Seymour," 45.

28 Legislative Council, *Journals*, 17 December 1868, in Hendrickson, *Journals*, 172.

29 Legislative Council, *Journals*, 21 December 1868, in Hendrickson, *Journals*, 175.

30 Dorothy Blakey Smith, "Carrall, Robert William Weir," *DCB*, vol. 10 (Toronto: University of Toronto Press, 1972), 138–39, also available online at: http://www.biographi.ca/en/bio/carrall_robert_william_weir_10E.html.

31 Legislative Council, *Journals*, 17 February 1869, in Hendrickson, *Journals*, 226. Seymour's covering letter to the Colonial Office noted that the difficulties with union were "almost insuperable and the advantages remote": Howay, "Seymour," 42.

32 The uprising in Red River that began in November 1869 delayed that arrangement, but did not seriously interfere with the arrangements for British Columbia.

33 Macdonald to Young, 25 May 1869, Macdonald Papers quoted in Creighton, *John A. Macdonald*, 35.
34 Ormsby, "Seymour," 18, n. 62.
35 Granville to Musgrave, 14 August 1869. Printed in *Papers on the Union of British Columbia with the Dominion of Canada*, 30-31.
36 *Colonist*, 11 September 1869.
37 *Colonist*, 11 September 1869.
38 Helmcken, *Reminiscences*, 252.
39 Helmcken, *Reminiscences*, 254. Helmcken claimed that his draft formed the basis of much of the Executive Council's discussion.
40 Musgrave to the Legislative Council, 15 February 1870 reprinted in Hendrickson, *Journals*, 271–72.
41 Musgrave to Governor-General, 25 February 1870, *Papers Relating to British Columbia*.
42 The debate on responsible government occupied twenty-seven printed pages, and was often mentioned in discussions of other terms.
43 Legislative Council, *Debates*, 18 March 1870, reprinted in Hendrickson, *Journals*, 526 and 527, reproduced by *The Confederation Debates*, http://hcmc.uvic.ca/confederation/en/lgBCLC_1870-03-18.html.
44 Legislative Council, *Debates*, 21 March 1870, reprinted in Hendrickson, *Journals*, 531, 536, reproduced by *The Confederation Debates*, http://hcmc.uvic.ca/confederation/en/lgBCLC_1870-03-21.html.
45 Legislative Council, *Debates*, 9 March 1870, reprinted in Hendrickson, *Journals*, 449, reproduced by *The Confederation Debates*, http://hcmc.uvic.ca/confederation/en/lgBCLC_1870-03-09.html.
46 Legislative Council, *Debates*, 10 March 1870, reprinted in Hendrickson, *Journals*, 459, reproduced by *The Confederation Debates*, http://hcmc.uvic.ca/confederation/en/lgBCLC_1870-03-10.html.
47 Legislative Council, *Debates*, 24 March 1870, reprinted in Hendrickson, *Journals*, 566, reproduced by *The Confederation Debates*, http://hcmc.uvic.ca/confederation/en/lgBCLC_1870-03-24.html.
48 Helmcken, *Reminiscences*, 251 and 262.
49 Legislative Council, *Debates*, 14 March 1870, reprinted in Hendrickson, *Journals*, 487 and 495, reproduced by *The Confederation Debates*, http://hcmc.uvic.ca/confederation/en/lgBCLC_1870-03-14.html.
50 Legislative Council, *Debates*, 16 March 1870, reprinted in Hendrickson, *Journals*, 498, reproduced by *The Confederation Debates*, http://hcmc.uvic.ca/confederation/en/lgBCLC_1870-03-16.html.
51 Legislative Council, *Debates*, 16 March 1870, reprinted in Hendrickson, *Journals*, 506, reproduced by *The Confederation Debates*, http://hcmc.uvic.ca/confederation/en/lgBCLC_1870-03-16.html. The idea of a railway to link with the railways of Canada came from Trutch: Helmcken, *Reminiscences*, 255.

52 Wilson Duff, *The Indian History of British Columbia* (Victoria: Provincial Museum of British Columbia, 1969), 42–43.

53 De Cosmos cited these numbers, 14 March 1870, Hendrickson, *Journals,* 488.

54 Legislative Council, *Debates,* 23 March 1870 reprinted in Hendrickson, *Journals,* 567–68, reproduced by *The Confederation Debates,* http://hcmc.uvic.ca/confederation/en/lgBCLC_1870-03-23.html.

55 Musgrave asked Robson to serve on the delegation, but for reasons of private business, Robson did not accept, *British Columbian,* 8 July 1882, cited in F.W. Howay, "Governor Musgrave and Confederation," *Transactions of the Royal Society of Canada,* Section II, (1921): 25.

56 Helmcken, *Reminiscences,* 259.

57 Helmcken, *Reminiscences,* 260, 352, 351, and 261.

58 In A. I. Silver, *The French-Canadian Idea of Confederation, 1864–1900* (Toronto: University of Toronto, 1997), 71-72. Silver says that Cartier proposed the time limit, but does not provide documentation to support this.

59 Helmcken, *Reminiscences,* 355 and 353.

60 Helmcken, *Reminiscences,* 262 and 349.

61 Robin A. Fisher, *Contact and Conflict: Indian-European Relations in British Columbia, 1774–1890* (Vancouver: University of British Colombia Press, 1992, 2nd ed.), 176.

62 Cartier told Parliament that some public lands had been set aside for Indigenous Peoples, "the only guarantee that was necessary for the future good treatment of the Aborigines was the manner in which they had been treated in the past" (Canada, Parliament, *House of Commons Debates* [hereafter HCD], 28 March 1871, 278). A. T. Galt in dealing with the number of BC's Members of Parliament, said "these aborigines should not be placed on an equal footing with the whites for the purpose of framing the financial basis of the Union. They could not be regarded as the equal of the whites for revenue purposes at least": *HCD,* 28 March 1871, 279.

63 See Robin A. Fisher, "Joseph Trutch and Indian Land Policy," *BC Studies* 12 (Winter 1971–72): 3–33.

64 The Canadian government named Trutch, who opposed responsible government, as the first lieutenant-governor. On taking his appointment, Trutch said it was his duty to "ensure its successful working" but would not introduce responsible government until after a general election. So gradually did Trutch institute responsible government that no precise date, save possibly his calling of Amor de Cosmos to form a government after the McCreight government lost a vote of confidence in 1872, can be given for its introduction: John Tupper Saywell, "'Sir Joseph Trutch,' British Columbia's First Lieutenant-Governor," *BCHQ* XIX (January-April 1955): 71–92.

65 Helmcken, *Reminiscences,* 263.

66 Musgrave to Colonial Office, 5 April 1870, 4924, CO/38, p. 290, quoted in Howay, "Governor Musgrave," 21.

67 Musgrave to Lisgar, 5 December 1870 and enclosures in. Printed in *Papers Relating to the Proposed Union of British Columbia with the Dominion of Canada,* 18-22.

68 Howay, "Musgrave," 26.
69 Helmcken, *Reminiscences,* 266.
70 *HCD,* 15 February 1871, reproduced by *The Confederation Debates,* http://hcmc.uvic.ca/confederation/en/lgHC_BC_1871-02-15.html.
71 Macdonald to Musgrave, 29 September 1870, quoted in Creighton, *John A. Macdonald,* 74 and 105.
72 *HCD,* 28 March 1871, 277 and 278, reproduced by *The Confederation Debates,* http://hcmc.uvic.ca/confederation/en/lgHC_BC_1871-03-28.html.
73 Morris to Macdonald, 1 April 1871 quoted in Creighton, *Macdonald,* 106.
74 *HCD,* 1 April 1871, 315, reproduced by *The Confederation Debates,* http://hcmc.uvic.ca/confederation/en/lgHC_BC_1871-04-01.html.
75 *HCD,* 30 March 1871, 301, reproduced by *The Confederation Debates,* http://hcmc.uvic.ca/confederation/en/lgHC_BC_1871-03-30.html.
76 Galt, *HCD,* 28 March 1871, 279, reproduced by *The Confederation Debates,* http://hcmc.uvic.ca/confederation/en/lgHC_BC_1871-03-28.html.
77 Jones, *HCD,* 30 March 1871, 298, reproduced by *The Confederation Debates,* http://hcmc.uvic.ca/confederation/en/lgHC_BC_1871-03-30.html; Dorion, HCD, 30 March 1871, 305, reproduced by *The Confederation Debates,* http://hcmc.uvic.ca/confederation/en/lgHC_BC_1871-03-30.html.
78 The published debates do not record any division. The *Colonist* reported that it passed with a majority of only eighteen.
79 *Cariboo Sentinel,* 8 July 1871. In 1871, the Americans at nearby Williams Creek did not hold their traditional July 4 celebrations.
80 *Mainland Guardian,* 18 and 22 July 1871.
81 *Colonist,* 20 July 1871.
82 *Victoria Daily Standard,* 19 and 20 July 1871.
83 *Mainland Guardian,* 21 July 1871.

8

"It is better to have a half loaf than none at all": The Yukon and Confederation

P. WHITNEY LACKENBAUER AND KEN S. COATES

> ... The Yukon was the locale of a fascinating contrast between two different North American political philosophies. The American version stressed local autonomy and the right of settlers to establish their own system of government and frame their own regulations. ... Against this stood the tradition of Canadian administration, sprung from British roots—a tradition of authority, of rules and regulations established from outside, of development controlled and directed in the presumed general, or national, rather than the particular local, or regional, interest.
>
> Morris Zaslow, 1971[1]

The year 1867 represented a political turning point in the history of what would become the Yukon Territory, although few if any one residing in the northwestern corner of what became the Dominion of Canada would have seen it as such. For millennia, Indigenous peoples of the region (mostly Athapaskan or Dene, with Inuit along the Arctic coast and Tlingit and Inland Tlingit people in the southwest corner) followed a subsistence economy rooted in hunting and gathering, with small groups following a seasonal cycle of movement within their traditional territories.² Throughout the region, the resources of the land and rivers (and sea, in the case of Inuit) determined their complex social and political systems, land use patterns, and material culture. There were no rigid boundaries. Following Russian colonization efforts in Russian America (Alaska) as part of a growing fur trade empire in the early nineteenth century, the Anglo-Russian Treaty of 1825 set an international border along the 141st meridian. This was done without any consultation with the local Indigenous Peoples, and it had little practical meaning in Indigenous homelands with little to no European presence. As was the case in many parts of the Canadian North, Hudson's Bay Company fur traders represented the vanguard of European penetration into the region and the first sustained contact with the Indigenous population. With only a handful of Euro-Canadian fur traders (soon joined by a couple of missionaries) in their midst, however, the Indigenous Peoples retained significant power or "agency" in their economic, spiritual, and political affairs through the middle of the nineteenth century.³

After US Secretary of State William H. Seward negotiated the purchase of Alaska from the Russians, the American government quickly made Alaska a military district and imposed laws regulating customs, commerce, and navigation. Speculators, developers, settlers, traders, and frontiersmen began to head North, and an agreement with Tlingit leaders allowed miners to cross the Chilkoot Pass and more easily access the Yukon River valley. By contrast, Canadians showed little interest in the far-flung corners of the fur trade preserve still controlled by the Hudson's Bay Company. Although the re-imagination of the Prairie West as a civilized, agrarian frontier served as a catalyst for the young dominion to purchase Rupert's Land and the North-Western Territory, the distant north remained a remote hinterland far removed from the mental maps of Ottawa politicians. Accordingly, the Canadian government's commitment to the Yukon River valley consisted of a few brief attempts to survey its resources and geography and little else until the mid-1890s.⁴

In the 1880s, gold discoveries—overwhelmingly by American prospectors—along the Yukon River near the international boundary led to the emergence of a small, isolated community at Fortymile that, by geographic happenstance, fell on the Canadian side of the 141st meridian.⁵ The absence of any Canadian official for hundreds of kilometres meant that the community was left to govern itself. When any resident had a grievance, they could call a "miner's meeting" that would bring together the entire community to render a decision based upon "common sense." Although this mechanism did not conform with British law, the miners' meetings served to maintain order on a distant frontier. When William Ogilvie led an official survey party to the region on behalf of the Canadian government in 1887–88, he offered a favourable assessment of this method of local governance. The Canadian government was certainly content to let the miners manage their own affairs, given its preoccupation with more pressing national policies such as completing the Canadian Pacific Railway and settling the southern Prairies. The struggle for responsible government in southern districts of the North-West Territories, discussed by Bill Waiser in his contribution to this volume, paid no attention to the Yukon.

The catalyst for Canadian government action came from two local voices in Fortymile. The owners of the Northwest Trading Company, Fortymile's principal merchant, appealed to the Crown in 1894 for regular law enforcement and a customs collector after being challenged at a local miners' meeting. Furthermore, Anglican missionary William Carpenter Bompas demanded that Ottawa preserve order, expressing particular concern about the effects of liquor supplied by Americans crossing the international boundary on First Nations and, along the Arctic coast, of American whalers wintering at Herschel Island. Ogilvie also began to recommend a more formal Canadian presence to ensure that, in the case of a major gold strike, the growing American influence in the region did not threaten Canadian sovereignty.

The Canadian government acquiesced to Ogilvie's appeals in 1894 when it sent North West Mounted Police Inspector Charles Constantine to investigate. His report revealed that American miners dominated the region and, because they simply carried their supplies and gold to and from the United States directly, Canada was losing thousands of dollars in potential customs duties. Accordingly, Ottawa established the Yukon as a separate district of the North-West Territories the following year and sent Constantine back in to set up a permanent post, impose dominion authority, and establish "law and order among a community of not less than 2000 miners of various nationalities, many of whom have hitherto known no law but that of their own making."[6] Constantine, a customs agent, and eighteen Mounties who arrived in Fortymile immediately asserted control by ending the miners' meetings and registering mining claims. The miners complied, seeking no confrontation with well-armed police, and Canada successfully asserted its first semblances of authority over a territory that would soon face a stampede of outsiders.[7]

The Klondike Gold Rush

The Klondike Gold Rush (1896–99) drew global attention to the Yukon. Although controversy remains about who deserves the credit for finding the first gold in the Klondike in August 1896,[8] the reports of gold lying "thick between the flaky slabs [of rock], like cheese sandwiches" on Rabbit Creek (soon renamed Bonanza Creek) sent shockwaves throughout North America and beyond. Miners from the area quickly staked claims along the full extent of Bonanza and the surrounding creeks, and hundreds of men began to descend on the Yukon from Fortymile mining camps in Alaska, and over the Chilkoot Pass from Juneau and Skagway. That fall and winter, while miners toiled in the muck in hopes of hitting paydirt, a ramshackle, fire-prone town emerged at the junction of the Klondike and Yukon rivers about 14 km from the discovery. Dawson City, conveniently located on the Yukon River, offered an easy day's travel from a major navigable river to the main gold-bearing creeks. By the spring of 1897 about fifteen hundred people resided in the town, and by the summer about thirty-five hundred. The arrival of ships in Seattle and San Francisco carrying the first hauls of gold from the initial rush that July electrified the public imagination and set in motion the "stampede" to the Yukon. Within two years, Dawson would swell to become the largest town in Canada west of Winnipeg.

Politicians and civil servants in Ottawa, increasingly aware of the magnitude of the stampede to the Klondike, hastily responded to the progressively chaotic situation. The Department of the Interior, headed by the energetic power-broker Manitoba Member of Parliament Clifford Sifton (who visited the Yukon in the fall of 1897), bore principal responsibility for determining the Laurier Government's policies in the region and organizing the new Yukon administration.[9] The federal government appointed Major James Morrow Walsh, one of the great figures of the early pioneering days on the Prairies and a retired Mounted Police officer, as its chief executive officer in the Yukon district with the title of "commissioner."

(Major Walsh could not be made "lieutenant-governor"—as had been the case with senior territorial officials in the NWT—because the Yukon was still a District of the North-West Territories, which already had a lieutenant-governor in Regina.) He was charged with coordinating and supervising all the federal employees in the region, including the North-West Mounted Police. Through his special commission from the federal cabinet, Walsh was empowered to alter or amend federal mining regulations under the authority of the Governor in Council without seeking advice or approval of any local council. He exercised this authority to reduce royalties on gold, establish mechanisms to settle disputed claims, and create incentives for miners to prospect in more remote locations.[10] "Although possessing autocratic powers," Territorial Secretary Dr. J.N.E. Brown noted, the commissioner frequently called upon other federally-appointed officials for advice at this time, particularly the judge, the Crown prosecutor, the gold commissioner, and the mining inspector.[11]

Given that the Yukon District still legally fell within the North-West Territories, the territorial government in Regina also cast its attention northward in 1897—and fixated on the possibility of reaping financial rewards from liquor revenues. The NWT government had assumed powers to license and regulate liquor traffic, and since the laws of the Territories applied in the Yukon, the Territorial Executive Council sent its member G.H.V. Bulyea to Dawson City to sell permits. The federal government had assumed the costs of administrating the Yukon, however, and Clifford Sifton (whose department issued liquor permits) disputed the Territorial government's jurisdiction. This created a strong incentive for Ottawa to separate the Yukon Judicial District from the NWT. "Now we stand in the position of having had our authority over-ruled, and our self governing rights invaded," an angry NWT Premier F.W.G. Haultain noted, "and we shall be obliged to protest as strongly as we can against what we consider an unwarrantable and unnecessary diminution of the self governing rights which we were so grateful to you for having procured for the Territories last year." Sifton conceded that Major Walsh's commission was "in some respects ultra vires" [meaning outside the law, in this case of federal jurisdiction], and the parliamentary session of 1898 provided the first opportunity since the gold rush began for the Liberal government in Ottawa to formally legitimize the Yukon as a distinct jurisdiction.[12]

The *Yukon Territory Act*, which received formal assent on 13 June

Fig 8.1 Yukon miners being chased from power by the Yukon Council and Ottawa "monsters." *Dawson Daily*, 19 May 1903.

1898, established the Yukon as a separate territory with the boundaries that the federal cabinet had set for the Yukon Judicial District the previous year and laid out its executive, legislative, and judicial institutions.[13] Speaking in the House of Commons, Sifton explained that he had adopted the philosophy that had guided governments of John A. Macdonald and Alexander Mackenzie in organizing the West a quarter-century earlier, with "the only radical departure" being the absence of "any elective members of the council." He considered the Act an interim measure until the "permanent character" of the community became clearer. He and his government were particularly concerned about the large number of Americans in the area, a demographic and political force of considerable potential consequence. In his view, a system of popular representation would be premature, "especially as all the information we possess goes to show that perhaps nine out of ten persons in the district are aliens, totally unacquainted with our method of representation, and the population will in all probability be a very nomadic character, at least for the present." Later on, "as a matter of course, if a permanent population establishes itself in the district," he anticipated that the federal government would provide "some representative system similar in principle to what was given to the North-West Territories."[14]

The head of the Yukon administration was the commissioner, appointed by, instructed by, and responsible to the federal Cabinet. Although this title did not have the royal connotation associated with the position of "lieutenant-governor" used in the other provinces and territories, retaining it was not intended to suggest a lesser status for the Yukon than for the NWT.[15] Indeed, historian L.H. Thomas observed that "the powers of the commissioner were unprecedented—in addition to heading the local administration he was given authority over all officers of the federal government in the territory, because of the obstacles to communication with Ottawa. He was also given the traditional power to reserve approval of any ordnance and send it to Ottawa for decision by the federal cabinet."[16] Walsh, who had quarrelled with the police and others over the previous year, resigned and was succeeded by William Ogilvie, who knew the country, was popular with the miners, and had solid political connections (as the uncle, by marriage, of Clifford Sifton).[17]

The commissioner presided over an appointed territorial council that held similar powers to the lieutenant-governor and legislative council of the North-West Territories in the period up to 1875. Commissioner Walsh had recommended a council consisting of three appointed and three elected members, but the federal government rejected the elective principle. Instead, the cabinet in Ottawa would appoint all of the members of a territorial council of up to six members. The Council consisted of the commissioner, the NWMP superintendent, the Territorial court judge (ex-officio, meaning by virtue of his status), the gold commissioner, the registrar, and the legal adviser. In Sifton's view, this paternalistic policy was both necessary and fit within the British tradition. An appointed council, designed to implement Ottawa's vision and impose a certain form of government, prevented it from serving as a channel through which the local "grass roots" (predominantly Americans) could voice their grievances to Ottawa. "The effect was rather like trying to clamp a lid on a simmering pot without a safety valve," Ken S. Coates and William Morrison described. "The members of the council . . . neither represented nor understood the problems of the miners, labourers, and others. The steam had to escape somewhere, and Sifton's efforts to cap it simply led to heightened frustration on both sides."[18]

Under the provisions of the 1898 Yukon Act, the Governor in Council (the federal cabinet in Ottawa) retained the power to make laws for the general "peace, order and good government" of the territory. The Yukon Commissioner in Council was granted "the same powers to make ordinances for the government of the territory" as the lieutenant-governor and legislative assembly in the North-West Territories at that time, except insofar as the federal cabinet decided to limit them. The Act required that the Yukon administration forward all of its ordinances to Parliament in Ottawa within ten days, with the federal cabinet having the power to disallow any of them within two years. Neither the territorial administration nor the federal cabinet could impose any tax or duty above $100, alter or repeal any punishment enacted by Parliament, or appropriate any Canadian public land, money, or property without Parliamentary authority. Existing criminal and civil laws, as well as NWT ordinances, remained in force unless explicitly amended or repealed.[19] Both levels of government would appoint certain administrative officials, paid from federal revenues (accrued from gold royalties, mining licenses, land sales, timber fees, customs duties, and liquor imports) and from territorial revenues (generated from retail liquor licenses and taxes for lawyers, auctioneers, ferry operators, and dance halls). Although this model resembled the *North-West Territories Act* from 1875, whereby the territories were governed partly from Ottawa and partly from capitals within the territorial borders, the Yukon Act did not provide for the development of representative institutions. "Feared by federal authorities because of the frontier and cosmopolitan nature of the mining community," historian David Morrison explained, "this aspect of political evolution had to await a response to organized pressure from within the Klondike basin."[20]

Pushing for Responsible Government

By excluding any direct participation by Euro-Canadian residents of the territory in formulating policy, the regime established through the 1898 Yukon Act provoked a strong local backlash. Immediately after the legislation came into force, miners held mass meetings and began agitating for elected representatives in the territorial council as well as representation in federal parliament. "The pre-1897 style of constitutional agitation in the North-West Territories reappeared," L.H. Thomas observed, with four competing newspapers (three American- and one Canadian-owned; two with anti-Ottawa editorial policies) reporting on incompetence and blatant corruption by Liberal patronage appointees, disputes over federal royalties on gold exports, and controversial new mining regulations—and the absence of meaningful self-government in the territory.[21] One angry editorial in the *Klondike Nugget* asserted that Ottawa treated Yukoners akin to "underdeveloped races which have given unmistakeable evidence of the lack of those qualities of self-government which have made our own race famous," insisting that Anglo-Canadians needed a vote—as did Americans who deserved it "by virtue of their prominence in opening up the country."[22]

Mass protests through miners' and citizens' committee meetings, newspaper pressure, and Conservative opposition members in parliament soon prompted reforms to territorial governance.[23] The 1899 amendments to the Yukon Act provided for two locally-elected members, with two-year terms, to join four federally-appointed officials on the Yukon Council. (Only "natural born and naturalized male British subjects 21 years of age who had resided continuously in the territory for a year" could vote—thus excluding women and status Indians.) The commissioner and appointed officials remained the executive arm of the Yukon Territorial Government, but the commissioner now presided over council meetings thus "ensuring, by his presence, a measure of co-ordination between executive and legislative functions."[24] The following year, the Yukon Council opened its meetings to the public for the first time and adopted some aspects of parliamentary procedure. "With the Council functioning as a legislative institution in open session and as a cabinet *in camera*," Yukon historian Linda Johnson notes, "the Yukon was poised for its first elections [in 1900] and the next important step towards more democratic government."[25]

With the addition of the elected members, the Yukon Council became an active legislative body, with members sending petitions and protests to Ottawa in hopes of inspiring federal action on issues important to territorial residents. Commissioner James H. Ross, who replaced Ogilvie in early 1901, promoted and secured legislation to provide for municipal institutions in Dawson and Bonanza (Grand Forks), thus reducing the burden on Council to provide local services.[26] Ross also convinced Ottawa to pass a series of amendments to the Yukon Act in May 1902, increasing the number of elected members on the Council to five and clarifying various legislative and judicial powers. *An Act Respecting the Representation of the Yukon Territory* received Royal Assent at the same time, specifying that the Yukon, as an electoral district, would return one member to the House of Commons. Although Ross resigned in July 1902 after suffering a stroke, he was duly elected the Yukon's first Member of Parliament before the end of the year.[27]

The Yukon Act made no mention of, or provision for, Yukon's Indigenous Peoples who, as a small minority of the territorial population during the gold rush era, were pushed to the political margins in the same way as they were across Canada. Several provisions of the federal *Indian Act* of 1876 and subsequent amendments applied to the Yukon, although the absence of any treaties with the First Nations and the lack of official Indian reserves meant that federal officials tended to ignore Indigenous Peoples rather than actively impose assimilationist agendas in the region. Where the government signed Treaty No. 8 in what is now northern Alberta and northeast British Columbia, ostensibly to clear the way for Klondike travellers, the reality is that the government was concerned that treaties and a reserve might preserve valuable gold bearing ground for the First Nations. While some Indigenous People tried to capitalize off of the gold rush activity as woodcutters, labourers, or working on steamboats, those who did not live along the main Yukon River corridor largely continued their traditional ways. Seeing the negative impacts that the influx of outsiders wrought on indigenous homelands, Chief (and business man) Jim Boss (Kishwoot) of present-day Ta'an Kwach'an and surrounding area retained a Whitehorse lawyer to write strong letters to the Superintendent

General of Indian Affairs in Ottawa and to the Commissioner of the Yukon in 1901 and 1902, explaining his people's concerns about the alienation of their lands and resources and their rights to control their own affairs and governance. Ottawa turned down his request to initiate land claim or treaty negotiations within the Yukon Territory. Yukon First Nations would have to wait for more than seven decades before the federal government agreed to initiate such a process.[28]

The politics of frustration continued amongst the non-Indigenous population of the territory as well. In 1903, the elected members of the Yukon Council began to advocate for responsible government—meaning (in a Canadian context) an executive that is dependent upon the support of an elected assembly rather than simply on the Crown.[29] This reform current was subsumed by concerted and virulent opposition by virtually everyone in the Territory over the "Treadgold Concession"— the federal cabinet's decision to grant control over much of the richest gold-bearing creeks, as well as special water rights, to a mining syndicate headed by British entrepreneur A.N.C. Treadgold that sought to introduce large-scale, mechanized mining to the region.[30] The situation threatened the Stampeder identity, forged around the individual placer miner, and reflected the declining economic prospects that jeopardized their communities. Adding fuel to the political fire, Frederick Tennyson Congdon, Ross' replacement as commissioner, was an unabashed "Liberal machine politician"[31] who proved an ineffective and blatantly corrupt leader, dividing Yukoners as well as the Liberal Party.[32] Congdon resigned as commissioner in 1904 to contest the federal election as the Liberal candidate, but divisions between the "Tabs" (followers of Congdon) and "Steam Beers" (followers of brewery-owner Tom O'Brien) split the Liberal vote and brought victory to Dr. Alfred Thompson who represented the Yukon Independent Party (a coalition of Liberals and Conservatives). "Now that Congdon had been defeated," David Morrison explained, "some territorial politicians could turn again to the struggle to secure the [economic and political] reforms they desired."[33]

Frank Oliver, who followed Clifford Sifton as the Minister of the Interior, visited Dawson City in 1905, met with citizens, and announced various changes to mining regulations that the Laurier government hoped would address local complaints. During that year's parliamentary session in Ottawa, however, Yukon MP Dr. Thompson argued ardently for a ten-member elected Yukon Council and responsible government. Prime Minister Laurier responded in the House of Commons, defending the government's approach to Yukon governance owing to how recently the region had been "brought into civilization" by the gold rush. "My hon. friend will agree with me that it would have been extremely unwise if we had given to this new population coming in from all over the world representative institutions," Laurier insisted. The prime minister now supported an elected Yukon Council, but reiterated that this "should not have been done before, and that the government has not been remiss in the character which it has given to the institutions of the Yukon."[34] Back in Dawson, the Council sessions in 1905 and 1906 proved relatively calm compared to previous years, with Commissioner William Wallace Burns McInnes who, along with the Dawson Board of Trade, the Yukon Independent Party, Yukon Liberals, and Opposition MPs, continued to lobby the federal cabinet to consider more substantive political reforms for the territory.[35]

"The people's desire for a wholly elective Yukon Council has not yet been granted," J.N.E. Brown noted in his 1907 reflection on the evolution of government in the territory. "More or less political unrest may be expected in the Yukon until a wholly elective Council is granted; for the struggles of this youngest territory are but the repetition of the struggles of Ontario, Quebec, and the North-West for fully responsible government."[36] Dr. Thompson raised the issue yet again in the 1907 session of Parliament, reassuring the House that he had the non-partisan support of most Yukoners and they did not seek complete provincial autonomy. As things stood, the five appointed members of the existing Council drew "salaries as occupants of various positions under the government, and they are, therefore, necessarily not as closely in touch with the people as would be men who were elected directly by the people." He complained that the Yukon "is the only territory in all this vast Dominion which has not full and complete autonomy, the only portion of Canada that has not directly representative institutions." In response, Frank Oliver anticipated that the upcoming 1907 election would "be the last that will be held in the Yukon where a council not fully elective will be chosen."[37]

The persistent agitation of newspaper editors, pressure groups, and politicians for a wholly elected Yukon Council was finally paying off. Senior officials in the Department of the Interior instructed their legal staff to prepare an amended Yukon Act which would model territorial governance after the most recent iteration of the North-West Territories Assembly. Their first draft included provisions for a lieutenant-governor and an elected, eleven-member Yukon Legislative Assembly which would exercise all the powers and duties previously assigned to the Commissioner in Council. Minister Oliver approved the draft bill, which was sent to the King's printer for copying in March 1908, but the following month the Deputy Minister of Justice reviewed the bill and informed his colleagues that "it appears to me to be quite unnecessary to repeal the existing Act, and that it would be a mistake to do so. All that is really required may be accomplished by a short amending Act." The Department of the Interior accepted his advice and abandoned early plans, assigning "new roles, responsibilities and relationships" to the Yukon Council and Commissioner and creating "an unwieldy version of representative but not responsible government" that proved difficult to administer—and difficult to reform, as time would show.[38]

The July 1908 amendment to the Yukon Act provided for a fully-elected Yukon Council of ten members, who would now choose their own speaker and sit separate from the commissioner.[39] This separation of powers meant that the commissioner and Council, respectively, now had a monopoly over executive and legislative powers. "The Commissioner, granted the powers of reservation and disallowance over Council legislation, was to continue his administration of federal responsibilities on advice from Ottawa, and to retain his supervision over employees of the Canadian and Yukon governments," David Morrison summarized. In short, the commissioner kept full executive powers and responsibility for the territorial administration. "The representatives of the people, prohibited from considering financial legislation not recommended by the chief executive, were to have control—but no initiative—over the public purse, power to conduct their proceedings as they saw fit under their own speaker, and freedom to legislate on non-financial matters."[40]

The Laurier government decided to provide for "self-government" by granting a fully elected legislature (in keeping with British parliamentary tradition)—but without conferring responsible government (an affront to the Westminster model). Frank Oliver, in sponsoring the 1908 amendment, proclaimed that "there is naturally a desire on the part of every community in this country to have the fullest possible measure of self-government," but that "in the organization of new territories it has not always been thought desirable, nor has it always been possible, to give entirely elective legislatures." He asserted that the government's proposal would provide for "a form of government generally that will be in accord with the general principle that pervades our constitution namely, that the people shall govern in certain well-defined affairs and within well-defined limitations."[41] Oliver's position reflected the long-standing belief, stated often by Clifford Sifton before him, that the Klondike was destined to be a short-term mining camp, with few prospects for longevity, let alone substantial population growth. The government, in turn, favour small and short-term solutions.

During the three-day parliamentary debate on the amendment, Conservative MP George Foster found it "a little peculiar to have the people elect their own representatives to do their legislation and then have the whole of the administration vested in someone appointed by the Crown." Senator James Lougheed also found it odd that if the commissioner, as the federal representative, initiated a money bill and the Council disagreed with it, there was no cabinet-like body to push Council members to compromise. To break a deadlock, the commissioner was empowered to simply dissolve the Council and call another election—a strange situation that deviated from the system of government prevailing in the rest of Canada. From the Liberal government's standpoint, however, Secretary of State R. W. Scott summed up the logic of the situation: "it would be rather a farce ... to invest a community of that kind [with less than 10,000 inhabitants] with powers given to a province. ... Surely it would be making a toy of government if you were to give all the ceremonial incident to the constitution of a province to a community of that number."[42] The political debates were followed with interest in the North, but by this time many northerners had fallen into a pattern of working in the Yukon in the summer and relocating to the South during the long winter months when placer mining was not possible. The steady decline of the post-Klondike Yukon was exacerbated by the creation of seasonal migratory patterns that reinforced the transient nature of the regional population.

The achievement of representative and not responsible territorial government did not provoke a serious backlash in the Yukon, in part because of shifting relationships. "Partly because they could not foresee the problems that would arise, but mostly because of apathy, the men who fought so hard for an elective council and an increase in popular control over government did not seem upset by the compromise Oliver and his colleagues effected," Morrison noted. "Even Dr. Thompson, who was not in Ottawa when the amendment was debated, said he regretted that the changes had not been more sweeping, 'but it is better to have half a loaf than none at all'."[43] R.G. Robertson would later suggest that "this clear division of executive and legislative responsibility—reminiscent of United States territorial practice—was a new, though apparently unrecognized, departure from Canadian precedents, and from the principles of parliamentary government."[44] But as Morrison astutely noted, "the new formal relationship between the Commissioner and the Council was similar to that between the governor and the legislature in any British system of government." By separating the chief executive from the Yukon Council without any cabinet to exercise executive powers, however, the 1908 amendments "created a hybrid system half-way between two British constitutional patterns."[45]

The 1908 amendments reflected the government's best guess about how to manage a distant territory, still with a large American population and close proximity to the Territory of Alaska. Their assumptions about the transient, impermanent nature of Yukon life proved to be prescient.[46] The population had plummeted from over twenty-seven thousand in 1901 to less than ten thousand, gold production declined precipitously, and the civil service in the territory shrank accordingly. Mining had changed from the hardy placer miner working his claim by hand to large-scale, capital-intensive, industrialized mining, with the Yukon economy dominated by the great "concessionaires": the Guggenheims of New York, A.N.C. Treadgold, and "Klondike Joe" Boyle.[47] Control of water supplies—the centrepiece of the concessions—had taken over from prospecting guile, good luck, and hard work as a determinant of financial success. "The glamour of the Yukon has passed, the days of the individual miner and the romance of great fortunes picked up in a week, have altogether gone," the Canadian *Annual Review* reported in 1908.[48] As the energy of the gold rush dissipated, the Yukon became less and less a priority in southern corridors of power. Representative government had arrived by 1908, but "like a hothouse plant exposed to a cold wind," Robertson observed, "it then stopped developing for over forty years."[49]

The Yukon's heyday passed, and the far northwest corner of the country slipped back into political irrelevance. Not until the 1970s would the

Yukon once again appear on the nation's constitutional and political radar in a significant manner. The First World War had accelerated the decline. Yukoners threw heart and soul—plus a large portion of their workforce and a lot of money—into the war effort. The population decline continued as did the hollowing out of Dawson City. Mining continued with the Klondike dredges operating into the mid-1960s, but the discoveries proved small and often short-lived. The government of Canada considered in 1918 eliminating the elected territorial council all-together and reluctantly settled on maintaining a three-person representative council. With the major exception of a potential troubling contretemps over a 1930s merger with British Columbia (a process overturned by the discovery that the Yukon government provided a small payment to the Catholic school in Dawson City), the Yukon did not factor much into national affairs. The Second World War thrust the far northwest back into the continental spotlight, although the government of Canada's engagement in the construction of the Alaska Highway, the Northwest Staging Route (airfields leading to Alaska), the CANOL pipeline, and related projects was restricted to near-total acquiescence and minimal government oversight.

Change accelerated after the Second World War. The government of Canada assumed greater responsibilities, matching a nation-wide expansion of the social welfare state with larger and rapid investments in the North. A region-wide mining boom further renewed southern interest in the Yukon, leading to an expansion of government operations in the territory, the relocation of the territorial capital from Dawson City to Whitehorse, and the expansion of the Yukon's population (although not to Gold Rush levels). The growing population, particularly in Whitehorse, agitated for greater political autonomy, particularly after the widely-admired James Smith stepped down as commissioner (1966–76). Yukon politicians, known for being obstreperous at times, demanded responsible and cabinet-style government. A major shift occurred in 1979, when the short-lived government of Prime Minister Joe Clark was in office. Clark, supporting Yukon Member of Parliament Erik Nielsen (who had backed his leadership campaign), promised provincehood for the Yukon, only to discover that Yukoners were lukewarm to this expensive proposition. Instead, the Conservative Government agreed to establish responsible government in 1979, by way of a letter issued by Indian and Northern Affairs Minister Jake Epp.

Yukoners' demand for autonomy during this era was matched by the rise of Indigenous political activism and, in particular, the emergence of the Yukon Native Brotherhood (later the Council for Yukon Indians/ Council for Yukon First Nations). Indigenous leaders, led by Elijah Smith, demanded a modern land claims settlement, which the Government of Canada reluctantly agreed to in 1973. This launched a twenty-year negotiation process that resulted in the signing of an umbrella final agreement in 1993 and the emergence of Indigenous self-government as a major force in territorial affairs. Yukon governance had been marked by decline for nearly seventy years, with changes sparked by restless Yukon politicians and the emergence of the Yukon land claims process. The passage of a renewed and modernized Yukon Act in 2002, combined with an extensive program of devolution of federal powers (including control of land and natural resources) and the steady re-establishment of Indigenous governance in the territory, gave the Yukon province-like authority while retaining access to large annual transfers from the Government of Canada.

Even in Canada's 150th year, Confederation is not constitutionally complete. The Yukon, Northwest Territories, and Nunavut are not provinces and are probably blocked, by way of the constitutional amending processes, from achieving that status in the coming decades. The Yukon Territory stands as a corrective to the standard Whiggish expectations about political reform that treat it as a linear, if bumpy, progression from colony to self-governing jurisdiction. The Yukon gained a measure of political autonomy after 1900, only to have it set aside due to the economic distress caused by the First World War and the doldrums that settled in after that time. Consequently, the Yukon holds a special place in the constitutional history of Canada, as a sign of the country's reluctance to turn its full attention northward and its uneven treatment of the country's northern colonies.

Further Reading

Coates, Ken S. *Canada's Colonies: A History of the Yukon and Northwest Territories.* Toronto: James Lorimer & Company, 1985.

Morrison, David R. *The Politics of the Yukon Territory, 1898–1909.* Toronto: University of Toronto Press, 1968.

Thomas, Lewis Herbert. *The Struggle for Responsible Government in the North-West Territories, 1870–97*, rev. ed. Toronto: University of Toronto Press, 1978.

Zaslow, Morris. *The Opening of the Canadian North, 1870–1914.* Toronto: McClelland & Stewart 1971.

NOTES

1. Morris Zaslow, *The Opening of the Canadian North, 1870–1914* (Toronto: McClelland & Stewart 1971), 139.

2. For a map of traditional territories, see http://www.env.gov.yk.ca/animals-habitat/documents/traditional_territories_map.pdf.

3. Ken S. Coates, *Best Left as Indians: Indian-White Relations in the Yukon Territory* (Montreal: McGill-Queen's, 1991).

4. Ken S. Coates, "Controlling the Periphery: The Territorial Administration of the Yukon and Alaska, 1867–1959," *Pacific Northwest Quarterly* 78, no. 4 (1987): 146.

5. See Michael Gates, *Gold at Fortymile Creek: Early Days in the Yukon* (Vancouver: University of British Columbia Press, 1994).

6. Comptroller F. White of the NWMP quoted in D.J. Hall, *Clifford Sifton. Vol. 1: The Young Napoleon, 1861–1900* (Vancouver: University of British Columbia Press, 1981), 160.

7. David R. Morrison, *The Politics of the Yukon Territory, 1898–1909* (Toronto: University of Toronto Press, 1968), 7-9; Thomas Stone, "The Mounties as Vigilantes: Perceptions of Community and the Transformation of Law in the Yukon, 1887–1897," *Law and Society Review* 14 (1979): 83–114; and William R. Morrison, *Showing the Flag: The Mounted Police and Canadian Sovereignty in the North, 1894–1925* (Vancouver: University of British Columbia Press, 1985), ch. 2.

8. See Great Unsolved Mysteries in Canadian History, "Who Discovered the Klondike Gold?" http://www.canadianmysteries.ca/sites/klondike/home/indexen.html.

9. Hall, *Clifford Sifton*, vol. 1, 172.

10. R.G. Robertson, "The Evolution of Territorial Government in Canada," in *The Political Process in Canada*, ed. J.H. Aitchison (Toronto: University of Toronto Press, 1963), 40.

11. J.N.E. Brown, "Evolution of Law and Government in the Yukon Territory," in *University of Toronto Studies. History and Economics*, vol. II, ed. S.M. Wickett (Toronto: Librarian of the University of Toronto, 1907), 199.

12. Hall, *Clifford Sifton*, vol. 1, 190–91; and C.E.S. Franks, "How the Sabbath Came to the Yukon," *Canadian Public Administration* 10 (March 1967): 123–35.

13 *The Yukon Territory Act*, 1898, 61 Victoria, c.6 (Canada).

14 Hall, *Clifford Sifton*, vol. 1, 191.

15 Linda Johnson, *With the People Who Live Here: The History of the Yukon Legislature 1909–1961* (Whitehorse: Legislative Assembly of Yukon, 2009), 11.

16 Lewis Herbert Thomas, *The Struggle for Responsible Government in the North-West Territories, 1870–97*, rev. ed. (Toronto: University of Toronto Press, 1978), 268.

17 Ken S. Coates and William Morrison, *Land of the Midnight Sun: A History of the Yukon* (Montreal and Kingston: McGill-Queen's University Press, 2005), 105.

18 Coates and Morrison, *Land of the Midnight Sun*, 191.

19 *The Yukon Territory Act*, 1898, 61 Victoria, c.6 (Canada). The Commissioner in Council powers included "direct taxation for territorial and local expenditure; the establishment of a territorial civil service to be financed by the territory; the establishment, maintenance and management of prisons; the incorporation of municipal institutions; the imposition of shop, saloon, tavern, auctioneer and other licenses; the incorporation of certain companies; the solemnization of marriage; the protection of property and civil rights; the administration of justice; the imposition of punishments—by fine, penalty, or imprisonment—for infractions of territorial ordinances; the expenditure of funds appropriated by Parliament for territorial purposes; superintendence over all matters of a merely local or private nature; and the provision of educational facilities." Quoted in Johnson, *With the People Who Live Here*, 12.

20 Morrison, *Politics of the Yukon Territory*, 20. See also Johnson, *With the People Who Live Here*, 11.

21 Thomas, *The Struggle for Responsible Government in the North-West Territories*, 269–70.

22 Quoted in Morrison, *Politics of the Yukon Territory*, 28.

23 See Morrison, *Politics of the Yukon Territory*, 25–32.

24 Robertson, "Evolution of Territorial Government," 141.

25 Johnson, *With the People Who Live Here*, 16.

26 Thomas, *The Struggle for Responsible Government in the North-West Territories*, 271; and Morrison, *Politics of the Yukon Territory*, 39–41.

27 See Steven Smyth, *The Yukon Chronology (1897–1999)*, vol. 1, 2nd ed. (Whitehorse: Clairedge Press, 1999), 6–7.

28 Ken S. Coates, *Best Left As Indians: Native-White Relations in the Yukon Territory, 1840–1973* (Montreal: McGill-Queen's University Press, 1991).

29 Careless, J.M.S., "Responsible Government." Accessed from http://www.thecanadianencyclopedia.ca/en/article/responsible-government/.

30 On the Treadgold Concession, see D.J. Hall, *Clifford Sifton*, vol. 2: *A Lonely Eminence, 1901–1929* (Vancouver: University of British Columbia Press, 1985), 132–44; and Morrison, *Politics of the Yukon Territory*, 43–56.

31 Thomas, *The Struggle for Responsible Government in the North-West Territories*, 271.

32 Hall, *Sifton*, vol. 2, 141.

33 Morrison, *Politics of the Yukon Territory*, 71.

34 *House of Commons Debates*, 1905, cols. 7074–79. Quoted partially in Thomas, *The Struggle for Responsible Government in the North-West Territories*, 272; and Morrison, *Politics of the Yukon Territory*, 74.

35 Appointed commissioner by P.C. 968 on 27 May 1905. See Steven Smyth, *The Yukon Chronology: The Yukon's Constitutional Foundations*, vol. 1 (Whitehorse: Northern Directories, 1991), 8.

36 Brown, "Evolution of Law and Government," 211.

37 *House of Commons Debates*, 1906–7, cols. 4521–23. Morrison, *Politics of the Yukon Territory*, 88. On Thompson's hopes for representative and responsible government, see his article "Government of Yukon," *Alaska-Yukon Magazine* 5 (1908): 414.

38 Johnson, *With the People Who Live Here*, 20–21.

39 Yukon Act, 1908 amendment, 7–8 Edward VII, c.76.

40 Morrison, *Politics of the Yukon Territory*, 88. The act also provided a three-year term for Council, but gave the commissioner power to dissolve it and call a new election at any time. During the three-day Parliamentary debate on the 1908 amendment, Conservative Opposition members raised concerns with this issue, but did not insist that it be changed. See R.L. Borden and G.E. Foster, Hansard, 1907–08, cols. 10528–10545.

41 *House of Commons Debates*, 1908, quoted in Thomas, *The Struggle for Responsible Government in the North-West Territories*, 272.

42 Morrison, *Politics of the Yukon Territory*, 89.

43 Morrison, *Politics of the Yukon Territory*, 90.

44 Robertson, "Evolution of Territorial Government," 141–42.

45 Morrison, *Politics of the Yukon Territory*, 88.

46 Robertson, "Evolution of Territorial Government," 141–42.

47 Coates and Morrison, *Land of the Midnight Sun*, 157–65; and Lewis Green, *The Gold Hustlers* (Vancouver: J.J. Douglas, 1972).

48 *Canadian Annual Review* (1908), 542, quoted in Morrison, *Politics of the Yukon Territory*, 87.

49 Robertson, "Evolution of Territorial Government," 142–43.

9

Creating New Provinces: Saskatchewan and Alberta

BILL WAISER

Bringing the Prairie West into Confederation was a decades-long struggle that must be understood as a contested process right up until the 1905 creation of the provinces of Saskatchewan and Alberta. The creation of the new western provinces is consequently not simply a story of achievement or celebration, but rather a protracted, at times acrimonious, experience.

Canada Acquires the North-West

The question of Western Canada's entry into Confederation actually had its formal beginnings in 1857, when the British government struck a select committee to consider whether the Hudson's Bay Company should continue to administer and govern Rupert's Land (the land that drained into Hudson Bay) in response to the company's request for a renewal of its exclusive trading privileges in the region (granted by royal charter in 1670). The Province of Canada (Canada East [Quebec] and Canada West [Ontario]) participated in these deliberations by sending a representative to the committee hearings. Since the late 1840s, Toronto *Globe* publisher George Brown had derided the HBC and its charter for standing in the way of westward expansion from the confines of the lower Great Lakes.[1] What lay behind this campaign against the HBC was the urgent need for Canada West to expand. The province, hemmed in by the Canadian

Shield to the north, was running out of agricultural land; if it was not going to stagnate and see its booming population siphoned off by the United States, then its boundaries would have to expand westward beyond Lake Superior. The answer lay to the North-West and the plains of the western interior. Once dismissed as a frozen wilderness, Canadian expansionists extolled the region in the 1850s as an agricultural Eden that would serve as the new home for thousands, maybe even hundreds of thousands, of farmers and provide a profitable western market for the Toronto business community.[2] Brown and other Reform (Liberal) members of parliament insisted that Canada was the rightful heir to Rupert's Land because the Montreal-based fur trade, especially the North West Company, had been active in the western interior for almost a century, and that this claim had not been extinguished in 1821 when the NWC joined with the HBC.[3]

The British select committee concluded that "it is essential to meet the just and reasonable wishes of Canada" to provide for the annexation of territory in the southern reaches of Rupert's Land.[4] This recommendation suggested that the way was clear for Canada to take over the western interior. That transaction, though, was still more than a decade away. Annexing the North-West necessarily meant a new political arrangement—namely, representation by population—that would undermine the equal representation of Canada West (Ontario) and East (Quebec) in the united parliament. Confederation of the colonies of British North America had to be achieved first, with adequate constitutional protections for the future province of Quebec, before expansion westward could become a reality. Even then, some Canadian political leaders were uneasy about assuming responsibility for so much territory—a land empire that would have enlarged the Canada of 1867 by seven times.[5] Conservative leader John A. Macdonald and his largely Montreal-based supporters subscribed to the old commercial empire of the St. Lawrence, while the drive to settle the British North-West was a Reform plan, spearheaded by George Brown, in order to satisfy Toronto's economic ambitions.[6] If the Great Coalition of 1864 was to bring about constitutional renewal in place of deadlock, then territorial expansion into the western Prairies had to be a planned feature of the Confederation deal. Section 146 of the 1867 BNA Act provided for the future admission of the British North-West.

Canadian negotiators finally sat down with the HBC directorship in London over the winter of 1868–69. No representatives from Rupert's

Land, including First Nations and Métis Peoples, were consulted, let alone invited to participate. Discussions soon reached a stalemate, largely over Canada questioning whether the company actually owned the territory in question. At this point, British Colonial Secretary Lord Granville, acting as an intermediary, forced a settlement on the two parties. The HBC agreed to surrender its charter rights to Rupert's Land in exchange for £300,000 compensation from the Canadian government. Canada, in return, secured title to Rupert's Land and the British North American mainland that was not drained by Hudson Bay, officially known as the North-Western Territory (literally northwest of Rupert's Land).

Dominion Rule Absolute in the North-West Territories

By occupying and developing the North-West, expansionists insisted that Canada would become stronger, more powerful, but most of all, more secure on a continent now dominated by the aggressive United States. It was therefore imperative that the West be settled and developed as quickly as possible—even if that process conflicted with the interests of the local Indigenous population.[7] Nor could this task, given the singular importance of the region to Canada's success, be handed over to any territorial or provincial government. Federal oversight, particularly the administration of western lands and resources, was a "national necessity."[8] The transfer consequently represented a new beginning in the history of the western interior.

At the same time, despite all the rhetoric about Canada's new western empire and how it would provide the means to greatness for the young dominion, the Conservative government of John A. Macdonald did the minimum possible to incorporate the region into Confederation. Canada planned to assume control of the three-million-square-mile territory on 1 December 1869 by means of a temporary government based in Red River. But the Red River Métis, led by Louis Riel, resented the lack of consultation and forced Ottawa to negotiate the entry of the region into Confederation. The 1869–70 Red River Resistance foiled the Canadian intention to treat the vast land transfer as little more than a simple real estate transaction. It did not, however, prevent the federal government from directing western settlement and development over the next few decades. Manitoba may have joined the dominion as Canada's fifth province on 1 July 1870, but it was kept deliberately small. It also did not exercise control over its public lands and resources, a provincial right enshrined in the 1867 British North America Act and enjoyed by all other provinces at the time. Instead, Manitoba had to depend on annual federal subsidies that did not always keep pace with the demands of provincial settlement and development.

The North-West Territories, meanwhile, became a separate federal territory in 1870 (sections 35 and 36 of Manitoba Act), but beyond that, "effective government remained almost completely unknown."[9] Some might reasonably have wondered whether the imperialism of the HBC had simply been superseded by that of the government of Canada, especially since the territorial government was located outside the region in Winnipeg and headed by the lieutenant-governor for Manitoba. There was not even provision for territorial government staff. The Alexander Mackenzie Liberal government tried to correct some of these deficiencies in the 1875 *North-West Territories Act* (approved 8 April 1875; effective 7 October 1876) by providing for a separate government, based in the territories, and elected council members as the newcomer population increased. But territorial government still offered limited representation and limited voice in running the affairs of the region. It could not, in any sense, be considered responsible government.

Canadian administration of its new western frontier in the second half of the century was based on the desire for order and stability—a desire to implant the best features of British civilization on the northern plains. This vision could only be realized, though, if the defining values and principles of the new society were imposed from outside. There was no allowance for local or democratic initiatives, no recognition that the Indigenous Peoples of the region might foresee a different future. Backing this Canadian plan, moreover, was a supreme confidence—bordering on arrogance—that the re-making of the region would proceed smoothly, if not quickly.[10]

The incorporation of the North-West Territories into Confederation was to be achieved through a handful of federal initiatives—collectively known as the national policies. Ottawa arranged for the surveying of the land, established a mounted police force, chartered a transcontinental railway, introduced a protective tariff to promote east-west trade, and negotiated treaties with western First Nations. All of these settlement and development policies encountered problems and/or challenges. The federal government believed that it knew what was best for the region—that it alone could determine and shape its future—and consequently treated the North-West Territories as little more than a colony with attendant consequences.[11]

Negotiating with the First Nations

Ottawa had no immediate plans to negotiate treaties with those First Nations bands living west of the new province of Manitoba. The Cree consequently took matters into their own hands—stopping a telegraph construction crew and turning back a Geological Survey of Canada party—and forced Canada to deal with them.[12] If the dominion wanted to guarantee the peaceful, orderly settlement of the region, then Ottawa had to reach an agreement with the Cree for their lands—sooner rather than later. But it drew the line at negotiating with bands from the boreal forest region whose lands were considered unsuited for agriculture.

In making the Numbered Treaties with western First Nations (Treaties 1–7 between 1871 and 1877), Canada was following a British tradition that had been established by the Royal Proclamation of 1763. In recognition of the important role that First Nations had played as allies in the military struggle between Great Britain and France, the British promised not to allow agricultural settlement of First Nations territory until title had been surrendered to the Crown by means of treaties. This policy of negotiating through the Crown for First Nations lands had been followed, albeit imperfectly, in the late eighteenth and early nineteenth centuries and had become well-entrenched by the time Canada acquired its North-West empire in 1870.[13] The motives underlying the process, though, had changed. Whereas British military officials had been anxious to secure and maintain Indigenous allies in their struggle with an aggressive, expansionist United States, Canadian civil authorities now wanted to avoid costly so-called "Indian" wars over western lands. In other words, negotiation was the cheaper course of action. The merits of this policy were clearly borne out by the experience south of the border, where the United States spent more money fighting Indian wars in 1870 than the entire Canadian budget for the year.[14]

The treaty process was also imbued by an imperialist ideology which held that First Nations Peoples would inevitably vanish as a distinct race in the face of the white man's "superior" civilization, and that it was Canada's duty to remake them into loyal subjects of the Crown. This notion that the Cree and other groups faced certain extinction unless saved by Canadian humanitarian efforts did not jibe with reality. Although the Cree faced a number of difficulties in the early 1870s, they were not a defeated or doomed people. They not only practiced an opportunity-based economy, exploiting a range of resources from season to season and from district to district, but were also an extremely dynamic, resilient people who had faced similar challenges in the past and adapted accordingly. The Cree saw themselves as equals in their dealings with Canada and were prepared to negotiate in order to guarantee their future security and well-being in the region as an independent nation. They had no interest in or need for a Canadian crutch. They recognized, though, that the rapid decline of the bison necessitated a shift to agriculture in order to compete with newcomers. Indeed, they regarded an alliance with the Crown—similar to the relationship that they had enjoyed with the HBC in the past—as the best hope of restructuring their economy.[15]

The agreement negotiated at Fort Carlton in August 1876 was the sixth of seven numbered western treaties (from present-day southern Manitoba west to the Alberta foothills). Treaty No. 6 covers some 120,000 square miles in present-day central Saskatchewan and Alberta—lands crucial to Canada's westward expansion. It is also one of the few treaties where the First Nations' perspective has been documented—in this case, by Métis interpreter Peter Erasmus who had been hired by Cree leaders Mistawasis and Ahtahkakoop. The treaty deliberations proved to be a long, at times protracted, process because First Nations negotiators insisted on better terms than those offered in the formal treaty and tried to build on the concessions that had been won in previous agreements. The treaty commissioners, in turn, were under strict orders to concede as little as possible to First Nations and not make any additional or "outside" promises to the original terms. Securing the consent of First Nations leadership, however, was neither straightforward nor certain.

Treaty No. 6 negotiations got underway in mid-August 1876 at a traditional camping area, known to the Cree as *pehonanihk* or the waiting place, about a mile from Fort Carlton. There were no photographers present for this momentous event; in fact, despite the widespread use of the camera during this period, no photographs exist of any of the treaty meetings in the 1870s. From the start, Indian Commissioner Alexander Morris, accompanied by a North-West Mounted Police escort, assured the assembled Cree that the Queen, the so-called "Great Mother," was genuinely concerned about their welfare and future well-being. "My Indian brothers," he began, "I have shaken hands with a few of you, I shake hands with all of you in my heart." He also implored First Nations leaders to take his words seriously and to think of the future: "what I will promise, and what I believe and hope you will take, is to last as long as that sun shines and yonder river flows."[16]

Commissioner Morris, who was also the lieutenant-governor of the North-West Territories and Manitoba, told the Cree that the Queen had no intention of interfering with their traditional form of making a living by hunting, fishing, and gathering. Such activities were guaranteed for future generations. He pointed out, however, that the wild game was disappearing and that First Nations Peoples had to learn how to grow food from the soil if they were to provide for their children and their children's children. To facilitate this transition to farming, the Canadian government would set aside reserve lands for each band based on the formula of one square mile for every family of five. He then listed the specific agricultural items—from tools and implements to animals and seed—that would be given to the bands to help them become farmers. He also emphasized the cash payment that every man, woman, and child could expect to receive for the life of the treaty. And he promised special gifts for the chiefs and headmen. These presents included symbols of the new order: treaty uniforms, silver medals, and a British flag. "I hold out my hand to you full of the Queen's bounty," Morris concluded, "act for the good of your people."[17]

Mistawasis and Ahtahkakoop, the two leading Carlton chiefs, responded that they needed time to discuss the treaty among themselves. The detractors, who were given the opportunity to speak first at the First Nations leadership's private council, acknowledged the hardship caused by the disappearance of the bison, but placed little faith in agriculture: to trade their land for an uncertain future was an admission of defeat. Mistawasis, on the other hand, could see no other future for his people. "Have you anything better to offer our people?" he directly challenged those who opposed the treaty. "I ask, again, can you suggest anything that will bring these things back for tomorrow and all the tomorrows that face our people?" He went on to argue that the bison would soon disappear and

Pîhtokahanapiwiyin Poundmaker
Cree First Nations Leader (later Chief)

19 AUGUST 1876

> This is our land! It isn't a piece of pemmican to be cut off and given in little pieces back to us. It is ours and we will take what we want.

CONFEDERATION QUOTE 9.1
Quotation from Peter Erasmus, *Buffalo Days and Nights*, Calgary: Glenbow-Alberta Institute, 1976, page 244
Photograph by O.B. Buel, from Library and Archives Canada, C-001875

Mistawasis (Big Child)
First Nations Chief

21 AUGUST 1876

CONFEDERATION QUOTE 9.2

Quotation from Peter Erasmus, *Buffalo Days and Nights*, Calgary: Glenbow-Alberta Institute, 1976, page 247
Photograph from Saskatchewan Archives Board, R-B2837

> I speak directly to Poundmaker and The Badger and those others who object to signing this treaty. Have you anything better to offer our people? I ask, again, can you suggest anything that will bring these things back for tomorrow and all the tomorrows that face our people?

that the treaty offered the best protection against future uncertainty. "I for one will take the hand that is offered," he concluded. Ahtahkakoop also voiced his support. "Let us not think of ourselves but of our children's children," he argued. "Let us show our wisdom by choosing the right path now while we yet have a choice."[18] This right path, according to the Cree leader, was the adoption of agriculture. There was no reason that they could not make a living from the soil, especially when the Queen's representatives promised assistance and instruction.

When the negotiations resumed, Commissioner Morris warned the First Nations leaders that his time was limited. Poundmaker then stepped forward and stated that while his people were anxious to make a living for themselves, he wanted assurances that they would receive adequate help when needed. This request clearly went against what the government was prepared to do at the time. It was also generally assumed that First Nations peoples would be able to learn how to farm fairly rapidly and that the bison would be around long enough to smooth the transition to agriculture. Morris consequently refused, insinuating that the real problem was Indigenous laziness. "I cannot promise . . . that the Government will feed and support all the Indians," he replied. "You are many, and if we were to try to do it, it would take a great deal of money, and some of you would never do anything for yourselves." The Badger then attempted to clarify their motives: "we want to think of our children; we do not want to be too greedy; when we commence to settle down on the reserves that we select, it is there we want your aid, when we cannot help ourselves and in case of troubles seen and unforeseen in the future." When Morris countered that the Cree had to trust the Queen's generosity, Mistawasis responded: "it is in case of any extremity . . . this is not a trivial matter for us."[19]

This request for famine relief was one of several counter-demands presented to Morris. The list also included additional tools, implements, and livestock; a supply of medicines free of charge; exemption from war service; the banning of alcohol; and schools and teachers on the reserve. Realizing that the negotiations were in danger of collapse, Morris granted most of the new demands. He agreed, for example, that a medicine chest (medical supplies) would be kept at the house of each Indian agent. He also promised, albeit reluctantly, to add a clause to the treaty providing famine assistance. The Alexander Mackenzie administration later criticized these terms for being too generous. But it is difficult to deny that the treaty, which settled First Nations claims to several thousand square miles of rich agricultural land, was a good bargain for Ottawa. The majority of the Cree chiefs and headmen, on the other hand, realized they had to adjust to new circumstances and affixed their mark to the revised treaty on the understanding that the Great Mother and her representatives would keep a "watchful eye and sympathetic hand."[20] The references that Morris made to family and kin, then, were not just empty rhetoric to the Cree participants who valued the spoken word. They fully expected and looked forward to a beneficial and meaningful relationship with the Crown.[21] Little did they realize that the House of Commons had passed the Indian Act in April 1876 that essentially defined First Nations as wards of the state.

Western Grievance Fuels Drive for Constitutional Reform

By the early 1880s, the white settler population was disillusioned, if not thoroughly frustrated, with the federal government and the ponderous pace towards responsible government and eventual provincehood for the North-West Territories. Those Anglo-Canadians who emigrated West in the 1870s and early 1880s had come from a tradition where they enjoyed a popular interest in political affairs and exercised a voice in governing themselves. The reality was a NWT lieutenant-governor who not only had sole control over the territorial budget, limited as it was, but exercised wide discretionary power over many other territorial matters. The 1875 NWT Act did allow for elected representation on the council, but not until there were one thousand people in a district. It was consequently not until 1880 that Lorne, the first electoral constituency in the future province of Saskatchewan, was created in the Prince Albert area. It could actually have been worse. In 1880, Ottawa floated the idea of removing the capital to Winnipeg. Even though it never happened because of a storm of regional protest, the proposal underscored the federal government's obvious contempt for territorial government.[22] Westerners, in turn, complained that federal promotion of immigration and settlement—spoken in terms of the region's importance to the future prosperity of the dominion—was not being materially supported by the building of infrastructure or the provision of government services.

After the 1885 North-West Rebellion, the campaign for a different political arrangement within Canadian Confederation became essentially a

Fig 9.1 The North-West demanding "justice" for the North-West. *The Grip*, November 1883.

white settler movement. Indeed, a new relationship between the territories and Ottawa seemed to be in the offing when the region finally secured parliamentary representation in 1886—a magnanimous four seats in the 215-seat House of Commons and two Senate members. There were also more elected members on the Territorial Council—fourteen in 1885—but the lieutenant-governor still administered the federal appropriation. Then, in 1888, the *North-West Territories Act* was finally amended to create a legislative assembly of twenty-two elected members. At best, it was a half-measure. There was still no executive cabinet drawn from the assembly and no assembly control of the annual federal grant.

Territorial politicians did, however, take steps to reinforce the Anglo-Canadian character of the region by trying to do away with French language and separate school guarantees. French had been employed in territorial government business as early as 1874 when the NWT Council published a consolidation of its ordinances in both French and English. But it was not given official recognition in the 1875 *North-West Territories Act*. Nor did the Alexander Mackenzie government plan to include French language rights in the 1877 modifications to the act until Francophone Marc-Amable Girard, a former Conservative premier of Manitoba, introduced an amendment during the third reading of the bill in the Senate that called for the use of either French or English in territorial debates, council publications, and territorial courts. This last-minute amendment passed without division—but not before Interior Minister David Mills sarcastically observed that since "almost everyone in that part of the country spoke Cree . . . [it] should be chosen for that purpose."[23] Separate schools, by contrast, were part of the 1875 NWT Act. The religious minority in any district (Catholic or Protestant) could establish a separate school and support it through self-assessment. This system was formalized by the Territorial Council in 1884 through the establishment of a board of education with distinct Roman Catholic and Protestant sections responsible for the supervision of their own schools. An unusual feature of the ordinance was that the public school in a school district could be either Catholic or Protestant, depending on the religious majority, and that the separate school was formed by the minority.

These aspects of territorial life had generated little controversy—hardly any comment—up until 1885. But any toleration quickly evaporated after the rebellion as the Anglo-Canadian majority moved to affirm the British character of the North-West. The general mood was that separate schools and the use of French had been foisted on the region by Ottawa and were not representative of the wishes and interests of the dominant society. There was also a widespread belief that French Canadians had failed the country because of their sympathetic support of the Métis "traitor" Riel, while Roman Catholics could not be trusted because they owed their allegiance to Rome and the Pope.[24] The territorial government in Regina was expected to set things right. "One nation, one language" should be the territorial motto, urged the Qu'Appelle *Vidette* in 1888, and the surest way to promote a unity of purpose and a true national identity was to abolish the use of French in the government, the courts, and schools. Legislators responded in 1889 by preparing two petitions to parliament—one calling for the repeal of French as an official territorial language, the other the repeal of separate schools. During the debate over the resolutions, the vocal majority questioned the legitimacy of official bilingualism and separate schools, repeatedly pointing out that local opinion had never been taken into consideration. Those few brave enough to oppose the measures countered that French had been a distinctive feature of the North-West since fur trade days. Nothing was done at the federal level, though, because politicians in Ottawa were already grappling with the thorny Manitoba schools question and did not want more controversy. The simmering issues were simply dropped back in the lap of the territorial government, effectively leaving it up to Regina to take action. That it did in early 1892, when the territorial government passed resolutions abolishing the official use of French and discontinuing the religious control of schools in favour of a single government-run Council of Public Instruction (replaced by a Department of Education in 1901).[25]

What the language and school controversy demonstrated to westerners was that the Regina government lacked political independence in keeping with the British parliamentary system. In fact, it had reached the point by the late 1880s, in the words of a Qu'Appelle merchant, where the region was "not prepared to accept dictation from Ottawa."[26] There had been several steps towards responsible government since the 1877 *North-West Territories Act*. But westerners objected to the glacial pace—and the fact that Ottawa had to be repeatedly prodded. What ultimately brought the campaign for constitutional reform to a successful conclusion was the election of Wilfrid Laurier Liberals in 1896. When responsible government finally took effect the following year (1 October 1897), Frederick Haultain was appointed the territory's first and only premier. He quickly found, though, that having control over government spending did not mean much if the legislature did not have much to spend, especially since any revenue from North-West lands and resources went to the federal treasury.

This financial need became more acute with the immigration and settlement boom of the late 1890s. Now that the United States had exhausted its homestead land, the great agricultural promise of the Canadian North-West was finally being realized—albeit, almost three decades late—and the territorial government simply did not have enough money to meet the growing service and infrastructure demands. There appeared to be only one solution. In May 1900, the territorial government submitted a petition to the Laurier government reviewing the constitutional evolution of the

Frederick William Alpin Gordon Haultain
Premier, NWT

4 APRIL 1902

CONFEDERATION QUOTE 9.3
Quotation from Northwest Territories,
North-West Legislative Assembly,
4 April 1902
Photograph from Saskatchewan
Archives Board, R-B446

" [Moved] Whereas the larger powers and income incidental to ...provincial status are urgently... required to aid the development of the Territories and to meet the ... necessities of a large and ... increasing population. Be it resolved, that this House regrets that the Federal Government has decided not to introduce legislation ... granting provincial institutions to the Territories. "

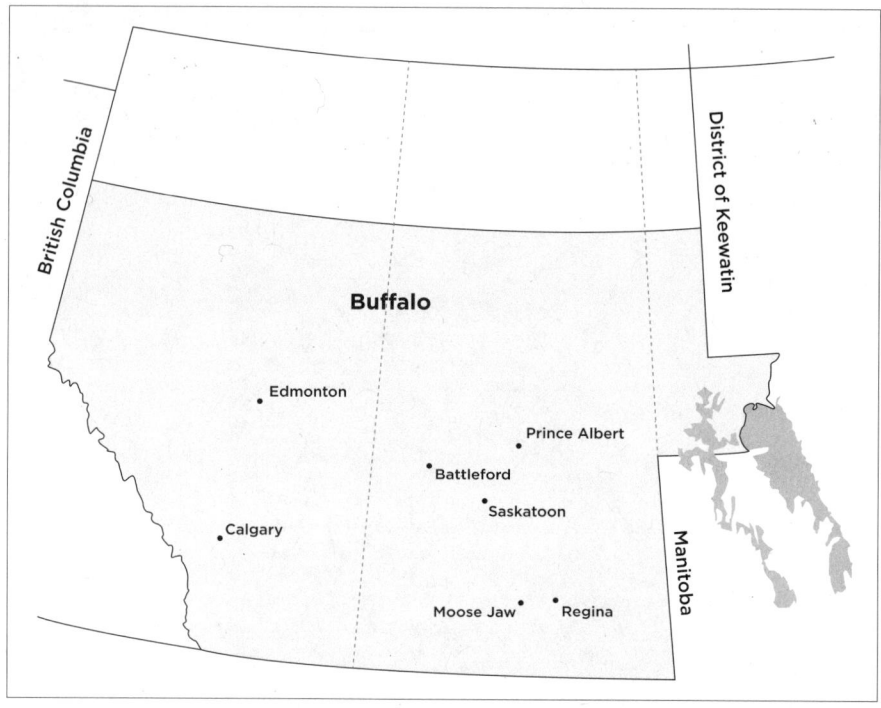

Fig 9.2 The proposed province of "Buffalo." Reproduced with permission from Bill Waiser, *Saskatchewan: A New History* (Calgary: Fifth House, 2006).

region and calling for the next logical step—namely, drafting the terms for provincehood. Ottawa turned down the request as premature, a position it repeated twice more in response to similar petitions.[27]

One of the stumbling blocks to finding common ground was Premier Haultain's dream of one large western province, to be called "Buffalo," between Manitoba and British Columbia and the 49th and 54th parallels.[28] Some argued that a western super province would upset the balance of Confederation, while others insisted that the territorial provisional districts (created in 1882 for administrative purposes) should be provincial material. Calgary, for example, had ambitions to be a territorial capital—as did Prince Albert. What also made Liberal negotiation with Haultain difficult was his decision to actively campaign on behalf of the federal Conservative party in the 1904 general election. It was a serious lapse in judgement and one that crippled his future political career. From his first days in territorial government, Haultain's strategy for securing concessions from the federal government was to adopt a non-partisan approach and speak with a single, territorial voice. Unfortunately, he had become so disillusioned with the Liberal government's intransigence that he cozied up to federal Conservative leader Robert Borden who not only promised provincehood for the West, but local control of lands and resources. These actions turned the autonomy question into a party issue—ironically, something that went against Haultain's own philosophy of putting territorial interests before political considerations.[29]

Securing Provincehood

By January 1905, the prime minister could no longer hold off autonomy because of the unparalleled success of federal immigration policy and invited Haultain to Ottawa to discuss the entry of the region into Confederation. The territorial leader outlined his vision of a single province with full constitutional powers. But the federal government had other plans and was confident of western support, especially given the strong Liberal showing in the November 1904 general election (seven of the nine territorial seats in the House of Commons were held by Liberals). Prime Minister Laurier personally introduced autonomy bills to create two roughly equal, north-south provinces, Saskatchewan and Alberta, on 21 February 1905.

The tabling of the two autonomy bills precipitated the longest debate in Canadian parliamentary history. It was so acrimonious that the date of entry for the new provinces had to be pushed back two months—to 1 September 1905—because the legislation did not receive royal assent until after the original entry date had passed. The source of the furor was the educational clauses. In the draft bills, the ambiguous phrase, "existing system," suggested that Laurier wanted to revive the old territorial dual school system and thereby secure legislative protection for Catholic minority rights. Members of the House on both the government and opposition benches reacted angrily to this seemingly blatant attempt to turn back the clock on educational matters, when the largely Protestant population of the territories had been moving towards secular education and public schools. Faced with a spiraling crisis—including the abrupt resignation of his Interior minister Clifford Sifton—that threatened to tear apart the administration and arouse latent Ontario-Quebec animosities, Laurier

Fig 9.3 Laurier as the proud father of two provincial "twins." *Montreal Daily Star,* 23 February 1905.

unceremoniously backed down and allowed a re-drafting of the offending clauses to bring them in line with current practice in the territories.[30]

The heated controversy over the educational clauses deflected attention away from the fact that Saskatchewan and Alberta were not full partners in Confederation. They, along with neighbouring Manitoba, were treated differently. Under the terms of the 1867 British North America Act, provinces exercised control over the public lands and resources within their boundaries. But that right was denied Manitoba in 1870, and it was denied Saskatchewan and Alberta in the autonomy bills. Clifford Sifton justified federal retention of western lands on the grounds that they were needed to promote immigration and settlement and that provincial control "would be ruinous . . . disastrous" to this national endeavour. "Do not yield," he admonished Laurier.[31] The prime minister, for his part, took a different tack in defending his government's policy. "Those lands were bought by the Dominion government," he reminded the House of Commons about the HBC deal in 1870, "and they have remained ever since the property of the Dominion government and have been administered by the Dominion government."[32] Ottawa attempted to make up for the loss of revenue by awarding the new provinces generous subsidies based on population. Haultain, however, wanted no part of the compensation package—he considered it "a matter of expediency"—and demanded the same right as other provinces in Canada.[33] He was gamely supported by the Calgary *Herald* which decried federal control of lands and resources as "Autonomy that Insults the West."[34]

Once the autonomy bills became law, the Liberal party turned its attention to securing power in the new provinces. In Alberta, over the protestation of the new provincial Conservative leader (and future Canadian prime minister) R.B. Bennett and other fellow Calgarians, Edmonton was named temporary capital until confirmed by a vote in the new Alberta legislature. It was no coincidence that the city was a Liberal stronghold. Or that Liberal G.H.V. Bulyea was appointed Alberta's lieutenant-governor and that he called on new provincial Liberal leader A.C. Rutherford to become premier.[35] A similar charade was played out in Saskatchewan. Despite Frederick Haultain's defining role in defending the interests of Western Canada, his opposition to the autonomy bills made him a liability and he was passed over as premier or lieutenant-governor. As one western historian remarked, "the territorial premier was almost as much an embarrassment to Laurier and his cabinet as the Métis leader [Louis Riel] to [Prime Minister J.A.] Macdonald and the Conservatives."[36] In Haultain's place, A.E. Forget, a lifelong Liberal who had first come West in 1876 as clerk for the North-West Territories Council, was retained as lieutenant-governor. He, in turn, invited Walter Scott, a Liberal backbencher in the House of Commons and the new provincial Liberal leader, to serve as premier. So confident were the Liberals of their hold on Saskatchewan that Prime Minister Laurier went to Edmonton first for Alberta's inauguration. Haultain's fall from power and influence, meanwhile, was so complete and so precipitous that he was not asked to speak at the delayed Regina ceremonies.[37]

Full Provincial Rights

Provincial control of public lands and resources for Saskatchewan and Alberta was still a quarter century away. At first, not wanting to lock horns with the friendly Laurier administration in Ottawa, the Scott and Rutherford provincial governments quietly pocketed the generous federal subsidy they received in lieu of their lands. But when the new Borden government extended the northern boundary of Manitoba, Ontario, and Quebec to Hudson and James Bays in 1912 (making the central provinces much bigger than Haultain's "Buffalo" province), Saskatchewan and Alberta began demanding control of their resources. Repeated attempts to hammer out an agreement foundered over the question of compensation for lands that had already been alienated. In 1927, for example, Premier Jimmy Gardiner claimed that Saskatchewan's right to compensation should date back to 1870. These demands delayed settlement of the matter until 1930. It was only then—sixty years after the region became part of the new Dominion of Canada—that Saskatchewan and Alberta secured full provincial rights.

Further Reading

Bovey, John A. "The Attitudes and Policies of the Federal Government Towards Canada's Northern Territories, 1870–1930." Master's thesis, University of British Columbia, 1957.

Carter, Sarah. *Capturing Women: The Manipulation of Cultural Imagery in Canada's Prairie West*. Montreal: McGill-Queen's University Press 1997.

Lingard, Charles C. *Territorial Government in Canada: The Autonomy Question in the Old North-West Territories*. Toronto: University of Toronto Press, 1946.

Miller, J.R. "The Aboriginal Peoples and the Crown." In *The Crown and Canadian Federalism*. Edited by D.M. Jackson. Toronto: Dundurn Press, 2013.

Owram, Douglas. *Promise of Eden: The Canadian Expansionist Movement and the Idea of the West, 1856–1900*. Toronto: University of Toronto Press, 1980.

Owram, Douglas, ed. *The Formation of Alberta: A Documentary History*. Calgary: Historical Society of Alberta, 1979.

Stonechild, Blair and Bill Waiser. *Loyal till Death: Indians and the North-West Rebellion*. Saskatoon: Fifth House Publishers 1997.

Thomas, L.G. *The Struggle for Responsible Government in the North-West Territories, 1870–97*. Toronto: University of Toronto Press, 1956.

Waiser, Bill. *Saskatchewan: A New History*. Calgary: Fifth House Publishers, 2005.

Waiser, Bill. "Teaching the West and Confederation: A Saskatchewan Perspective." *Canadian Historical Review* vol. 98, no. 4 (2017): 742-64.

Waiser, Bill. *A World We Have Lost: Saskatchewan before 1905*. Markham: Fifth House Publishers, 2016.

NOTES

1. J.M.S. Careless, *Brown of the Globe, v. 1* (Toronto: Macmillan 1959), 230.

2. See W.L. Morton, "The Geographical Circumstances of Confederation," *Canadian Geographical Journal* 70, no. 3 (1965): 74–87.

3. Arthur S. Morton, *A History of the Canadian West to 1870–1871* (London: Thomas Nelson 1939), 827–31.

4. Great Britain, *House of Commons*, Report from the Select Committee on the Hudson's Bay Company, 1857, iii.

5. What changed Macdonald's reluctance and that of others was the apparent threat of American encirclement. On 30 March 1867, only one day after Queen Victoria had signed the British North America Act (effective 1 July 1867), the United States and Russia reached an agreement for the purchase of Russian Alaska. Even before Confederation became a reality, then, the United States seemed to have been manoeuvring to outflank the new dominion and threaten its future takeover of the North-West.

6. See Donald G. Creighton, *John A. Macdonald: The Young Politician* (Toronto: University of Toronto Press, 1952).

7. Douglas Owram, *Promise of Eden: The Canadian Expansionist Movement and the Idea of the West, 1856–1900* (Toronto: University of Toronto Press 1980), 4–5, 101–02.

8. Chester Martin, *Dominion Lands Policy* (Toronto: McClelland and Stewart 1973), 9.

9. John A. Bovey, "The Attitudes and Policies of the Federal Government Towards Canada's Northern Territories, 1870–1930," Master's thesis, University of British Columbia, 1957, 27.

10. Owram, *Promise of Eden*, 137–38.

11. Bill Waiser, *A World We Have Lost: Saskatchewan Before 1905* (Markham: Fifth House Publishers 2016), 439–527.

12. John L. Tobias, "Canada's Subjugation of the Plains Cree, 1879–1885," in *Sweet Promises: A Reader in Indian-White Relations in Canada*, ed. J.R. Miller (Toronto: University of Toronto Press 1991), 216.

13 See J.R. Miller, *Skyscrapers Hide the Heavens: A History of Indian-White Relations in Canada* (Toronto: University of Toronto Press 1989), ch. 4–5.

14 Rod C. Macleod, *The North-West Mounted Police and Law Enforcement* (Toronto: University of Toronto Press 1976), 3.

15 This notion of reciprocity is examined in Jean Friesen, "Magnificent Gifts: The Treaties of Canada with the Indians of the Northwest 1869–76," *Transactions of the Royal Society of Canada* series 5, vol. 1 (1986): 41–51.

16 Quoted in Alexander Morris, *The Treaties of Canada with the Indians of Manitoba and the North-West Territories* (Saskatoon: Fifth House 1991), 199, 202, reproduced by *The Confederation Debates*, http://hcmc.uvic.ca/confederation/en/Morris_Chapter_09.html.

17 Quoted in Morris, *The Treaties of Canada*, 205, 208, reproduced by *The Confederation Debates*, http://hcmc.uvic.ca/confederation/en/Morris_Chapter_09.html.

18 Quoted in Peter Erasmus, *Buffalo Days and Nights* (Calgary: Glenbow Museum 1974), 247, 249–50, reproduced by *The Confederation Debates*, http://hcmc.uvic.ca/confederation/en/Erasmus.html.

19 Quoted in Morris, *The Treaties of Canada*, 210–13, reproduced by *The Confederation Debates*, http://hcmc.uvic.ca/confederation/en/Morris_Chapter_09.html.

20 Quoted in Morris, *The Treaties of Canada*, 212, reproduced by *The Confederation Debates*, http://hcmc.uvic.ca/confederation/en/Morris_Chapter_09.html.

21 See J.R. Miller, "The Aboriginal Peoples and the Crown," in *The Crown and Canadian Federalism*, ed. D.M. Jackson (Toronto: Dundurn Press, 2013), 255–69.

22 Lewis H. Thomas, *The Struggle for Responsible Government in the North-West Territories, 1870–97* (Toronto: University of Toronto Press 1956), 94, 98–9, 108–9.

23 Canada, *House of Commons Debates*, 27 April 1877, 1872.

24 Arthur Silver, *The French-Canadian Idea of Confederation, 1864–1900* (Toronto: University of Toronto Press, 1982), 67–217; J.R. Miller, "Anti-Catholic Thought in Victorian Canada," *Canadian Historical Review* 66, no. 4 (1985): 474–94.

25 Manoly R. Lupul, *The Roman Catholic Church and the North-West School Question: A Study in Church-State Relations in Western Canada, 1870–1905* (Toronto: University of Toronto Press 1974), 21–79.

26 Thomas, *The Struggle*, 180.

27 Douglas Owram, ed., *The Formation of Alberta: A Documentary History* (Calgary: Historical Society of Alberta 1979), xxiv–xxxix.

28 Quoted in Thomas, *The Struggle*, 258.

29 James W. Brennan, "A Political History of Saskatchewan, 1905–1929," PhD diss., University of Alberta, 1976, 28–32.

30 David J. Hall, "A Divergence of Principle: Clifford Sifton, Sir Wilfrid Laurier, and the North-West Autonomy Bills, 1905," *Laurentian University Review* 7, no. 1 (November 1974): 11–19.

31 Quoted in Owram, ed., *The Formation of Alberta*, 270.

32 Quoted in Owram, ed., *The Formation of Alberta*, 279.

33 Quoted in Owram, ed., *The Formation of Alberta*, 293.

34 Quoted in Owram, ed., *The Formation of Alberta*, 333.

35 Charles C. Lingard, *Territorial Government in Canada: The Autonomy Question in the Old North-West Territories* (Toronto: University of Toronto Press 1946), 232–51.

36 Lewis G. Thomas, *The Liberal Party in Alberta: A History of Politics in the Province of Alberta* (Toronto: University of Toronto 1959), 3.

37 Brennan, "A Political History of Saskatchewan, 1905–1929," 49, 56; J.T. Saywell, "Liberal Politics, Federal Policies, and the Lieutenant-Governor: Saskatchewan and Alberta," 84, 87–8; J. Courtney and D.E. Smith, "Saskatchewan," in *Canadian Provincial Politics*, ed. M. Robin (Toronto: Prentice-Hall 1978), 285; Archer, *Saskatchewan*, 136.

10

Newfoundland and Canada: Confederation and the Search for Stability

Raymond B. Blake

In September 1864 when Maritime politicians met at Charlottetown to consider union, Newfoundlanders were not invited. They were, however, asked to Quebec City, when delegates reassembled there a month later. Conservative Deputy Premier and Protestant, F.B.T. Carter, and Ambrose Shea, Liberal Leader and representative of the Catholic minority, were excited about Confederation. They saw Confederation as Newfoundland's best hope to deal with its depressing isolation, reliance on a single staple commodity (codfish), and a way to spur economic diversification. Though Confederation had its proponents, union was overwhelmingly rejected in the 1869 election because voters saw no economic or political benefit. The issue of Confederation arose periodically after 1869, but it was not seriously debated again until after the Second World War. During this later debate, proponents of union argued that Confederation would provide economic and social security as well as rid Newfoundland of its long history of underdevelopment and poverty. The opponents of Confederation again fought to maintain the country's independence and sovereignty, promising never to sell their birth-right to Canada. While the debate might have been similar, the outcome was not. Confederation had a powerful champion in Joseph R. Smallwood and a rural population that demanded the state take a great interest in their social and economic well-being. In 1949,

Newfoundlanders opted for union with Canada by majority vote.

Newfoundland in the 1860s

In the 1860s Newfoundland was neither great in population nor wealth. Many of its 162,000 residents were dispersed along the coastline and depended on the cod and seal fisheries, which together accounted for 95 percent of exports. Any decline in catch, such as had occurred in the 1860s, created social and economic paralysis. In the four years to 1865 the debt grew from £18,000 to £36,000 as the country experienced its worst economic depression in twenty years. The government ran a deficit on current account, and relief payments accounted for 23 percent of current revenue as poverty levels rose dramatically.[1]

In the mid-nineteenth century, Newfoundland struggled with the quality of its human capital as defined by literacy and education, which had become an essential tool for fostering a better personal and national life and for spurring a lively intellectual debate about a nation's goals. High levels of education and literacy are necessary for social transformation and liberation, but those were lacking in Newfoundland, especially outside St. John's. Alan Macpherson's analysis of parish records for Hermitage on the South Coast estimated a literacy rate among the young married population of only 18 percent in the years 1867 to 1880, which improved only to 53 percent in 1901-10. In the 1890s, at least 32 percent of population were totally illiterate—a much higher rate than in Canada. In the 1860s, rather than "face the world with pride and confidence," as Ambrose Shea and Frederick Carter suggested, Newfoundland turned inward to pursue its own economic development.[2]

Newfoundland was also marked by sectarian and ethnic divisions for much of the nineteenth century and even into the twentieth century. Immigrants came either from the Protestant west of England or the Catholic south of Ireland, although there were small numbers of French, either from France or Acadia, who settled predominantly on the Port-au-Port Peninsula. Most settlers to Newfoundland arrived between 1760 and 1830. The Irish settled mostly on the Avalon Peninsula, the English further north and west, into Conception Bay and along the South Coast; St. John's became home to both groups who often brought with them the prejudices and hostilities of their homeland and which found their way into

Ambrose Shea
Liberal Leader, Newfoundland and Labrador

2 FEBRUARY 1865

CONFEDERATION QUOTE 10.1
Quotation from Newfoundland, House of Assembly, 2 February 1865
Photograph from The Rooms Provincial Archives Division, Newfoundland and Labrador, B 1-145

" . . . we cannot remain as we are if the other provinces confederate. We shall probably have to contend with their commercial restrictions, and our isolation will be more complete than ever, and more injurious. "

the Island's political life. The sectarian lines became further entrenched with the establishment of denominational schools in 1843, a practice that remained until 1998. The dominant religious groups forged an unwritten agreement in the 1860s for proportionate representation in the Legislature Assembly, in the Executive Council, and in patronage more generally. It was hoped that by informally institutionalizing such sectarian practices the country would be somewhat free of religious animosity.[3] Sometimes it worked.

Most of the wealth in Newfoundland was in the hands of a small group of merchants, primarily in St. John's and Conception Bay. The fisheries operated on a credit system whereby fishers were advanced supplies in the spring, with the hope that at the end of the season the catch was sufficient to settle their account with the merchants. Merchants charged as much as they could for the items advanced on credit and paid as little as possible for the fish delivered in the fall. Most fishers consequently lived in poverty or on its boundaries, but the fish merchants and the country's elite, known as Water Street merchants, exerted a powerful hold over the country, controlling all aspects of the economy, including local banking and the Island's meagre manufacturing sector. They also controlled the Legislative Council and their proxies, the Legislative Assembly, and the powerful Chamber of Commerce. They saw the economy, particularly the fisheries, as their own and ensured that the state did not intervene in their domain. As a result—unlike the fisheries of other countries—there was no strict and sustained government regulatory involvement in the sector in Newfoundland until the 1930s.[4]

The Confederation Debate, 1869

Ambrose Shea and Frederick B. T. Carter were impressed with the notion of Confederation when they gathered with other delegates in Quebec in October 1864, but they found no great enthusiasm for it upon returning to St. John's. Premier Hugh Hoyles and Governor Anthony Musgrave expressed some interest, but the Newfoundland Assembly was divided. When the 1865 throne speech called for a "calm examination" of union, eighteen members spoke against and twenty-one expressed some support, though the latter also identified problems with the Quebec Resolutions. Merchants and the Roman Catholic Church also opposed the deal.[5]

Newfoundland had little reason to be excited about continental integration. Its trade and traffic were to Europe and North America's Eastern Seaboard rather than with Canada and the continent's interior. There was no fear of an American threat of invasion or of the Fenians as was the case in much of British North America. Moroever, the Royal Navy provided all of the defence Newfoundland needed. Westward continental expansion held no appeal with Newfoundlanders while the promise of a railway from Halifax to Quebec similarly stirred no excitement. Political squabbling and deadlock in the Canadas was not their concern, and Newfoundland's debt—compared to that of the other colonies—was minimal. Confederation, moreover, was unlikely to resolve the French Shore issue whereby France enjoyed considerable rights in northern and western Newfoundland that had their roots in the eighteenth century. Finally, the terms of union did not allay fears of competition—in fisheries and manufacturing from Canada. Opponents of union believed that Canadian protectionism would have been catastrophic for Newfoundland, and some claimed that if the Canadian tariff of 1864 had been applied to Newfoundland, it would have raised taxes by 44 percent.[6]

The country's political elite agreed that the economy had to be diversified, and saw Confederation as possibly providing economic growth, improving social and economic conditions for most citizens, and stemming out-migration from the island. The island's future economic growth, many felt, lay in the interior of the Island; new investment in mineral and timber resources and in industrialization might boost the productive capacity of the country. Confederation, an arrangement that the British government favoured, might spur Canadian investment in Newfoundland and raise the standards of public services to that of the mainland colonies. Carter was most optimistic and in a speech in the Assembly, he said " . . . it would be well . . . to travel a little and visit that magnificent province [Canada], as well as Nova Scotia and New Brunswick, which were advancing so rapidly in material prosperity, and in all that tended to make a people great and respected. . . . These countries were all more prosperous than we are." Confederation would also provide cheaper imports, he promised. Like those who successfully pursued Confederation in 1949, he encouraged voters to "support this confederation on account of their children." In addition to its economic potential, Carter also hoped that Confederation would bring an end to the religious strife in Newfoundland as it would have

Charles Bennett
Anti-Confederation leader and future Premier, Newfoundland and Labrador

29 SEPTEMBER 1869

CONFEDERATION QUOTE 10.2
Quotation from "No Confederation," the *Morning Chronicle*, 29 September 1869
Photograph from Library and Archives Canada, C-054438

> What is Confederation? It is Taxation without limit upon our imports, our Exports, and upon all kinds of property, to be levied— not by our own people, but—by Canadians, residing more than a thousand miles from us, and who know nothing of our resources or requirements, and care less.

Newfoundland's politicians playing a role on a larger national stage. In 1869, the terms of union were agreed upon by Newfoundland and Canada. Canada was generous, offering just about everything Newfoundland demanded, including a special annual grant of $175,000 for surrendering its Crown lands, a promise that there would be no export levy placed on Newfoundland fish, and even modifications to the *Dominion Militia Act* that would exempt Newfoundlanders from serving in Canada.[7]

It was a tired government that entered the fray promoting Confederation in the 1869 election called in part to seek a mandate to complete union with Canada. In power for eight years, the Carter Administration had made unpopular decisions, especially on poor relief during the period of economic distress, even though recovery was well underway by 1869. The government faced, moreover, a determined and vigorous opponent in Charles Fox Bennett, a Protestant Tory and one of the country's leading merchants. He vowed to protect Newfoundland from the Canadians. To do so, Bennett forged a strange coalition, linking the St. John's Protestant oligarchy which feared commercial competition from Canada, and Irish Catholics who harboured a profound dislike of the British and had traditionally supported the Liberals. The Irish Catholic minority viewed Confederation as a British plot akin to that of the Act of Union of 1801 that had brought their beloved Ireland under English domination. Bennett played upon those fears and appealed to local patriotism: "The sending of Delegates to Canada," he said "would be the sacrifice of our independent legislation and the control of our own rich colonial resources for the benefit of that nationality which, so far as I can at present conceive, can confer but few and trifling benefits on us."[8] Shea, who was one of a few Catholics to support Confederation, was deemed a traitor by many of his faith; at Placentia, a Catholic community, he was "met by a priest and people bearing pots of pitch and bags of feathers, and the moaning of cow bells."[9]

The election held on 13 November 1869 was marked by sectarianism: all of the country's Catholic constituencies, and some Protestant ridings, too, voted against Confederation, with anti-Confederates taking twenty-one of the thirty Assembly seats.[10] The defeat was overwhelming, and the Conservatives quickly abandoned the idea of union. When Governor Stephen John Hill suggested adding Newfoundland to Canada by imperial fiat, Prime Minister John A. Macdonald declined, recognizing that for the time being the Confederation movement in Newfoundland was dead.[11]

Confederation, 1869-1939

After 1869, there were further discussions of union between Newfoundland and Canada, but none resulted in union. In the 1890s, when Newfoundland once again faced an economic crisis that devastated its banking sector and led to the demise of several Water Street firms, the government once again contemplated Confederation. The Bank of Montreal subsequently established operations in Newfoundland and helped to stabilize the fiscal and economic crisis. Worried that Newfoundland might forge an independent reciprocity treaty with the United States, Canada expressed some interest in union, but it worried that the associated costs and opposition to the French Shore in Newfoundland had the potential to generate additional political discontent, particularly in Quebec if the federal government intervened on the island's behalf.[12]

In 1906, as Newfoundland Prime Minister Robert Bond quarrelled with Britain and Canada over reciprocity and fishing rights with the Americans, some in Canada and in Great Britain again encouraged union between the two countries. Lord Grey, the Governor General of Canada, and Lord Elgin, the British Colonial Secretary, promoted union as did the Newfoundland Governor Sir William MacGregor, officials at the Bank of Montreal, the Canadian iron ore companies, and the Reid Family of Montreal that had secured a monopoly on the Newfoundland Railway in 1898. They hoped that Edward Morris would break with Bond—who had earlier used his own money to save the colony from bankruptcy—and lead the campaign for Confederation in the 1908 election, but Morris recognized Confederation's unpopularity. In that campaign, both parties accused each other of being insincere in their opposition to union, and even though it was a tied result, Morris formed a majority government in 1909 but had no interest in promoting Confederation. Confederation arose again during the economic and political turmoil in the 1930s that eventually led Newfoundland to surrender responsible government in 1933. Charles A. Magrath, a Canada banker and a member of the Newfoundland Royal Commission, wrote Canadian Prime Minister R.B. Bennett suggesting that Newfoundland's destiny lay with Canada and urged "generosity on the part of Canada." With Canada's own economic and fiscal situation deteriorating rapidly, however, Confederation would not be an option during the Great Depression.[13]

Canada and Newfoundland Rekindle Interest in Union, 1939-45

Canada's attitude towards Newfoundland changed during the Second World War. The United States had, through the 1941 Leased Bases Agreement with Great Britain, secured a ninety-nine-year lease to construct several military bases in Newfoundland, and Canada was determined not to be shut out of Newfoundland to have an Alaska on its eastern flank. Officials in the Canadian Department of External Affairs pushed Prime Minister Mackenzie King to be more proactive on Newfoundland, and he announced subsequently that Newfoundland would be included in Canada's defence preparations. He also made it clear that Canada would welcome Newfoundland into Confederation "should they make their decision clear and beyond all possibility of misunderstanding."[14] Canada appointed its first High Commissioner to Newfoundland in 1941, a clear sign of its growing interest in the country. At the same time, Britain realized that it could not afford to pay for postwar reconstruction in Newfoundland, and believed that union with Canada was the best solution. King remained cautious on Newfoundland, however, and was worried that its addition might spur political turmoil, especially in the Maritime Provinces, if Ottawa offered terms of union that were more generous than contemporary agreements with the Maritimes. On several occasions in 1945, King and his officials, nonetheless, suggested that if the British withheld financial assistance, it might "assist Newfoundlanders to turn their thoughts to Canada." King continued to insist, however, that "Newfoundland could not be forced into Confederation."[15]

Reconsidering Confederation During the 1940s

Newfoundland had been governed by a British-appointed Commission of Government since 1933, and it became solvent during the economic boom created by the Second World War with a forty-million dollar surplus. The future for the country was far from secure, however, and by the end of the war there was little public appetite to continue with the Commission of Government. After all, the war had been fought for freedom and democracy. Democracy had to be restored in Newfoundland. Yet, the wartime boom had seen "no new productive capacity to help

Joey Smallwood
Member of Newfoundland National Convention and future Premier

28 OCTOBER 1946

CONFEDERATION QUOTE 10.3
Quotation from Newfoundland,
Newfoundland National Convention,
28 October 1946
Photograph by Duncan Cameron, from
Library and Archives Canada, PA-113253

" These, then, are the conditions of my support of confederation: that it must raise our people's standard of living, that it must give Newfoundlanders a better life, that it must give our country stability and security and that it must give us full, democratic responsible government under circumstances that will ensure its success. "

Michael F. Harrington
Member of Newfoundland National Convention

28 OCTOBER 1946

CONFEDERATION QUOTE 10.4
Quotation from Newfoundland, Newfoundland National Convention, 28 October 1946
Photograph from Archives and Special Collections, Queen Elizabeth II Library, Memorial University of Newfoundland, Coll. 309

> "The members of this Convention are supposed to have an open mind... I am doing my honest best, whatever my personal opinions, to fairly appraise the situation... Mr. Smallwood's antics may provide a great deal of humorous conversation, but it goes beyond a joke when even one individual is asked, cajoled or invited to sell his integrity, to further the cause of confederation, or any cause at this stage."

sustain the economy in peacetime" and no new alternative sources of employment.[16] On almost any index—from employment rates, income per capita, education levels, hospital beds, electrification, or number of indoor flush toilets—Newfoundland ranked below any jurisdiction in Canada. The Newfoundland Tuberculosis Association claimed in 1948, for instance, that the country's health services equalled those of England and Wales in 1910. More than ten thousand suffered from tuberculosis in Newfoundland, but its sanatoria could accommodate less than four hundred. Death rates exceeded those in Canada: the Newfoundland death rate per 100,000 of population was 122.0 while Ontario's was 25.7, Nova Scotia at 62.4, and Quebec's at 72.4. Infant mortality was much higher than that in the Maritime Provinces, and total public hospital expenditure in 1946 ($1.68 million) paled in comparison to New Brunswick's ($4.13 million) and Nova Scotia's ($5.06 million).[17]

On 11 December 1945 British Prime Minister Clement Atlee announced the formation of a National Convention to study Newfoundland's economic and social conditions and then recommend possible forms of future government to the British government. It would then put several constitutional options before the people in a national referendum.[18] Attlee imposed a residency requirement for election to the National Convention, fearing vested interests might otherwise control the body.[19] Less than 50 percent of eligible voters cast a ballot in the National Convention elections on 21 June 1946. The new body first met on September 11 and deliberated for the next eighteen months; its debates were broadcast nightly on the Newfoundland Broadcasting Corporation. Nine investigative committees studied various aspects of Newfoundland's economy, government, and society, and the reports stimulated considerable debate in the Convention and throughout the country as audiences considered how their country would transition from war to peace and, at the same time, find economic and political stability. The Convention awakened Newfoundlanders to some harsh realities, including their poverty and the comparative lack of public services.[20]

Two groups emerged during the National Convention proceedings. The larger group advocated returning to responsible government and restoring democracy. A smaller group rallied around the promise of Confederation, arguing that responsible government had collapsed, in part, because the population had been demoralized by the state's long-term neglect.[21] This group focussed on the problems facing the country, and demanded that the state introduce a series of programmes to address citizens' social and economic needs. Joseph R. Smallwood and F. Gordon Bradley were already proponents of Confederation, and they became the leaders of a small group within the Convention who believed that Newfoundland, like other countries such as Britain and Canada, must also adopt a form of government that included an expansion of social rights and the provision of social security programs that would see the implementation of such programs as family allowances and veterans' benefits to citizens. The supporters of Confederation promoted a new relationship between the state and its citizens.

Smallwood became the *de facto* leader of the Confederates. His first speech to the Convention proposed sending a delegation to Ottawa to investigate the possibility of Confederation; it was also a plea to extend social citizenship to Newfoundland. In that speech, which might be titled "We are not a Nation," Smallwood fully embraced the necessity of a new social citizenship. "In the North American family Newfoundland bears the reputation of having the lowest standards of life, of being the least progressive and advanced of the whole family," he said. "Our people never enjoyed a good standard of living, and never were able to yield enough taxes to maintain the government. . . . We are not a nation. . . . We are living in a world in which small countries have less chance than ever before of surviving. . . . Confederation I will support if it means a higher standard of living for our people."[22] This was the major narrative of his Confederation campaign.

Although Smallwood's resolution on 28 October 1946 to send a delegation to Ottawa failed, a wider resolution introduced on 4 February 1947 to send delegations to London and Ottawa succeeded. The governor rejected another resolution to send representatives to Washington in hopes of negotiating an economic union with the United States. The delegation that travelled to London found no support for an independent Newfoundland. The delegation to Ottawa sought to learn whether a fair and equitable basis could be found for federal union of Newfoundland and Canada. It was greeted enthusiastically. Bradley, who had been a Confederate since his studies at Dalhousie University in 1914, chaired the meetings in Ottawa. He had written earlier "I don't care two straws for Newfoundland as an abstraction." He believed that Newfoundland as "small, remote and economically weak . . . [and] could not survive and prosper was an independent unit."[23] Like

Fig 10.1 The Ottawa Delegation of the National Convention, 1947. Photographer: G. Hunter. LAC, MIKAN 3362966.

Shea and Carter decades earlier, Bradley believed Confederation might address Newfoundland's peculiar economic and social situation.

Canada welcomed union with Newfoundland for several reasons. Its inclusion would fulfill the Canadian dreams of 1867 to thwart any designs the Americans might have on Newfoundland. It would bring considerable resource wealth, including expansive fisheries, mineral and potential hydro-electric resources. It would also safeguard the Newfoundland market for Canadian exporters, valued at between twenty-five and forty million dollars, and it would also secure Canadian defence and civil aviation privileges in Newfoundland. Ottawa's only concern was the financial cost of union.

The Canadian and Newfoundland delegations agreed upon the "Proposed Arrangements for the Entry of Newfoundland into Confederation." On 29 October 1947 when King despatched to Sir Gordon MacDonald, governor of Newfoundland, the proposed terms, he wrote "I feel I must emphasize that as far as the financial aspects of the proposed arrangements for union are concerned, the Government of Canada believes that the arrangements go as far as the Government can go under the circumstances." Yet, on matters of primarily provincial concern, such as education, he said that "Canada would not wish to set down any rigid conditions, and it would be prepared to give reasonable consideration to suggestions for modification or addition."[24] The "Proposed Arrangements" were presented to the National Convention on 6 November 1947.[25]

Debate in National Convention on Constitutional Options

Debate in the National Convention on the Canadian proposal began on 20 November 1947 and continued for thirty-four days, generating considerable interest across Newfoundland and Labrador.[26] "These terms," Smallwood said in his final speech to the National Convention, "would make a new country for the people of Newfoundland—a new country where . . . the poor man would have a chance to live and breathe, a chance to bring up his family decently. The terms would give our people a chance, and that is something they have never had yet." As a small nation, Smallwood asserted, Newfoundland could not prosper on its own; Canada promised security and an improved standard of living as well as a return to responsible and a democratically elected government.[27]

The National Convention debated the inclusion of responsible government for four days. On 19 January 1948 the Convention unanimously passed a resolution introduced by Gordon Higgins recommending that both Responsible Government—as it existed in 1933—as well as the continuation of the Commission of Government be placed before the electorate in a national referendum. Smallwood then moved that Confederation also appear on the ballot, but it was defeated twenty-nine to sixteen. The Confederates reacted by launching an appeal to the country for Confederation's inclusion. Even before the governor received over twenty-four thousand telegrams demanding Confederation be placed on the ballot, the British Government (which had long favoured the union of Newfoundland with Canada) decided that all three options be included in the referendum.

Referendum Campaigns

In the referendum campaigns that followed, the Confederate Association led the fight for union with Canada. Those who wanted to return to responsible government fell into two groups that often shared resources and people: the Responsible Government League (RGL) and the Economic Union Association (EUA) which campaigned for an economic union with the United States, though that option was not on the ballot. It had first to achieve responsible government and then work for an economic union. There was no organized campaign for Commission of Government.

The Responsible Government League (RGL) was established in St. John's on 11 February 1947. It was dedicated to securing the return of "Responsible Government for Newfoundland and to encourag[ing] the people of Newfoundland to accept their full, personal and collective responsibilities for the good government of our country." The RGL was perceived as an organ of Newfoundland's business and professional elite. Nearly all of the founding members came from this particular group and many who later joined were primarily merchants with close ties to Water Street.[28]

The Responsible Government League never embraced the notions of social citizenship then circulating throughout much of the developed world. In fact, J.S. Currie, the owner of the *Daily News* and stalwart advocate for the return of responsible government, said "people should accept the responsibility of self-government with the restraints and discipline that it should impose on the individual." Many in the RGL worried that "materialism" had become the order of the day, and insisted that even if Newfoundland did not possess the material wealth that other nations enjoyed, it might be better off. Materialism, the RGL members often asserted, breeds selfishness and greed and embitters the lives of great sections of the populations and gives rise to avaricious politicians. The RGL believed that citizens were content with the level of services that the current tax system could support and accused the Confederates of bribing voters with the promise of Canada's social programs.[29]

The RGL faced an uphill struggle. First, responsible government was not remembered with any great enthusiasm by voters, and it had become associated with the economic deprivation that many had experienced in the 1920s and 1930s. The Hollis Walker report of 1924, for instance, had

Fig 10.2 Anti-Confederate Campaign, 1948. Anti-Confederate posters were often patriotically displayed in the windows of many Newfoundland homes and businesses. Courtesy of the Rooms Provincial Archives Division, George Carter Collection, Box 5, MG910.

been charged with investigating alleged corruption in several government departments, and provided not only an indictment of a number of individuals but also of a political system that allowed such actions within the state apparatus. Less than a decade later, the Newfoundland Royal Commission (the Amulree Commission) also popularized the notion that Newfoundland's experiment with responsible government had resulted in widespread corruption and mismanagement. The RGL inherited all of the negativity associated with responsible government.

On the other hand, the Confederate Association, established on 21 February 1948, emphasized the social benefits of Confederation, stressing how Canadian social programs and a general higher standard of living would improve the lives of all Newfoundlanders. It also waged a well-organized and effective campaign. Its ideas were communicated over the radio and in a successful tabloid, *The Confederate*, first published on April

Fig 10.3 The pro-Confederation movement promised that union would bring change to Newfoundland. *The Confederate*, 31 May 1948, 3.

7 and whose appealing political cartoons were professionally drawn by a *Globe and Mail* cartoonist under Smallwood's direction. The 31 May 1948 edition of *The Confederate* asked voters "to give yourself a chance. Give the

Children a chance. Give Newfoundland a chance. Vote for Confederation and a healthier, happier Newfoundland." To mothers, Smallwood and the Confederates promised the benefits of a modern social state, claiming "Confederation would mean that NEVER AGAIN would there be a hungry child in Newfoundland." He also reminded parents that their children under the age of sixteen would receive "EVERY MONTH a cash allowance for every child you have or may have."[30]

Smallwood travelled widely throughout the campaign and wrote open letters to a large number of communities that he could not visit. He explained in a 29 May 1948 letter "To the People of Lower Island Cove" why he favoured Confederation: "It is the people who earn small incomes who will benefit the most by Confederation. They are the ones who deserve our greatest consideration: because they get very little out of life." He suggested further that those who argued for a return to responsible government had not considered the interests of others: "Don't forget the struggle is between a better living for you, or more profits for the merchants and a still lowering of your standard of living. It is a struggle in which you have only one advantage, and that is the ballot paper." He asked voters to compare their situations with their relatives in Canada, and "you know they are enjoying a better standard of living than here." His message was clear: "I ask you in all sincerity to consider carefully the issue. Your decision will mean a better standard of living for you if you vote for Confederation." Smallwood made similar arguments during his radio broadcasts.[31]

The RGL never matched the Confederate Association in attracting support in rural Newfoundland because it failed to present to the voters an alternative to the St. John's dominated political system that had failed in 1933. Many voters in rural and outport Newfoundland harboured a great deal of resentment towards St. John's and were not attracted to "responsible government as it existed in 1933". The RGL also failed to create a country-wide political organization and did not campaign aggressively outside the Avalon Peninsula. Nor did it present an economic and social agenda to compete with the prospect of Newfoundland's membership in Canada. Thus, by opting for union with Canada, voters were effectively rejecting the political system that had existed before the establishment of Commission of Government.

The results of the first referendum on 3 June 1948 failed to produce a majority for either side, though Responsible Government led with

44.5 percent of the vote to Confederation's 41.1 percent. Commission of Government with 14.3 percent was dropped from the second referendum held on 22 July 1948 which gave Confederation a narrow victory with 52.3 percent of the vote. Responsible Government won in seven districts, all on the Avalon Peninsula while the Confederates carried the remainder of the country. Because most of the support for Responsible Government came from districts with Catholic majorities, it might appear that denominationalism was the deciding factor in the referendum.[32] It was not; region was decisive. Sixty-six percent of voters on the Avalon Peninsula supported Responsible Government, compared to 34 percent for Confederation; the rest of the Island voted 70 percent for Confederation. Two Avalon districts, those furthest from St. John's (Port de Grave and Carbonear-Bay de Verde), voted Confederation and two predominantly Catholic districts off the Avalon Peninsula (Placentia West and St. George's-Port-au-Port) supported Confederation. Catholic votes outside the Avalon Peninsula may have carried Confederation to victory. Still, Catholic and Protestant organizations exchanged a number of barbs during the campaign leading to the second referendum. As Jeff A. Webb suggests, Newfoundlanders held different conceptions of national identity and different political and economic expectations depending on their place of residence.[33] While those on the Avalon Peninsula were committed to a Newfoundland state, many outside of the Avalon Peninsula were not. Perhaps also pivotal to the outcome was the decision of several well-known members of the economic elite as well as several of the Newfoundland members of the Commission of Government to embrace Confederation. More important, Confederation was a vote for the welfare state which a return to responsible government could not deliver because of the limitations of the local economy.

Newfoundland's Delegation to Ottawa, 1948

On 27 July 1948, the Canada government announced that it would accept Newfoundland as a province and preparations began in St. John's and in Ottawa for the final negotiations between the two countries. The 1948 Newfoundland delegation to Ottawa was chaired by Albert J. Walsh of the Commission of Government. It also included Smallwood and Bradley, and was primarily concerned with the financial prospects of Newfoundland after union. Even though Canada had insisted that the amount of the subsidy offered to Newfoundland was proportionately higher than that paid to any of the Maritime Provinces, the delegation worried that Newfoundland's fiscal capacity would be insufficient to meet normal expenditures as a province of Canada.[34] Its memorandum to the Canadian government pointed out that the level of public services in Newfoundland was below that of any Province of Canada and even without including for new services, Newfoundland would face a deficit of approximately ten million dollars per annum within four years of union (when it was expected that its surplus of approximately forty million dollars would be exhausted). The delegation warned that the existence of such a financial gap would result in an unworkable union.

The Newfoundland and Canadian delegations first met on 6 October 1948. The meetings were not a series of negotiations between the two delegations, but more of a discussion of how Newfoundland might fit into the existing Canadian system. Canada did not bargain directly with the Newfoundland delegation, trying to ascertain what price had to be paid to induce the Newfoundlanders to join. The Canadian government had decided what was fair, reasonable, and compatible given the arrangements that existed in the Maritime Provinces and left it to the Newfoundland delegation to decide whether it was justified in recommending union.[35]

On 22 November 1948 the two sides began drafting an agreement that became the Terms of Union. On the fiscal side, Newfoundland won a small victory. Canada increased the twelve-year sliding transitional subsidy in the 1947 proposals from twenty-six to forty-two million dollars. Canada also promised in Term 29 a review of Newfoundland's finances after eight years of union, but Newfoundland did not insist on playing a role in that investigation. On December 11 the two sides completed their work, but one member of the Newfoundland delegation, Chesley Crosbie, refused to sign, claiming that the arrangement did not secure Newfoundland's financial future. Smallwood, too, realized that some uncertainties about Newfoundland's financial future remained, but he believed that Canada and Newfoundland would address any lingering problems over fiscal matters through Term 29.

The Canadian Parliament passed the appropriate legislation by the end of February 1949, which allowed the British Parliament to pass the Newfoundland Act, providing for the union of Newfoundland and Canada. By the time Newfoundland became a province on 1 April 1949, the

Fig 10.4 Rt. Hon. Louis St. Laurent speaking during the ceremony which admitted Newfoundland into Confederation. Ottawa, Ontario, 1 April 1949. LAC, MIKAN 3408569.

Government of Canada had already made arrangement for the integration of Newfoundland, including the payment of Canada's social programmes in the first month of union. Little attention was paid to the Indigenous Peoples in Newfoundland and Labrador during the negotiations leading to union in 1949, and there was considerable ignorance of the affairs of Indigenous Peoples even if they had full rights of citizenship. It was decided to settle the administration of Indigenous Affairs after Confederation, when the Indian Act was proclaimed in Newfoundland, but only in 1987 did the Conne River Miawpukek become a reserve under the Indian Act, and in 2013 did the Government of Canada recognize the Qalipu Mi'kmaq Band as a landless band for the Mi'kmaq of Newfoundland. In 2007 the Innu of Labrador won recognition for its members as status Indians under Canada's Indian Act, but land claims remain an issue of contention.[36]

From its earliest days, Newfoundland faced many difficult economic problems, and poverty was abundantly evident throughout the country.

In 1869, voters rejected Confederation as the best path forward because of concerns over the economic costs of union with Canada and because of the opposition of Irish and Catholic voters. In 1949, however, Smallwood and other Confederates won a narrow victory by promising a variety of programs already provided throughout Canada by the federal government. Those who supported Confederation in 1869 and 1949 believed that union with Canada held the best promise of a decent, prosperous future with a better and more secure standard of living than they had enjoyed as an independent country. As Smallwood often repeated throughout his long political career, "Newfoundland joined Canada mostly for Newfoundland's sake. Newfoundland was the smaller of the two, the poorer of the two, the weaker of the two; and it was because we believed that Newfoundland would get the better of the bargain that Newfoundlanders agreed to unite their country with Canada."[37] In 1949, a majority of Newfoundlanders hoped that would be the case and voted to join Canada.

Further Reading:

Baker, Melvin. "Falling into the Canadian Lap: The Confederation of Newfoundland and Canada, 1945–49." In *Royal Commission on Renewing and Strengthening our Place in Canada*. Research Volume 1. St. John's: Office of the Queen's Printer, 2003, 29-88.

Blake, Raymond B. *Canadians as Last: Canada Integrates Newfoundland as a Province*. Toronto: University of Toronto Press, 1994.

Bridle, Paul, ed. *Documents on Relations Between Canada and Newfoundland*. Vol. 2, 1940–1949. Confederation, Part II. Ottawa: Minister of Supply and Services, 1984.

Hiller, James. "Confederation Defeated: The Newfoundland Election of 1869." In *Newfoundland in the Nineteenth and Twentieth Centuries: Essays in Interpretation*. Edited by James Hiller and Peter Neary. Toronto: University of Toronto Press, 1980.

Hiller, J. K and M.F. Harrington, eds. *The Newfoundland National Convention, 1946–1948. Debates*. Volume 1. Montreal: McGill-Queen's University Press, 1995.

MacKenzie, David. *Inside the Atlantic Triangle. Canada and the Entrance of Newfoundland into Confederation, 1939–1949*. Toronto: University of Toronto Press, 1986.

Neary, Peter. *Newfoundland in the North Atlantic World*. Montreal and Kingston: McGill-Queen's University Press, 1988.

Webb, Jeff A. "The Responsible Government League and the Confederation Campaigns of 1948." *Newfoundland Studies* 5, no. 2 (1989): 203–20.

NOTES

1 James K. Hiller, "Newfoundland Confronts Canada, 1867–1949," in *The Atlantic Provinces in Confederation*, eds. Ernest Forbes and D.A. Muse (Toronto: University of Toronto Press, 1993), 351–2.

2 David Alexander, "Literacy and Economic Development in Nineteenth Century Newfoundland," in *Atlantic Canada and Confederation. Essays in Canadian Political Economy*, compiled by Eric Sager et al. (Toronto: University of Toronto Press, 1983), 113 and 137. These points are also made in S.J.R. Noel, *Politics in Newfoundland* (Toronto: University of Toronto Press, 1971).

3 Noel, *Politics in Newfoundland*, 23–25.

4 Hiller, "Newfoundland Confronts Canada, 1867–1949," 352–55.

5 Phillip Buckner, "The 1860s: An End and a Beginning," in *The Atlantic Region to Confederation: A History*, eds. Phillip Buckner and John G. Reid (Toronto: University of Toronto Press, 1994), 382–83.

6 James K. Hiller, "Confederation Defeated: The Newfoundland Election of 1869," in *Newfoundland in the Nineteenth and Twentieth Centuries: Essays in Interpretation*, eds. James Hiller and Peter Neary (Toronto: University of Toronto Press, 1980), 75.

7 H.B. Mayo, "Newfoundland and Confederation in the Eighteen-Sixties," *Canadian Historical Review* 29 (1948): 125–42.

8 C. F. Bennett to *The Newfoundlander*, December 5, 1864. http://www.heritage.nf.ca/articles/politics/charles-bennett-objections.php.

9 Hiller, "Confederation Defeated: The Newfoundland Election of 1869," 79.

10 Frederick Jones, "The Antis Gain the Day," in *The Causes of Canadian Confederation*, ed. Ged Martin (Fredericton: Acadiensis Press, 1990), 147, and Buckner, "The 1860s: An End and a Beginning," 383.

11 J. K. Johnson and P. B. Waite, "Macdonald, Sir John Alexander," *Dictionary of Canadian Biography*, vol. 12, University of Toronto/Université Laval, 2003–, accessed 4 February 2017, http://www.biographi.ca/en/bio/macdonald_john_alexander_12E.html.

12 Hiller, "Newfoundland Confronts Canada, 1867–1949," 360.

13 Quoted in Noel, *Politics in Newfoundland*, 211.

14 Paul Bridle, ed., *Documents on the Relations between Canada and Newfoundland*, vol. 2, *1940–49, Confederation* (Ottawa: Minister of Supply and Services, 1984), 73–74.

15 Raymond B. Blake, *Canadians at Last: Canada Integrates Newfoundland as a Province* (Toronto: University of Toronto Press, 1994), 11–14.

16 Noel, *Politics in Newfoundland*, 263.

17 Rooms Provincial Archives (RPA), GN 154, Newfoundland Delegation to Ottawa (1948) Fonds, GN 154.6, Memorandum from the Newfoundland Tuberculosis Association to Ottawa Delegation, September 1948.

18 Great Britain, *House of Commons Debates*, 11 December 1945, 210–11.

19 Peter Neary, "Clement Attlee's Visit to Newfoundland, September 1942," *Acadiensis* 13, no. 2 (1984): 101–09; Nicklaus Thomas-Symonds, *Attlee: A Life in Politics* (New York: Palgrave Macmillan, 2010).

20 Newfoundland National Convention, 1946–1948, *vol. 6: Report of the Fisheries Committee of the National Convention*: 47–48. Digital Archives Initiative link: http://collections.mun.ca/PDFs/cns/NationalConventionReportsAgriculture1946-1948.pdf.

21 Great Britain, *Newfoundland Royal Commission 1933: Report* (London: HMSO, 1933). See also, Peter Neary, *Newfoundland in the North Atlantic World* (Montreal and Kingston: McGill-Queen's University Press, 1988), and Noel, *Politics in Newfoundland*.

22 Joseph R. Smallwood, *I Chose Canada. The Memoirs of the Honourable Joseph R. "Joey" Smallwood* (Toronto: Macmillan of Canada, 1973), 255–61.

23 J.K. Hiller, "The Career of F. Gordon Bradley," *Newfoundland Studies* 4, no. 2 (1988): 165.

24 Bridle, *Documents, vol. 2, Confederation*. Part 1, 682–83.

25 RPA, Albert Walsh Fonds, MG 302.13, Box 1, Meetings between Delegates from the National Convention of Newfoundland and Representatives of The Government of Canada, Summary of Proceedings, Part II, Ottawa, 25 June–29 September 1947, 67–69.

26 Bridle, *Documents, vol. 2, Confederation*, Part I, 526 and 528.

27 Hiller and Harrington, eds., *The Newfoundland National Convention*, vol. 1, 1187, reproduced by *The Confederation Debates*, http://hcmc.uvic.ca/confederation/en/lgNFNC_1948-01-14.html.

28 Quoted in Jeff A. Webb, "The Responsible Government League and the Confederation Campaigns of 1948," *Newfoundland Studies* 5, no. 2 (1989): 205.

29 Centre for Newfoundland Studies Archives, Memorial University, Senator John G. Higgins Collection, Coll. 0-87, Box 19, file 3.01.032, Speech by J.S. Currie, 14 February 1948; file 3.01.033, Broadcast Speech by A.B. Butt, 10 April 1948; Radio Speech, F.W. Marshall, Dominion President of the Great War Veterans' Association, 5 May 1948; Radio Speech by Frank Fogwill, 6 March 1948.

30 Peter Neary, ed., *Political Economy of Newfoundland* (Toronto: Copp Clark, 1973), 140–41.

31 Centre for Newfoundland Studies Archives, Memorial University of Newfoundland, Coll-075, J.R. Smallwood Papers, Box 299, file 4.01.001 Nfld. Confederate Association, "To the People of Lower Island Cove from C.F. Garland (Secretary Treasurer, Confederate Association), 29 May 1948. Letter from Confederate Headquarters; and file 4.01.004 Speech, "Why I favour Confederation," 6 April 1948 and 23 April 1948.

32 Patrick O'Flaherty, *Leaving the Past Behind. Newfoundland History from 1934* (St. John's: Long Beach Press, 2011), 193–98.

33 Jeff A. Webb, "Confederation, Conspiracy and Choice: A Discussion," *Newfoundland Studies* 14, no. 2 (Fall 1998): 169–87.

34 The Rooms, GN 154, Newfoundland Delegation to Ottawa (1948), GN 154.1, Minutes, 25 August–24 September 1948, Minutes 28 August 1948.

35 Blake, *Canadians At Last*, 29–30.

36 David Mackenzie, "The Indian Act and the Aboriginal Peoples of Newfoundland at the Time of Confederation," *Newfoundland and Labrador Studies* 25, no. 2 (2010): 161–81, and Peter Neary, "The First Nations and the Entry of Newfoundland into Confederation, 1945–54, Part 1," *Newfoundland Quarterly* 105, no. 2 (Fall 2012): 36–42.

37 Smallwood Papers, Coll-075, file 4.03.007, Speech by Smallwood during the 1959 election campaign, no date, 3.

11

"A More Accurate Face on Canada to the World": The Creation of Nunavut

P. Whitney Lackenbauer and André Légaré

> *For a long, long time Canada was described as a nation founded by two peoples, the English and the French. Eventually, the Indian people of this country started making a lot more noise than they had previously. They started getting some official recognition. Then, Inuit came along, and created this new territory. The creation of Nunavut in some ways has put a native face on the country. People can no longer talk about Canada being a country founded by two nations. Most people now accept the fact that Canadian history has been a three way partnership between the English, the French and the Aboriginal People. In that sense, the creation of Nunavut puts a more accurate face on Canada to the world.*
>
> John Amagoalik, *Changing the Face of Canada*[1]

On 1 April 1999, two new territories—a new Northwest Territories and Nunavut ("our land" in Inuktitut)—were created when the federal government redrew the boundaries in Canada's North, splitting off the central and eastern Canadian Arctic north and east of the tree-line from the rest of the Northwest Territories. Nunavut became the largest political unit in Canada, covering one-fifth of the country's land mass (more than two million km²) with a population of twenty-seven thousand people, about 85 percent of whom were Inuit, dispersed in twenty-eight communities (see Figure 11.3: map of Nunavut). This event marked the first significant change to the map of Canada since Newfoundland joined Confederation in 1949, and the culmination of a process negotiated over several decades. In the end, it provided the Inuit with powerful mechanisms to control their future through a public territorial government.

The lengthy road to Nunavut becoming a distinct territory within the Canadian Confederation is inextricably linked to the negotiation and settlement of an Aboriginal land claim between Inuit of the central and eastern Arctic and the government of Canada. First proposed in 1976 by the Inuit Tapirisat of Canada (ITC), the institution representing the political interests of Canadian Inuit, the Nunavut idea was aimed at settling the outstanding Aboriginal rights of Inuit of the Northwest Territories (NWT) and creating a territory within which the vast majority of people were Inuit. Inuit pushed for their own political unit for three main reasons. First, they had not concluded any land cession treaty with the Canadian government. Second, they possessed a demographic majority in the central and eastern Canadian Arctic. Third, they desired to control their own political, social, and economic agendas. Accordingly, ITC promoted the idea that a Nunavut Territory, split from the rest of the NWT, would better reflect the geographical extent of Inuit traditional land use and occupancy in the central and eastern Canadian Arctic, while its institutions would adhere to Inuit cultural values and perspectives.

This chapter provides an overview of the political contexts, debates, and lengthy processes that surrounded the settling of the Inuit land claims and the division of the NWT, which culminated with the creation of Nunavut in 1999. Dispossessed of political power by expanding colonial control in the first six decades of the twentieth century, Inuit used the federal comprehensive land claims policies, from the 1970s–90s, to seek and eventually secure a new relationship with the federal government, linking the search for Nunavut to the long-recognized benefits of dividing the NWT. The long, winding path to Nunavut reveals Inuit resilience and pragmatism in overcoming "many rough spots and roadblocks" (as MP

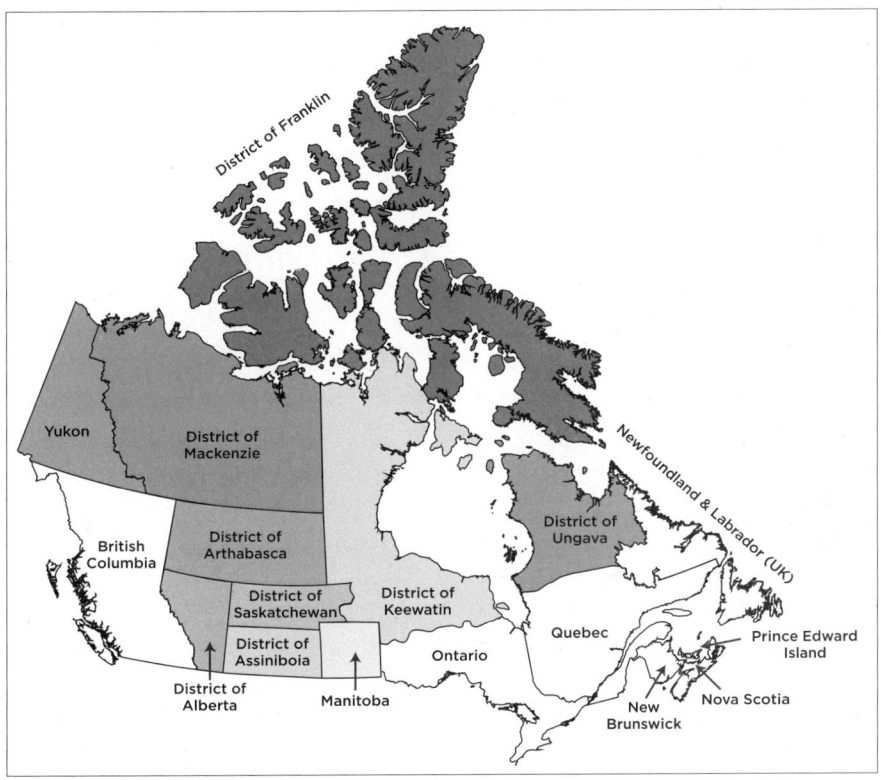

Fig 11.1 Canada at the beginning of the 20th century, before the federal government created Alberta as well as Saskatchewan, and extended the northern boundaries of Manitoba, Ontario, and Quebec. Developed from Natural Resources Canada, "Map 1898," *Library and Archives Canada*, https://www.collectionscanada.gc.ca/confederation/023001-5009-e.html.

Jack Anawak put it)[2] to achieve their political objectives and reconfigure Canada's northern political boundaries. "Governments, territorial and federal, have made constitutional attempts to separate our political rights from our rights to the land, and Inuit have had to drag those governments, kicking and screaming, to the negotiating table to discuss our political rights as Aboriginal People and as Canadians," John Amagoalik noted in 1992.[3] These efforts yielded a unique political outcome. "The creation of the [Government of Nunavut] in the 1990s was as close to fashioning a government on a blank piece of paper as anyone is likely to see," consultant Jack Hicks and political scientist Graham White observe. "Certainly nowhere in Canada had there ever been an opportunity to, in effect, design a government of this scale or importance virtually from scratch."[4] In the case of Nunavut, Inuit of the central and eastern Canadian Arctic managed to link land ownership and self-government, in the form of a public government at the territorial level, more successfully than any other Indigenous group in Canada.[5]

Governing the Northwest Territories after 1905

With the creation of the provinces of Saskatchewan and Alberta in 1905, the NWT lost its most populous areas. Accordingly, the federal government restructured the form of the territorial government in the residual parts of the NWT, rescinding the territory from an elected representative government to a state of outright colonial dependency controlled by appointed bureaucrats in Ottawa. Amendments to the Northwest Territories Act in 1905 provided for a commissioner (a position held by the Comptroller of the RCMP from 1905–18, and then by the deputy minister of the Interior and its successor departments until 1963) and a federally-appointed council of four. No appointments were actually made until 1921, when the Council increased to six members. The Council, "or government," of the NWT was an interdepartmental committee comprised entirely of senior federal civil servants based in Ottawa until after the Second World War. With the federal government still preoccupied with the development of Western Canada, the North occupied a peripheral place on the political agenda of federal politicians and administrators in southern Canada.

Until the late 1940s, there was little Canadian political presence in the North. "The human population of the territorial North was left largely in a 'state of nature'", Frances Abele aptly describes. Non-state institutions (particularly the fur trading companies and churches) provided social services. "While Dominion policy towards Native people in southern Canada had the official objective of making them 'good, industrious and useful citizens' by settling them on reserves and replacing the hunt with agriculture," she explains, official consensus held that "*northern* Native people ought best 'follow their natural mode of living and not . . . depend upon white men's food and clothing which are unsuited to their needs.'"[6]

In 1952, following requests from non-Indigenous residents of the Mackenzie District (the mainland portion of the NWT lying directly north of British Columbia, Alberta, and Saskatchewan), Ottawa agreed that those residents could elect representatives to the NWT Council. Other NWT residents (mostly Inuit) living in the central and eastern Arctic (i.e., Keewatin and Franklin Districts) were denied the same privileges. Inuit did not have the right to vote in territorial elections until the federal parliament amended the Northwest Territories Act in 1966. Up to that point, all four elected seats to the Council came from the western part of the NWT. This amendment also added three seats to the Council from the central and eastern Arctic, so that Inuit voters could elect their representatives to the NWT Council for the first time.[7]

The challenges of effectively administering the vast NWT from far-away Ottawa had long perplexed federal officials and politicians. In the early 1960s, the government of John Diefenbaker considered a proposal to separate the Mackenzie District (western part of the NWT) from the Keewatin and Franklin Districts (central and eastern Arctic). In a July 1961 speech to the NWT Council, the prime minister suggested that northerners should assume more responsibility, including "self-government," through "a division of this vast northern area into two districts," which he believed would receive "sympathetic consideration on the part of the federal government."[8] Although Prime Minister Diefenbaker failed to implement these changes before his government fell, the Pearson Liberal government followed suit and proposed, in May 1963, Bills C-83 and C-84 to amend the Northwest Territories Act and to create two separate territories: one to be named Mackenzie, the other *Nunassiaq* ("the beautiful land" in Inuktitut). During the ensuing debates, Minister Arthur Laing became "satisfied" that the Mackenzie District in the west, which contained most of the main populated centres, "is quickly going to be able to take care of itself." *Nunassiaq*, encompassing the central and eastern Arctic area above the tree-lines, with a smaller population posed a "more difficult" dilemma. Consequently, the government chose not to divide the NWT. Instead, they looked at the possibility of decentralizing the political administration of the NWT from Ottawa to a new hub to be located in the NWT.[9]

In 1965, the NWT Council proposed a commission to study and to make recommendations on the political, social, and economic future of the territory. The Advisory Commission on the Development of Government in the Northwest Territories (the Carrothers Commission) was the first consultative body to travel throughout the NWT to elicit the views of all of the residents. The ensuing Carrothers Report, published the following year, heralded a sea change in the approach on how to govern the NWT.[10] In April 1967, the seat of the territorial government moved from Ottawa to Yellowknife, with the new Government of the Northwest Territories (GNWT) assuming responsibility for some of the federal northern bureaucracy and governance legislative authorities heretofore administered from Ottawa. The Council increased in size from nine to twelve members, with seven elected and five appointed, thus reversing the traditional power balance which had been weighted towards Ottawa since 1905.[11]

Inuit and Political Change in the Twentieth Century

The ancestors of Inuit ("the people"), known to scholars as the Thule, replaced the Dorset people in what is now the Canadian Arctic around 1000 CE. Social and environmental factors (particularly cooling climate during the Little Ice Age from the sixteenth to nineteenth centuries) led Inuit to move from large coastal communities onto the sea ice and in smaller snow house (igloo) villages, following a seasonal cycle with extended family groups living together and hunting as a unit for most of the year.[12] Decision-making processes were often informal, highly consultative, consensus-based, and egalitarian.[13] The oldest male played a leadership role in deciding when to go hunting or fishing, when to migrate, or where to set up camp.

Apart from relatively brief encounters with the Norse around 1,000 CE and European explorers searching for the Northwest Passage, beginning with Martin Frobisher's expeditions to Baffin Island in 1576, contact between Inuit and *Qallunaat* (non-Inuit people) remained limited until the nineteenth and even twentieth centuries. Inuit contact with Euro-Canadians and Americans should be seen as a process, given that there was no single moment when the Inuit as an entire people entered into sustained relationships with these newcomers. In the late nineteenth and early twentieth centuries, whaling activities, the establishment of Hudson's Bay Company trading posts, and the arrival of Catholic and Anglican missionaries certainly influenced Inuit behavior, but most early contact has been described as "harmonious."[14]

A growing Canadian state presence in the Arctic in the 1920s and 30s, however, began to challenge Inuit political control. The Canadian government's only permanent representatives in the North (and only in a few locations) were the Royal Canadian Mounted Police, who began to assert legal jurisdiction through a few high-profile Inuit murder cases and wildlife management infractions. Non-Inuit traders and missionaries certainly sought to reshape Inuit economic and spiritual life, but they had no intent to fundamentally disrupt kin-based sharing networks or to pull the Inuit off the land. During and after the Second World War, however, when global forces redirected strategic attention towards the Arctic for the first time, political concern about Inuit living conditions prompted the federal government to intervene in Inuit lives to an unprecedented degree.

In the 1940s and 50s, power structures changed fundamentally as Inuit were drawn into sedentary villages along the Arctic coast and into the web of the welfare state. They received health, education, and social services from *qallunaat* government administrators who, by assuming high status positions within the newly created Inuit settled villages (spread throughout the Arctic) alongside non-Inuit clergy and traders, ushered in a period of "internal colonialism" by the Canadian state.[15] Increasingly alienated from their traditional way of life, with their role diminished over their lands and waters, and their political voices marginalized, Inuit leadership lost confidence. As Inuit awakened to the complex social challenges emanating from the transition to settlement life, the federal Northern administration in Ottawa came under growing pressure to encourage and enable Inuit to play a more direct role in community development. Accordingly, Northern Service Officers and other non-Inuit residents supported Inuit in setting up elected community councils in the late 1950s in an attempt to train Northern Indigenous peoples in democratic governance. Language barriers and limited education levels (in the *qallunaat* governance model) hindered these efforts, as did the foreign concept of having Inuit meet to discuss and try to solve community problems (from dog control to housing allocation to garbage collection) using representative majority decision-making procedures. Yet, these initiatives contributed to an increased political Inuit consciousness, which would lead to the ground-breaking Inuit political initiatives of the 1970s. New local governance structures were implemented to give Arctic communities a more direct say in running their own affairs. "The strategy of developing local autonomy before increasing autonomy at higher levels proved successful," Duffy observed.[16]

The Inuit Tapirisat Proposals: Linking Land Claims and the Proposal for a Nunavut Territory

In the 1970s and 80s, the political evolution of the NWT became increasingly intertwined with the assertion of Indigenous rights, the emergence of a new federal comprehensive land claims process, and Inuit self-government. Vast reserves of oil and gas were discovered in Alaska and in the Canadian Arctic in the late 1960s, thus drawing national attention to the region. Concurrently, federal reports and policies focused on the social, economic, and legal concerns of Indigenous Canadians. The Trudeau government's 1969 White Paper, which proposed to abolish the Department of Indian Affairs and Northern Development (DIAND) and denied any notion of Indigenous land or political rights, elicited a strong backlash from Indigenous organizations across Canada. Elsewhere, Inuit groups in Greenland and Alaska were also asserting their rights at this time. The emergence of transnational Inuit political networks ensured that these ideas influenced their Canadian counterparts and, within this context, Canadian Inuit developed a heightened sense of political self-awareness and confidence.

In 1971, Inuit from across Canada decided to form the Inuit Taparisat of Canada (ITC) so that they could speak with a united voice on issues related to Northern development, education, culture, and Indigenous rights. As the national umbrella organization for six regional Inuit organizations spanning Arctic Canada from Labrador to the Beaufort Sea, the ITC began to lobby for land claims in the NWT and northern Quebec. The landmark 1973 Supreme Court of Canada Calder decision recognized that Aboriginal rights in Canada pre-existed the 1763 Royal Proclamation, thus setting up a context for the settlement of Aboriginal land claims (where land had not been ceded through treaties) and later for Aboriginal self-government as an inherent right. Accordingly, the federal government adopted an Aboriginal Comprehensive Land Claims Policy in 1973, based on the idea that once an Indigenous group proves its use and occupancy of the land, it may hold land ownership and resources management authority over its traditional territory.[17] Towards this end, the federal government offered financial assistance to various Indigenous organizations, including the ITC, to determine the land areas (i.e., settlement areas) over which they may claim land resources management authority and land ownership rights.[18]

The Inuit of the NWT set forth to work preparing their land claims, cognizant of the urgency of advancing their claim before private interests encroached on their traditional lands. During the early 1970s, oil and gas industries and the federal government contemplated the construction of a pipeline in the Mackenzie Valley to transport Alaskan and Beaufort Sea oil and gas from northern Canada to southern North American markets. In 1974, the government of Canada appointed a Commission of Inquiry, under Justice Thomas Berger, to study the potential environmental and socio-economic impacts of the proposed project. The Berger Inquiry, which ran from 1975–77, proved to be a watershed in catalyzing the political voices of the Indigenous Peoples of the NWT to articulate their future aspirations for their homeland. In the end, Berger recommended that no Mackenzie Valley pipeline project should go ahead until Aboriginal land claims were settled in the region.[19]

To launch its land claims process, ITC initiated a land use and occupancy study in 1974 to determine the spatial extent of Inuit culture traditions in Canada's Arctic. The study, published two years later in a report entitled *Inuit Land Use and Occupancy Project*,[20] set out to prove that Inuit have used and occupied virtually all of the land and oceans in the Canadian Arctic for more than four thousand years. Some one thousand and six hundred map biographies, collected from Inuit hunters and depicted in the report, trace the territory over which each hunter has ranged in search of game animals. Inuktitut place-names also played a crucial role in determining the spatial extent of Inuit occupancy, as well as old camp sites, burial grounds, and cairns, which culminated in the publication of an Inuit cultural space map (or Inuit traditional territory) for the Canadian Arctic.

Armed with these maps, ITC delegates, attending a conference in Pond Inlet during the fall of 1975, passed a resolution authorizing the organization to begin land claims negotiations with the federal government. As a result of its land use study, the ITC presented *An Agreement-in-Principle as to the Settlement of Inuit Land Claims in the Northwest Territories and the Yukon Territory between the Government of Canada and the Inuit Tapirisat of Canada* to Prime Minister Pierre Trudeau and his cabinet on 27 February 1976. The Inuit of the NWT hoped that their proposed agreement would create a new political relationship whereby they could "preserve Inuit identity and their traditional way of life so far as possible."

It also sought to create a new territory to be known as Nunavut—*Our Land*—where, "through numbers and voting power, the Inuit will have control for the foreseeable future." Because Inuit would form the majority of the population, the proposal argued that "this Territory and its institutions will better reflect Inuit values and perspectives than with the present Northwest Territories."[21] The ITC indicated that the proposed government would be closer to the people, both physically and culturally, suggesting that the decentralization process[22] that had already started in the NWT offered less appeal to Inuit than the formation of their own government.[23]

Practical and political considerations confused this plan, and negotiations between ITC and federal government representatives soon reached an impasse. By September 1976, ITC withdrew the original Nunavut proposal after extensive consultations with the people of the North affirmed that much of ITC's initial vision was unrealistic. Inuit expressed concern about its excessive complexity and a sense that the proposal "had been drafted by southern lawyers, with little input from the communities it was designed to benefit."[24]

After years of debates and failed proposals,[25] the ITC General Assembly approved *Political Development in Nunavut* in September 1979, which articulated four key objectives: (1) ownership rights over portions of land rich in non-renewable resources; (2) decision-making power over the management of land and resources within the settlement area; (3) financial compensation and royalties from resource development in the area; and (4) a commitment from Ottawa to negotiate self-government and to create a Nunavut Government once a land claim agreement-in-principle was signed.[26] In exchange, Inuit would have to surrender their Aboriginal rights to all lands in the North. Most of these objectives complied with Ottawa's Comprehensive Land Claims Policy. The fourth one, negotiating self-government, would force the federal government to compromise so that it could open a dialogue with ITC. The Government of Canada felt that this latest proposal was acceptable and, in August 1980, federal and Inuit representatives met for the first time to begin the long process of drafting a final land claims agreement.

The Debate over Dividing the Northwest Territories and the Search for a Boundary Line

The question of dividing the NWT, so as to create Nunavut, continued to invite conflicting opinions about the best course of action to serve Northern Canadian interests. Prime Minister Trudeau appointed a commission to look into the matter in 1977. The Drury's Report on the *Constitutional Development in the Northwest Territories* (released in March 1980) concluded that dividing the NWT would not solve the conflicting political interests of Inuit, Dene/Métis, and non-Indigenous residents of the NWT, because the long-term consequences of division remained unclear. Instead, he urged for further devolution of federal political power to the GNWT and decentralization of territorial responsibilities to empower NWT regional and community-level governments. The NWT's fiscal dependence on the federal government (which provided more than 80 percent of the territory's budget) made dreams of greater autonomy unrealistic according to C.M. Drury.[27] However, other political stakeholders disagreed. Former Minister of DIAND Warren Allmand and NDP MP Peter Ittinuar proposed private members' bills to divide the NWT. These received their first reading in Parliament on 2 May 1980, but neither was ever debated. Instead, political initiatives emanating from the GNWT would ultimately force Ottawa's hands in negotiating the division of the NWT and in creating the Nunavut Territory.

Following the November 1979 territorial election (which brought in a majority of Indigenous members for the first time), the NWT Legislative Assembly created a special unity committee to discern how best to generate a political consensus amongst Northerners on the controversial issue of dividing the territory. In its October 1980 report, the committee noted that "the Northwest Territories as a geo-political jurisdiction simply does not inspire a natural sense of identity amongst many of its indigenous peoples; its government does not enjoy in the most fundamental sense the uncompromising loyalty and commitment of significant numbers of those who are now subject to it." The report concluded that "Aboriginal and non-Aboriginal citizens of the NWT supported the idea of dividing the Territory."[28] With these recommendations in hand, the Members of the Legislative Assembly (MLAs) committed in principle to dividing the territory and submitted the question to the population in a territory-wide plebiscite.[29]

Fig 11.2 Northern NDP MP Peter Ittinuar. NWT Archives/©GNWT. Department of Public Works and Services/G-1995-001: 0539.

The April 1982 plebiscite resulted in a small majority (56 percent) favouring the idea of dividing the NWT into two political entities: Denendeh in the west and Nunavut in the east.[30] The federal government accepted the overall verdict in favour of division and, six months later, DIAND minister John Munro announced that Ottawa was willing in principle to divide the Territory as long as three pre-conditions were met. The first was a settlement of the Inuit land claims. The second was the establishment of an agreed-upon boundary line that would divide the NWT in two parts. The third involved concluding a political accord which would define the basic structural arrangements of the future Nunavut territorial government.

Inuit-Crown negotiations in the early 1980s were challenged by Canada's refusal to discuss Aboriginal self-government along with land claims. This precluded ITC from pursuing a core component part of its negotiating agenda: the creation of a Nunavut government.[31] Nonetheless, Inuit pragmatism kept momentum moving forward. In 1982, Inuit leaders acquiesced to a land claim negotiation process that did not deal directly with the creation of a new territory.

The path forward, however, also revealed deep internal divisions that ended pan-NWT Inuit solidarity on the Nunavut project. The Committee for Original People's Entitlement (COPE), the regional organization representing the Inuvialuit of the Western Arctic, had been enthusiastic supporters of the 1976 original proposal. However, they became increasingly frustrated with the form and pace of negotiations. Because Inuvialuit economic and transportation links along the Mackenzie River connected them to the western part of the NWT and Alberta, and because the pan-Inuit Nunavut claim focused largely on the central and eastern Arctic, COPE applied to Ottawa for funding when pressures mounted to allow oil and gas development in the Beaufort Sea. COPE used these funds to prepare its own separate Inuvialuit Nunangat land claim, which it submitted in 1977. The Inuvialuit leadership broke away from the ITC in 1982 and signed their own land claim the following year, leaving Inuvialuit political questions (including self-government) for future negotiations.[32] The Inuvialuit would ultimately decide to remain with the NWT rather than joining Nunavut.

With the Inuvialuit pursuing their independent course, the Baffin, Keewatin, and Kitikmeot regional Inuit associations created a new organization, the Tunngavik Federation of Nunavut (TFN), to legally represent the Inuit of the central and eastern Canadian Arctic in land claim negotiations with the federal government. From October 1982 onward, the national Inuit organization ITC no longer represented the political and land claim interests of the Inuit of the NWT. Negotiations between TFN and federal representatives were quite tense throughout the 1980s.[33] One of the key outstanding issues was the lack of advancement over the discussions surrounding the creation of the Nunavut Territory due to the debate over where to divide the NWT.

Determining where to put the line that would divide the NWT in two parts dominated political discussions throughout the 1980s. The NWT Constitutional Alliance, which was founded in July 1982 and comprised of MLAs, Dene/Métis leaders, Inuvialuit, and Inuit representatives, faced the challenging task of proposing a boundary line that would bring a possible consensus among all of the NWT's Indigenous groups, particularly the Dene-Métis of the Mackenzie valley and the Inuit of the central and eastern Arctic. The Inuit requested that the borders of Nunavut be in close congruence with other political boundaries already in existence in the NWT (the Nunatsiaq federal electoral district created in 1979[34]), with boundaries that existed in the past (such as the Arctic Islands Game Preserve, 1926–46) and with proposed past boundaries (such as the Nunassiaq Territory proposal of 1962) as well as the 1984 Inuvialuit Settlement Area.

However, overlapping Indigenous land claims interests between the Inuit and the Dene/Métis around the tree-line rendered the discussion over the boundary difficult. NWT Dene/Métis claimed traditional hunting and trapping rights to lands that the Inuit had selected as being solely occupied and utilized by them.[35] Nevertheless, through the Constitutional Alliance, both sides agreed on a compromise boundary in February 1987, but the agreement broke down a few months later when Dene chiefs refused to endorse the proposal.[36] Having failed to settle the boundary issue, the Constitutional Alliance was disbanded in July 1987, and negotiations on this critical issue stalled for the next three years.

After land claim negotiations between the Crown and the Dene/Métis of the Mackenzie Valley collapsed in 1989, TFN was ready to sign a land claim boundary agreement with Canada without Dene/Métis involvement. The anticipated conclusion of an agreement-in-principle with the Inuit of the NWT forced Ottawa to act on the question of the boundary dispute. After ten years of intense negotiations, TFN and federal representatives signed a land claims agreement-in-principle in April 1990, but Inuit leaders threatened that they would refuse to ratify any final land claim deal unless the federal government committed to the creation of a Nunavut Territory through a distinct negotiation process and settled the boundary dispute. "Inuit leaders believe strongly that the ratification of the Nunavut land claims by Inuit is likely only if there is a commitment to the creation of a Nunavut Territory and Government," their 20 January 1990 letter asserted. "In response to these considerations, we are proposing that Canada agree to introduce legislation to Parliament creating a Nunavut Territory on or before the time the Nunavut land claims ratification legislation is expected to be introduced."[37] To solve this political dilemma, the NWT premier and TFN president asked Prime Minister Brian Mulroney to intervene and propose a compromise boundary line.

This brought a new political imperative to solve the boundary imbroglio. Former NWT Commissioner John Parker, armed with a federal mandate to do so in April 1990, consulted with Inuit and Dene/Métis representatives over the next year and recommended a compromised boundary. Dubbed the "Parker Line," it generally followed the border line proposed by the Dene/Métis and Inuit three years earlier (which the Dene/Métis Chiefs had subsequently rejected). In a May 1992 plebiscite, 54 percent of NWT residents approved this proposed boundary. "Whereas the Nunavut region was overwhelmingly in support (nine to one in favour)," White and Cameron observe, "the people of the west voted three to one against the boundary line (but failed to turn out in sufficient numbers to defeat the proposal)."[38] The Government of Canada, the GNWT, and TFN accepted this democratic verdict, however narrow, because it dovetailed with momentum on the land claims front. They agreed on the proposed "Parker Line" as the border to divide the NWT.

The Completion of the Nunavut Land Claims Agreement and Political Accord

On 16 December 1991, the federal government and TFN reached a final agreement on the Inuit Land Claims in the central and eastern Arctic. The Nunavut Land Claims Agreement (NLCA) became the most far-reaching settlement ever signed in Canada between an Indigenous group and the federal government. The agreement established clear rules of ownership and control over lands and resources in a settlement area covering one-fifth of Canada's land mass (1,963,000 km^2). In exchange for relinquishing Aboriginal claims, rights, title, and interests to their traditional lands and waters, Inuit secured a wide range of benefits and provisions to encourage self-reliance and the cultural and social well-being of Inuit. The agreement recognized Inuit ownership over an area of 353,610 km^2, including 36,257 km^2 with subsurface mineral rights. It also created public boards comprised equally of Inuit- and federally-appointed representatives to manage the lands and resources throughout the Nunavut settlement area. Inuit also obtained royalties from all current and future non-renewable resources development (up to $2 million per year). Inuit received $1.15

billion dollars from Canada over a fourteen-year period (1993–2007) as compensation for extinguishing their Aboriginal land rights.[39] Although the extinguishment clause led some Inuit to remain opposed to the agreement, an Inuit plebiscite, held in early November 1992, ratified the contents of the NLCA, with 69 percent voting in favour.

On 25 May 1993, the NLCA was signed in Iqaluit between the TFN, representing Inuit of Nunavut, and the federal government. It was a defining moment for Canada, described by Prime Minister Mulroney as an expression of nation-building. "The Inuit of Nunavut have broken the mold of the past," the Canadian Arctic Resources Committee extolled at the time. "They have done this openly and democratically, using powers of persuasion. They are now better equipped to determine their own future, and can participate more fully in national decision-making." No longer simply another interest group vying for the federal government's ear, the creation of the new territory of Nunavut would mean Inuit approaching "Ottawa as a fellow government. This is the beauty—and the simplicity—of Nunavut."[40]

With the land claim settled and the Parker boundary line approved, representatives from TFN and the federal and territorial governments had initiated discussions in April 1992 to draft a political accord to divide the NWT and to create the Nunavut Territory. By 30 October 1992, their work was completed. James Eetoolook, the acting president of TFN, proclaimed at the historic signing of the Nunavut Political Accord in October 1992, "[w]e are pleased to be turning dreams into reality."[41] The Nunavut Political Accord[42] became the federal Nunavut Act on 1 June 1993, establishing Nunavut as a territory (as of 1 April 1999) with a public government—meaning that all residents of the territory,[43] regardless of their ethnicity—would be eligible to vote and hold public office, and that all territorial programs and services would be provided on a universal basis. "The *Nunavut Act* contains no high-flown rhetoric about Inuit self-determination, the rights of Nunavummiut, or anything else for that matter," Hicks and White observe. "Rather, it sets out in practical language the structure, powers, and main operating principles of the [Government of Nunavut] and, crucially, its relation with the federal government." The Canadian model of responsible government would apply, with executive authority vested in a federally-appointed commissioner who, in turn, would appoint members of the territorial cabinet based on the recommendation of the legislature.

Fig 11.3 Nunavut, as established in 1999. Reproduced from: "Nunavut with Names," *Natural Resources Canada*, http://ftp.geogratis.gc.ca/pub/nrcan_rncan/raster/atlas_6_ed/reference/bilingual/nunavut_names.pdf.

11 | "A More Accurate Face on Canada to the World"

Now that the Inuit comprehensive land claim was settled, TFN morphed into a new organization, Nunavut Tunngavik Incorporated (NTI), and focused on the implementation and the administration of the NLCA. NTI and the three regional Inuit associations in Nunavut (Kivalliq, Kitikmeot, Qikiqtani) would administer Inuit financial assets and would hold title to Inuit-owned lands on behalf of Inuit beneficiaries. As mandated by the claim, NTI would also play "significant governance functions" within the new territory, "making it, within Nunavut, an enormously powerful political entity."[44]

There was little debate in Parliament about the bills to create the territory of Nunavut and to approve the NLCA: it took only one day in the House of Commons and two in the Senate. In fact, the House read and passed the bills in three successive motions taking less than five minutes.[45] With the Mulroney-Campbell government coming to an end of its mandate, all of the federal political parties seemed determined to approve the enabling legislation prior to the end of the parliamentary session. DIAND Minister Tom Siddon noted the "tears of happiness and joy" in the eyes of Inuit elders at the signing ceremony in Iqaluit the week before, as well as "the confidence, joy and pride, especially of the children, as they anticipated a new future relationship with the people of Canada."[46] This new partnership theme also infused the statements of Jack Anawak, MP for Nunatsiaq. "Both these bills change the course of history," he proclaimed. "Canada is evolving and the Inuit of Nunavut are in the forefront of that evolution. . . . For the Inuit the settlement of the land claim and the creation of Nunavut represent a bold new start and a chance to participate as partners in the development of our homeland and our country."[47]

The Establishment of the Government of Nunavut

With the land claim and political accords in place, the final phase remained: defining the structures of the Government of Nunavut. Although the Nunavut Act offered little direction in terms of the structure and operation of the territorial government (instead focusing on the scope of jurisdictions in which Nunavut could legislate), it did provide for an interim commissioner of Nunavut (a role filled by John Amagoalik) and a ten-member Nunavut Implementation Commission (NIC). The NIC was established to provide recommendations to the federal government on how Nunavut's administrative and political structures should be designed. The consultation process initiated by the NIC produced a comprehensive report, *Footprints in New Snow* (1995), with 104 recommendations articulating political concepts and the inner workings of the future Nunavut administrative and legislative branches. The Canadian government, the GNWT, and NTI endorsed this first report as well as a follow-up one (*Footprints in New Snow 2*) published the following year.[48]

According to the Nunavut Act, the Nunavut Territory would be led by a non-ethnic public government whose legislative authority would rest among the elected members of the Nunavut Legislative Assembly. The Government of Nunavut would have the same political institutions as the GNWT (a Commissioner, an Executive Council, a Legislative Assembly, a public service sector, and tribunals), and existing NWT laws would apply in Nunavut until repealed or modified by the new Nunavut legislature. Thus, the form of "Inuit government" embodied in Nunavut would not replicate the elements of Aboriginal self-government regimes in southern Canada, Hicks and White explain. "Rather, the goal was to create a 'public government' structured and operated according to Inuit ways and values, a government whose organization and culture would reflect Nunavut's unique demographics, geography, and culture rather than simply replicating the conventional governance institutions of the provinces and other territories."[49]

The establishment of the government of Nunavut would put into the hands of Inuit (as the vast majority of Nunavummiut) legislative powers over social and economic issues such as culture, education, health, social services, sustainable development, and finances that could not have been held in a simple land claims agreement. In the matter of language, for instance, the NIC anticipated a territorial government role to protect Inuit culture and language by making Inuktitut (one of three official languages in the territory) the primary working language of the Nunavut government. "We can give the language of a majority of our people (Inuktitut) a role in the workplace that it could never have in an undivided NWT," a 1992 newsletter explained.[50] This idea that the government of Nunavut would have a special role in protecting the Inuktitut language and culture bears resemblance to the political weight that the French language is assigned in Québec, making these two linguistic situations unique in Canada. The

NIC recommended that the Nunavummiut consider gender parity in the territorial legislature through two-member constituencies system (one male candidate and one female candidate per electoral district). The proposal was, however, rejected by Nunavummiut in a non-binding plebiscite on 26 May 1997.[51] The NIC also proposed, based on consultations with Nunavummiut, that the Nunavut legislature operate under a consensus system, blending the principles of British parliamentary democracy with Inuit values of cooperation, egalitarianism, and communal decision-making. The federal government accepted this proposal.[52]

On 15 February 1999, Nunavut held its first election to vote for the nineteen members of the Nunavut Legislative Assembly. As is the case with the GNWT, there were no political parties, so candidates ran as individuals and sat as independents. Following the election, the MLAs gathered together as the "Nunavut Leadership Forum" to select the speaker, premier, and cabinet members in a secret ballot election. During its first sitting, the newly constituted assembly chose Paul Okalik as the territory's first premier,[53] while the federal government appointed Helen Maksagak as the first Commissioner of Nunavut.

In their important study *Made in Nunavut*, Hicks and White observe that, ultimately, the Government of Nunavut "emerged as a decidedly conventional government, leavened with a few distinctive features: its departmental structure, which included such distinctive developments as sustainable development and culture, language, elders, and youth; a commitment to Inuktitut as the working language of government; and an attempt to imbue both public policy and government operations with traditional Inuit values (*Inuit Qaujimajatuqangit*—IQ)." It also implemented a decentralized form of government that, by seeking to disperse government functions and jobs in small communities across the territory, would better reflect Inuit values and avoid the centralization of power in Iqaluit.[54] Nunavut unquestionably rearranged the relationship between the Inuit of the central and eastern Arctic and Canada, by creating a territorial jurisdiction dominated by Inuit that would have a seat at inter-governmental fora alongside other provincial and territorial governments. The creation of Nunavut significantly expanded the political weight of Inuit within the Canadian federation.

When Nunavut became the newest Canadian territory on 1 April 1999, it not only created a third territory and a thirteenth member of the

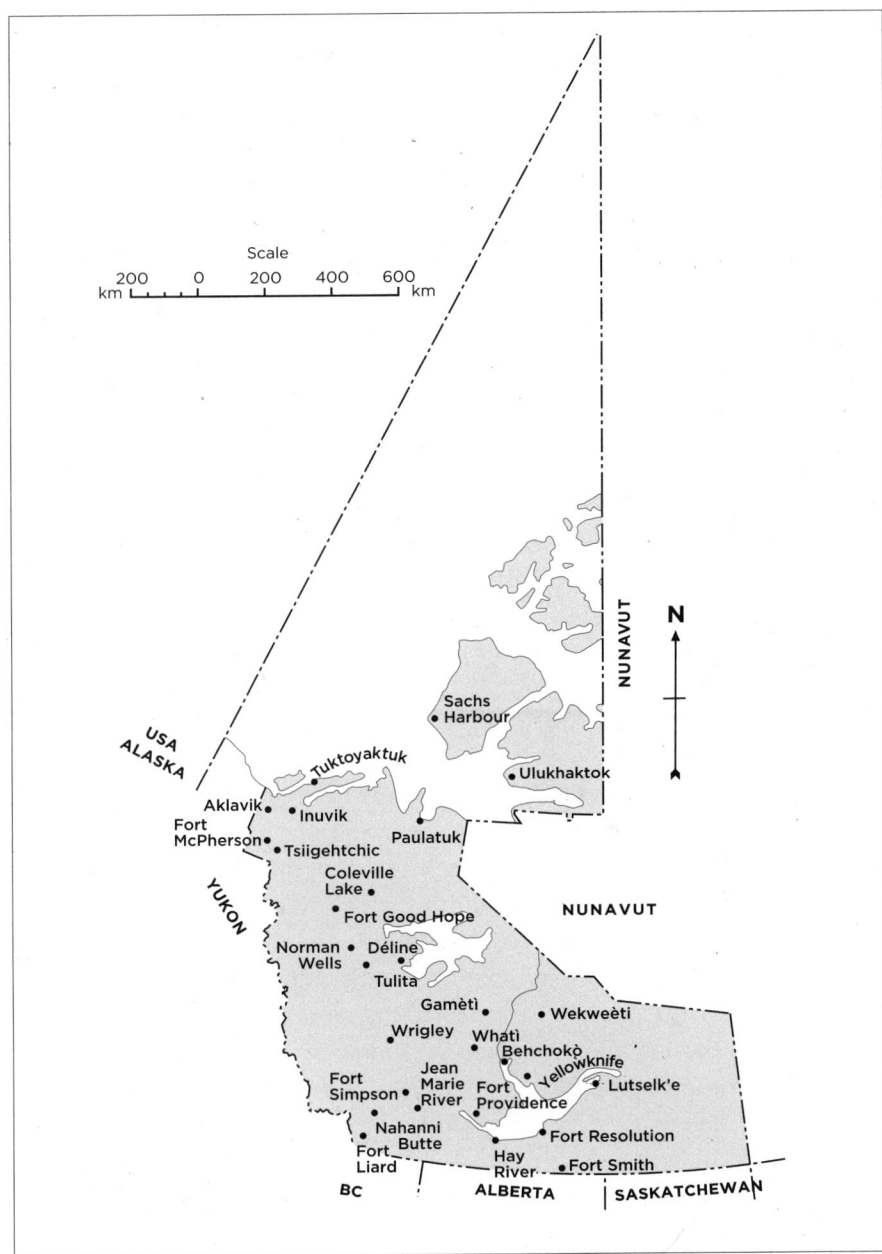

Fig 11.4 The Northwest Territories after the establishment of Nunavut in 1999. Reproduced from: "Northwest Territories with Names," http://ftp.geogratis.gc.ca/pub/nrcan_rncan/raster/atlas_6_ed/reference/bilingual/nwt_names.pdf.

Canadian Confederation, it also dramatically reshaped the NWT. The fourteen MLAs elected in 1995 to serve the constituencies in the Western Arctic decided to retain the name "Northwest Territories" and voted to increase the size of the Legislature to nineteen members after division. Furthermore, a "Special Committee on Western Identity" appointed in 1998 made several changes to official symbols and heraldry for the Northwest Territories.[55] The iconic polar bear license plate remained, but a new mace was designed by three NWT artists bearing the words "One land, many voices" in all ten official languages of the territory and included symbols representing the distinct cultures of the Inuvialuit, Dene/Métis, "and the many non-aboriginals from around the world who have made the NWT their home."[56] With the predominantly Inuit areas of the central and eastern Arctic carved out, the NWT population became almost evenly split between Indigenous and non-Indigenous people.

"It could well be that imaginative political development in the North, with full involvement of the native peoples there, is just the thing we need to remove that nagging doubt whether Canada really is different and really has a character of its own," former NWT Commissioner Gordon Robertson noted in 1987.[57] When Nunavut was officially created twelve years later, Inuit of the central and eastern Canadian Arctic had a territorial government in their homeland which was closer to the people in its make-up and philosophy than the GNWT and its remote capital—Yellowknife. While the new public, territorial government of Nunavut did not bring Inuit self-government in a strict constitutional sense, the simple fact that more than 80 percent of Nunavummiut were Inuit meant a *de facto* form of Inuit self-government. By wedding Inuit interests to the new territorial government, Nunavut has "an explicit constitutional role" that no other province or territory enjoys. "The provincial model of government, founded on British parliamentary structures and traditions, has been modified to give Aboriginal People of the Nunavut region extensive jurisdiction over their inherent Aboriginal interests," Cameron and White explain. "The creation of Nunavut, in other words, is a powerful and visionary step forward for Canada's Aboriginal People and for Canada itself."[58]

As the youngest political jurisdiction in the Canadian Confederation, Nunavut faces numerous challenges. Social, economic, and health conditions in the territory remain far below national averages, despite much higher per capita transfer payments to Nunavut than any other jurisdiction in the country.⁵⁹ While the process of devolving most of the remaining federal responsibilities to the GNWT and Yukon has been completed, negotiations on federal devolution of powers to Nunavut continue.⁶⁰ Unfulfilled provisions of the land claim, such as commitments to employ Inuit at a level "representative" of their proportion of the territorial population, have led to lawsuits and an out-of-court settlement that provides federal funding for enhanced Inuit training and education.⁶¹

The preamble to the NLCA recognizes "the contribution of Inuit to Canada's history, identity and sovereignty in the Arctic." The creation of Canada's third territory equally reflects this Indigenous contribution to nation-building. Because the Territory of Nunavut and the Nunavut land claim Settlement Area cover largely the same geographic space, the two are inextricably linked, providing the clearest example of how modern Indigenous-Crown treaty-making is tied to the formal definition of Canada's geopolitical boundaries. As it has been the case throughout the history of Indigenous-Crown treaty relations and jurisdiction-making in the Dominion of Canada, the "settlement" of the Inuit land claims and the creation of Nunavut was not primarily about achieving finality, it was about laying the foundation for new relationships. Inuit "negotiated from a premise that an Agreement should enable them to sustain their culture and wildlife-based economy, and bring their traditional values to bear in a modern democratic state," Alastair Campbell, Terry Fenge, and Udloriak Hanson explain. The NLCA, "like most constitutional instruments, . . . contains very specific provisions, [but] its central purpose is to describe an idea. Its framers were drafting a document to establish a new relationship between Canada and the Inuit of Nunavut that would last for generations; they were not simply setting out performance requirements in a contract."⁶² Canadian history has revealed the limitations of conceiving Indigenous Treaties as contracts, rather than compacts or covenants. In an era of Truth and Reconciliation, where all Canadians are officially encouraged to envisage themselves as "Treaty peoples" and bear all of the responsibilities that it entails, Nunavut stands as a litmus test of what this means in political practice and, arguably, as a key representation of the evolving process of Confederation-building more broadly.

Further Reading

Amagoalik, John with Louis McComber. *Changing the Face of Canada: The Life Story of John Amagoalik.* Iqaluit: Nunavut Arctic College, 2007. Available online at http://www.traditional-knowledge.ca/english/changing-the-face-canada-b33.html.

Cameron, Kirk and Graham White. *Northern Governments in Transition: Political and Constitutional Development in the Yukon, Nunavut and the Western Northwest Territories.* Montreal: Institute for Research on Public Policy, 1995.

Duffy, R. Quinn. *The Road to Nunavut: The Progress of the Eastern Arctic Inuit since the Second World War.* Montreal and Kingston: McGill-Queen's University Press, 1988.

Henderson, Ailsa. *Nunavut: Rethinking Political Culture.* Vancouver: University of British Columbia Press, 2008.

Hicks, Jack and Graham White. *Made in Nunavut: An Experiment in Decentralized Government.* Vancouver: University of British Columbia Press, 2015.

Légaré, André. *The Evolution of the Government of the Northwest Territories (1967–1995).* Québec City: Université Laval, Gétic, Collection Recherche, 1998.

Merritt, John, Terry Fenge, Randy Ames, and Peter Jull. *Nunavut: Political Choices and Manifest Destiny.* Ottawa: Canadian Arctic Resources Committee, 1989.

Parker, John H. *Arctic Power: The Path to Responsible Government in Canada's North.* Peterborough: Cider Press, 1996.

NOTES

1. John Amagoalik with Louis McComber, *Changing the Face of Canada: The Life Story of John Amagoalik* (Iqaluit: Nunavut Arctic College, 2007).

2. Canada, *House of Commons Debates*, 4 June 1993, 20358.

3. John Amagoalik, "The Land Claim and Nunavut: One Without the Other Isn't Enough," *Arctic Circle* (January-February 1992): 20.

4. Jack Hicks and Graham White, *Made in Nunavut: An Experiment in Decentralized Government* (Vancouver: University of British Columbia Press, 2015), 4.

5. See, for example, Kirk Cameron and Graham White, *Northern Governments in Transition: Political and Constitutional Development in the Yukon, Nunavut and the Western Northwest Territories* (Montreal: Institute for Research on Public Policy, 1995), 90.

6. Emphasis in original. Frances Abele, "Canadian Contradictions: Forty Years of Northern Political Development," *Arctic* 40, no. 4 (1987): 312.

7. R. Quinn Duffy, *The Road to Nunavut: The Progress of the Eastern Arctic Inuit since the Second World War* (Montreal and Kingston: McGill-Queen's University Press, 1988), 227.

8   Quoted in R. Quinn Duffy, "Canada's Newest Territory: The Formation of Nunavut," in *Canada: Confederation to Present,* ed. Bob Hesketh (CD-ROM, Edmonton: Chinook Multimedia, 2001).

9   *History in the Making: Under Northern Skies* (Yellowknife: Legislative Assembly of the Northwest Territories, 1999), 3; Duffy, "Canada's Newest Territory"; and Mark O. Dickerson, *Whose North? Political Change, Political Development, and Self-Government in the Northwest Territories* (Vancouver: University of British Columbia Press, 1992), 84–85.

10 Department of Indian Affairs and Northern Development, *Commission on the Development of Government in the Northwest Territories,* 2 vols. (Ottawa: DIAND, 1966).

11 Duffy, "Canada's Newest Territory." Only in 1975 did the Council become a fully elected body with fifteen members. In a further growth spurt in 1976 the Council increased to twenty-two. Fourteen of these members were Indigenous. On the early political development of the GNWT, see André Légaré, *The Evolution of the Government of the Northwest Territories (1967–1995)* (Québec City: Université Laval, Gétic, Collection Recherche, 1998). See also John H. Parker, *Arctic Power: The Path to Responsible Government in Canada's North* (Peterborough: Cider Press, 1996).

12 There were about fifty Inuit "tribal" groups in the Canadian Arctic whose size varied between thirty to one hundred individuals. See David Damas, "Copper Eskimo," in *Handbook of North American Indians, vol. 5, Arctic* (Washington: Smithsonian, 1984), and Robert McGhee, *The Last Imaginary Place: A Human History of the Arctic World* (Toronto: Key Porter, 2004).

13 On different models of Inuit decision-making, see Marc Stevenson, "Traditional Inuit Decision-Making Structures and the Administration of Nunavut," report prepared for the Royal Commission on Aboriginal Peoples (September 1993), 17 July 2017, http://publications.gc.ca/collections/collection_2016/bcp-pco/Z1-1991-1-41-25-eng.pdf.

14 David Damas, "Shifting Relations in the Administration of Inuit: The Hudson's Bay Company and the Canadian Government," *Études/Inuit/Studies* 17, no. 2 (1993): 5.

15 See, for example, Hugh Brody, *The People's Land. Inuit, Whites and the Eastern Arctic* (Vancouver: Douglas & McIntyre, 1991); Renée Fossett, *In Order to Live Untroubled: Inuit of the Central Arctic* (Winnipeg: University of Manitoba Press, 2001); and David Damas, *Arctic Migrants, Arctic Villagers: The Transformation of Inuit Settlement in the Central Arctic* (Montreal & Kingston: McGill-Queen's University Press, 2002).

16 Duffy, "Canada's Newest Territory"; and Abele, "Forty Years," 313.

17 Department of Indian Affairs and Northern Affairs, *Indian Affairs Policy Statement* (Ottawa: DIAND, 1973).

18 On the stages that led to the conclusion of a land claims agreement, see André Légaré, "The Process Leading to a Land Claims Agreement and its Implementation: The Case of the Nunavut Land Claims Settlement," *Canadian Journal of Native Studies* 16, no. 1 (1996): 139–163.

19 Thomas R. Berger, *Northern Frontier, Northern Homeland: Report of the Mackenzie Valley Pipeline Inquiry,* 2 vols. (Ottawa: DIAND, 1977).

20 Milton Freeman et al., *Inuit Land Use and Occupancy Project,* 3 vols. (Ottawa: DIAND, 1976).

21 Gurston Dacks, ed., *Devolution and Constitutional Development in the Canadian North* (Ottawa: Carleton University Press, 1990); André Légaré, "The Government of Nunavut (1999): a Prospective Analysis," in *First Nations in Canada. Perspectives on Opportunity, Empowerment, and Self-Determination*, ed. R.J. Ponting (Toronto: McGraw-Hill Ryerson, 1997); G.R. Weller, "Self-Government for Canada's Inuit: the Nunavut Proposal," *American Review of Canadian Studies* 18, no. 3 (1988): 341–57; and W. Hamley, "The Nunavut Settlement: A Critical Appraisal," *International Journal of Canadian Studies* 12 (1995): 221–34.

22 On the decentralization process in the NWT, see Légaré, *Evolution of the Government of the Northwest Territories*.

23 On the key components of the proposal, see Inuit Tapirisat of Canada, *Agreement-in-Principle As to the Settlement of Inuit Land Claims in the Northwest Territories and the Yukon Territory between the Government of Canada and the Inuit Tapirisat of Canada* (Ottawa: ITC, 1976), 14–15.

24 John Merritt, Terry Fenge, Randy Ames, and Peter Jull, *Nunavut: Political Choices and Manifest Destiny* (Ottawa: Canadian Arctic Resources Committee, 1989), 66.

25 Duffy, "Canada's Newest Territory."

26 Inuit Tapirisat of Canada, *Political Development in Nunavut* (Ottawa: ITC, 1979).

27 Department of Indian Affairs and Northern Development, *Constitutional Development in the Northwest Territories. Report of the Special Representative C.M. Drury* (Ottawa: DIAND, 1980).

28 1980 Special Unity Committee report quoted in Jull, "Nunavut," *Northern Perspectives* 10, no. 2 (1982): 6.

29 See Parker, *Arctic Power*.

30 The Inuit of the central and eastern Arctic voted overwhelmingly in favour of division, with more than 80 percent of eligible voters casting ballots in some communities. In the Western Arctic, however, residents were more apprehensive and the results were mixed, with most voters casting their ballots against division. See Frances Abele and Mark Dickerson, "The Plebiscite on Division of the Northwest Territories: Regional Government and Federal Policy," *Canadian Public Policy* 11, no. 1 (1982): 1–15.

31 *In All Fairness: A Native Claims Policy—Comprehensive Claims* (Ottawa, 1981); Sheilagh Dunn, *The Year in Review 1981: Intergovernmental Relations in Canada* (Kingston: Institute of Intergovernmental Relations, Queen's University, 1981), 167. Substantial amendments were made to the Comprehensive Land Claims Policy in 1986 after the release of the Coolican Report and by the introduction of the Inherent Right Self-Government Policy in 1995.

32 COPE negotiators signed a draft agreement in December 1983, which cabinet approved the following March and the House of Commons passed as the *Western Arctic (Inuvialuit) Claims Settlement Act* in June. Christopher Alcantara and Adrienne Davidson, "Negotiating Aboriginal Self-Government Agreements in Canada: An Analysis of the Inuvialuit Experience," *Canadian Journal of Political Science* 48, no. 3 (2015): 553–75.

33 On the challenges that surrounded the Nunavut negotiations, see Tom Molloy, "Negotiating the Nunavut Agreement—A View from the Government's Side," *Northern Perspectives* 21, no. 3 (1993): 11.

34 In 1976, a special federal Electoral Boundaries Commission recommended dividing the NWT federal electoral district into two constituencies that would "give recognition to the traditional life and cultural patterns of the majority of the indigenous peoples," Doug Neill in Canada, *House of Commons Debates*, 5 April 1976. The Mackenzie constituency became Western Arctic and the new Eastern Arctic riding became Nunatsiaq, with Peter Ittinuar becoming the first Inuk elected to the House of Commons in 1979.

35 The heart of the problem lay in the ongoing harvesting activities of both groups around Contwoyo Lake and the Thelon Game Sanctuary, with both groups arguing that these areas should be on their side of the border. The Denesuline of Saskatchewan and Manitoba also voiced concerns with respect to the proposed southern boundary of Nunavut, given their continued use of the land. In this situation, Canada decided to deal with the Denesuline's overlapping claim in a separate process and stated that the Denesuline would not be entitled to influence the negotiations in the NWT. Malloy, "Negotiating the Nunavut Agreement."

36 William Wonders, "Overlapping Native Land Claims in the Northwest Territories," *American Review of Canadian Studies* 18, no. 3 (1988): 359–68.

37 GNWT, TFN, letter to Mulroney, 20 January 1990.

38 Cameron and White, *Northern Governments in Transition*, 96.

39 Department of Indian Affairs and Northern Development, *Nunavut Land Claims Agreement. Agreement between the Inuit of the Nunavut Settlement Area and Her Majesty the Queen in Rights of Canada* (Ottawa: DIAND, 1993).

40 "Creating Nunavut and Breaking the Mold of the Past," *Northern Perspectives* 21, no. 3 (Fall 1993): 1.

41 Eetoolook quoted in White and Cameron, *Northern Governments in Transition*, 89.

42 On the negotiations leading to the Nunavut Political Accord, see Gurston Dacks, "Nunavut: Aboriginal Self-Determination through Public Government" (report prepared for the Royal Commission on Aboriginal Peoples, 1995) and Légaré, "The Government of Nunavut."

43 Nunavut's residents are known as "Nunavummiut," meaning "inhabitants of Nunavut" in Inuktitut.

44 Hicks and White, *Made in Nunavut*, 47–48. On NTI's role, see Alastair Campbell, Terry Fenge, and Udloriak Hanson, "Implementing the 1993 Nunavut land claims agreement," *Arctic Review* 2, no. 1 (2011): 25–51. See also André Legaré, "The Nunavut Tunngavik Inc.: An Examination of its Mode of Operation and Its Activities," in *Natural Resources and Aboriginal People in Canada*, eds. Robert Anderson and Robert Bone (Concord, ON: Captus Press, 2009), 193–214.

45 Canada, *House of Commons Debates*, 4 June 1993, 20392.

46 Canada, *House of Commons Debates*, 4 June 1993, 20353.

47 Canada, *House of Commons Debates*, 4 June 1993, 20357.

48 The Commission's members were appointed by the federal government from a list of nominees submitted by the GNWT, DIAND, and NTI. Each of these political actors nominated three members to the Commission. The Chairman of the Commission, John Amagoalik, was selected by the consensus of all parties. Following the release of a discussion paper on the design and operations of the future Nunavut Territorial Government in January 1994, the Commission conducted consultations with Nunavummiut regarding the

administrative structure of the territory, the composition of its Legislative Assembly, and the training of future Nunavummiut civil servants. In total, twenty-six hundred citizens (predominantly Inuit) participated in sixty-two meetings held in communities throughout the central and eastern Arctic between September 1994 and January 1995. The whole process culminated with a public conference in Iqaluit in February 1995, which brought together about one hundred delegates from all parts of Nunavut. See, for example, John Anawak in Canada, *House of Commons Debates*, 4 June 1993, 20399, and the comprehensive discussion in Hicks and White, *Made in Nunavut*.

49 Hicks and White, *Made in Nunavut*, 7, 50.

50 *Nunavut Newsletter*, 1992, 26.

51 On the failed two-member constituencies proposal, see Lisa Young, "Gender Equal Legislatures: Evaluating the proposed Nunavut Electoral system," *Canadian Public Policy* 23, no. 3 (1997): 306–15.

52 See Government of Nunavut, "The Consensus Style of Government in Nunavut," accessed 17 July 2017, http://www.gov.nu.ca/consensus-government. See also André Légaré, "An Assessment of Recent Political Development in Nunavut: The Challenges and Dilemmas of Inuit Self-Government," *Canadian Journal of Native Studies* 18, no. 2 (1998): 271–99; Graham White, "Nunavut: Challenges and Opportunities of Creating a New Government," *Public Sector Management* 9, no. 3 (1999): 3–7; and Natalia Loukacheva, *The Arctic Promise: Legal and Political Autonomy of Greenland and Nunavut* (Toronto: University of Toronto Press, 2007).

53 On his experience as Nunavut's first premier see Paul Okalik, *Let's Move On: Paul Okalik Speaks Out* (Montreal: Baraka Books, 2018).

54 Hicks and White, *Made in Nunavut*, 5.

55 Legislative Assembly of the Northwest Territories, "Creation of a New Northwest Territories," accessed 17 July 2017, http://www.assembly.gov.nt.ca/visitors/creation-new-nwt.

56 Legislative Assembly of the Northwest Territories, "The Mace," accessed 17 July 2017, http://www.assembly.gov.nt.ca/visitors/mace.

57 Gordon Robertson, "Nunavut and the International Arctic," *Northern Perspectives* 15, no. 2 (Fall 1987), 9.

58 Cameron and White, *Northern Governments in Transition*, 111.

59 See, for example, John Amagoalik, "There's little to celebrate on Nunavut's 10th birthday," *Toronto Star*, 1 April 2009; and "Is Nunavut a failure of Canadian nation building?" *Globe and Mail*, 1 April 2011. See also André Légaré, "Nunavut, the Unfulfilled Dream: The Arduous Path Towards Socio-Economic Autonomy," *The Northern Review* 30, no. 1 (2009): 207–40.

60 On devolution, see Kirk Cameron and Alastair Campbell, "The Devolution of Natural Resources and Nunavut's Constitutional Status," *Journal of Canadian Studies* 43, no. 2 (2009): 198–219.

61 NTI, "NTI Launches Lawsuit Against Government of Canada for Breach of Contract," 6 December 2006, accessed 17 July 2017, http://www.tunngavik.com/blog/news/nti-launches-lawsuit-against-government-of-canada-for-breach-of-contract/. On the settlement, see NTI, "Settlement Agreement Signed in Iqaluit," 4 May 2015, accessed 17 July 2017, http://www.tunngavik.com/blog/news/settlement-agreement-signed-in-nti-lawsuit/.

62 Campbell et al., "Implementing the 1993 Nunavut land claims agreement," 50.

Confederation Quotes: Sources and Further Reading

These quotes highlight some of the thought provoking, notable or humorous comments made while Canadian Confederation was being debated. These documents can be found in their entirety online at *The Confederation Debates*' website: https://hcmc.uvic.ca/confederation.

CONFEDERATION QUOTE 1.1

John A. Macdonald, quotation from Province of Canada, Legislative Assembly, 6   4
February, 1865. Reproduced from Province of Canada, *Parliamentary Debates on the Subject of the Confederation of the British North American Provinces*. Quebec: Hunter, Rose and Co., Parliamentary Printers, 1865, 27–28.

Photograph: Library and Archives Canada, C-006513

Confederation Debates: See Province of Canada—Legislative Assembly

CONFEDERATION QUOTE 1.2

Kenneth McKenzie Brown, quotation from Newfoundland National Convention, 28   5
October 1946. Reproduced from Newfoundland, *The Newfoundland National Convention, 1946–1948. Vol. 1: Debates*. Edited by J.K. Hiller and M.F. Harrington Montreal: Memorial University of Newfoundland by McGill-Queen's University Press, 1995.

Photograph: *Who's Who in and from Newfoundland* 1930, 198.

Confederation Debates: See Newfoundland National Convention—Debates

CONFEDERATION QUOTE 3.1

George Brown, quotation from Province of Canada, Legislative Assembly, 8 February,   60
1865. Reproduced from: Province of Canada, *Parliamentary Debates on the Subject of the Confederation of the British North American Provinces*. Quebec: Hunter, Rose and Co., Parliamentary Printers, 1865, 92.

Photograph: William Ellisson, Library and Archives Canada, C-008359

Confederation Debates: See Province of Canada—Legislative Assembly

Confederation Quote 3.2
Matthew Crooks Cameron, quotation from Province of Canada, Legislative Assembly, 24 February 1865. Reproduced from: Province of Canada, *Parliamentary Debates on the Subject of the Confederation of the British North American Provinces*. Quebec: Hunter, Rose and Co., Parliamentary Printers, 1865, 92.

66

Photograph: Notman & Fraser, Library and Archives Canada, PA-028639

Confederation Debates: See Province of Canada—Legislative Assembly

Confederation Quote 3.3
Mawedopenais, quotation from Alexander Morris' book, *The Treaties of Canada with the Indians of Manitoba and the North-West Territories Including the Negotiations on Which They Are Based, and Other Information Relating Thereto*. Toronto: Willing & Williamson, 1880, page 59.

69

Photograph: Library and Archives Canada, Acc. No. 1986-79-1638

Confederation Debates: See Treaty Negotiations—Alexander Morris, *The Treaties of Canada*, Chapter 5

Confederation Quote 4.1
George-Étienne Cartier, quotation from Province of Canada, Legislative Assembly, 7 February 1865. Reproduced from: Province of Canada, *Parliamentary Debates on the Subject of the Confederation of the British North American Provinces*. Quebec: Hunter, Rose and Co., Parliamentary Printers, 1865, 57.

78

Photograph: Library and Archives Canada, MIKAN 2242461

Confederation Debates: See Province of Canada—Legislative Assembly

Confederation Quote 4.2
Thomas D'Arcy McGee, quotation from Province of Canada, Legislative Assembly, 9 February 1865. Reproduced from: Province of Canada, *Parliamentary Debates on the Subject of the Confederation of the British North American Provinces*. Quebec: Hunter, Rose and Co., Parliamentary Printers, 1865, 144.

79

Photograph: William Notman, Library and Archives Canada, C-016749

Confederation Debates: See Province of Canada—Legislative Assembly

Confederation Quote 4.3
Étienne-Paschal Taché, quotation from Province of Canada, Legislative Council, 3 February 1865. Reproduced from: Province of Canada, *Parliamentary Debates on the Subject of the Confederation of the British North American Provinces*. Quebec: Hunter, Rose and Co., Parliamentary Printers, 1865, 9.

84

Photograph: Library and Archives Canada, PA-074100

Confederation Debates: See Province of Canada—Legislative Council

CONFEDERATION QUOTE 4.4
Christopher Dunkin, quotation from Province of Canada, Legislative Assembly, 27 February 1865. Reproduced from: Province of Canada, *Parliamentary Debates on the Subject of the Confederation of the British North American Provinces*. Quebec: Hunter, Rose and Co., Parliamentary Printers, 1865, 511.
Photograph: Topley Studio, Library and Archives Canada, PA-026325
Confederation Debates: See Province of Canada—Legislative Assembly

86

CONFEDERATION QUOTE 4.5
Antoine-Aimé Dorion, quotation from Province of Canada, Legislative Assembly, 16 February 1865. Reproduced from: Province of Canada, *Parliamentary Debates on the Subject of the Confederation of the British North American Provinces*. Quebec: Hunter, Rose and Co., Parliamentary Printers, 1865, 261.
Photograph: Topley Studio, Library and Archives Canada, PA-025755
Confederation Debates: See Province of Canada—Legislative Assembly

87

CONFEDERATION QUOTE 4.6
Henri-Gustave Joly de Lotbinière, quotation from Province of Canada, Legislative Assembly, 20 February 1865. Reproduced from: Province of Canada, *Parliamentary Debates on the Subject of the Confederation of the British North American Provinces*. Quebec: Hunter, Rose and Co., Parliamentary Printers, 1865, 350.
Photograph: Topley Studio, Library and Archives Canada, PA-025470
Confederation Debates: See Province of Canada—Legislative Assembly

89

CONFEDERATION QUOTE 5.1
Samuel Leonard Tilley, quotation from New Brunswick, Legislative Assembly, 28 June 1866. Reproduced from *House of Assembly*. St. John: G.W. Day, 1865–1867. Microfilm copies provided by the Provincial Archives of New Brunswick, 38.
Photograph: Topley Studio, Library and Archives Canada, PA-026347
Confederation Debates: See New Brunswick—Legislative Assembly

110

CONFEDERATION QUOTE 5.2
Albert J. Smith, quotation from New Brunswick, Legislative Assembly, 1 June 1865. Reproduced from: New Brunswick, *Reports of the Debates of the House of Assembly*. St. John: G.W. Day, 1865–1867. Microfilm copies provided by the Provincial Archives of New Brunswick, 118.
Photograph: Topley Studio, Library and Archives Canada, PA-025258
Confederation Debates: See New Brunswick—Legislative Assembly

113

CONFEDERATION QUOTE 5.3
Adams George Archibald, quotation from Nova Scotia, Legislative Assembly, 12 April 1865. Reproduced from: New Brunswick, *Reports of the Debates of the House of*

119

Assembly. St. John: G.W. Day, 1865–1867. Microfilm copies provided by the Provincial Archives of New Brunswick, 226.

Photograph: Library and Archives Canada, MIKAN 3214517

Confederation Debates: See New Brunswick—Legislative Assembly

CONFEDERATION QUOTE 5.4

William Annand, quotation from Nova Scotia, Legislative Assembly, 12 April 1865. Reproduced from: New Brunswick, *Reports of the Debates of the House of Assembly*. St. John: G.W. Day, 1865–1867. Microfilm copies provided by the Provincial Archives of New Brunswick, 238.

120

Photograph: Nova Scotia Legislature, Province House Collection

Confederation Debates: See New Brunswick—Legislative Assembly

CONFEDERATION QUOTE 5.5

William Henry Pope, quotation from Prince Edward Island, House of Assembly, 24 March 1865. Reproduced from: Prince Edward Island, *The Parliamentary Reporter of Debates and Proceedings of the House of Assembly as Printed in the Examiner*, 1866, 43.

131

Photograph: Topley Studio, Library and Archives Canada, PA-027027

Confederation Debates: See Prince Edward Island—Legislative Assembly

CONFEDERATION QUOTE 5.6

James Colledge Pope, quotation from Prince Edward Island, Legislative Assembly, 7 May 1866. Reproduced from: Prince Edward Island, *The Parliamentary Reporter of Debates and Proceedings of the House of Assembly as Printed in the Examiner*, 1866, 101.

132

Photograph: Topley Studio, Library and Archives Canada, PA-027027

Confederation Debates: See Prince Edward Island—House of Assembly

CONFEDERATION QUOTE 6.1

Louis Riel, quotation from Convention of Forty, Second Provisional Government of Manitoba, 27 January 1870. Reproduced from: Convention of Forty, "Third Day," edited by Norma Jean Hall. Digitized by the Province of Manitoba, 2010.

155

Photograph: Duffin and Co., Library and Archives Canada, C-052177

Confederation Debates: See Convention of Forty

CONFEDERATION QUOTE 6.2

Donald Alexander Smith, 1st Baron Strathcona, quotation from Convention of Forty, Second Provisional Government of Manitoba, 27 January 1870. Reproduced from: Convention of Forty, "Third Day," edited by Norma Jean Hall. Digitized by the Province of Manitoba, 2010.

158

Photograph: Library and Archives Canada, C-5489

Confederation Debates: See Convention of Forty

CONFEDERATION QUOTE 7.1
Amor de Cosmos, quotation from British Columbia, Legislative Council, 10 March
1870. Reproduced from: British Columbia. *Legislative Council: Debates on the Subject of
Confederation with Canada*. Victoria: William H. Cullin, 1912, 38.

Photograph: Courtesy of the Royal BC Museum and Archives, Image A-01224

Confederation Debates: See British Columbia—Legislative Council

174

CONFEDERATION QUOTE 7.2
Robert William Weir Carrall, quotation from British Columbia, Legislative Council, 11
March 1870. Reproduced from: British Columbia. *Legislative Council: Debates on the
Subject of Confederation with Canada*. Victoria: William H. Cullin, 1912, 48.

Photograph: Topley Studio, Library and Archives Canada, PA-026366

Confederation Debates: See British Columbia—Legislative Council

177

CONFEDERATION QUOTE 7.3
John Sebastian Helmcken, quotation from British Columbia, Legislative Council, 9
March 1870. Reproduced from: British Columbia. *Legislative Council: Debates on the
Subject of Confederation with Canada*. Victoria: William H. Cullin, 1912, 11.

Photograph: Courtesy of the Royal BC Museum and Archives, Image A-01351

Confederation Debates: See British Columbia—Legislative Council

180

CONFEDERATION QUOTE 9.1
Chief Poundmaker, quotation reproduced from Peter Erasmus, "Buffalo Days and
Nights," Calgary: Glenbow-Alberta Institute, 1976, 244.

Photograph: O.B. Buel, Library and Archives Canada, C-001875

Confederation Debates: Peter Erasmus—Buffalo Days and Nights

220

CONFEDERATION QUOTE 9.2
Mistawasis (Big Child), quotation reproduced from Peter Erasmus, *Buffalo Days and
Nights*, Calgary: Glenbow-Alberta Institute, 1976, 247.

Photograph: Saskatchewan Archives Board, R-B2837

Confederation Debates: Peter Erasmus—Buffalo Days and Nights

221

CONFEDERATION QUOTE 9.3
Frederick William Alpin Gordon Haultain, quotation from Northwest Territories,
North-West Legislative Territories Assembly, 4 April 1902. Reproduced from: the
Regina Leader, 10 April 1902.

Photograph: Saskatchewan Archives Board, R-B446

Confederation Debates: See North West Territories—North-West Legislative Assembly

227

Confederation Quote 10.1

Ambrose Shea, quotation from Newfoundland, House of Assembly, 2 February 1865. Reproduced from: *The Newfoundlander*, 13 February 1865.

239

Photograph: The Rooms Provincial Archives Division, Newfoundland and Labrador, B1-145

Confederation Debates: Newfoundland—House of Assembly

Confederation Quote 10.2

Charles Bennett, quotation reproduced from "No Confederation," the *Morning Chronicle*, 29 September 1869.

242

Photograph: Library and Archives Canada, C-054438

Confederation Quote 10.3

Joey Smallwood, quotation from Newfoundland, Newfoundland National Convention, 28 October 1946. Reproduced from: Newfoundland. *The Newfoundland National Convention, 1946–1948. Vol. 1: Debates.* Edited by J.K. Hiller and M.F. Harrington Montreal: Memorial University of Newfoundland by McGill-Queen's University Press, 1995, 96.

246

Photograph: Duncan Cameron, Library and Archives Canada, PA-113253

Confederation Debates: Newfoundland—National Convention

Confederation Quote 10.4

Michael F. Harrington, quotation from Newfoundland, Newfoundland National Convention, 28 October 1946. Reproduced from: Newfoundland. *The Newfoundland National Convention, 1946–1948. Vol. 1: Debates.* Edited by J.K. Hiller and M.F. Harrington Montreal: Memorial University of Newfoundland by McGill-Queen's University Press, 1995, 98.

247

Photograph: Archives and Special Collections, Queen Elizabeth II Library, Memorial University of Newfoundland, Coll. 309

Confederation Debates: Newfoundland—National Convention

Contributors

RAYMOND B. BLAKE is professor and head of the Department of History at the University of Regina. He has published widely on Canadian history. His most recent publications include *Lions or Jellyfish: A History of Newfoundland-Ottawa Relations* and *Celebrating Canada: Holidays, National Days and the Crafting of Identities,* co-edited with Matthew Hayday.

PHILLIP BUCKNER is a professor emeritus at the University of New Brunswick where he taught for thirty-one years. He was founding editor of *Acadiensis: Journal of the History of the Atlantic Region*, the founder of Acadiensis Press, and author/editor of a number of books and articles on the history of Atlantic Canada. A past President of the Canadian Historical Association, he also created and edited the series of CHA booklets on Canada's ethnic groups. Since moving to England in 1999, he has served as a visiting professor at several research institutes and has edited/written a number of books and articles on Canada's place within the British World.

COLIN M. COATES teaches Canadian Studies and History at Glendon College, York University. A specialist in the history of French Canada, the history of utopias in Canada, and environmental history, he is currently working on a project on colonial statecraft under the French régime. He has edited or co-edited two collections in environmental history with the University of Calgary Press. He has also published *The Metamorphoses of Landscape and Community in Early Quebec* (McGill-Queen's University Press) and with Cecilia Morgan, *Heroines and History: Madeleine de Verchères and Laura Secord* (University of Toronto Press).

KEN S. COATES is Canada Research Chair in Regional Innovation, Johnson-Shoyama Graduate School of Public Policy, University of Saskatchewan. He holds a PhD in Canadian history from the University of British Columbia, where he studied Native-newcomer relations in the Yukon. He has taught at universities across Canada, including Brandon University, University of Victoria, University of Northern British Columbia, University of New Brunswick (Saint John), University of Saskatchewan, and University of Waterloo. Ken has written extensively on Northern and Canadian history and Indigenous affairs. His books include *Best Left as Indians: Indian-White Relations in the Yukon*, *A Global History of Indigenous Peoples* and, with Bill Morrison, such works as *Land of the Midnight Sun: A History of the Yukon*, *The Alaska Highway in World War II*, *The Sinking of the Princess Sophia*, among others. He is currently working on a study of the continental significance of the Klondike Gold Rush.

BARRY FERGUSON is Professor of History and the Duff Roblin Professor of Manitoba Government at the University of Manitoba. He has written on Canadian political ideas, contemporary Canadian society, and Prairie and Manitoba politics. His books include *Remaking Liberalism: the Intellectual Legacy of Adam Shortt, O.D. Skelton, W.A. Mackintosh, and W.C. Clark* (1993), *Recent Social Trends in Canada* (2006), *Multicultural Variations* (2013), and also *Manitoba's Premiers of the 19th and 20th Centuries* (2010) co-edited with Robert Wardhaugh.

MAXIME GOHIER is a professor of history at the Université du Québec à Rimouski. A specialist of Aboriginal history during French and British rule, his research deals with the political history of Indigenous communities and their dealings with the state. His main interest is in Aboriginal political discourse as observed through diplomatic rituals and petitioning. He is equally interested in the toponomy of Indigenous places and the place occupied by Aboriginals in the Saint-Lawrence Valley during the seigneurial period. He is the author of *Onontio le médiateur : la gestion des conflits amérindiens en Nouvelle-France (1603–1717)*.

DANIEL HEIDT, PhD, is the Project Manager for *The Confederation Debates* and the Manager of Research and Administration at *The Centre on Foreign Policy and Federalism*. The author of several academic articles, his doctoral research focused on Ontario federalism to 1896. He also has a strong interest in Arctic history, and has partnered with P. Whitney Lackenbauer to co-edit *Two Years Below the Horn: Operation Tabarin, Field Science, and Antarctic Sovereignty* and *The Advisory Committee on Northern Development: Context and Meeting Minutes, 1948–66*.

P. WHITNEY LACKENBAUER is a Professor in the Department of History at St. Jerome's University in the University of Waterloo, Ontario. He is Honorary Lieutenant-Colonel of 1st Canadian Ranger Patrol Group based in Yellowknife, Northwest Territories. He is also a Fellow with the Canadian Global Affairs Institute; the Bill Graham Centre for Contemporary History; the Arctic Institute of North America; and the Centre for Military, Security and Strategic Studies. His recent books include *China's Arctic Ambitions and What They Mean for Canada* (co-authored, 2017), *Blockades or Breakthroughs? Aboriginal Peoples Confront the Canadian State* (co-edited 2014), *A Historical and Legal Study of Sovereignty in the Canadian North, 1870–1942* (edited 2014), *The Canadian Rangers: A Living History, 1942–2012* (2013, shortlisted for the Dafoe prize), and *Arctic Front: Defending Canada in the Far North* (co-authored 2008, winner of the 2009 Donner Prize). He is also co-editor of the Documents on Canadian Arctic Sovereignty and Security (DCASS) series and has contributed four volumes to it.

ANDRÉ LÉGARÉ holds a PhD from the Department of Geography at the University of Saskatchewan. He also holds Bachelor's and Master's degrees in Geography as well as a Master's degree in Political Science from Laval University. For the past twenty-five years, he has written extensively on Indigenous self-government and on political development in the Canadian North. His research interests focus on Indigenous identity and on governance in Nunavut and in the Northwest Territories. André Légaré lives in Yellowknife, where he works as a chief negotiator on Indigenous land claims and self-government. He is also a research associate at the International Centre for Northern Governance and Development at the University of Saskatchewan.

MARCEL MARTEL is professor and holder of the Avie Bennett Historica Chair in Canadian History at York University in Toronto. He has published on public policy, language rights, and moral regulation. His most recent publications include *Le Canada français et la Confédération. Fondements et bilan critique* (with Jean-François Caron, Les Presses de l'Université Laval, 2016), *Canada the Good? A Short History of Vice Since 1500* (Wilfrid Laurier University Press, 2014), *Langue et politique au Canada et au Québec: Une synthèse historique* with Martin Pâquet, Boréal, 2010), translated by Patricia Dumas: *Speaking Up. A History of Language and Politics in Canada and Quebec* (Toronto: Between the Lines, 2012). He has also published two collections of essays on Confederation: *Globalizing Confederation: Canada and the World in 1867* (with Jacqueline D. Krikorian and Adrian Shubert, University of Toronto Press, 2017) and *Roads to Confederation: The Making of Canada, 1867* (with Jacqueline D. Krikorian), and *Vers la Confédération: La construction du Canada, 1867* (Jacqueline D. Krikorian, ed., Presses de l'Université Laval, 2017).

MARTIN PÂQUET is a professor of history at Laval University and director of the *Chaire pour le développement de la recherche sur la culture d'expression française en Amérique du Nord*. A specialist in the history of political culture, migration, and cultures of North American Francophones, he has authored numerous works including *Tracer les marges de la Cité. Étranger, immigrant et État au Québec (1626–1981)* (Montreal, Boréal, 2010) as well as *Langue et politique au Canada et au Québec: Une synthèse historique* (with Marcel Martel, Montreal, Boréal, 2010).

J.R. MILLER, a fellow of the Royal Society of Canada and professor emeritus at the University of Saskatchewan, has been studying the relationships between Aboriginal Peoples and non-Aboriginal "Newcomers" who have migrated to Canada over the last four centuries. He has written or co-authored nine books including *Skyscrapers Hide the Heavens: A History of Indian-White Relations in Canada (1989), Shingwauk's Vision: A History of Native Residential Schools (1996)* as well as *Compact, Contract, Covenant: Aboriginal Treaty-Making in Canada (2009)*. Recently named an Officer of the Order of Canada, his engaged scholarship has been influential both inside and outside the university, deeply shaping Canadians' understanding of issues such as treaty rights and residential schools, and encouraging

Canadians—both Aboriginal and non-Aboriginal—to rethink our history together and to envision our future together.

PATRICIA E. ROY is professor emerita of history at the University of Victoria. Her major work has been on the response of British Columbians and other Canadians to immigration from China and Japan. Her most recent book is *Boundless Optimism: Richard McBride's British Columbia* (2012).

BILL WAISER is an author and historian at the University of Saskatchewan who specializes in western Canadian history. He has published over a dozen books—many of them recognized by various awards. His most recent book, *A World We Have Lost: Saskatchewan Before 1905*, won the 2016 Governor General's Literary Award for Non-Fiction. Bill is a frequent public speaker and contributor to radio, television, and print media. He has also served on a number of national, provincial, and local boards. Bill has been awarded the Saskatchewan Order of Merit, elected a fellow of the Royal Society of Canada, named a distinguished university professor, and granted a D.Litt.

ROBERT WARDHAUGH is Professor of History at the University of Western Ontario. He has worked on national and Prairie politics and society in the twentieth century as well as contributed general studies on Canadian history. His books include *Mackenzie King and the Prairie West* (2000) and *Behind the Scenes: The Life of William Clifford Clark* (2010). He is the co-editor of *Manitoba's Premiers of the 19th and 20th Centuries* (2010) as well as co-author of the two-volume survey of Canadian history, *Origins* and *Destinies* (2016).

Index

1837–1838 Rebellions, 54, 76

A

Acadians, 31-32, 95, 96, 114, 117, 238
Advisory Commission on the Development of Government in the Northwest Territories (the Carrothers Commission), 267-68
Ahenakew, Canon Edward, 27
Ahtahkakoop, Chief, 218, 219, 222
Alberta, 2, 7, 12, 231-32, 266. *See also* North-West
Amagoalik, John, 265,280
Anawak, Jack, 264-65, 280
Anglin, Timothy Warren, 114, 115, 116, 117, 118, 130, 186
Annand, William, 3, 120, 122, 125
Archibald, Adams George: Nova Scotia, 118, 119, 121; Manitoba, 160-61, 163, 164
Attlee, Clement Richard, 248

B

Badger, 222
Baldwin, Robert, 57
Begbie, Matthew Baillie, 173
Bennett, Charles James Fox, 242, 243
Bennett, Richard Bedford, 231, 244
Berger Inquiry: *see* Mackenzie Valley Pipeline Inquiry
Black, John, 154, 156-57
Bompas, William Carpenter, 195
Bond, Robert, 244

Borden, Robert Laird, 229, 232
Boulton, Major Charles, 154
Bourassa, Henri, 7
Bourget, Bishop Ignace, 94
Bradley, Frederick Gordon, 249, 256
Brecken, Frederick, 133
British Columbia, 2, 11, 91, 202, 208; opposition to Confederation, 175-81; pro-Confederation viewpoints, 173, 175-76, 178, 183-85; responsible government, 11, 172, 173, 175, 179, 181, 184, transportation connection with Canada, 175, 181-86, Yale Convention, 176; Indigenous Peoples, 39, 44, 46, 182, 183
British North America (defence), 56, 104, 106, 115, 126, 241, 243, 245, Confederation as defence, 57, 61, 62, 105, 215; Confederation as inadequate defence, 63-64, 88, 114, 121-22, 180. *See also* Fenians; United States
Brown, George, 3, 56, 57, 59, 60, 61, 62, 77, 97, 107, 114, 172, 213-14
Brown, J.N.E., 197
Brown, Kenneth McKenzie, 5
Bruce, John, 150
Bruce, Victor Alexander (Lord Elgin), 244
Bulyea, G.H.V., 197, 231
Butler, General Benjamin F., 135

C

Calder et al. v. Attorney General of British Columbia, 270
Cameron, Matthew Crooks, 63, 64, 66

303

Campbell, Alexander, 81
Canada East. *See* Quebec
Canada West. *See* Ontario
Canadian Arctic Resources Committee, 278
Canadian Pacific Railway, 67
Carrall, Robert William Weir, 171, 176-79, 182, 183
Carrothers Commission. *See* Advisory Commission on the Development of Government in the Northwest Territories
Carter, Frederick Bowker Terrington, 237, 238, 240, 241, 243, 250
Cartier, George-Étienne, 3, 56, 57, Quebec, 77, 78, 80, 82, 83, 85, 92, 94, 97; Indigenous rights, 81; Manitoba, 147, 156-57, 159; British Columbia, 172, 184, 185-86
Cauchon, Joseph-Édouard, 92-93
Chandler, Edward Barron, 111
Chapais, Jean-Charles, 77
Charlottetown Conference, 9, 57-58, 75, 77, 81, 101, 118, 237
Clark, Joe, 208
Coles, George, 128-29, 134, 135
Committee for Original People's Entitlement (COPE), 275
Confederate Association. *See* Newfoundland and Labrador: pro-Confederation viewpoints
Confederation (concept), 6-8, 13-15, 285. *See also* federalism; local autonomy; regionalism
Confederation Debates: The, ix
Congdon, Frederick Tennyson, 203
Conne River Miawpukek, 258
Connell, Charles, 112
Connolly, Archbishop Thomas, 121
Connolly, Bishop Thomas Louis, 95-96
Constantine, Charles, 195
Constitutional Development in the Northwest Territories (Drury Report), 273
Costigan, John, 114, 117, 118
Crease, Henry Pering Pellew, 179
Crosbie, Chesley, 257
Cudlip, John W., 112, 116, 118
Currie, John Stewart, 252

D

de Cosmos, Amor (William Smith), 3, 11, 173, 174, 176, 185, 187
de Salaberry, Colonel Charles, 152
democracy, 9, 65, 105, 111, 117, 125, 127, 128
Dene, 193, 273-77, 284
Dennis, Colonel J.S., 150, 151-52
Dickey, Robert Barry, 121
Diefenbaker, John George, 267
Dorion, Antoine-Aimé, 3, 87, 88, 91
Drury Report. *See Constitutional Development in the Northwest Territories*
Dunkin, Christopher, 85, 86, 88, 90, 91

E

Economic Union Association (EUA). *See* Newfoundland and Labrador: responsible government (as alternative to Confederation)
Eetoolook, James, 278
Epp, Jake, 208
Erasmus, Peter, 218

F

federalism, 6, 10, 14, 56, 61-62, 64, 67, 90; compact theory, 7. *See also* legislative union; local autonomy; regionalism
Fenians, 104, 116, 117, 130, 241
First Nations: 11, 19-51, 56, 67-70, 163-66, 188, 195, 202, 203, 209, 215-23. *See also* Indigenous Peoples; Mi'kmaq; Treaties
Fisher, Charles, 111, 112, 115
Forget, Amédée Emmanuel Marie, 231
Foster, George, 206

G

Galt, Alexander Tilloch, 56, 57, 77, 80
Gardiner, Jimmy, 232
Geoffrion, Félix, 93
Gibbs, Mifflin Wistar, 176
Gillmor, Arthur Hill, 115

Girard, Marc-Amable, 225
Gordon, Arthur Hamilton, 112, 116
Goulet, Elzéar, 161
Gray, Colonel John Hamilton (Prince Edward Island), 129, 130, 133, 134
Gray, John Hamilton (New Brunswick), 109, 111, 112
Grey, Albert Henry George (Lord Grey), 244

H

Hankin, Philip, 179
Harrington, Michael F., 247
Hatheway, George Luther, 111, 115, 116
Haultain, Frederick William Alpin Gordon, 197, 226-29, 231-32; "Buffalo" province, 228, 232
Haviland, Thomas Heath, 129, 133, 134, 138
Haythorne, Robert Poore, 135, 136, 137
Helmcken, John Sebastian, 171, 173, 178, 180-85
Henry, William Alexander, 121, 124
Higgins, Gordon, 251
Hill, Stephen John, 243
Hincks, Sir Francis, 160, 184
Holbrook, Henry, 181, 182
Holland, Augustus Edward Crevier, 138
Holloway, Robert, 187
Howatt, Cornelius, 134, 138
Howe, Joseph, 122, 125, 130, 135, 149-52, 156, 160, 173
Howlan, George, 133, 137, 138
Hoyles, Hugh, 240
Hudson's Bay Company (HBC), 10, 11, 145, 146-47, 149, 151, 194, 213-15, 231. *See also* Rupert's Land; Treaties

I

imperial pressures, 104-6, 108-9, 115, 116-17, 123, 133-34, 135, 172, 215, 243, 245, 251
imperialism (Canadian), 146, 147, 162, 209, 215-18, 264, 269
Indian Act, 46, 202, 223, 258
Indigenous Peoples: agency, 217-18; lack of consultation with, 80-82, 182, 183, 215, 216; residential schools, 81. *See also* First Nations; Inuit; Inuit Tapirisat of Canada; Métis; Mi'kmaq; Nunavut; Nunavut; Implementation Commission; NWT Constitutional Alliance; reconciliation; Treaties; Tunngavik Federation of Nunavut
Intercolonial railway, 62, 63, 67, 83, 102-3, 105, 106, 109, 115, 121, 123, 124, 241
interprovincial trade, 56, 61, 83, 90, 102-3, 109, 110, 214, 241
Inuit, 13, 82, 193, 194. *See also* Inuit Tapirisat of Canada; Nunavut
Inuit Tapirisat of Canada (ITC), 264, 270-72, 275
Ittinuar, Peter, 273

J

Johnson, John Mercer, 111, 112
Joly de Lotbinière, Henri-Gustave, 88-90, 91

K

Kakatcheway, Chief, 68
Kakishiway, Chief, 42
Kelly, Francis, 134
Killam, Thomas, 122, 124, 125
King, William Lyon Mackenzie, 245, 250
Kishwoot, Chief (Jim Boss), 202-3

L

La Fontaine, Louis-Hippolyte, 57, 76
Laflèche, Louis-François, 94
Laframboise, Maurice, 93
Laing, Arthur, 267
Laird, David, 42, 136, 137
Landry, Amand, 117
Langevin, Bishop Jean, 93-94
Langevin, Hector-Louis, 77, 80, 81, 92, 95-96
Laurier, Wilfrid, 11; Alberta and Saskatchewan, 226, 229-30, 231-32; Yukon, 204-5
legislative union, 6, 61, 64, 67, 80-81, 108, 115. *See also* federalism

local autonomy, 3; Indigenous, 12-13, 165;
——provincial, 6-7, 10, 12, 13-14; Alberta and Saskatchewan, 223-31; British Columbia, 178, 179, 180-81; Manitoba, 150, 153, 154; New Brunswick, 107-8, 114; Newfoundland and Labrador, 237, 243; Nova Scotia, 122; Ontario, 57-59, 61-62, 65; Prince Edward Island, 126, 133; Quebec, 80, 83-85, 88-93; Yukon, 199-209.
See also federalism; Indigenous Peoples; natural resources (jurisdiction); Nunavut; regionalism; Senate; Treaties
London Conference, 77, 96, 117-18, 123-24, 134
Lougheed, James, 206
Lower Canada. *See* Quebec
Loyalists, 109, 111, 159

M

Macdonald, Andrew Archibald, 129
Macdonald, Gordon, 250-51
Macdonald, John, 64
Macdonald, John Alexander, 3, 4, 6, 13, 198; British Columbia, 11, 171-72, 178, 185; Indigenous rights, 81-82; Manitoba, 149, 151, 156-57, 159, 160; Newfoundland and Labrador, 243; Ontario, 56, 57, 61, 77, 80; Prairies, 214, 215
Macdonald, John Sandfield, 63, 65
MacGregor, William, 244
Mackenzie, Alexander, 91, 159, 186, 198, 216, 222, 225
Mackenzie Valley Pipeline Inquiry, 271
MacTavish, William, 149, 150, 154
Magrath, Charles Alexander, 244
majority rule, 3, 59, 60, 96-97. *See also* federalism; minority rights; representation by population
Maksagak, Helen, 282
Manitoba, 10-11, 215-16, 39, 97, 218, 226, 231, 232; amnesty 161; Canada First, 156; Canadian Party, 154, 156; *Comité National des Métis de la Rivière Rouge*, 150-51, 153; Convention of Forty, 154, 156; Council of Assiniboia, 146, 149, 150, 156; Council of Twenty-Four, 151, 153; List of Rights, 153, 154, 156, 157, 163; Métis scrip, 157, 159, 160, 161; Provisional government 153-54, 160; Red River delegation 156-57. *See also* natural resources (jurisdiction)
Maritime union, 101, 123, 133
Mawedopenais, Chief, 69
McClelan, Abner Reid, 112
McCully, Jonathan, 121
McDougall, William, 81, 147, 149-52, 159
McGee, Thomas D'Arcy, 3, 64, 77, 79, 80, 130
McInnes, Commissioner William Wallace Burns, 204
McKay, James, 166
McMillan, John, 112
Métis, 10, 67, 73n37, 95, 145, 149-51, 154, 156-57, 159-61, 163-64, 166, 215, 218, 225, 231, 273, 275, 276, 277, 284. *See also* Indigenous Peoples; Manitoba; Riel, Louis
Mi'kmaq, 31-32, 82, 258
Miller, William, 123
Mills, David, 225
minority rights, 3; 10; biculturalism, 7, 13, 75, 76, 80, 88-90, 94-97, 154, 159, 176, 224-26, 239-40; education, 12, 80, 96-97, 160, 162, 208, 224-26, 229-30. *See also* majority rule; religion
Mistawasis, Chief, 218, 219, 221, 222
Mitchell, Peter, 111, 116
Morris, Alexander, 41, 42, 68, 164-65, 186, 219, 222, 223
Morris, Edward, 244
Mulroney, Brian, 276-77, 278, 280
Munro, John, 274
Musgrave, Anthony, 171, 178-79, 182, 185, 240
Musqua, Danny, 40

N

National Policy, 216-17
national unity, 3, 6-7, 13-14, 64, 67, 83, 85-86, 108-9. *See also* local autonomy; regionalism

natural resources (jurisdiction), 11, 13, 145; 157, 160-62, 209, 216, 230-31, 232
New Brunswick, 1, 10, 31, 63, 64, 65, 90, 95, 96, 123, 248; opposition to Confederation, 114-16, 117; pro-Confederation viewpoints, 109-12, 117-18
New France, 25, 28-32, 75
Newfoundland and Labrador, 2, 12, 13, 101, 107, 128, 264; Canadian desire for union, 245, 250; commission of government, 244, 245; demographics, 238; discussions with Canada, 249-51, 256-57; Indigenous Peoples, 258; National Convention (establishment), 248; opposition to Confederation 2, 237, 241, 243, 259; pro-Confederation viewpoints, 237, 241, 243, 248-49, 251, 253-56, 259; referendums, 255-56; responsible government (as alternative to Confederation), 248, 251-53
Nielsen, Erik, 208
Nolin, Charles, 166
North West Company, 214
North West Mounted Police, 195-97
North-West, 2, 9, 10, 55, 59-60, 83; initial governance, 216-17, 223-24; responsible government, 223, 226-28. *See also* Alberta; Hudson's Bay Company; natural resources (jurisdiction); North-West rebellion; *North-West Territories Act*; Rupert's Land; Saskatchewan
North-West rebellion, 145, 166, 223
Northwest Territories (NWT), 2, 263; governance, 266-68, 273, 284
North-West Territories Act, 200, 216, 224, 225, 266, 267
Northwest Trading Company, 195
Nova Scotia, 1, 10, 31-32, 35, 38, 53, 64, 67, 88, 95-96, 105, 107, 248; opposition to Confederation, 118, 120, 121-22, 124-25; pro-Confederation viewpoints, 119, 121, 123
Nunavut, 2, 12-13, 263-66; created, 277-78; demographics, 264; governance, 278, 281-82; land ownership and management, 264-66, 270-72, 274-75, 276, 277-82; plebiscites, 274, 277, 278, 282; proposals to divide the Northwest Territories, 267, 272, 273-77; reasons for establishment, 264. *See also* Inuit; Inuit Tapirisat of Canada; Nunavut Land Claims Agreement (NLCA)
Nunavut Implementation Commission (NIC), 280-82
Nunavut Land Claims Agreement (NLCA), 277-78, 280, 285
Nunavut Tunngavik Incorporated (NTI), 280
NWT Constitutional Alliance, 275-76

O

O'Brien, Tom, 203
Ogilvie, William, 195, 199, 202
Okalik, Paul, 282
Oliver, Frank, 203, 204, 205-6
Ontario, 1, 9, 10, 37, 95, 97, 107, 108, 154, 156-57, 160, 165, 204, 213, 214, 229, 232; opposition to Confederation, 62-66, 67; pro-Confederation viewpoints 59-62, 67. *See also* Province of Canada

P

Palmer, Edward, 128-29, 134
Parker Line, 277, 278
Pearson, Lester Bowles, 267
Pîhtokahanapiwiyin (Poundmaker), 220
Political Development in Nunavut, 272
Pope, James Colledge, 130, 132, 133, 134, 136, 138
Pope, William, 129, 130, 131, 133, 136
Prince Edward Island, 1, 10, 13, 31, 95, 105, 107, 124; absentee landlord question, 126, 127, 128, 129, 134-35, 138; demographics, 126-27; opposition to Confederation, 125-28, 132, 133, 134; pro-Confederation viewpoints, 130, 131, 133, 134, 135, 136, 137, 138; railway construction, 136-37; representation in the House of Commons, 128, 138

Prince, Henry, 151
Province of Canada, 53-57, 76, 83-84, 213-14; Great Coalition, 57, 77, 82, 214; Confederation votes, 90-91. *See also* Ontario; Quebec

Q

Quebec, 1, 7, 9-10, 44, 57, 67, 107, 160, 213, 214, 229, 232, 244, 270; clerical influence, 92-94; demographics, 94-95; Indigenous Peoples, 80-82; opposition to Confederation, 85-90, 91-92; pro-Confederation viewpoints 7, 82-85, 92. *See also* Province of Canada
Quebec Conference, 9, 58-59, 75, 77, 81, 118, 237; Maritime positions, 101-9

R

reciprocity, 102, 104, 106, 109, 114-17, 121-23, 126, 128, 135, 136, 244. *See also* tariffs; trade
reconciliation, 7-8, 14-15, 70; Royal Commission on Aboriginal Peoples, 8; Truth and Reconciliation Commission, 7-8. *See also* Indigenous Peoples; Treaties
Red River Expedition, 159, 160-61, 183
Red River Settlement, 145, 146, 148
regionalism, 6, 145. *See also* federalism; local autonomy; Senate
Reilly, Edward, 130
religion: intolerance, 12, 32, 54, 57, 94, 97, 104, 117-18, 129, 154-56, 159, 208, 229-30, 243, 256; tolerance, 79, 80, 96, 159, 225
Rémillard, Édouard, 93
representation by population, 9, 56, 59, 60, 76, 106-8, 116, 128, 214. *See also* majority rule; minority rights; Senate
Responsible Government League (RGL). *See* Newfoundland and Labrador: responsible government (as alternative to Confederation)
Ressor, David, 63

Riel, Louis, 3, 7, 150, 153-56, 161, 215, 225.
Ritchot, Rev. Noël-J., 156-57, 159
Robertson, Gordon, 284
Robson, John, 11, 171, 173, 176, 179, 181, 182, 184, 186, 187
Rogers, Bishop James, 117
Ross, Commissioner James H., 202, 203
Ross, James, 154
Royal Canadian Mounted Police, 269. *See also* North West Mounted Police
Rupert's Land, 2, 10, 11, 175; purchase of, 147-49, 160, 213-15. *See also* Alberta; Manitoba; McDougall, William; North-West; Saskatchewan
Rutherford, Alexander Cameron, 231, 232

S

Sanborn, John Sewell, 64
Saskatchewan, 2, 7, 12, 231-32, 266. *See also* North-West
Schmidt, Louis, 154
Scott, Alfred H., 156-57
Scott, Richard William, 206
Scott, Thomas, 154, 156-57
Scott, Walter, 231, 232
Seelye, Henry, 171
Senate, 59, 63, 65, 88, 107, 117, 122, 124, 127, 160. *See also* representation by population; regionalism
Seymour, Frederick, 172-73, 175-76
Shea, Ambrose, 237, 238, 240, 243, 250
Sicotte, Louis-Victor, 63
Siddon, Tom, 280
Sifton, Clifford, 196, 197, 198, 199, 200, 203, 206, 229-31
Simpson, John, 65
Simpson, Wemyss, 163, 164
Smallwood, Joseph ("Joey") Roberts, 3, 237, 246, 249, 251, 254, 255, 256, 257, 259
Smith, Albert, 3, 113-16, 117, 118
Smith, Donald Alexander (Lord Strathcona), 152, 154, 157, 158
Smith, Elijah, 209
Smith, James, 208
Steeves, William Henry, 111
Sweeny, Bishop John, 114, 117

T

Taché, Bishop Alexandre-Antonin, 149, 156
Taché, Étienne-Paschal, 77, 84, 85
Tariffs, 10, 103, 137, 181, 184, 241. *See also* reciprocity; trade
Thibault, Jean-Baptiste, 152
Thompson, Alfred, 203-4, 207
Thompson, Joshua, 176
Thunderchild, Chief, 27
Tilley, Samuel Leonard, 65, 90, 107, 109-12, 116, 117-18, 138, 171, 175, 178, 183
trade, 102-3, 127-28. *See also* reciprocity; tariffs; Western Extension
Treadgold, Arthur Newton Christian, 203, 207
Treaties, 7-8, 11, 13, 217, 285; as compacts, 8, 19, 20-27, 45; as contracts: 8-9, 19, 36-39, 45-46; as covenants: 9, 19-20, 39-45, 46; James Bay and Northern Quebec Agreement, 44; Nisga'a Treaty, 44;
——Numbered Treaties, ix, 2, 20; Treaty no. 1, 39-40, 163-64; Treaty no. 2, 163-64; Treaty no. 3, 67-68, 164-65; Treaty no. 4, 40, 42; Treaty no. 5, 42, 165; Treaty no. 6, 41, 42, 218-23; Treaty no. 7, 42; Treaty no. 8, 36, 202; Treaty no. 9, 68; Treaty no. 11, 44;
Peace and Friendship Treaties, 8, 27-31; Robinson Treaties 38-39, 56; Royal Proclamation of 1763, 32-35, 37, 39, 55, 147, 217, 270; Selkirk Treaty (1817), 36-37, 39; Vancouver Island Treaties, 39. *See also* Nunavut; Nunavut Land Claims Agreement
Treaty of Utrecht, 31-32
Trudeau, Pierre Elliott, 271. *See also* White Paper (1969)
Trutch, Joseph, William, 171, 173, 181-85
Tunngavik Federation of Nunavut (TFN), 275-76, 278, 280. *See also* Nunavut Tunngavik Incorporated
Tupper, Charles, 3, 6, 107, 118, 121, 123-24, 133

U

United States, 2, 241, 249; annexation, 11, 92, 105, 118, 125, 129, 151, 172, 179; Civil War, 6, 56, 61, 64, 88, 90, 102, 103-4, 109, 121, 123, 128. *See also* British North America (defence); Fenians
unity. *See* national unity
Upper Canada. *See* Ontario
Upper Fort Garry, 149, 150, 151, 182, 183

W

Walsh, Albert Joseph, 256
Walsh, Major James Morrow, 196-97, 199
Western Extension, 112, 115, 117
Whelan, Edward, 130, 133, 134
White Paper (1969), 45, 270
Wilmot, Robert Duncan, 114, 115, 116
Wolseley, Col. Garnet 160, 183. *See also* Red River Expedition

Y

Young, Sir James, 135
Young, Sir John, 152
Yukon, 2, 11-12; early miner's meetings 195; Indigenous Peoples, 193-94, 201, 202-3, 209; Klondike Gold Rush, 196-201; office of the commissioner, 199-200; provincial status, 206, 209; responsible government, 199-209; territorial Council established, 199-200